2001)

HUNGA...   ...OMANIA

D0374871

WESTERN
SLAVONIA

Danube R.

Horgos

VOJVODINA

EASTERN
SLAVONIA

Vukovar

Novi Sad

Sava R.

Bosanski
Brod

Belgrade

Keraterm   Banja Luka

Brcko

Batajica
Airfield

Danube R.

BOSNIA–
HERZEGOVINA

Tuzla

Drvar   Jajce

Zvornik

Srebrenica

Kakanj   Sarajevo

S E R B I A

Pale   Visegrad

Gorazde

Drina R.

HERZEGOVINA

Mostar

DALMATIA

Area of
detail

Nis

Kursumilja

BULGARIA

MONTENEGRO

Pristina

Sofia

KOSOVO

Dubrovnik

Podgorica

Shkoder

Kukes

Skopje

A D R I A T I C

S E A

Durres

Tirana

Lake
Ohrid

MACEDONIA

A L B A N I A

G R E E C E

CORFU

Ioannina

	Yugoslavia prior to 1991
	Present-day Yugoslavia

© A·Karl/J·Kemp, 2001

WAGING MODERN WAR

Staying in Command

Wes Clark

WAGING MODERN
WAR

*Bosnia, Kosovo,
and the Future of Combat*

GENERAL WESLEY K. CLARK
U.S. Army (Retired)

PublicAffairs NEW YORK

Library of Congress Cataloging-in-Publication data
Clark, Wesley K.
Waging modern war: Bosnia, Kosova, and the future of combat / by General
Wesley K. Clark.—PublicAffairs ed.
p.   cm.
Includes index.
ISBN 1-58648-043-X
1. Yugoslav War, 1991–1995—Personal narratives, American. 2. Yugoslav War,
1991–1995—Bosnia and Hercegovina. 3. Kosovo (Serbia)—History—Civil War,
1998—Personal narratives, American. 4. Wesley Clark K. I. Title.
DR1313.8 .C58 2001
949.703—dc21   2001019717

FIRST EDITION
10 9 8 7 6 5 4 3 2 1

This book is dedicated to the men and women of the Armed Forces of NATO member nations, to the Secretary General, statesmen and leaders of NATO's member nations. They found themselves in NATO's first operations—the Balkans—after a half century of peace. We should have celebrated our success, but because we couldn't call it a war, we couldn't call it a victory, even though it was.

And to my family—my wife, Gert, and our son, Wes, who believed, sacrificed and trusted during my thirty-four years as an officer in the U.S. Army. Without their love and support, neither the book nor my military service would have been possible.

CONTENTS

CONTENTS

PART IV: Endgame

CAST OF CHARACTERS

STEVE ABBOTT. Admiral, U.S. Navy; Deputy Commander in Chief, U.S. European Command, 1998–2000.

MADELEINE ALBRIGHT. U.S. Ambassador to the United Nations, 1993–1996. U.S. Secretary of State, 1997–2001.

MARIO ARPINO. General, Italian Air Force; Chief of Defense, Italy, 1999–present.

HARTMUT BAGGER. General, German Army; Chief of Defense, Germany, 1996–1999.

SAMUEL R. "SANDY" BERGER. Deputy National Security Adviser to the President, 1993–1996. National Security Adviser to the President, 1997–2001.

TONY BLAIR. Prime Minister, United Kingdom, 1997–present.

EDWIN H. BURBA. General, U.S. Army (retired); Senior Mentor, U.S. Army Battle Command Training Program.

GEORGE CASEY. Brigadier General, U.S. Army; Deputy Director, Strategic Plans and Policy (J-5), The Joint Staff 1997–1999.

PETER CHIARELLI. Brigadier General, U.S. Army; Executive Officer, Office of the Supreme Allied Commander, Europe, 1999–2000.

WILLIAM J. CLINTON. President of the United States, 1993–2001.

WILLIAM S. COHEN. U.S. Secretary of Defense, 1997–2001.

RASIM DELIC. Lieutenant General, Army of Bosnia-Herzegovina; Chief of Defense, Bosnia-Herzegovina.

JAMES DOBBINS. U.S. Ambassador; President's Representative for the Balkans, 1999. Assistant Secretary of State for European Affairs, 2000.

MICHAEL DURKEE. Minister-Counselor, U.S. Foreign Service; Poltical Adviser to the Supreme Allied Commander, Europe, 1995–present.

JAMES ELLIS. Admiral, U.S. Navy; Commander-in-Chief, Allied Forces Southern Europe; Commander-in-Chief, U.S. Naval Forces, Europe. Commander, U.S. Joint Task Force Noble Anvil.

ROBERT H. "DOC" FOGELSONG. Lieutenant General, U.S. Air Force; Assistant to the Chairman of the Joint Chiefs of Staff.

ROBERT GELBARD. U.S. Ambassador; President's Representative for Dayton Implementation, 1996–1999.

SIR CHARLES GUTHRIE. General, U.K. Army; Chief of Defense Staff, United Kingdom.

JAY HENDRIX. Lieutenant General, U.S. Army; Commanding General, U.S. V Corps, 1997–1999. Commanding General, Task Force Hawk, 1999.

GEORGE HIGGINS. Brigadier General, U.S. Army; Executive Officer to the Commander-in-Chief, U.S. Southern Command, 1996–1997. Executive Officer to the Supreme Allied Commander, Europe, 1997–1998.

CHRISTOPHER HILL. Office Director, Bureau of European Affairs, Department of State, 1995–1996; U.S. Ambassador to Macedonia, 1996–1999.

RICHARD C. HOLBROOKE. U.S. Ambassador; Assistant Secretary of State for European Affairs, 1994–1996. Consultant to the Department of State, 1996–1999. U.S. Ambassador to the United Nations, 1999–2001.

IGOR IVANOV. Deputy Foreign Minister, Russia, 1995; Foreign Minister, 1998–present.

ALIJA IZETBEGOVIC. President of the Republic of Bosnia-Herzegovina, 1992–1996. Member of the Tri-Presidency, Bosnia-Herzegovina, 1996–2000.

SIR MICHAEL JACKSON. Lieutenant General, U.K. Army; Commander, Allied Command Europe Rapid Reaction Corps, 1997–2000.

JAY JOHNSON. Admiral, U.S. Navy; Chief of Naval Operations, 1996–2000.

GEORGE JOULWAN. General, U.S. Army; Supreme Allied Commander, Europe, 1993–1997.

JOHN JUMPER. General, U.S. Air Force; Commanding General, U.S. Air Forces, Europe, 1997–2000.

RADOVAN KARADZIC. President of Bosnian Serbs, 1992–1995. Indicted war criminal, currently hiding.

JEAN-PIERRE KELCHE. General, French Marines; Chief of Defense, France, 1998–present.

HANS-PETER VON KIRCHBACH. General, German Army; Chief of Defense, Germany, 1999–2000.

MOMCILO KRAJISNIK. Serb colleague of Karadzic; Serb member of Bosnian Tri Presidency, 1996–1998. Indicted war criminal, currently awaiting trial in the Hague.

ANTHONY LAKE. National Security Adviser to the President, 1993–1996.

SIR JEREMY MACKENZIE. General, U.K. Army; Deputy Supreme Allied Commander, Europe, 1994–1998.

RATKO MLADIC. Colonel General, Yugoslav Army; Commander, Bosnian Serb Army, 1992–present.

MONTGOMERY MEIGS. General, U.S. Army; Commander, Stabilization Force (SFOR), 1998–1999. Commanding General, U.S. Army Europe, 1998–present.

SLOBODAN MILOSEVIC. President of Serbia, 1990–1997; President of the Federal Republic of Yugoslavia, 1997–2000.

MILAN MILUTINOVIC. Foreign Minister, Federal Republic of Yugoslavia, 1995–1998; President of Serbia, 1997–2000.

KLAUS NAUMANN. General, German Army; Chairman of the NATO Military Committee, 1996–1999.

DRAGOJUB OJDANIC. Colonel General, Yugoslavian Army; Chief of Defense, Yugoslavia, 1999. General, Minister of Defense, 1999–2000.

ROBERTS OWEN. U.S. lawyer; member of Holbrooke Delegation, arbitarator for Brcko.

MOMCILO PERISIC. Colonel General, Yugoslav Army, Chief of Defense, 1995–1998.

WILLIAM PERRY. U.S. Secretary of Defense, 1994–1997.

BILJANA PLAVSIC, President, Republika Srpska, 1996–1998.

JOSEPH RALSTON. General, U.S. Air Force; Vice Chairman, Joint Chiefs of Staff, 1996–2000. Supreme Allied Commander, Europe, 2000–present.

DENNIS REIMER. Major General, U.S. Army; Commanding General 4th Infantry Division, Fort Carson, Colorado, 1988–1990. General; U.S. Army Chief of Staff, 1995–1999.

JOHN REITH. Major General, then Lieutenant General, U.K. Army; Commander, ACE Mobile Force (Land) and the NATO Force in Albania (AFOR).

MICHAEL RYAN. Lieutentant General, U.S. Air Force, assistant to the Chairman, JCS, 1993–1994. General, U.S. Air Force, U.S. Air Force Chief of Staff, 1997–2001.

NIKOLA SAINOVIC. Yugoslav minister for Kosovo.

JOHN SHALIKASHVILI. General, U.S. Army; Chairman, Joint Chiefs of Staff, 1993–1997.

HENRY H. "HUGH" SHELTON. General, U.S. Army; Chairman, Joint Chiefs of Staff, 1997–present.

ERIC SHINSEKI. Lieutenant General, U.S. Army; Deputy Chief of Staff for Operations and Plans, 1995–1997. General; Commander, Stabilization Force (SFOR) and Commanding General, U.S. Army, Europe, 1997–1998; U.S. Army Vice Chief of Staff, 1998–1999; U.S. Army Chief of Staff, 1999–present.

MICHAEL SHORT. Lieutenant General, U.S. Air Force; Commander, Air Forces Southern Europe and U.S. 16th Air Force, 1998–2000.

HARIS SILAJDIC. Prime Minister, Republic of Bosnia-Herzegovina, 1995–1998.

WALTER SLOCOMBE. Undersecretary of Defense for Policy, 1994–2001.

SIR RUPERT SMITH. Lieutenant General, U.K. Army; Commander, U.N. Protective Forces (UNPROFOR) in Bosnia-Herzegovina, 1995. General; Deputy Supreme Allied Commander, Europe, 1999–present.

JAVIER SOLANA. Secretary General, North Atlantic Treaty Organization, 1995–1999.

DIETER STOCKMANN. General, German Army; Chief of Staff, Supreme Headquarters Allied Powers Europe (SHAPE), 1998–present.

STROBE TALBOTT. U.S. Deputy Secretary of State, 1993–2001.

GUIDO VENTURONI. Admiral, Italian Navy; Chief of Defense, Italy, 1995–1998. Chairman, NATO Military Committee, 1999–present.

ALEXANDER "SANDY" VERSHBOW. Special Assistant to the President for European Affairs, National Security Council Staff 1994–1997. U.S. Ambassador to NATO, 1998–2001.

LIST OF ABBREVIATIONS

ACTORD: Activation Order—The third and final stage in the NATO authorization procedure for military action.

ACTREQ: Activation Requirement—Second stage in the NATO authorization procedure for military action.

ACTWARN: Activation Warning—First stage in a three-phase authorization procedure for NATO military action.

AFSOUTH: Allied Forces Southern Europe.

ALLIED FORCE: Official operation name of NATO action in Kosovo.

ARRC: Allied Command Europe Rapid Reaction Corps, created as part of the military implementation of the Alliance Strategic Concept.

ATACMS: Long-range rocket fired from an MLRS (Multiple Launch Rocket System).

CAOC: Combined Air Operations Center.

CHOD: Chief of Defense (top military leader of a nation's armed forces).

CINC: Commander in Chief.

CINCEUR: Commander in Chief, European Command. The regional commander for European Command, who is also the NATO Supreme Allied Commander, Europe.

CJCS: Chairman of the Joint Chiefs of Staff.

CMC: Chairman, NATO Military Committee.

COMSFOR: Commander, SFOR.

CBU: Cluster Bomb Unit.

DOD: Department of Defense.

EU: European Union.

EUCOM: U.S. European Command. Area of responsibility includes Europe, Turkey, Israel, Syria, Lebanon, and most of Africa.

IFOR: Implementation Force—The NATO-led force responsible for upholding the Dayton Peace Accords from December 1995 through December 1996.

JCS: U.S. Joint Chiefs of Staff, comprised of the Chairman, Vice Chairman, and Chiefs of each of the Armed Forces.

JOINT STAFF: the staff serving the Chairman and Vice Chairman, the JCS, comprised of permanent staff officers J-1–8 and their subordinates.

J-1: Joint Staff, Manpower and Personnel Directorate.

J-2: Joint Staff, Intelligence Directorate.

J-3: Joint Staff, Operations Directorate.

J-4: Joint Staff, Logistics Directorate.

J-5: Joint Staff, Strategic Plans and Policy Directorate.

J-6: Joint Staff, Command, Control, Communications, and Computer Systems Directorate.

J-7: Joint Staff, Operational Plans and Interoperability Directorate.

J-8: Joint Staff, Force Structure, Resources, and Assessment Directorate.

KLA: Kosovo Liberation Army.

KFOR: Kosovo Force. International force organized and commanded by NATO to enforce an agreement in Kosovo.

MLRS: Multiple Launch Rocket System.

MOD: Minister of Defense.

NAC: North Atlantic Council, the NATO policy making group.

NATO: North Atlantic Treaty Organization, a collective defense organization (Member nations are: Belgium, Canada, Czech Republic, Denmark, France, Germany, Greece, Hungary, Iceland, Italy, Luxembourg, Netherlands, Norway, Poland, Portugal, Spain, Turkey, United Kingdom, United States).

NSC: National Security Council, senior U.S. policy making body often represented by the National Security adviser to the President and its staff.

OSCE: Organization for Security and Cooperation in Europe.

PFP: Partnership for Peace, nations associated with NATO, but not member nations. (Member nations include: Albania, Armenia, Austria, Azerbaijan, Belarus, Bulgaria, Croatia, Estonia, Finland, Georgia, Ireland, Kazakhstan, Kyrghyz Republic, Latvia, Lithuania, Moldova, Romania, Russia, Slovakia, Slovenia, Sweden, Switzerland, Former Yugoslav Republic of Macedonia, Turkmenistan, Ukraine, Uzbekistan).

QDR: Quadrennial Defense Review.

SACEUR: Supreme Allied Commander, Europe—who is also the U.S. CINCEUR.

SECDEF: U.S. Secretary of Defense.

SECGEN: Secretary General, the highest official in NATO.

SHAPE: Supreme Headquarters, Allied Powers Europe (Headquarters for Allied Command Europe, commanded by SACEUR).

SFOR: Stabilization Force—Second phase of the Implementation Force, IFOR. Created to implement the Dayton Peace Accords.

UNHCR: U.N. High Commissioner for Refugees.

UNPROFOR: U.N. Protection Force, deployed to Bosnia and Croatia. The first U.N. deployment to the Balkans.

VTC: Video Teleconference.

INTRODUCTION

Casteau, Belgium,
Supreme Headquarters, Allied Powers Europe,
March 31, 1999.

NOTEBOOK IN HAND, grimacing a little but calm, Brigadier General Pete Chiarelli walked into my office. "Sir, you've got Solana's office calling in," he said. Javier Solana was the Secretary General of NATO, the highest ranking official in the Alliance. Seven days earlier, NATO had begun bombing targets in Yugoslavia in response to President Slobodan Milosevic's refusal to halt his systematic campaign of repression and violence against the ethnic Albanians in the Serbian province of Kosovo.

"They sound a little agitated this morning," Chiarelli went on. "Said he wants to speak to you right away."

Forty-eight years old, twenty-six years in the Army, unfailingly cheerful and optimistic, Pete Chiarelli was my executive officer, my closest personal assistant. I swiveled around from the desk to pick up the phone—the unclassified line, lots of nations probably listening in, I thought—and pushed the speaker switch so Chiarelli could take notes for me. He had to know what I knew and back me up on the coordination with Washington and the direction of the personal assistants here.

Solana was a former Socialist foreign minister of Spain who had, in his earlier days, strongly opposed Spain's membership in the North Atlantic Treaty Organization. Now he was directing the Alliance in war. In recent months we had become fast friends. We were about the same age. He was a former Fulbright Scholar who had studied in the United States; I was a former Rhodes Scholar who had studied in England. He was a physicist by training; I was a scientifically inclined "wannabe."

"Wes, Wes, can you hear me?" Solana asked. It was unusual for him, I thought, not to ask first how I was doing. I could hear the tension and urgency in his voice.

"Yes, Javier, I'm here," I replied.

"Wes," he said, coming straight to the point, "many governments are calling me to complain that I'm not giving you enough freedom to pick targets. And you are showing me pictures and telling me about the technical details of weapons that I am not familiar with. You are the expert on these things, you are the military man..."

"Yes, Javier." He sounded a little on edge. Target selection had quickly emerged as the toughest issue of the campaign, with most of the military leaders in NATO seeking to strike more high-value targets closer to Belgrade, the Yugoslavian and Serbian capital, while a number of foreign ministries were urging cautious and carefully measured escalation. I had been pressing hard for approval to strike Serb police headquarters in Belgrade, and after conferring with the head of the British military the previous evening, I knew that other military leaders were likewise pressing their governments for such authorization. But the request still had not been granted. We were quickly learning how difficult it is for a nineteen-nation alliance to wage a coherent military campaign.

"The Chairman of the Military Committee has spoken to me about this, also," Solana said, referring to General Klaus Naumann, the German general who headed the NATO Military Committee in Brussels. "And your country has called me to complain." The edge had definitely sharpened.

I was not surprised. I had been discussing the issue of target selection every day with the U.S. Chairman of the Joint Chiefs of Staff,

General Hugh Shelton, focusing on the approval process and the nature of Alliance support, explaining what was needed and expressing my frustration over the time that was required to get political approval, including in Washington. Perhaps my complaints to Shelton had led to more pressure on Solana.

Before I could get a sentence out in reply, the Secretary General cut me off. "So, you will have your targets," he said—a pronouncement that impacted like the smack of a fastball in a catcher's mitt. "You will pick the targets you want to strike. You will keep me informed, and I would like to know if the targets will be in Belgrade. If there are difficulties, I will tell you, but I will support you, and you will pick the targets. You will take your responsibility and you will accept the consequences. Do you understand?"

"Yes, Javier." Good, I thought. This sounded like a significant change in procedures. I would not have to justify and explain every target in sensitive areas, and he would support me. I needed that support.

"And you will take your responsibilities, do you understand?" He underscored his message once again; it was about as sharply as I had ever heard Javier Solana speak to me.

"Yes, Javier, thank you," I said. "This is what we need. It will definitely move things along." But flashing simultaneously through my mind was the series of high-ranking European generals who "took responsibility" in World War I and World War II. They were the losers. And they were gone, their names long forgotten.

In war, you don't just lose. Not if you're a commander. It's what General Douglas MacArthur told Major General Robert Eichelberger in New Guinea in 1942: "Take Buna, or don't come back alive."

Of course, there were many other people who were responsible in this war, too. The heads of government of the nineteen NATO member nations, their foreign ministers and defense ministers, as well as their Chiefs of Defense, the military leaders in each country. These men and women were responsible for their own nations and for helping to provide direction for the alliance. There was the NATO leadership, too—Secretary General Javier Solana and General Klaus Naumann, the Chairman of the Military Committee. They were responsible for forging consensus in NATO, shaping its strategy, and representing it privately and publicly.

As Supreme Allied Commander, Europe, I was working for each of these people. I was responsible for the conduct of the military operations against Yugoslavia, as well as for the 30,000 troops on the ground in NATO's other operation in the nearby country of Bosnia-Herzegovina. There was no doubt in my mind that I was the one responsible. Above me, everything was political or political-military. Below me was just the military. I was at the waist of the hourglass, and the grains of sand were pouring past in both directions.

I looked over at the picture on the wall of the first Supreme Allied Commander, General Dwight D. Eisenhower. I looked down at my desk, the same desk he had used to sign the activation orders of our command almost fifty years ago. I was the first of his successors to have to lead NATO to war, and I wasn't going to lose.

As a first-year cadet at West Point, in 1962, I was required to memorize General MacArthur's words and recite them again and again. "There is one single message, one sole idea, written in red on every beachhead from Australia to Tokyo: there is no substitute for victory!"

Military leaders carry their early education and experiences with them for the rest of their service. The good ones read, study, and reflect on their own until they are steeped in history and tradition, and have a broad perspective and a rich base on which to address specific military and diplomatic issues. For most of the nineteenth and twentieth centuries, wars were fought for territory. The survival of nations—or at least, their systems of government—was at stake. It was national warfare, relying on the mobilization of populations, vast conscript armies, and national controls over the economy and the flow of public information.

This was the form of warfare that Napoleon had taught us, nation-state against nation-state. Cohorts of young men were organized and drafted; large, bureaucratic organizations and state ministries were created just to be able to handle the logistical planning required in case of mobilization for war. The ideal was the battle of annihilation, surrounding an enemy force through a series of maneuvers ambiguous to him, forcing him to fight on your chosen ground, bringing to bear the superior firepower of well-trained artillery, and then closing the fight with infantry and the bayonet. Horse cavalry would be used for reconnaissance, feints, and screening, and when the enemy's ranks were broken, cavalry would sweep in, with pistol and heavy saber, to finish the fight and ensure that a retreating enemy was defeated and destroyed.

Napoleonic strategy was part of our instruction in military art in 1965 at West Point. We studied the Italian campaign and the battles of Marengo, Ulm, Austerlitz, and Leipzig. God is on the side of the big battalions, Napoleon taught us, and it is better to be lucky than good. War is decided by battle, we learned. You focused on the enemy force. The strategic art was to bring the enemy to battle at the time and place of your choosing, where you had the advantage and could finish him.

I began my study of the profession early in my cadet career, reading the histories and biographies, writing articles and reflecting on contemporary challenges, and trying to soak up others' experiences. Over the years I came to understand the uniqueness of each conflict, and the failure of most theorists to understand or predict the nature of battle and the alternatives available to commanders and national leaders. Twentieth-century war seldom matched its Napoleonic ideal in terms of decisiveness. But the mobilization of the nation-state, the conscription, the large organizations, the extreme destructiveness of the weaponry, the focus on battle and the enemy force, the prodigious losses of men and material, and the dreadful burdens to the civilian populations were certainly features of war as we knew it.

Eisenhower and NATO itself were the product of such a war. World War II was to be a fight to the finish, as the United States and its Allies called for the unconditional surrender of Germany, Italy, and Japan, and civilian populations were targeted by all sides. In a war that saw the only use of the atomic bomb, almost no weapon was spared. And when it was over, and Europe and the United States sensed the threat of Joseph Stalin and the Red Army, NATO was established and Eisenhower recalled to service in Europe to protect against another such terrible conflict.

Operation Allied Force, NATO's military action against Yugoslavia in the spring of 1999, wasn't meant to be that kind of war. In fact, we were never allowed to call it a war. But it was, of course. This was modern war, the first war fought in Europe in half a century, and the first ever fought by NATO. The Alliance and its member nations weren't under attack. This war wasn't about national survival, or the survival of our democratic systems of government. We didn't mobilize our populations or do anything significant to control information. The conscripts remaining among the NATO nations never came close to getting to the fight, because there were national laws in most cases prohibiting their service outside their own countries. The economies of the West weren't taken over by governments or turned to war production. The choice of weapons was carefully considered, and ultimately, not left up to the military. Civilian populations and purely civilian facilities were not targeted.

Operation Allied Force was modern war—limited, carefully constrained in geography, scope, weaponry, and effects. Every measure of escalation was excruciatingly weighed. Diplomatic intercourse with neutral countries, with those opposed to NATO's actions, and even with the actual adversary continued during and around the conflict. Confidence-building measures and other conflict prevention initiatives derived from the Cold War were brought into play. The highest possible technology was in use, but only in carefully restrained ways. There was extraordinary concern for military losses, on all sides. Even accidental damage to civilian property was carefully considered. And "victory" was carefully defined.

This is a book about modern war, using the NATO action in Kosovo as the best, most recent example. These are my recollections, supplemented by notes and records. The quotations are as I remember them, cited to help tell the story from the perspective of the overall commander. It is not a complete record of the war nor a history that explains all the simultaneous activities and events in Washington, London, Brussels, or other capitals. Usually I acted on time-sensitive and incomplete information. My perceptions weren't formed by full knowledge of all happening above and around me.

The stakes in this conflict were huge, and success was not inevitable. In fact, many predicted that NATO would fail in its mission to end the ethnic cleansing in Kosovo. Had we failed, the consequences would have been profoundly damaging to NATO, to its many member nations, to the Kosovar Albanians, and to many nations in the region that need stability and democracy. NATO could likely not have survived in its present form, and a wave of fear and insecurity would have raced through eastern Europe. I was warned that a NATO failure would bring the collapse of several European governments, as well.

Failure would have meant another one and a half million refugees and accepting ethnic cleansing as an unalterable fact. Failure would have deepened instability in the Balkans and raised moral outrage in Europe. For the United States, there would have been worldwide repercussions on United States credibility and the significance of American commitments.

But we did not fail—we succeeded. This was a result of many factors and forces that were not necessarily visible on the surface. Many people contributed to the successful outcome of this effort, and each will have seen it from his or her perspective. Inevitably, there will be important considerations not covered in this book, and important contributions unrecognized. Many people made extraordinary efforts in the political and military channels above me to give direction and help forge consensus. I am enormously grateful to those for whom I worked in both the NATO and the U.S. chains of command—the Presidents and Prime Ministers, Secretary General Solona, the Secretaries and ministers, Generals and Admirals—for their guidance and support and the confidence they had in me during this operation. I hope their full contributions will one day be known and acknowledged. But this book is from my perspective: how I worked as a strategic commander in modern war, dealing with modern weaponry, instantaneous communications, and a highly complex political-military environment.

This war was nothing if not complex. Every facet is difficult to understand, masked by acronyms, procedures, security arrangements, and national sensitivities. It was a war waged by a nineteen-nation alliance that habitually looked to the United States for leadership but ultimately made decisions on the basis of consensus and then delegated their implementation to a multinational military chain of command.

As the Supreme Allied Commander, Europe, I was the head of the NATO military chain of command within Europe and responsible for implementing those decisions. And though decisions were made at higher political levels, much of the information to make those decisions came from my commanders and me. I also held another command position simultaneously, that of U.S. Commander in Chief, European Command. It was a process known as "dual-hatting," complete with two different, geographically dispersed headquarters—NATO's Supreme Headquarters Allied Powers Europe (SHAPE), near

Mons, Belgium, and the U.S. European Command (EUCOM), in Stuttgart, Germany—two different staffs, and two entirely different reporting chains. It was a linkage designed by General Eisenhower himself. My effectiveness was in part a function of my authority as a U.S. commander to call upon U.S. capabilities and resources, but, perhaps more important, of my ability to keep the trust and support of the Europeans. I had to use my leverage with the Americans to gain influence with the Europeans and vice versa. I was straddling the Atlantic divide in perspective and actions.

Of course, a crucial challenge to NATO was to harmonize American and European interests and perceptions during the campaign. On some issues there were almost as many viewpoints as there were nations. This was the first war the Alliance had fought, and there was no assurance in this novel undertaking that differing interests could be made to converge. NATO needed continual shoring up from me and others, or it could have crumbled. In fact, it came close to crumbling more than once. The successes achieved stemmed from hard work by many people. But part of my work was also this effort to recognize and accommodate different perspectives and to fight the campaign in a manner that helped strengthen Allied unity, not break it.

The weight of modern history lay heavily upon everyone involved from the European side. The memories of the destruction of World War II, the millions of refugees and displaced persons, the young men in uniform lost forever, and the lasting tragedy and shame of aggressive attacks on civilians were always present. As a leading Italian statesman told me after the Kosovo campaign, "In Italy, we couldn't use the word *war*. Too many bad memories. War meant destruction, death, defeat and occupation."

And in Germany, especially, many of the leaders, military and civilian, had deep personal scars from World War II. The historical pessimism was deeply reflected in the popular culture. As General Naumann told me, "I will never forget the sight of the bombs falling on Munich when I was a small child." The German battlefield cemeteries, paid for not by the government but by popular donations raised by the armed forces, extol not the virtue and valor of sacrifice but the tragedy and futility of war. In the German cemetery near Omaha Beach, site of the Allied invasion of France in 1944, the German soldiers are buried, two to a grave, the headstones a somber brown, with the inscription on the cemetery reading:

> Darkly rises the mound
> Over the graves of soldiers.
> Darkly stands God's command
> Over the dead of the war.
> Yet brightly glows the sky
> Above the towering crosses
> More brightly still shines their comfort:
> The final word is God's.

Even countries that didn't suffer extensive war damage in World War II were scarred psychologically. In a visit to Denmark in late 1997, I was escorted past the harbor in Copenhagen by a Danish military officer, who pointed out, "This is where we scuttled the Danish fleet in 1940 so the Germans couldn't get use of it when they marched in and took over. And over there lies the house where twelve members of the Danish resistance were taken in 1944 by the Germans and later they were executed. But the resistance was slow in forming, and not many participated. In fact, a number of Danes joined up with the Germans to fight on the Eastern Front in 1941." This was said with the air of apology I found often among the smaller nations that had learned earlier in the century that for them war against a larger power usually ended badly, that courageous resistance was seldom rewarded, and the use of military power was best exercised through an Alliance with larger powers.

But for America, the Second World War was a distant and dim memory, battles fought in far-off lands against people now our friends. We had significant losses and a large and proud population of veterans and their families. But the pain and horror lacked immediacy. The pain of the losses was dulled by time and victory.

Americans, of course, learned about limited war from the experiences of Korea and Vietnam and, to some extent, the Gulf War. The impact of Vietnam was especially strong. Policymakers who had participated in student demonstrations against the war thirty years earlier now found themselves on the receiving end of antiwar sentiment. President Bill Clinton, National Security Adviser Samuel L. Berger, and

Deputy Secretary of State Strobe Talbott knew the power of the student movements well from their own personal experiences. Now they found themselves responsible for directing the American role in a military conflict. They knew that for large democracies, the home front is the critical theater of war, and words and images are the key weapons. Everyone in top leadership positions in uniform knew it, too.

United States policy was not monolithic. Rather there was another divide that also had to be bridged, the persistent struggle between the U.S. Department of State and the U.S. Department of Defense. One department is responsible for recommending and leading the execution of U.S. foreign policy. It is a department of diplomats and policy analysts, schooled in language, compromise, and consensus-building, present in embassies around the world, but perpetually short of the direct resources necessary to implement foreign policy if it proceeded beyond the "talking" stage. The Department of Defense, on the other hand, saw its responsibilities as primarily in the areas of deterrence and warfare. There were many among the officers and leaders of all ranks who believed the purpose of the Armed Forces, and especially of the Army, was to "fight and win America's wars." They drew a strong distinction between their responsibilities in warfighting and the State Department's articulation and peacetime efforts to advance American interests. It was a distinction that some leaders, like former Chairman of the Joint Chiefs of Staff Colin Powell, had tried to blur by advancing the notion of "peacetime engagement" for the Armed Forces. Most at the top of the military hierarchy supported this as it evolved, at least as it was a way to defend and use American military resources until they were needed for war.

But this construction bridged a chasm of differing education, perspective, and style. The State Department in the post-Cold War period, with White House encouragement and direction, found itself seeking to advance American interests and ideals and seeking to leverage Defense resources in the effort. The Defense Department found itself struggling to protect its own programs and priorities from the grasping reach of the policy planners at State and among the National Security Council staff, as the military coped with a 30 to 40 percent contraction in defense resources and capabilities. And the struggle was played out not only within the Washington interagency process but also within NATO itself, as the Secretaries of State and Defense brought their differing perspectives to the issues in the Balkans.

It was characteristic of NATO that the foreign ministries, or in the American case, the State Department, ran the day-to-day process at NATO headquarters through nations' ambassadors, who met in the North Atlantic Council or NAC. The defense ministries were represented within the ambassadors' teams and also by a military representative of the Chief of Defense who sat on the NATO Military Committee, a body subordinate to the NAC. Thus the foreign ministries had the upper hand and the last word in working the issues. This was doubly the case for the United States, where the White House and Secretary of State seemed to place a higher priority on NATO's requirements and responsibilities than did the Defense Department. It was perhaps for this reason that Secretary General Solana seemed to speak more often with the White House and the Secretary of State than with the Secretary of Defense.

For me, then, I was torn between the guidance and perspective I gained from NATO, heavily influenced by the Department of State and the White House, and what I would hear in my U.S. military chain reporting to the Pentagon. From one side I was continually exhorted to "do the best I could" to accomplish the task at hand; from the other I was often implicitly or explicitly constrained in seeking resources and authority to act. Many times, I had to set my own compass and follow it.

Partly by consequence of having a foot in these different camps, I was also at an odd place within the military hierarchy. I had a perspective that other U.S. military leaders didn't share and responsibilities they only partially understood. That is another element of the story of modern war: my relationship with the leaders of the U.S. Armed Forces, and especially with some of the men in top positions in the Army.

Personalities are important factors in history and in military affairs, even though we don't like to admit it to ourselves. This story is often told to groups of new U.S. Army brigadier generals: "If we put you all on a plane and it crashed and we lost all of you, we could pick another fifty, and they'd be just as good as you." Maybe so, but they wouldn't be the same fifty, and individuals do make a difference.

From the outside, of course, officers in the top leadership positions probably look mostly the same. There is no "lateral entry" to leadership in the U.S. Armed Forces. You can't go out and raid a "competitor" to find a good corps commander or strategist. Everyone starts at the bottom and works his way up. Advancement is basically by age and years of service, with a little acceleration at the margin for a select few. So we end up about the same age, with about the same decorations on our uniforms, much the same formal training and education, and many shared experiences and friends. And there is a common culture, though it's a little different for each of the U.S. Armed Forces, and for each branch within each service. The Army and the Air Force, in my experience, were a little better in "rounding off the rough edges" or eliminating those who weren't easily "rounded."

Still, there are enormous differences underneath, defined by individual character and insight, distinctive competencies, shared relationships as junior officers, loyalties to particular senior officers, or perhaps just differences in basic personality and proclivities. As in many organizations, people in the U.S. Armed Forces make it to the top because their immediate superiors and their superiors' superiors believe in them. But when something happens to those "sponsors," then it often spells the end for the followers, too. In the Army there was an old legacy of the "airborne mafia," dating back into the period after World War II and Korea. Some believed that an "artillery mafia" was present in the 1990s. I heard others speak in fear of an "armor mafia." In the Navy there were aviators and submariners, and in the Air Force, the men from Strategic Air Command and the fighter pilots.

As an Army armor officer, I never considered that I belonged to one of the classic "mafias." I had commanded a mechanized infantry company in Vietnam, not a tank company or an armored cavalry troop. I believed that officers had to strive to learn as much, and gain as broad a perspective as possible. Those perspectives ranged from a White House Fellowship on the one hand, to assignment to the Army's National Training Center on the other. I sometimes found myself challenging conventional wisdom—no "hiding in the pack." Like everyone who was successful, I definitely had my supporters and some doubters. And as I was moved upwards in responsibility, many of my strongest supporters retired.

What I saw in the Kosovo conflict was the significant difficulty the U.S. Armed Forces faced in adapting to the requirements of a new situation. These difficulties were in part due to organizational factors, such as the Armed Forces' effort to cling to the 1991 Gulf War, Operation Desert Storm, as the model for future operations, rather than facing up to an ambiguous, tense, highly political coalition environment in which military actions would face tight restraints, constant high-level oversight, and continuing public scrutiny. In part these difficulties were due to the competing pressures being brought to bear on the senior military leaders in Washington, as well as their own preference for staying with their focus on a two-pronged strategy centered on the Persian Gulf and Korea. The Europeans had difficulties, too, especially in matching the high-technology requirements for the campaign. At the same time I saw strong and continuing personal support from my European colleagues. Perhaps they were just closer to the conflict. But I can't deny that personal factors might have played a role, too.

For me the war was professional, but it was also personal. It drew on the experiences and insights of my full thirty-seven years of military service; it placed heavy demands on character and stamina, and it strained my relations with some American colleagues. It was personal, because in war, you accept your responsibilities and give every ounce of your character and experience to accomplish the mission.

This is the story of how we won, seen from the cockpit of strategic command. It is also a record of modern warfare, with important implications for the future of NATO, for the Armed Forces of the United States and its Allies, and for U.S. diplomacy.

PART I

INTO THE BALKANS

ONE

THE COLD WAR IS OVER

I ENTERED MILITARY SERVICE during the Cold War. Fortunately, we never had to fight the war in Europe that NATO was formed to deter. Nevertheless, we saw a continuing evolution in the conduct of war. Modern war, as defined here, emerged as a function of history and culture, as a result of NATO, the media, and technology. Local factors, such as the environment or the particular characteristics of the enemy forces, had a significant impact as well. From the Korean War of 1950–53, through the American war in Vietnam, and into the United Kingdom's 1982 campaign in the Falklands, the U.S. 1989 intervention in Panama, and the 1991 Gulf War, and into Kosovo in 1999, the divergence from the World War II model of warfare has grown more and more pronounced. The evolution hasn't been linear or particularly well understood, even within the armed forces in most Western countries—but it's there.

The divergence began with the Soviet Union's acquisition of nuclear weapons. After the wholesale tragedy of World War II and the advent of the nuclear age, it soon was obvious that many conflicts could not be pushed to "unconditional surrender." It was too risky, or too expensive, or too much in conflict with other goals and priorities.

Lesser objectives usually had to suffice. When contemplating conflict with the Soviet Union, it became axiomatic in the West, as the Soviet Union acquired greater numbers of nuclear weapons, that nuclear war wasn't winnable in the usual sense; the consequences of widespread use of nuclear weapons by both sides would simply be too destructive. The point was to deter it. The absence of war was the victory, because if you fought, you couldn't win. If fighting did begin, the idea was to defend as long as possible using conventional weapons without resorting to the use of nuclear weapons. Then, if conventional defense wasn't succeeding, use nuclear weapons in some limited way and hope the other side would see the results as so terrible that the conflict could be terminated. You would have to convince the other side that if the aggression wasn't called off, we would use all of the nuclear weaponry in our arsenal. To put it another way, crossing the threshold to use force wasn't necessarily a decision for all-out war. Hearkening back to World War II and the mutual decision among the major belligerents not to use chemical weapons in Europe, this theory rested on the belief that if the belligerents were rational, both sides would see that that it was in their best interests to limit a war once it had begun.

This strategy in NATO was known as Flexible Response. Defend with conventional weapons for as long as possible, then use nuclear weapons selectively, keeping full-fledged nuclear strikes in reserve. Naturally, the strategy had to be trained and rehearsed. In its nuclear exercises, NATO had established procedures for political decision-making and ordering the use of nuclear weapons, and these were extensively practiced. The procedures were immaculate: clear, carefully controlled, double checked, and carefully secured. Entire communications systems were constructed to meet the needs of "nuclear release." NATO was defensive. It didn't seek victory, it sought "conflict termination."

As a major at Supreme Headquarters, Allied Powers Europe (SHAPE) in 1978–79, I watched NATO go through training and exercises for this strategy. Observing the heavy emphasis on the decision-making and procedures for the first nuclear releases, I was one of many who sensed that our approach was incomplete. We never seemed to work our way through what happened after the first nuclear release. Disturbingly, during this period and into the 1980s, the evidence began to accumulate that the Soviets didn't always have the same view, but rather might believe that with adequate preparations and stout, integrated air and missile defenses around Moscow, the center of their military-industrial complex, nuclear war might be survivable and for the best prepared, "relatively" won.

We recognized a growing asymmetry in the Western and Soviet view of the problem, but NATO stuck with its strategy. There was another strand of thought that had crept into the thinking of some of the European members of NATO, from work done in the United States in game theory. This work aimed to take the influence of the military beyond "deterrence"—causing someone to refrain from doing something by threat of punishment or threat of taking away his means to act—and into something called "compellence," which was to cause someone to act in a certain way. It was a peculiar, or perhaps more generalized form of limited war, a conflict not necessarily fought for territory or to turn back aggression but perhaps for other purposes. In military terms compellence seemed to translate into a certain implicit or explicit bargaining through the graduated use of force, inflicting ever increasing punishment to convince an opponent to change his behavior. It was to be applicable against the smaller, nonnuclear states.

Many of us in the United States and the Armed Forces had seen early on the fallacies of gradualism. It was, after all, the thinking that lay behind the early, unsuccessful years of the deepening American involvement in the Vietnam War. My personal concerns stemmed from an analysis of the 1965–68 air campaign in Vietnam known as Rolling Thunder. Writing a thesis for a master's degree in military art and science as a captain and student at the U.S. Army Command and General Staff College, I reviewed as much as I could find about Vietnam, reread the Pentagon Papers, and researched the problem of contingency operations—operations in unanticipated areas that had political aims less sweeping than unconditional surrender.

It was clear that the U.S. effort to halt North Vietnamese support of the fighting in South Vietnam by "signalling" U.S. resolve through carefully constrained, politically designed bombing, which avoided seeking decisive military impact, had been a failure. The question was, why? The answer seemed to have to do with the pace and intensity of the campaign, in relation to North Vietnamese willpower and determination, and North Vietnam's ability to build up resistance to the strikes and repair the damage even as it was being inflicted. To successfully "compel," I realized, the force applied must be much greater than we had been willing to commit at the time, must be intensified more rapidly, and must be directed at achieving significant military ends. Only when the targeted state realizes that its military efforts cannot succeed will it be "compelled" to consider alternatives.

But apparently this was quite difficult, as I reflected on such operations, because in modern democracies, the political leaders were usually too hesitant, imposing tough constraints on military actions, and military leaders were not bold enough in pushing for the real military muscle required to achieve significant military objectives. The results, I thought, were extended campaigns that could leave democratic governments vulnerable to their own public opinion. Forbearance in the strikes could be misinterpreted at home or abroad as irresolution or incompetence. As mistakes and losses accumulated, the policy would appear incompetent in application and foolish in design. Campaigns like this were therefore subject to domestic political defeat. And that was part of what happened to the United States in Vietnam. Once fighting had begun, you had to escalate rapidly and achieve "escalation dominance" over an adversary, if you were to succeed. And you had to go after meaningful military objectives.

I came out of the study convinced that the United States would again find itself engaged in problems of not only deterrence but also "compellence." Little did I suspect that I would be in the middle of the action as Supreme Allied Commander, Europe, when it occurred.

I had my first chance to weigh in with my concerns about gradualism when I was a lieutenant colonel. One afternoon in late May 1983, I sat in a basement office of the Pentagon with Brigadier General Colin Powell as we put the finishing touches on a transition plan for the incoming Chief of Staff of the Army, General John Wickham. Powell was a rising star, even then, a man who had commanded a brigade in General Wickham's division in the mid-seventies and was considered one of the best among his contemporaries. He had been put in charge of the project. The papers had been prepared, addressing such topics as personnel, relations with Congress, force structure, and so on. The group of fourteen officers who had worked the report had broken up. But as we put the papers together in a substantial volume, I noticed that we seemed to be missing an introduction.

I suggested to Powell that we add a "one-pager" up front, containing the two or three most important things for the new Chief to consider, and he agreed. Emboldened, I suggested a line of argument: "Isn't the most important thing never to commit U.S. troops again unless we're going in to win? No more gradualism and holding back like in Vietnam, but go in with overwhelming force?" Again, Powell agreed, and we put it in the introduction. This argument captured what so many of us felt after Vietnam. Perhaps this idea made it into U.S. military action, when we intervened with overwhelming forces in Grenada in 1983. Certainly the work General Powell did leading up to the Gulf War and the Powell Doctrine of decisive force were a wholehearted refutation of the failed gradualism of Vietnam.

Unfortunately, the idea of decisive force never quite made it into NATO thinking. It seemed incompatible with nuclear realities, and perhaps the limitations of the armed forces of our European allies. And, if not well understood, it could seem to be a kind of naïve throwback, to an earlier, simpler era of warfare that saw a relatively clear separation between the political and the military: the fighting started when the talking ended, it seemed, and the talking would resume when the fighting stopped. This was the kind of misinterpretation that American military students and some of their leaders could hang onto, though, because it seemed to reflect our American military traditions—that when the war begins the civilian leadership will turn us loose to win it, applying all the skills and judgment of our many years of accumulated professional military experience. In fact, that was a misinterpretation: the doctrine of decisive force was not incompatible with continued diplomacy, explicit or implicit. On the contrary, decisive force—rather than gradualism—was precisely what was required to make "compellence" a sure success, along with the diplomacy to produce the "way out" for the loser.

One factor that did make its way into the diplomatic and military dialogue within the Alliance was the century-long trend to establish legal and diplomatic barriers against the outbreak of war, and then to limit war's destructiveness. Extraordinary institutions were established to smooth the flow of communications between governments. The European Union was itself first and foremost a means of binding nations' interests together so that they would never again want to go to war against each other. For states outside the EU, various legal and political confidence-building measures were put in place, intrusive measures that made it awkward and difficult for nations to take the opening moves of conflict. Building on precedents set at the Nuremberg War Crimes Trials of 1946, the prosecution of war crimes became a fact, in several different venues, and the standards of permissible military actions—the so-called accidents of war—were tightened. The use of military force was increasingly constrained. The Allies' hideous firebombing of Dresden, which reduced the city to ashes and rubble in February 1945, would never recur.

Hand-in-hand with the growing effort to restrict, hobble, and outlaw war-making was a revolution in communications. American and European leaders were acutely sensitive to the vast change in the flow of information. In Vietnam the battlefield was isolated in space and time from the policymakers at home. Instructions and guidance from Washington was transmitted electronically, of course, but in what we would consider today very small "pipes." Military communications thirty years ago flowed in organized channels, controlled and monitored by the military itself. The TV reports and press copy that came out of Vietnam were also delayed for hours or days. It took years for the media to build the reporting networks and data flow to bring battlefield events in Vietnam out to the public.

In the 1990s, all of the information age technologies were available—satellite transmission of TV imagery, fax, the Internet, a plethora of long-distance phone lines, and cellular telephones.

The new technologies impacted powerfully at the political levels. The instantaneous flow of news and especially imagery could overwhelm the ability of governments to explain, investigate, coordinate, and confirm. We called it the "CNN factor," and people began to speak jokingly of the need to follow the itinerary of CNN correspondent Christiane Amanpour, whose stunning on-the-scene visuals and reporting could make a distant crisis an instant domestic political concern. It was clear that the new technologies could put unrelenting heavy pressure on policymakers at all levels from the very beginning of any operation.

New technologies also changed warfare for the military. The advent of twenty-four hour news coverage and satellite relays for TV meant that the world would certainly be present on every battlefield where Western forces were engaged. During the U.S. operation against Manuel Noriega in Panama in 1989, the entire focus of attention for several hours was the action by U.S. forces to rescue a civilian aircrew and others trapped in a hotel. Then the whole world heard the daily doses of psychological warfare as Noriega attempted to take refuge inside the Papal Nuncio's residence and was bombarded out with unrelenting rock music. The bright lights of the TV crews that observed the U.S. Marines coming ashore in Somalia in December 1992 were a foretaste of the spotlight under which all NATO actions against Yugoslavia would be assessed. Future actions could anticipate even more intrusive information collection and more intense top-down, media-driven focus. There would be few spaces in which blunders or mistakes could remain unnoticed.

The technical side of war changed, too. The Gulf War brought the first public awareness of new precision-guided, aerial-delivered weapons. Though only a small percentage of the total weapons used, these systems accounted for a disproportionate share of the targets destroyed. It was clear within the U.S. Armed Forces that these were the weapons of the future. The Navy, which had possessed only a limited precision-strike capability in 1990, rushed to retrofit the capabilities of much of its air fleet.

Consider the almost revolutionary impact of precision strike weapons. These pinpoint bombs and missiles were able to strike within a few feet, and sometimes a few inches, of the designated aim point on a target. The first-generation weapons were optically guided, and they required clear weather conditions for some portion or perhaps all of their flight. The second generation used lasers for precision guidance and also required clear weather. The third generation, available during Operation Allied Force, relied on the satellite-based Global Positioning System, enabling the weapons to work at night or in bad weather. Precision weaponry greatly reduced the number of weapons and aircraft needed to bring destruction to the battlefield or to a strategic target array. This meant that the days of the massed air fleets were over. And this, in turn, meant a more rapid buildup of forces against a potential adversary, a buildup that could occur without national mobilization—political, economic, or military.

Long-range delivery of precision weaponry further extended the reach and blurred the distinctions between war and peace. With air-to-air refueling, long-range strike aircraft can strike across continents and around the world, reducing even further the preparation time before launching an attack. The U.S. Air Force reformulated its doctrine, titling it Global Reach–Global Power.

The precision bombs and long-range delivery platforms were just the tip-end of a system that relied on precision intelligence, much of it imagery, that enabled the weapons strikes to be planned, checked, and approved. This system, in turn, was a result of long-term, sustained investment in high-speed global communications, imagery, and analysts. And this technology made more detailed and stringent civilian, political-level control possible. When political leaders can receive updates in real time, they can take a more active role in directing the pace and conduct of military engagements.

Ground forces had a few new weapons also, but they lacked the combination of reliable striking power, action from a distance, and controlled risk-taking that airplanes and missiles can provide. Ground combat retained the possibility of turning nasty and unpredictable at close quarters; its weapons—tanks, ground artillery, and infantry fighting vehicles—tend to be more numerous and less controllable than the air platforms; and the crews are less experienced, and more vulnerable. No wonder that political leaders conditioned by the twentieth century's profligate losses of military manpower tend to opt first to use airpower.

One consequence of all these factors was that the old separations in time between the military and the political and between the echelons of military command were no longer the same. Political leaders don't give orders and wait days and weeks for results. What we discovered increasingly was that the political and strategic levels impinged on the operational and tactical levels. Or, to put it another way, any event in modern war has four distinct, unequal components: tactical, operational, strategic, and political. Sometimes even insignificant tactical events packed a huge political wallop. This is a key characteristic of modern war.

These common perceptions of the needless slaughter of warfare, the impact of NATO and its Cold War doctrine, the efforts to restrict the violent nature of war and to limit its effects, and the impact of the new technologies on policymakers and the military itself converged to shape the operations in Kosovo. Modern war is the response developed by the democratic West after a century of trauma in Europe. It is the answer to the trenches and wholesale slaughter of World War I, and it is the answer to the devastation of civilian populations by the "total war" of World War II. But its concept has been incomplete, and the application of military and diplomatic means to wage it and win it have not been well understood.

Modern warfare is likely to recur in the years and decades to come. It remains a fact that military force is the ultimate arbiter in international affairs. Diplomacy, the process of international relations, has always required the use of influence and power, played out to achieve gains or protect against losses. In classic diplomacy, military power has always been the ultimate card. But there were also diplomatic suasion, economic relations, and all other measures of intercourse between nations. Ideally, diplomacy relies on the positive, as nations cooperate for their mutual benefit. But sometimes issues arise for which positive inducements to cooperation don't suffice, or in which positive inducements are simply inappropriate. International legal pressures, such as war crimes indictments, have now also begun to be used to augment diplomatic pressures.

In recent years, economic pressures, such as trade and investment restrictions, and even cutoffs of trade have become a staple of international affairs. During the past decade and a half the United States has become accustomed to using its economic muscle to sanction nations whose behavior we wish to change. But the limitations of the economic instruments of power have become increasingly apparent. In the Balkans, for example, the economic sanctions implemented against Serbia during the early 1990s are widely credited with helping Serb President Slobodan Milosevic strengthen his control, through the encouragement of black market and smuggling activities. At the same time these sanctions imposed burdens on neighboring countries like

Bulgaria, Macedonia, and Romania, whose leaders were unanimous in opposing any extension of the sanctions regime.

The imminent entry of China into the World Trade Organization will spell the end of trade sanctions as an element of coercion against that country. Iraqi oil is back on the world market today, though the proceeds are supposed to be used only in procuring humanitarian goods. The experience with the total economic embargo imposed against Haiti was also instructive, in that after the Aristide government was restored to power in 1994, economic recovery was made far more difficult by the impact of the preceding embargo on small and family-owned businesses. While economic sanctions have certainly produced punishment for the affected nations, the punishment has often been indiscriminant, causing economic deprivation and in some cases contributing to more hunger and poverty without impacting those directing the offensive policies and practices of the targeted state.

If other means of diplomatic suasion fail, the limited efficacy of economic sanctions will leave military power as the last recourse when pressure is required. It may not be used, or even threatened, overtly. In Korea, for example, U.S. forces have been stationed in the south for almost fifty years, since the end of the Korean War, and demonstrate the determination of the United States to assist the Republic of Korea in the event of renewed aggression from North Korea. Though the troops have never been used, there can be no doubt in the minds of potential adversaries what they represent.

And there are cases where the deployment of military forces can be threatening but still ambiguous. In March 1996 Chinese missiles fired toward Taiwan led to American naval deployments into the immediate area. No specific public threats were made, and no commitments were given, so far as is known, to Taiwan. But the deployments nevertheless gave leverage to achieve the desired Chinese de-escalation of the crisis.

Finally, there are likely to be cases where, for one reason or another, it will be necessary to make a more open statement of possible military action. U.S. actions against Iraq are a case in point, where a continual series of air strikes have been conducted since the four-day series of strikes against Saddam Hussein's special weapons programs in December 1998. Here the United States and its allies have continued to enforce the no-fly zones in northern and southern Iraq that were established after the Gulf War. When Iraqi forces challenge the air patrols with air defense radars or manned aircraft, American and British aircraft are directed to strike designated targets. These actions serve as a continuing reminder to Hussein that military power will be brought against any move to threaten his neighbors, or the Kurdish tribes in the north that have been protected by the West since 1991.

In each of these cases, U.S. and Allied military power is in use, will be, or could be, in order to deter, to dissuade, or to compel. These, too, are examples of actions that could become modern war: not a fight for national survival, but carefully restrained and limited action, widely observed and reported by the media, and under real-time political control.

When it can, the United States will use military power in conjunction with its friends and allies. It is a matter of distributing the risks and burdens of military action, as well as securing essential access and support. And in the case of allied action, the United States will have to recognize that its own national interests will seldom be the same in nature, intensity, scope, or duration as those of its allies and partners. This is the unchangeable truth about groupings of states: they have differing interests. These may derive from different degrees of exposure to the damages of war, varying economic interests in the affected region, historical or cultural relationships with adversaries, or even different national election procedures or timing. Sustaining a common interest sufficient to support military power and its use is therefore a matter of high statesmanship. The United States will be fortunate indeed if it has alliance political and military "machinery" like NATO to assist in forging and sustaining shared interests and common commitments.

NATO has survived numerous crises over its half century of existence, crises arising from the differing perspectives and interests of its member nations. There was a crisis in 1956, caused by the U.S.'s refusal to support British and French military actions against Egypt, a crises in the early 1960s associated with the U.S.'s reneging on promises to share nuclear weapons technology with allies, and a crisis in 1966 when France withdrew from the NATO military structure. There were longstanding European questions about whether Washington would really risk American cities to deter attacks on Western European cities.

There was a perception of neglect as the United States turned its attention to Vietnam, and another crisis brought on by the buildup of Soviet theater nuclear forces and NATO's need to respond in the late 1970s and early 1980s. With the end of the Cold War and the breakup of the Warsaw Pact and the Soviet Union, there was concern that NATO would have no purpose, and that the profound underlying differences between nations on each side of the Atlantic would overshadow their common interest in security.

Yet, NATO has survived and adapted, binding together member nations on both sides of the Atlantic through its Charter document, its consensus-building institutions and procedures, and the continuing common interests of its members. NATO is a "consensus engine." It was designed and has evolved to harmonize varying opinions into a workable, cohesive whole. Economics, language, culture, and politics create rifts and rivalries from time to time, but on military matters the Atlantic Alliance has proved a durable force for teamwork. Leaders and staff from its nineteen member nations know each other through the frequent—some say, too frequent—meetings. There are summit meetings for heads of state, meetings for foreign ministers and defense ministers twice each year, and a third meeting only for the defense ministers. The top military leaders in each country, the Chiefs of Defense, or CHODs, meet separately three times per year and then accompany their defense ministers to their meetings. And each meeting has its social event the evening before, with the transatlantic participants sometimes numbed by jet lag and looking for the door early.

The mechanics of the Alliance are designed to promote agreement on essential minimums. NATO is led and represented on the diplomatic level by the Secretary General, always a European, normally someone with previous experience as a defense minister or foreign minister. The military work at the headquarters is led by the Chairman of the Military Committee, always a European general who has led his nation's military. This military work is the essential preliminary in generating agreement. Issues are identified, parsed out, worked, and resolved at the military level first in order to facilitate the subsequent political-level discussions and agreements that then become orders for NATO's military. The Supreme Allied Commander, Europe—known as the SACEUR—commands the Alliance's European-based military forces on land, sea, and air in accordance with approved directions and restrictions from NATO headquarters. He is always an American, due to the leading U.S. role in the Alliance and the coupling of its deterrent mission in Europe to the American strategic deterrent elsewhere.

NATO operates bilingually, with English and French as its two languages. But in truth, NATO has its own language of acronyms, out-of-syntax constructions, and insider code. There is a subtlety that reflects not only the nuances of complex issues but also the tortuous process of consensus building. Agreements are not voted; they are place "under silence." Disagreement is noted by "breaking silence" on a proposal. The North Atlantic Council meets in different groupings, "ambassadors only," or "ambassadors plus four," tailored to promote the most effective exchanges.

Javier Solana, NATO's Secretary General, proved himself to be a master at using the machinery and language to shape policies and build consensus. In a rare quiet moment, I once asked the Secretary General the secret of his success. He reflected briefly, then said, "Two things. Make no enemies. And ask no question unless you know what the answer will be and it is the answer you want."

The complexities of forging common purpose are today compounded by the emergence of the European Union's efforts to create a Common Foreign and Security Policy and by the fact that Russia is no longer perceived as a military threat to Western Europe or the United States. Many in the United States, over the past decade, looking at the rapidly growing economic strength of countries in the Pacific and east Asia, and especially China, have sought to reduce American foreign policy's long-term orientation toward Europe. This has added to the stress on transatlantic relationships and institutions like NATO.

War, of course, is first and foremost a political act. The U.S. Constitution assigns the power to declare war to the Congress, while the President serves as the U.S. Commander in Chief. Other Western nations see the problem similarly. During World War I, French Premier Georges Clemenceau famously said, "War is too important to be left to the generals." In fact, this realization is one of the points of origin for modern war. Political leaders make the ultimate decisions, decide the key policies, develop or approve the strategy, and supervise the execution. Even limited war requires the acceptance of risks and losses, embarrassment, and potential failure. Warfare disrupts peacetime patterns of commerce and political discourse and can consume alternate political goals and efforts. Warfare is thus one of the supreme tests for political leaders, and for leaders in democracies, it is something to be avoided if possible.

Each NATO nation has its own system for providing national guidance on matters affecting its security, including direction of its armed forces in war. In some parliamentary governments there are special groupings of ministers. In France the president had unique responsibilities in foreign affairs. In the United States, the Armed Forces are directed by the National Command Authority, consisting of the President and his Secretary of Defense. But the directives and orders themselves usually emerge from a system of interagency coordination that brings together the information, perspectives, and resources of the Department of State, the intelligence agencies, the Department of Defense, and sometimes others, under the coordination of the National Security Council staff. Issues are raised and developed, options considered, and consensus is formed. In some cases, where differing agency positions cannot be reconciled or the stakes are so high, the decisions are pushed upward, for resolution in small meetings of the cabinet secretaries or in the Oval Office itself. Of course, differing agency perspectives always remain, to bedevil policy execution or to resurface when similar issues arise in the future.

Thus within the U.S. system, military leaders receive their orders from a clear chain of command, but the orders may be influenced by a broader set of personalities and agencies. The military chain of command provides the hierarchy of leaders, institutions, and communications that actually commands the forces. Military leaders must give information and advice, prepare plans as directed, and respond to queries. However, this exchange of information also goes beyond the strict confines of the military chain of command. While it may seem desirable in theory to separate the military decisionmaking from policy formulation, in practice it is impossible. At the top levels the generals and admirals stay abreast of the issues and arguments, anticipating requests for information or orders for action, and engage in a variety of informal exchanges with members of the diplomatic community, policymakers in other agencies, and members of Congress and their staffs. The top leadership therefore not only carries out the orders it receives, it may heavily influence their formulation.

Military advice is not without profound professional and personal implications for the military itself, as well as civilians. War risks the loss and destruction of carefully honed armed forces, the disruption of well-laid plans for the future, and of course, personal embarrassment, failure, defeat, and loss of life. None knows better than the military leaders themselves the dangers of war; consequently, they are usually the last to advocate it.

The difficulties and complexities of modern war can be measured in part by the difficulties faced by the American military in coming to grips with Kosovo. The top leaders in the American Armed Forces were still heavily impacted by their early experiences in the Vietnam War. We knew about the dangers of "political micromanagement," when bombing targets were picked by Lyndon B. Johnson's White House and pilots were restrained from attacking key enemy airfields and air defense sites. All of us knew from personal experience the incredible power of the media, which, at least in Vietnam, turned increasingly adversarial to the Pentagon and the leadership of the Armed Forces as the long war continued. And in the Army, it had long been an article of resolve that there would be "no more Vietnams," wars in which soldiers carried the weight of the nation's war despite the lack of public support at home.

These were scars that I carried personally. Bullet wounds, I learned, healed in a few months, but the emotional isolation from our contemporaries, the sense of rejection that we felt, and the lack of public appreciation lingered. We wanted to believe that what we were doing in Vietnam was our duty, a public service—not just a personal preference. But that's not the way much of the country saw it. The Pentagon was harassed by massive demonstrations and blood thrown on the entrance. Around Washington military people seldom wore their uniforms; no point in stirring up protest and problems. Like other military men of my generation, I spent much of my military career helping to rebuild the war-shattered U.S. Army and to learn and embed in it the lessons to prevent another disaster like Vietnam. We changed the Army to a volunteer force, brought in new equipment, created sweeping new military doctrine and training techniques, and brought up a new generation of officers, much more combat-focused, much less academically inclined. We built an outstanding force, an organization that in December 1989 took down Panamanian dictator Manuel Noriega and his henchmen in a few days with innovative elite light units and bold tactics and a year later conducted a large-scale and highly successful action against Saddam Hussein in Iraq.

In 1991, as U.S. and coalition forces were engaged in the Persian Gulf, Americans tried to make up with their armed forces. There was a great outpouring of support and sympathy for the men and women who fought in the Gulf War. Popular songs were written, and extravagant welcomes were staged to greet the returning veterans. Many of those who had participated in the public demonstrations against the war in Vietnam seemed to feel strongly that this time war was right and that the men and women in uniform were America's heroes. Even men and women like me, who were serving in uniform but didn't fight in the Gulf, received some of the splash.

I was at Fort Irwin, California, commanding the National Training Center during the Gulf War. We had done some work on tactics and techniques against the Iraqi trench line defenses, had taken one group from the First Infantry Division through the training before they deployed, and then spent the period from January through March training the National Guard brigades from Georgia and Mississippi that might have to deploy if the war had continued. Of course, almost all the officers and soldiers would have preferred to deploy to the fight, and I was besieged with requests for reassignment, most of which I had to deny.

So it was a surprise when our public affairs officer came in one day in March, reporting that the honorary mayor of Hollywood, Johnny Grant, wanted to express his appreciation for our contribution. Several days later Grant and his team made the long drive into the high Mojave to visit us.

As a result, in April 1991, while the bulk of the forces that had deployed were still hard at work in the Gulf, several hundred soldiers and their families from Fort Irwin went to Hollywood, to receive the thanks of a grateful entertainment community at a Bob Hope Special at Universal Studios. It was warm and immensely moving, especially in contrast to the lack of appreciation twenty years previously, after Vietnam.

The warmth lasted a few weeks, amid the joyful homecomings, then the American people moved on to other issues, and the armed forces faded from the popular eye.

In the Army, though, and the other services, we diligently studied the lessons of the build-up and the forty-four days of fighting. We revised our techniques a little and defined some necessary enhancements in our equipment. For the youngsters who served in the war, marched in the parades, and received the big welcome homes, there was some sense of completion. But the Army and the other services were soon caught up in the process of downsizing that followed the war and the collapse of the Soviet Union. The instinct, especially the Army instinct, was to hang on, to preserve the memory and machinery of those brief moments of public acclaim, in preparing for the future. The organizations had proved themselves, and so had the weapons. We had had a foretaste of how we could do the same thing all over again, only better. It gave us the only road map we could see clearly in the new, post-Cold War world.

But the war in Kosovo was nothing like the Gulf War, not even close: no clear international consensus to fight, no sure cause, ambivalent public support, no long deployment and build-up, an incredibly complex theater environment, and difficult climactic, demographic, and geographic conditions on the battlefield. For the U.S. military, it was neither the conflict we had prepared for nor the war we wanted to fight. Still it was a fight that had to be won. We had to learn to fight a new kind of war—while we were fighting it.

Challenging as the task before us was, I had confidence in my senior officers at SHAPE and in the U.S. chain of command. They were experienced and able. They had risen into top positions. And the men and women they led were superb.

As for me, after graduating from West Point in 1966, I had worked on the streets of New York City in the poverty program for a few weeks, gone to airborne school, and then sailed on the ocean liner Queen Elizabeth with thirty-one other young men to commence two years of study at Oxford University as a Rhodes Scholar. Later, as an Army captain, I commanded tank companies in the United States and a mechanized infantry company in combat in Vietnam, where I received the Purple Heart and a Silver Star. I worked temporarily on the volunteer army program in the Pentagon. I taught economics and political philosophy at West Point and saw how Washington worked by serving as a special assistant to the Director of the Office of Management and Budget as a White House Fellow. Later, I worked in NATO, as a special assistant for General Alexander M. Haig, when he was the Supreme Allied Commander. Eventually, I commanded a tank battalion, a heavy brigade, and the First Cavalry Division. Between command tours with units, I ran the Army's National Training Center and helped start the higher level training program for Army divisions and corps. As a staff officer I helped draft the lessons from Army actions in Grenada and the Gulf War, and later served in a senior position on the Joint Staff in Washington. My postgraduate education and training included stints at the Ranger School, the Armor Officer Basic and Advanced Courses, the Command and General Staff College, and the National War College.

The way I saw it, I knew soldiering, joint operations, and national strategy, and also a little about diplomacy, NATO, Europe, the U.S. government, and politics. But I knew it wasn't enough. It was often said that people stopped growing once they assumed high office; they used the ideas and approaches they brought with them to the job. I never believed that. I tried to learn from every job and grow in it as I proceeded.

I was born in Chicago. My father, Benjamin Kanne, was a lawyer and Democratic Party politician there. His parents, Jacob and Ida, had immigrated from Minsk and become part of Chicago's thriving Jewish community. My father died when I was not quite four. My mother, who came from a long line of Scottish, Irish, and Dutch settlers, returned to live with her parents in Arkansas and remarried a former banker. I knew nothing of my father's family or my heritage—my mother, who wasn't Jewish, admitted years later that she just wanted to protect me from some of the prejudice she had witnessed—and when my mother remarried, I took my stepfather's name, Clark. I was raised as a Baptist (I later converted to Catholicism in Vietnam) and went to the local schools, except for a year at a Tennessee military school when the high schools closed in Little Rock in the late 1950s because of disputes over racial integration. When it was time to go to college, I turned down scholarships to several prestigious schools and selected West Point. I wanted to be an officer and a leader in the Army. I wanted public service.

I had learned a little about leadership and public service as a counselor at the Boys Club camp outside Little Rock, when I was fourteen. Responsibility for others, the teaching and the coaching that came with looking after the sixteen campers in the cabin gave me a keen sense of satisfaction. I had to get to know each one, learn his dispositions, strengths, and weaknesses, and help him to participate and achieve in the two-week-long camp programs. There was also a fellowship among the counselors and staff that made it fun. And I learned a lot from the others at the camp as well.

One of the first things I learned was that you have to have courage to attain your goals. The camp was run by our Boys Club swim coach, Jimmy Miller, a World War II veteran in his late thirties who had seen Army duty in the South Pacific. He was careful about who he picked to serve as counselors. After several months of Saturday morning leadership classes under Coach Miller at the Boys Club, I was selected to spend a weekend in early April with other prospects to help get the camp ready for opening in June. I figured it was just a matter of doing a little work. But it proved to be much more than that.

Ten of us prospective counselors headed out on a beautiful Saturday morning for the forty-minute drive to the camp. We spent the rest of the day taking down shutters from the cabins and moving beds and mattresses, sorting out the softballs, bases, gloves, horseshoes, basketballs, and other supplies, setting up the ball field, and doing the other things necessary. The camp's swimming pool wasn't ready either, so on Sunday morning early we took advantage of a break in the schedule to go out the gate and down the road to where Little Maumelle Creek widened to a shallow sparkling stream with a wide gravel bar. It was perfect for wading, catching frogs and crawfish, and running the electric model boats I brought out with us. Of course, it was a skinny-dip.

Soon Jimmy Miller passed by on the red iron girder bridge above the creek on his way to a nearby country store. He saw us there, stopped his pickup truck, asked what we were doing, and drove on. Whether he said anything more remains in some dispute.

A few minutes later he drove back by and again stopped. "I thought

I told you all to return to camp immediately," he said. "But you've disobeyed me and now you'll pay the price. Any of you that want to be counselors in June, get up here and go off the bridge. The rest of you, just head on back now, and you can come out as campers."

We had heard about this old iron girder bridge before but never paid much attention to it. The camp rumors were that Miller and some of the older guys would come out at night, shinny up to the top of the girders and dive off. Some were said to do back flips and gainers under the influence of a little beer. This was the legendary Red Bridge Club, and from the top of the girders to the water, the rumor was, it was forty-two feet. Surely, he didn't want us to do this, at our relatively young ages, on a Sunday morning, with no bathing suits.

Four of us stayed behind, half believing we could talk him into changing his mind. Six returned to camp. Ranny Treece, Larry Busbee, Mike Stewart, and I scrambled up the bank and onto the wooden planking, then began the climb up to the top girder. We went in order of age.

Ranny stood up on the top, balanced a little precariously, while the rest of us remained prone on the twelve-inch wide girder. He was a little older than the rest of us and had been on the swim team with Coach Miller a few years longer. And Ranny began the debate.

"Miller, there's not enough water down there." Right under the bridge the water was only two or three feet deep.

"Look out there to that deep green pool," Miller said. "That's six or seven feet of water. Just do a standing broad jump; you'll get out there,"

"But, Coach, I don't have a suit on. I'll get hurt." Ranny continued, all the while staring down at the water and swaying just a bit. It sounded like another good argument to us, but Miller wasn't about to be talked out of this.

"Just keep your legs together and you'll be fine," he said. "I'll count to three, and you jump!" He was the coach now, not the punitive disciplinarian of a few minutes earlier.

Once, and then again, he counted, but still Ranny didn't jump. The sun was getting warm on top of the girder, and this was starting to look like a long morning with an uncertain ending. Ranny was glancing around now, looking for a way off the top of the bridge.

Then we all heard it—the sound of gravel popping—and looked down the road to see a column of dust signaling the approach of a speeding vehicle. Perhaps this would be the distraction we needed. Maybe now Miller would change his mind.

In an instant a pickup truck became visible as it crested the rise and headed down toward the bridge. It was a green Chevy, with three women in the front seat, dressed for church, ribbons flying out the open windows. Coming down the slope toward the bridge, the truck was about even with the top girder. They could see us clearly.

Ranny saw them, too, as he stood naked on the top girder. He looked down, looked again toward the approaching truck and jumped. What ambition and good coaching couldn't do, a little embarrassment did. Now there was no way out for the rest of us.

I stood up and looked down. Yes, I might just make it into the deeper pool with a good broad jump. Was I really going to do this? Jimmy counted to three and I leaped, somewhat to my surprise.

The afterglow lasted a good two weeks, at least. Or maybe forty years. You have to have courage and faith. And you have to expect to go through some trials to be a leader.

I was wounded in Vietnam while commanding a mechanized infantry company. We were on patrol in the jungle, moving on foot in platoon strength, searching for the Viet Cong. By February 1970, two years after Tet, the Viet Cong were just remnants, hiding in the jungle, armed, lethal, and seeking to avoid us. Our force found a small group in an old bunker complex—the buzzing around my head wasn't hornets but AK-47 rounds whizzing by, the dark stains on my leg and shoulder weren't perspiration but blood, and there was a white bone sticking out from my right hand as I looked down to see why I had dropped my rifle.

I jumped back and took cover, directing one small element from our force of twenty-five to lay down a "base of fire" while another element maneuvered against the base camp from the flank.

In a few minutes it was over—an insignificant fire fight which perhaps disrupted a group of Viet Cong scouts and guides who may have been part of a larger plan to threaten Saigon. We had one other soldier wounded; we found blood stains from the enemy as we overran his positions. I was soon evacuated by helicopter and eventually returned to the States for two months in the hospital and a year of effort to recover fully.

Ground combat was a difficult, often dull, and potentially deadly business. But there was no other way to seek out and defeat the enemy force there.

Later, I was picked for a succession of what businessmen would call "turn-around situations and start-ups." From staff officer to commander to trainer for units, many of my positions involved muscling up an organization that had been "low-performing" or swimming upstream to start something new. So I learned a lot about the fundamentals, and how to work details that spelled the difference between success and failure. I worked on coaching subordinates into achieving what they didn't dare dream. It was challenging and satisfying, but it definitely brought out a hard-edge mentality and a determination to succeed.

In early 1980 I was placed in command of a tank battalion at Fort Carson, Colorado. The previous commander had been removed early due to the battalion's poor ability to maintain its equipment. The assistant division commander said, "Take six weeks, get the unit in top shape and pass the materiel readiness re-inspection." I walked the quarter-mile down to the motor pool for a look. Pitiful. The tanks were old, with thousands of hard miles on them. Most were reported to be inoperative. Twenty-five had their engines removed, with the hulking engines and transmission assemblies half covered in tarpaulins, sitting on the sloping concrete on the motor pool, bleeding oil slowly onto the ice and snow. The troops weren't anywhere to be seen.

Less than six weeks later we had met all standards in the reinspection. I gave a lot of pep talks, I made it a point personally to inspect the tanks, including a detailed technical inspection, and I met individually with the company commanders. One soldier sent a nice letter saying I was like Clint Eastwood. One of the company commanders said, "All right, sir, I can see I don't know how to inspect a tank correctly. But I will learn. This will never happen again." Another told me, over a beer, "Sir, you're going to make us the best battalion in the division." They had begun to believe in themselves. We went on to earn a reputation for the best maintenance in the division and became one of the top battalions with great esprit and morale, too.

I had found a command pattern that worked: Be personally competent. Know and work the details; set high standards; provide lots of personal, up-front leadership and good planning; and work to bring out the best in the people you have. Make them achieve more than they ever thought possible, but never forget that they are also human beings. Look after the families, and deal with the whole person.

I always remembered what Prime Minister Yitzhak Rabin had told me when I visited Israel as a White House Fellow in 1976. Seven of us had sat around the dinner table in Rabin's home. It was a few years after the Yom Kippur War, and with Rabin were Shimon Peres, at the time the defense minister; Yigal Allon, the foreign minister; and Yehoshua Rabinowitz, the finance minister. "Sir," I asked Rabin, "what advice could you, as a winning leader, give me as a young officer?"

Rabin told the story of his holding positions in the Old City of Jerusalem during the War of Independence in 1948. His brigade was almost out of ammunition, he said, and his battalion commanders all wanted to withdraw. They feared another Arab assault would carry their positions and they would be destroyed. Rabin refused their advice. We stay, he told them. It turned out the Arabs were also low on ammunition and were unable to mount another attack. "Persistence," he said. "It's the most important quality for a military leader."

It was a pattern I applied successfully again and again. But I slowly realized that I was going against the Army tide of the time, which emphasized older commanders and de-emphasized education and broadening experiences. It was a time of the "country-boy" and "jes' plain soldierin'." Lots of people with fancy masters degrees and Ph.D.s kept it quiet if they could. It was the Vietnam backlash, though it took a long time to develop. I couldn't help what I had already done or how I had worked my way up. After the Rhodes scholarship and finishing at the top of the class in the Command and General Staff College, I had gotten an Army-wide reputation, and I was stuck with it, for better or worse.

Still, I was returned to Fort Carson as a full colonel in 1986 to command a brigade for two years, an assignment I had long hoped to receive. Some months after I left that post, I came back to Fort Carson to visit friends, and I was pulled aside by one of the senior officers in the division. "The new Commanding General considers you a potential Army Chief of Staff," he confided. "I just thought you ought to know. He's watching you."

My friend said it with a matter-of-fact air, perhaps a little puzzled that I would have been discussed this way. I didn't know Major General

Dennis Reimer, the Commanding General, though I certainly knew his outstanding reputation. But his comment seemed favorable. He knows who I am, I thought; he thinks I might be in the running for the Big Job. I was flattered at the time—after all, I was only a colonel.

A few weeks later I was selected for promotion to brigadier general at age forty-three and subsequently given a plum assignment as commander of the National Training Center. Three years later I was tapped to command the First Cavalry Division, at Fort Hood, Texas. The Army had ten divisions, each consisting of 12,000 to 17,000 soldiers, but this was the one division that always had stood out from the rest, in my mind. The big, gold-colored shoulder patch, with the diagonal slash and the horse head, were a symbol recognized everywhere.

The "First Team," it was called: a full-strength division, recently returned from the Gulf War, placed at the top of the Army's priority list. It had a history, a great combat record, especially in Vietnam, and a tremendous esprit. This was an elite unit, with top-notch officers and sergeants at every level. It was a unit that just hummed with positive energy. This was not a "turnaround." And it really did almost run itself.

I put in the same command philosophy that had worked for me everywhere else. The division maintained its fine reputation. We were winning our key fights at the National Training Center. We actually defeated the opposing force in the division-level war fighting evaluation run by my old outfit, the Battle Command Training Program. We "made our mission" in reenlisting soldiers. We readied ourselves to redeploy to Saudi Arabia and Kuwait if need be.

One Saturday morning in 1993, as some of the generals on the post were riding horseback together, the Corps Commander, Lieutenant General Pete Taylor, leaned across his saddle and said to me, "Did you hear that President Clinton was talking about you with the Army Chief last week? Asked him if he knew 'my friend, Wes Clark.'"

"No, I didn't know that," I said. Of course, I was acquainted with the new president—we had both grown up in Arkansas, though in different towns, and I was two years older. We had first met at a student conference at Georgetown in 1965. I had also met Mrs. Clinton, at a French-American Young Leaders Conference in France in 1983. My wife and I had had dinner with the Clintons nine years earlier, when he was Governor of Arkansas, and I had talked to him once on the phone as I was passing through the state a few years later. But that was about the extent of it.

The president wasn't popular with the officers and troops at this point, particularly over his promise to admit gays to the military. Taylor's remark was another of those seemingly flattering comments that ought to raise red flags.

A few months later Lieutenant General Barry McCaffrey, the J-5 on the Joint Staff in Washington, came through Fort Hood on an official visit. It was a whiz-bang stopover by an important officer, and the briefings were vintage McCaffrey: hard-hitting and slightly irreverent. Barry was already famous, the most decorated general in the Army, a division commander in the Gulf War, and the general who had been insulted to his face by an anonymous White House staffer who said that they "did not want people in uniform at the White House unless absolutely necessary."

We talked briefly on his way out. "I'm going to be leaving my position as J-5 sometime in the next few months," he said. "I'm going to talk you up for it." The J-5. A principal position on the Joint Staff, the nation's highest military staff, responsible for strategic plans and political-military affairs around the world. It would mean horizons beyond the Army. And it sounded like it would mean leaving the division early. Well, I had learned that you can't control your assignments as a senior officer. If officially asked, I couldn't refuse it.

A few weeks later I was invited to Washington to meet with the new Chairman of the Joint Chiefs, General John Shalikashvili, to talk about the job. As Barry had explained the procedure, the Army, Navy, Air Force, and Marines would each nominate a two- or three-star officer, and Shali (as he was universally known) would decide whom he wanted for the post.

It was a good conversation. I had heard how much people respected Shali and liked him, and could see why. He was noncommittal but indicated he would be back in touch with me, one way or the other.

I dutifully reported back to the Army's General Officer Management Office, which controls generals' assignments. "How did it go, sir?" they asked. Obviously it was in the Army's interest to have their man picked.

"OK, I think. We talked about a lot of issues—Somalia and all."

"Well, sir, I guess we'll wait to hear about how everyone else did." It turned out that I wasn't actually the Army nominee, just one of ten Army officers who might be made available.

Oh, I thought. I was still a little ambivalent about the job, but I was happy knowing that I had the Army behind me. Now I was slightly adrift, like when you were expecting an A on your report card but got a B-.

A few weeks later I got a call from General Shali. "How soon can you be here?" he asked. I felt a thrill, a little shiver, at the news. I knew it was likely to be the end of my service with Army units, but I looked forward to the challenges ahead.

TWO

CRISIS MANAGEMENT

BY PENTAGON STANDARDS, it was an impressive "E-ring" office: two full windows, a meeting area with overstuffed furniture, a conference table, multiple telephones, and a full colonel to "guard the door." The E-ring was the outer ring, where offices could have windows and actually have views of the outside. In April 1994, reporting in to my new position as the J-5, the Director for Strategic Plans and Policies on the Joint Staff, I realized that I had arrived at the highest levels of the U.S. Armed Forces.

The J-5, is the senior staff officer responsible to the Chairman of the Joint Chiefs of Staff for worldwide political military policies and strategy. I was "armed" with several briefing books each day. Over 200 staff professionals, mostly senior lieutenant colonels and colonels from all the branches of the Armed Forces, assisted me. Daily packages of messages and intelligence from around the world were delivered periodically. I often accompanied the Chairman to key White House meetings. My assistants and I routinely went across the Potomac to represent the military at lower level meetings in the State Department and White House.

The Joint Staff is one of those mysterious organizations that none of us understands until we are actually part of it. It operated then in specially protected areas with distinctive security badges, behind locked doors, within private operations and information centers, deep inside the Pentagon. It was a large team, hundreds of officers, noncommissioned officers, and civilians. The officers were by law limited to no more than forty-eight months' continuous service.

I was one of eight J-Staff "principals," numbered J-1 through J-8, each with a different set of responsibilities, from personnel through resources, and we were drawn from each of the branches of the Armed Forces. When I arrived there, the J-1, J-4, and J-6 were Navy; the J-3 a Marine; the J-8 was Air Force; and the J-2, J-7, and I were Army. The -3, -4, -5, and -6 were authorized three-star officers; the other positions were filled by two-stars and one-stars.

Of course we worked for the Chairman of the Joint Chiefs, but the day-to-day staff coordination was usually done by a fellow three-star, the Director of the Joint Staff. The Chairman could also call on a four-star Vice Chairman and a three-star Assistant to the Chairman.

These were the top-quality men and women in the Armed Forces; the organization had a real "key insider" feel to it.

As I went around to meet my colleagues, Lieutenant General Jack Sheehan, the Marine officer who was the J-3, Director of Operations, clued me in. "You can count on a crisis this weekend, like almost every other weekend," he said. "I can't tell you what it will be, but they always break on a Friday night or a Saturday morning, just timed perfectly to screw up the weekend. It's been going like this for months."

Two days later, my executive officer, Colonel Tom Banks, came in to see me. "Sir, have you heard the reports that Belgian troops are on the ground in Kigali?" he asked. "Mideast-Africa Division heard it on CNN."

Wait a minute, I thought. This doesn't sound right. Shouldn't we have heard about this from our liaison with their armed forces? Let's get the facts, I thought. I summoned the staff officers who were working African issues up to the office.

Sure enough, it was a little after 6 on a Friday night.

Where is Kigali? What are the distances and en route airfields in case we have to do something? And the two tribes—are they Tutus and Hutsis, or Tutsis and Hutus? Do the Belgians need any assistance?

What about the French? Where is our European Command on all this? Are they in the coordination loop?

We looked at the maps, checked with others on the Joint Staff, called the Belgian and French attachés in Washington, checked with the operations center at the U.S. European Command in Stuttgart, Germany, and tried to sort out the incomplete and conflicting reports. Staff officers began preparing papers, the calls began to flow back and forth to the Department of State and the National Security Council staff. Gradually, we began to pull together a coherent picture of the situation on the ground.

I went home about 7:00 A.M., feeling good about our work. The J-5 staff had been taking criticism during the period after McCaffrey had left and before I arrived that they weren't "in the loop." In this crisis, we had taken the lead in the Joint Staff and in the "interagency," the committees of experts and policymakers from State, Defense, CIA, NSC, and the Joint Staff that reviewed all policy initiatives. I had two hours to clean up and return for a morning meeting with the Secretary of Defense, William Perry, to prepare for his forthcoming trip to Korea.

The meeting on Korea was my first chance to meet Secretary Perry. Everyone had been speaking so highly of him that I was eagerly anticipating the meeting, and also a little apprehensive. I had been cramming on Korea issues over the last couple of days.

I went upstairs to the big office looking across the river toward Washington and joined several of Perry's staff. Plush carpet, multiple sitting areas, a large desk set in the center, portraits on the walls, several phones, a computer. The room spoke authority from every angle. The Secretary gathered us around a conference table at one end of the room and we took seats. An aide came in with muffins and coffee.

Perry was exactly as described: focused, articulate, precise, and deep. He had a response to every issue, and the discussion proceeded clearly down unfolding alternatives in the pursuit of increased cooperation between the United States and South Korea. I went away impressed.

The hallways in the J-5 area were quiet, and most of the offices were closed as I came back downstairs. It was time for the next issue on the weekend agenda, the Balkans. A number of the staff officers had come in to help read me further into the situation. As of early April

1994, the war had been going on in Bosnia for two years. It was a three-sided fight, with cross-border assistance to two of the sides. The largest of the factions was the Muslims. The Muslims were the city-dwellers, generally the most prosperous and well-educated of the groups. But in military terms they were the most poorly equipped and had been the chief victims of the fighting thus far. They had been shoved out of many parts of Bosnia in sometimes vicious campaigns of murder, pillage, and rape by the Serbs, the second-largest of the factions in Bosnia. The Muslims had barely managed to retain most of the capital of Sarajevo but it was surrounded and cut off by Serb forces. In several places to the east of the capital, large civilian populations of Bosnian Muslims were similarly encircled and under fire.

The Serbs insisted that they would not live under the Islamic domination of the Muslims. And they had the Yugoslav Army supporting them. They had been the aggressors during the earlier fighting and currently held about 70 percent of the territory of Bosnia-Herzegovina. Traditionally, the Serbs in Bosnia had been country folk who had retained their customs and Orthodox Christianity during 400 years of Turkish occupation by remaining on the land. But the Serbs also constituted the largest ethnic group in Yugoslavia, from which Bosnia had declared its independence in 1992. Before the breakup of the country, the Serbs had managed to dominate the Yugoslav military, and it was clear that the fighting within Bosnia was supported by Serbia and Montenegro, the remaining republics within the now-truncated Yugoslavia, just to the east.

The third side in the conflict was the Croats, the smallest of the three principal ethnic groups in Bosnia. In 1992 they had been allied with the Muslims against the Serbs, but then had switched sides, and, in some of the most vicious fighting of the war, had forced Muslim families from many villages and towns. The Bosnian Croats were receiving aid and direction from neighboring Croatia (another former Yugoslav republic) and some considered themselves citizens of a "greater Croatia." In early 1994, the United States had arbitrated an agreement between the Muslims and Croats to cease fighting each other and work together against the Serbs.

There was also a U.N. Protective Force, UNPROFOR, deployed in Croatia and in Bosnia. More than twenty thousand of these blue-bereted U.N. troops were deployed within Bosnia. They came from NATO Allies like Britain and France, neutrals like Bangladesh, and even the newly independent states of the former Soviet Union, like Ukraine. Their mission was to assist in the delivery of humanitarian relief and, indirectly, to dampen the fighting and help protect the non-combatants. But they were a widely dispersed and lightly equipped group, not organized for heavy fighting and tied to fixed locations. They were basically in static positions or escorting convoys of humanitarian supplies, while the fighting continued around them.

The United States was not involved on the ground, but we were participating through NATO in an air operation to patrol the skies over Bosnia and prevent the Yugoslav or Bosnian Serb air forces from taking part in the action.

As I read into the situation, I recalled hearing estimates of up to 400,000 troops required to stop the fighting there and pacify the parties. And I remembered my conversations with retired General Dick Cavazos, a commonsense leader and a famed commander during the wars in Korea and Vietnam, who had advised me to do what I could to keep the United States out of the seemingly intractable problem of Bosnia.

The immediate problem was centered around the Bosnian town of Gorazde, located near the border with Serbia. Muslim defenders were under attack in what had become house-to-house fighting, with Serb artillery positioned on the high ground overlooking the Drina River and firing into the town. The United Nations had promised to protect the civilians in Gorazde, but the UNPROFOR personnel in the encircled city were powerless to halt the fighting by themselves. While there were no Americans among UNPROFOR the United States was involved because NATO aircraft were likely to be called in to support the embattled peacekeepers on the ground.

I ended up working most of the afternoon on the phone and with staff officers from my team trying to understand the issues involved and to formulate recommendations for the scheduled Sunday afternoon White House meeting. Then General Shalikashvili called and told me to come in on Sunday to go with him to the White House for a special meeting on Bosnia.

Sunday afternoon, in the White House Situation Room, I took a seat behind General Shali, who was at the table. Secretary Perry and Secretary of State Warren Christopher soon arrived, along with Vice President Gore's adviser, Leon Fuerth, and Sandy Berger, the President's Deputy National Security Adviser. Then Tony Lake, the National Security Adviser, came into the room to chair the meeting. The chairs around the table were packed, mostly with people I hadn't met. There was a hushed, somber atmosphere, and a slight sense of fatigue.

We were going to talk about the use of airpower to repel the Serbs' attacks on Gorazde. And we did in great detail. Much of the discussion was about the so-called rules of engagement—the practical and legally binding guidelines that specified when, under what circumstances, and how much force was to be used. The practical procedures for striking from the air—target identification, radiotelephone coordination procedures, and the like—were worked. These were not new issues to the principals. They were into the fine-grain details. By the end of the meeting I had a lot of respect for the tough issues and tough questions that had to be addressed in an operation of that sort.

Two weeks later I was off on a trip to Korea with Secretary Perry—all in all, a busy beginning to my assignment as the J-5. I was coming to realize just how challenging the national agenda in the post-Cold War world could be. The issues confronting us were not only numerous, but complex and politically destabilizing as well. There was the problem of North Korea's nuclear capability, and how we would respond to defiance of the International Atomic Energy Agency. There was the Nuclear Posture Review, which would determine whether the United States should retain a secure nuclear deterrent in the post-Cold War world. There was Operation Provide Comfort, the humanitarian relief and protection operation for the Kurds in northern Iraq. There was the fighting and genocide spreading in Rwanda. There was the refusal of General Raul Cedras and his thugs to leave Haiti, in response to which the United States was considering a total economic embargo. But how were we going to deal with the new waves of "economic migrants" that this might unleash? Finally, there were the U.S. troops still on the ground in Somalia, with the Joint Staff still trying to finish an after-action report on the humanitarian operation there that had ended so badly, with American troops killed and dragged through the streets of Mogadishu.

We were also required by law to produce a National Military Strategy, and Congress was holding our feet to the fire on this. General Shali had mentioned this task to me when I arrived, and I thought I would begin by trying to update my understanding of NATO. The action officers brought in a paper with a series of overlapping and intersecting rings showing how countries were associated with each other. It was an alphabet soup of semi-redundant organizations and concepts, they explained. There was the Western European Union, the European Union, NATO, the NATO Cooperation Council, Partnership for Peace (also part of NATO), and the Conference on Security and Cooperation in Europe. Some countries, like Germany, were in everything. Others, like Austria or Ireland, were in the EU but not the WEU or NATO, and Norway was in the WEU but not the EU. The WEU was the defense arm of the EU, except the WEU had no structure, command and control, or real military capacity. Each organization claimed some competency or turf in the area of security.

I could see that this was going to be hard. Don't worry, sir, my staff told me, nobody can really deal with all this. They were trying to be encouraging.

A few days later General Shalikashvili called me to his office to discuss the National Military Strategy. "Wes," he said, "I hired you as the J-5. You are supposed to be the strategist. So tell me, exactly what is our National Military Strategy?"

I began to lay out my concerns about whether or not we should retain a nuclear deterrent.

"You are probably right," Shali said. "But it seems we should be broader. Our strategy isn't any longer only to deter Russia, is it? Or to contain Russia?"

We agreed that it wasn't. "So," he said, "take a look at what Colin Powell was speaking about: this idea of peacetime engagement. What does it really mean? But don't get us involved everywhere. We are not Globocop."

I went to see one of my Joint Staff colleagues, Lieutenant General Mike Ryan, the Assistant to the Chairman, to work the ideas of engagement, containment, and deterrence. We concluded that these terms were a matter of intent as well as of the specific nature of the activities. In other words, we might be doing the same thing—positioning ships in the Mediterranean Sea—but now the purpose would be to help rein-force friendly governments rather than implicitly threaten a potential adversary.

Working with Air Force Colonel Bob Stratton, we recognized that "engagement" alone was a weak reed on which to base a strategy. The basic function of the Armed Forces is to fight, and so that had to be the most fundamental part of the strategy. But then, it would be better to deter or prevent conflict, if possible. So we put together the concepts of peacetime engagement, deterrence, conflict prevention, and fighting and winning. Seeking to avoid the potential of overcommitment, we labeled the strategy Flexible and Selective Engagement. And we wrote it, and rewrote it, and rewrote it again. Bob and I used to joke that we would hand this mission over to his successor—and mine.

Along the way we took a close look at the Bottom-Up Review (BUR), which was just being completed and sought to answer the question, How big a military does America need? The answer seemed to bear an important relationship to the strategy. In fact, how could you know how much was enough unless you knew what you needed it for? In the BUR the planners on the Joint Staff and in the Office of the Secretary of Defense had drawn on seven Illustrative Planning Scenarios. These were meant to explore military requirements arising from certain hypothetical situations, the two most demanding of which were a major regional conflict in Korea, against which we had maintained Armed Forces there since the end of the Korean War, and a renewed effort by Saddam Hussein to attack Kuwait or other neighbors. These hypotheticals had the additional virtue of being easily understood and generally non-contentious. No one was going to object if we cited these two cases as examples of where we might have to fight in the future. They seemed perfect for both sizing the force and explaining the rationale to the White House and Congress. What came to be known as the "two-MRC strategy" wasn't intended to be a strategy for employing the forces—it was meant to defend the size of the military.

Beneath all the other problems was always the nagging concern about the continued conflict in Bosnia. In excruciating detail the merits of the various aspects of rules of engagement continued to dominate debate at the highest levels. When could an aircraft engage a Serb aircraft violating the no-fly zone? On sight, if hostile intent were demonstrated, or only if there were a hostile act? What was a hostile act? What was hostile intent? It was a struggle between military leaders, lawyers, and common sense, waged in some effort at secrecy at some of the highest levels within and between governments. It consumed an inordinate amount of time, and it represented only the merest piece of a real policy.

In the meantime it seemed difficult to define the objectives, strategies, and means of the Bosnia policy. Of course, we wanted the fighting stopped. But on what conditions, and at what price?

For in truth the United States was progressively deepening its political and diplomatic commitment in the region. In early 1993, Secretary of State Christopher had suggested to the Europeans the so-called "lift and strike" policy, in which the U.N. arms embargo against the former Yugoslavia would be lifted, theoretically enabling the Bosnian Muslim forces to gain the means to defend themselves, and the NATO nations would threaten to strike the Bosnian Serb forces if they continued to attack the Muslims. But to the Europeans, this looked like a recipe for the expansion of the fighting, not its termination. The principle of allowing the Bosnian Muslims in Sarajevo to acquire the arms to defend themselves was directly in conflict with the principles of remaining neutral, containing the conflict, and ameliorating its humanitarian impact.

Lacking international support for "lift and strike," the United States tried various diplomatic tracks to seek to end the conflict, even while NATO was supporting the U.N. peacekeepers and helping to enforce the U.N. arms embargo. By the early summer of 1994, U.S. envoy Charles Redmond was leading the development of the so-called Contact Group peace plan. Working with the representatives of France, Russia, the United Kingdom, and Germany, Redmond was seeking an agreement between the parties on a territorial division that would end the fighting.

But as I began to understand the policy process in Washington, there seemed to be more of a military stake in this plan than at first met the eye. If the territorial agreement broke down, would we be militarily obligated to enforce it? And, was the division militarily sound, or did it split key topographic or economic features in such a way as to encourage the resumption of fighting at a later time?

I met with Redmond on one of his trips back to Washington and got a quick look at the territorial division that had emerged from his travels and discussions. The map did not follow any clear military principles in assigning the key terrain, but seemed instead to be purely the result of political brokering; it might contain the seeds of renewed conflict.

I recommended that General Shalikashvili engage with the Department of State to renegotiate some aspects of the proposed division of territories, and he did, but it was too late to reopen the agreement, according to State. In the future, I thought, we would need to build in the military advice as we commenced the negotiations—and we needed to take more care in getting the right military advice into the policy process early in the development of solutions. On instructions, I began the process of developing and drafting a policy paper on our options in resolving the Bosnian situation.

As the summer wore on, the internal debates on the proper policy toward Bosnia continued. I became increasingly concerned about our staff's lack of experience with the situation on the ground. No one had been there personally. We were relying exclusively on intelligence reports, diplomatic cables, and the press for our information. This didn't give us an adequate basis for understanding the full context of the policies under consideration. I wanted to become acquainted with the situation first hand.

I set up a trip to Bosnia-Herzegovina for late August as an add-on following a visit to Russia to do the first U.S.-Russian Joint Staff talks in Moscow. Preparations followed the usual routine of requesting country clearances from the State Department. In addition, I checked with retired General John R. Galvin, a former Supreme Allied Commander who had been serving as an on-call military adviser to Chuck Redmond. Galvin recommended that I see the generals on both sides, including General Ratko Mladic, the blustering military leader of the Bosnian Serbs. I checked with Redmond to be sure I had his support for the trip and believed that he would take care of the arrangements.

Our first stop coming out of Moscow was in Naples, Italy, to consult with the NATO regional command, Allied Forces Southern Europe, and the American chief of staff there, Lieutenant General Marv Covault. He was an experienced and very highly regarded officer, a Vietnam veteran, who, as commander of the Seventh Infantry Division in 1992, had deployed his outfit to Los Angeles to help reestablish civil order there. His word carried a lot of weight. He spoke with authority on the current issues, especially the planning for air operations and the potential for "lift and strike."

"Look," he said, "there aren't enough targets, and they don't represent any kind of a center of gravity. With five days of good weather we could take them all out, and then we would find that the Serbs would just keep on doing whatever they were doing. Air strikes just won't be decisive."

I filed the information away. It certainly was consistent with my Vietnam experience and some of what we had learned about airpower during the Gulf War.

We departed Italy the next morning for the flight into Sarajevo, and upon landing I was met by the U.S. defense attaché and by Lieutenant General Sir Michael Rose, the U.N. military commander and a British officer with a reputation as a thoughtful intellect as well as a distinguished warrior.

Rose had arranged for me to see Major General Rasim Delic, the Bosnian Muslim commander, and I was looking forward to hearing personally what military assistance Delic felt he would need if we were to lift the arms embargo and change U.S. policy. I told Rose that I also needed to see the Serbs, including General Mladic. Rose said he understood, and he agreed that this could be useful. Mladic, at the time, was popularly accused of war crimes for his role in directing many of the Serb activities in Bosnia but had not yet been indicted by the International Criminal Tribunal at the Hague.

I wanted to see what the Serbs really thought about the Contact Group plan, and thought that as a senior American military officer, I might be able to reinforce the dialogue. At this time the Contact Group peace proposal had been offered to the warring parties and had been accepted by the Bosnian Muslims and Croats. The Bosnian Serb leaders had rejected the plan but had agreed that they would abide by the results of a vote by their parliament in Pale.

The visit to Bosnia proved critical to my later understanding of the issues in the region. I met almost all the key players, from the U.N. team, the Bosnian Muslims (including President Izetbegovic, Prime

Minister Silajdic and General Delic), and the Serb military commander, General Mladic. I visited the troops of the Muslim forces
defending in the hills around Sarajevo, flew over the villages devastated
by ethnic cleansing, and saw the relatively unscathed Serb-controlled
city of Banja Luka. Along the way it was non-stop conversation with
Michael Rose, the Muslims, and the Serbs. The terrible passions of a
country rent by brutal war were visible at every stop.

Meeting with Mladic was especially useful. Although the United
States had not taken sides officially in the conflict, our concerns were
clear. How many people, I reflected at the time, have the opportunity
to size up a potential adversary face-to-face? He carried a reputation
among the U.N. forces for cunning and forcefulness, I found him
coarse and boastful. He knew far less than he thought about NATO,
airpower, and the capabilities of the United States.

But I learned even more about the problems of the Balkans when I
reported back to work in the Pentagon two days later. The staff, as
usual, was involved in dozens of important issues. There was time for a
brief discussion with Shali, reporting on the visit. I soon had the guidance I needed for the paper. Then a *Washington Post* reporter called.
He'd been tipped off about a cable from the American Embassy in
Sarajevo complaining that contrary to instructions I had visited
Mladic. It seemed that even though I had checked with Chuck Redmond about my itinerary, and I understood that it had been "worked,"
the U.S. ambassador hadn't approved the visit. Following my Army
public affairs training, I tried to say as little as possible. We later
released an innocuous statement.

The story ran in the next morning's paper: "Despite Warning, U.S.
General Met With Serb War Crimes Suspect." This was untrue—there
was no warning—but the story generated several phone calls and a
couple of letters from people disapproving of the visit, as well as a letter to the President from two members of Congress calling for my dis-
missal. It was my first experience in the rough and tumble of high
visibility—and a painful few days.

The fact was that I had not received instructions not to visit. Fortunately, I had strong support within the Defense Department, the
National Security Council staff, and at State for having visited both
sides to lay the basis for a proper policy analysis. I heard that the Pres-

ident sent a letter back to the Congress in my defense, and, after a few meetings with Congressional staffers, the controversy died.

The intense political interest in my trip to Bosnia left a profound impression. These were reputation-breaking issues, in some degree partisan, but also caught up with the whole debate about America's proper role in the world. And the sides were oddly switched. Those most interested in deepening our engagement were the liberals—the very people who, two decades earlier, had been most opposed to American activity in Southeast Asia. It was truly a different world, I thought.

I remembered that in July, General Shalikashvili had been musing about life at high levels in Washington. "If you're going to make a difference in this town," he said, "you've got to be able to take the heat that comes with it."

The Bosnia policy paper was prepared and submitted, and a consensus seemed to develop that lifting the arms embargo was going to be very dangerous, in view of the prospect of UNPROFOR withdrawal and the time required for any military assistance to make a substantial impact on the balance of forces. The Serb parliament rejected the Contact Group peace plan, and the international community seemed to need time to consider possible next steps. Policy seemed to move with glacial slowness, and only when forced by events on the ground.

In November, as part of an effort to make UNPROFOR more effective, I travelled to Zagreb, the capital of Croatia, to attend a U.N.-sponsored meeting with the U.N. Secretary General's Special Representative, Yasushi Akashi, the U.N. commanders, and national representatives. The subject was how to strengthen UNPROFOR. But the weather in the Balkans was closing in and, following its annual rhythm, fighting in the region had seemed to slow.

Checking into the hotel in Zagreb, I struck up a conversation with the middle-aged woman behind the desk. "Looks like the fighting will just taper off, doesn't it? Perhaps the lines will just gradually freeze where they are," I suggested.

She answered deliberately but forcefully. "My husband and I lived as the only Croat family in an apartment building with five Serb families. One day in 1991 our neighbors came to us and told us we had to leave. When we didn't leave, the Serb men came back and beat my husband—

they said they would kill him the next time—and then we left." The memories were sharp and unpleasant. "And the fighting will not be over until we get our home back in Knin!"

It wasn't the answer that I had expected. So long as the women were supporting continued fighting, there was going to be more fighting. This war wasn't over.

By November the Serbs were on the march to crush a feeble Bosnian offensive that had been launched out of the so-called Bihac pocket, one of the U.N.-designated safe zones in western Bosnia. It looked as if the Serb counterattack might carry them all the way into the pocket, and Washington was concerned.

Ambassador Richard Holbrooke had recently been appointed Assistant Secretary of State for European Affairs, and he quickly moved in to grip the Bosnia issues. There were several meetings over the Thanksgiving weekend, starting with one in his office, which I attended, followed by a meeting with Secretary of Defense Perry in his office. I gave Holbrooke a lift over to the Pentagon in my car.

"Don't you think we ought to bomb?" he asked. There it was again, the expectation that a demonstration of force would convince the Serbs to call off their aims. I went through the limitations of airpower as I saw it, replaying the arguments I had gained from my visit to Naples in August: difficult to strike targets on the ground, no centers of gravity, and what next if it's not effective? These were the standard Pentagon and military arguments, and Holbrooke didn't press me. But the question of whether NATO should bomb remained open in the interagency discussions.

Because the Bosnians' defense around Bihac survived, we avoided the hard issue of bombing. We recognized, instead, that we were going to have to do something to strengthen UNPROFOR or it was going to be either completely compromised or forced out. And the prospect of UNPROFOR's departure was highly worrisome. Our NATO allies were speculating that although the Serbs were now our most consistent problem, should we attempt to leave, the Muslims would resist our departure, possibly by force. The withdrawal, they anticipated, would be slow, difficult, and dangerous. Indeed, all of us knew from our own military studies that a withdrawal of troops in contact with an enemy is among the most difficult of all operations. We had been hearing the rumblings of concern from our allies for months.

In early December, with his top advisers sitting around the table in his office, General Shalikashvili asked, "If our allies on the ground in Bosnia need our help to get out, should we help them?" The Director of the Joint Staff, Air Force Lieutenant General Walter Kross; the new J-3, Air Force Lieutenant General Howell Estes; and I all answered, almost in unison, "Of course."

Shali said, "I think so, too." We began to actively consider how we could assist an extraction of UNPROFOR if necessary. General George Joulwan, the Commander in Chief of the U.S. European Command and the SACEUR, began to plan the options for extraction.

But we worked the other alternative, too—making UNPROFOR strong enough to be effective. General Shalikashvili and I flew to The Hague a few days later to try to craft some practical steps to strengthen the U.N. force. It was a question of determining what was needed, and then pressuring other nations to contribute. The U.S. contribution on the ground wasn't going to be very significant because our troops weren't there.

General Shalikashvili and the other Chiefs of Defense went to dinner and adjourned, turning the responsibilities over to their two- and three-star subordinates. The Dutch Vice-Chief of Defense, Lieutenant General Martin van Schouten, was in charge of the meeting, but Shali gave me my instructions as he broke off for the dinner. "Keep them at it all night if you have to, but get results. Don't come out with nothing." Van Schouten and I kept the meeting going until dawn, at the end of which we had created a menu of requirements and contributions that might help marginally. But we all knew that this would be no quantum improvement, even if fully implemented. Sure enough, as we entered the new year, it was clear that not much was going to be done. In many cases there were national legal problems or administrative delays, and in a few instances, the need for the additional equipment had apparently disappeared, perhaps met from other sources.

The Croatian defense minister, Goyko Susak, paid a visit to Washington in February 1995. He was a respected participant and interlocutor on Balkan issues. He had spent twenty years in Canada in the restaurant and construction business and then, as Yugoslavia was breaking up in the early '90s, he had returned home to play key roles in the new government. His relationships, financial clout, and charisma have brought him to the position of defense minister, but to us in the Pentagon he was often referred to as "Pizza Man," in reference to how he got his start in business.

Susak was a frequent visitor to the Pentagon, and considered himself a good friend of Secretary Perry. The United States had been working with the Croatian government closely since the previous spring, when it helped forge the Federation agreement, which ended the fighting between the Bosnian Muslims and the Bosnian Croats, and Susak had been instrumental in the effort. He always brought key insights on the situation on the ground.

In this case, though, he apparently had a specific item on his mind: he wanted U.S. support for a military effort to regain the Krajina, a Croatian territory on the border of Bosnia which had a heavily Serb population and was no longer under Zagreb's control. Susak laid out the general intent to take the area by force if it wasn't returned in some other way. It was a challenge to the international community; Croatian patience had run out. I was a little surprised at the baldness of his intent. Were we really going to see a Croatian offensive against the Serbs in the Krajina? The Serb forces maintained a fearsome reputation, while the Croats and Bosnian Muslims had been notably ineffective against them.

Susak was warned about the significant military challenge posed by the Serb forces and the difficulty of fighting in the rugged terrain of the Krajina. You could get bogged down and stalled for months, we said. Don't expect U.S. assistance. You won't get it. We believe in a peaceful resolution of this issue. Susak grunted acknowledgement and looked around the table at the body language. There was no give on our part. But his tough-minded attitude was an ominous sign.

We didn't need any more challenges in this post-Cold War world. Just during the past ten months, we had almost gone to war with North Korea, only to commence at last significant negotiations with the regime there; delivered relief supplies to Rwanda; invaded Haiti to restore its democratically elected president; and by quick action blocked Saddam Hussein's replay of the invasion of Kuwait. But we were also among the countries responsible for not permitting the U.N. forces in Rwanda to intervene as more than a half million people there were hacked to death with machetes, and we hadn't resolved the problems of the Balkans. Other nations looked to the United States for leadership, and we needed to work closely with them to help share the burdens that would otherwise fall on us alone. There were continuing claims on Defense resources, and suggestions from many quarters that if only our military could be used, many problems could be addressed. With good will, cooperation, and insightful leadership, however, the interagency process could work well. The weight of worldwide U.S. responsibilities, the need for American leadership, and the anxiety to protect defense resources: these were themes I would see repeated many times.

THREE

TO DAYTON AND BACK

I N THE WINTER and spring of 1995, it wasn't only the Balkans that occupied major blocks of time for the Joint Staff. The Republicans now controlled Congress, and they had intensified the questioning of the military policy and strategy for the U.S. Armed Forces. The Armed Forces were continuing to shrink, in accordance with plans drawn up during the Bush Administration in the early 1990s. Congress wanted to know why we needed the forces we had and whether we had enough. We were continuing to ask the same questions, as we always did in preparation for congressional testimony. The draft National Military Strategy was in its latest revision, but it wasn't yet published.

In the Pentagon, we had already completed the Bottom-Up Review, which established the requirement to fight two nearly simultaneous Major Regional Contingencies, or MRCs, one in response to our treaty commitments to defend South Korea, another to protect against another Iraqi invasion of Kuwait or other Persian Gulf states.

I was directed to rewrite basic national military plans to incorporate the two nearly simultaneous MRCs. This seemed like a good stroke because it addressed the needs of our commanders and the service chiefs. It also could be cited to prove to the critics that there were sufficient existing forces to fight these two Major Regional Contingencies nearly simultaneously and insured that any further cuts would be more difficult politically. It was a tight fit but was achievable. On a parallel track, the J-3, Air Force Lieutenant General Howell Estes, led an effort to develop a means of looking at Joint readiness, for the first time. The idea was to take one or both of the Major Regional Contingencies and ask the commands to describe their shortfalls or inadequacies in meeting the requirements prescribed in the war plans. Over a period of time we could then determine the needs and priorities for further improvements or investments.

The new system was met with interest and approval on the Hill and inside the Pentagon. It was logical and pertinent. But what I didn't realize was that we had constructed a closed-cycle bureaucratic instrument that would focus the U.S. Armed Forces' thinking on only two primary conflicts and then drive marginal investments of scarce resources to enhance these capabilities at the expense of other possible employments. While this system undoubtedly strengthened our ability to cope with the situations for which we were planning, it was to become a classic case of restricting consideration of other options. In other words, if a crisis were to emerge outside the regions of the two MRCs—that is, outside Korea or the Persian Gulf—the resources available to address it would detract from our readiness to meet the MRC requirements, and this in turn would lead the military to resist political direction to employ forces elsewhere.

Though we didn't recognize the full impact of what we were doing with the planning, we did recognize the significance of the new National Military Strategy, which was a strong assertion that the basic purpose of the Armed Forces was to fight and win America's wars. We maintained that we would seek coalitions where we could, but fight unilaterally where we must. Though we acknowledged the significance of trying to shape international events to deter or prevent the outbreak of war, the National Military Strategy focused the Armed Forces comfortably on their war-fighting mission and gave short shrift to the potential problems that our Allies were facing in Bosnia. We said we would size the force based on the Bottom-Up Review, and, at General Shalikashvili's specific direction, we put in a reminder, inside the section on sizing the Armed Forces, that "no one can predict with certainty where the next conflict will occur."

Around this time, however, we were also participating in the completion of a major NATO operations plan, a plan to assist the with-drawal of U.N. forces from Bosnia. It was going to be a major effort, with tens of thousands of troops over a period of three months or more, and with a real possibility of conflict during and after the with-drawal. It was the equivalent of a major war plan, and it was hammered out with some difficulty.

In the office with General Shalikashvili, I overheard the dialogue with General Joulwan, the SACEUR. "George, you're going to have to come up with the requirements so that the Transportation Command can work the movement data," the Chairman was imploring. Joulwan was in an unusual position. In his NATO capacity as SACEUR, he was asking each of the nations to tell him how many forces would be avail-able and by when, while in his U.S. capacity as Commander in Chief of the U.S. European Command, he was responding to a requirement that NATO had placed on the United States to answer precisely those questions. This was the consequence of actually running two different headquarters, one in Belgium, for NATO, and one in Germany for the United States.

In the American channel it was difficult to complete a step-by-step, bottom-up planning process, which required specific information from literally hundreds of subordinate American units, each in the correct format for an obsolescent automated movements planning system. "I can't get them to come up with the numbers. They just seem to be sit-ting on them," Joulwan replied.

It was frustrating. What does he mean he can't get anyone to come up with the numbers? They're his numbers; it's his command, we thought. I didn't suspect that a few years later I would understand per-fectly the difficulties facing Joulwan.

This was a major planning effort, from a theater that we had delib-erately left out of the list of regional contingencies in the National Military Strategy, despite General Joulwan's pleas. He argued repeat-edly that if we didn't assign to his theater an "MRC" designation, he would lose his priority on resources. And since the time of Eisenhower, we had always looked on the NATO mission and our Alliance in Europe as our top priority.

I could see at the time that the theater would lose its priority, but I couldn't foresee the consequences. Russia was no longer a threat, and the situation in Bosnia looked like a one-time effort, not something to build the U.S. Armed Forces for. I didn't recognize that this NATO plan, and all its ramifications, had the potential to invalidate the tighter focus on the two major regional conflicts. Nor did others in the Pentagon. But the truth was that if the Pentagon's warfighting strategy came to be focused closely on Asia and the Middle East—something we never intended—we'd have neither the preparations nor the inclination to respond if war should break out in Europe.

Meanwhile, in Bosnia, as the weather warmed, fighting began again. The Serbs announced in April 1995 that they would no longer observe the cease-fire they had declared, and, beginning in early May, they tightened their grip on Sarajevo, using tanks and heavy artillery to pressure the Muslim defenders. The flow of humanitarian aid to the city was disrupted and the U.N. troops were increasingly at risk. The U.N. commander, Lieutenant General Rupert Smith, gave the Serbs an ultimatum to cease the shelling or face NATO air strikes. Subsequently, two air strikes were conducted against ammunition bunkers.

Then the Serbs struck. In a series of actions in late May they seized almost three hundred U.N. soldiers and international personnel. Some were actually taken to potential target sites to be used as "human shields." The United Nations was humiliated, NATO nations were angered, the air strikes stopped, and the Serbian president, Slobodan Milosevic, apparently arranged for the piecemeal release of the hostages. By early June Britain and France had won backing from a group of Western nations to strengthen the forces on the ground. They announced the creation of a Rapid Reaction Force, which would be equipped with artillery and armor for a real military action. The deployment would take some weeks, but the policy decision had been made: the international community wasn't going to leave Bosnia yet.

Soon the fighting resumed again. Muslim forces built up around Sarajevo and began a strong but ultimately unsuccessful effort to break the siege. The Serbs renewed their attacks against the Muslim forces in Bihac and began to maneuver their forces in eastern Bosnia, where three U.N. safe areas had been isolated and surrounded. Meanwhile, Goyko Susak made another trip to Washington.

The Croatian defense minister promised us he would not allow the pocket in Bihac to fall to the Serbs. He raised again the subject of a

Croatian offensive to regain the Krajina. To us it seemed that a larger war was drawing ominously closer. On July 6, the enclave of Zepa, the smallest of the three Bosnian enclaves, fell to Serb attack. Most of the defenders, as well as the U.N. forces positioned there, fell back to the larger nearby enclave of Srebrenica. Then Srebrenica itself came under attack.

As always, the attacks appeared ambiguous from a distance. Strictly on military considerations, the superior Serb forces made the outcome a foregone conclusion. However, there were some who insisted that the Serbs didn't mean to take the enclave, for that would entail too great a cost in international approbation. Others asserted that perhaps the Serbs could be successfully restrained through a combination of limited force and diplomacy. On the ground the U.N. command repositioned forces and considered calling in air strikes.

With Walt Slocombe, the Undersecretary of Defense for Policy, we began to craft a renewed and different look at the Contact Group proposal. It seemed clear that the Bosnian enclaves in the east were indefensible, each vulnerable to defeat in detail by isolation and reduction of the defending forces. So why not cease the fighting, redraw the Contact Group map to emphasize defensible frontiers in the demarcation of the zones, and then provide some sort of security guarantee?

In Washington, the interagency discussions seemed to go nowhere for a few days, while we held our breaths on Srebrenica. Then Srebrenica fell. There were rumors and then confirmation of a huge massacre, and international outrage grew.

On July 21, the military leaders of NATO and UNPROFOR met in London to consider next steps. The remaining eastern enclave, the U.N. safe area of Gorazde, was clearly in jeopardy, if the Serbs dared attack to seize it. NATO had shown its vulnerability to hostage taking. The new Rapid Reaction Force was out of position. There was discussion about using U.S. helicopters to ferry French soldiers into Gorazde, but there were no U.S. helicopters there, and, in any event, if helicopters were needed, surely France and Britain had them in adequate numbers and could redeploy them there as rapidly as we could.

The London Conference decided to rely instead on the threat of airpower. New instructions were given to the U.N. military commanders, who were encouraged not to wait before calling for airpower. A consensus was reached that in the event of another outrage, airpower would be used against the Bosnian Serbs.

A few days later Secretary Perry held a Sunday evening meeting on the situation in Bosnia-Herzegovina at his townhouse in Alexandria. After reviewing the current situation, the Secretary outlined the importance of moving ahead with some form of a U.S.-brokered peace settlement. He announced that Ambassador Holbrooke would be leading an American negotiating team and that there would be a guaranteed commitment of American troops to keep the peace. Walt Slocombe and I pressed for a strong interagency team to do the negotiations. Mindful of the previous experience with Chuck Redmond and the Contact Group proposal from 1994, we wanted to be sure the Defense Department's views and interests were interjected from the outset. I volunteered to join Holbrooke's team.

On Tuesday, August 1, Walt Slocombe called from the White House. "Tony Lake wants you over here right away. The subject is what we discussed Sunday night."

I was shown right into Lake's office, where a small group was drafting the components of the proposed U.S. peace plan. Lake sketched out what had been agreed thus far and sought my views on the "train and equip" concept. There would be an offer of U.S. forces—up to 25,000 troops—as part of a NATO force to help enforce a territorial division between the Serbs and the Federation. If the Bosnians and Croats didn't agree we would stop providing them support; if the Serbs didn't agree we would do "lift and strike" against them, as we had threatened for years. There were to be positive and negative inducements for each side.

The question, Lake said, is whether, in the event the plan is accepted by both sides, we should still offer to train and equip the Bosnian Muslim and Croat armed forces. "Of course," I reasoned, "because in the event that there is a breakdown later on, your best guarantee against a resumption of hostilities would be a better balance of forces inside the country." Lake reflected for a moment, and then assented.

Over the next forty-eight hours the full plan came together. We formed an interagency team and departed the next Monday. The mission was to sell the plan to our Allies and to Russia. Tony Lake was our leader, and he brought with us Sandy Vershbow, the NSC staff director for Europe and NATO; Ambassador Robert Fraser, the Deputy Assistant Secretary of State who had been handling discussions with the parties in the region since the collapse of the Contact Group plan the previous year; and Dr. Joseph Kruzel, the Deputy Assistant Secretary of Defense who was the regional expert on the Balkans and NATO. I went along to represent General Shalikashvili.

For me this was a significant addition to my responsibilities. In the J-5 position I was a staff officer, preparing position papers, consulting military colleagues, and working interagency and international coordination. While I read most of the diplomatic cable traffic and met with international visitors who came to Washington, this was my first time to be the front man in selling a plan, dealing with international military and diplomatic counterparts.

At every stop we briefed the plan, with Tony Lake carrying the main load and others chipping in to give added credibility or dip into minor details. We met skepticism at first that there would really be 25,000 American troops committed on the ground, which was a major change in U.S. policy, to be sure. In fact, the American willingness to commit ground troops was the decisive factor in winning support. Without this pledge the plan would never have gotten to first base with our Allies.

During the travels we built a real sense of camaraderie on the small Air Force plane—sharing perspectives, playing a couple of games of hearts, and keeping up the chatter. "Nice suit, Tony," I offered one morning as Lake settled into his seat on the aircraft. "I'll trade you," he said, gesturing to my Army green uniform with the three stars, ribbons, and right shoulder combat patch.

It was a surprising rejoinder. It wasn't that I wasn't proud of serving or wearing the uniform—I hadn't realized the impact of a uniform in a group of civilians. It may be the ultimate "power suit," connoting authority and experience, and helping its wearer stand out in a crowd.

Camaraderie aside, we were working within a smoldering crisis, as our Allies began to speak more openly about unilaterally withdrawing their forces from UNPROFOR. The sense of urgency was intensified by the Croat attack on the Krajina in early August. Susak's warnings to us in February and July had come to be realized; Croatia wasn't going to wait. There was a sense that a real turning point had been reached in the conflict: whether Croatia succeeded or not, it had challenged the Serb military.

As we jumped from country to country, it was clear that the momentum of the discussions had to be maintained. Ambassador Holbrooke arrived on Monday, August 14, to take the handover from Tony Lake. Holbrooke had been pleading all summer to set up some sort of negotiation. He had recently married, but departed from his honeymoon in Colorado to pick up responsibility for leading the effort to end the war.

Along with Holbrooke came Colonel Nelson Drew, an Air Force officer who had just left my staff to work for Sandy Vershbow at the NSC staff. Drew was an expert on European affairs and had been my lead in the J-5 on Bosnia. His presence would enable Vershbow to return to Washington. Another key player who joined us was Holbrooke's special assistant, Rose-Marie Pauli. She was an incredibly energetic, competent, and sensitive administrator who was able to plan, coordinate travels, arrange logistics, and soothe feelings in a 360-degree arc.

Dick Holbrooke wanted an agreement to end the war. I was along to help him, of course, but I also had a distinct, military portfolio. My problem was what we were going to do with the 25,000 U.S. troops, and all the others who came in. We knew that we would have to focus on military tasks, not just presence, and certainly not police activities. But how could we match up what the military capabilities were with what the security requirements would be? Would this be enough? The art of the discussions for me would be to gain enough perspective on the diplomatic arrangements to be able to help craft an appropriate set of reinforcing military tasks that General Shalikashvili and General Joulwan would approve, prior to submitting the plan to NATO.

I was also interested in the proposed territorial division, which had important military implications. We had signed on in the overall plan for a 51 percent to 49 percent division of Bosnia-Herzegovina favoring the Croat-Muslim Federation (as had been the case in the Contact Group's plan), but the issue would be the precise delimitation of the territory. From a military perspective we would want to divide the ground along defensible lines, avoiding the kinds of isolated pockets

and peninsular-type arrangements that could encourage renewed conflict later or that would simply prove unenforceable in practice. If we
stuck by the Contact Group proposal, we would face some difficult
problems due to the way the group's proposed division of territory split
lines of communication and ignored the key terrain features that were
the more natural borders. I would have to engage in the discussions of
the map in order to influence the outcome.

Holbrooke put us into a "shuttle rhythm" to point toward an agreement. He said he had no fixed schedule; the intent was to improvise, end
the war, and secure the peace. At the end of the first week we had a tragic
accident on Mount Igman, near Sarajevo. Bob Frasure, Joe Kruzel, and
Nelson Drew were killed when the French armored personnel carrier in
which they were riding broke through the shoulder of the road and
tumbled several hundred meters down a steep hillside. It was a devastating and incomprehensible loss. Frasure was our star diplomat in eastern
Europe, held in the highest regard everywhere. Kruzel had been the
driving force behind NATO's Partnership for Peace and reaching out to
the new democracies. Drew was one of our most knowledgeable and
clever analysts dealing with NATO and western Europe. We were all
good friends from previously working together. But despite the tragedy,
the word from the White House was to continue the mission.

After returning to Washington for the memorial service, the new
team assembled. Ambassador Holbrooke and I were joined by Christopher Hill, from the European bureau at State; Jim Pardew, from the
Pentagon; Brigadier General Don Kerrick, who was brought back to
the White House from an Army assignment; and Roberts Owen, a distinguished Washington lawyer. Owen had been a legal adviser to Warren Christopher during the Carter Administration, and the Secretary
of State had great confidence in his skill and judgment.

We spent the next three months in frantic diplomacy, jammed in a
tiny aircraft for eighteen transatlantic flights, wheeling around Europe
visiting capitals and arguing diplomacy, and ultimately locked in
together at Wright-Patterson Air Force Base in Dayton. It was an
interagency team, bringing together a wide perspective on the issues. It
became a close team, as well. Together we would help end one war. And
I would learn how to fight another.

Over the next two months we met many times with the key leaders in the region—Franjo Tudjman of Croatia, Alija Izetbegovic of Bosnia-Herzegovina, and Slobodan Milosevic of Serbia—and their many lieutenants and military men. Apart from his skill in drawing out points of agreement or difference for the negotiations, Holbrooke had a clear sense for using military force to back diplomacy. It was a view that, as I traveled with him, I came to share. When the United States and NATO followed through on their pledge to strike the Serbs hard on their next violation, at our urging, we used the air strikes to help achieve a ceasefire and pullback of Serb heavy weapons around Sarajevo. We moved step-by-step in working the general principles of a peace agreement, the timing of elections, the nature of the government, its constitution, and even the division of territory.

As Holbrooke moved the broader negotiations forward, I worked on a parallel track to help devise the military component of the agreement. This included seeking a strong consensus with our key Allies, assisting in bringing the Russians into the force, and, above all, taking the lessons from the ongoing UNPROFOR experience to make a better mission for NATO. From the time we had begun the negotiations in early August, General Shalikashvili and I had been discussing what it was that the military could do. We had reaffirmed from Somalia that clarity of mission was essential. And we had learned from the experience in Haiti—when we deployed 20,000 U.S. troops to oust the Haitian coup leaders and their infamous military-police force—that we should never look to our military to do police work. From the observation of UNPROFOR on the ground we saw the need for strong, unambiguous authority enforced by well-equipped troops, capable of serious combat.

General Shalikashvili and I walked up to the missions, in continuing consultation with General Joulwan in Belgium. "Sir, one thing we can do is separate forces," I pointed out. "Another thing is to secure borders."

"Yes, I'm sure that's right," Shalikashvili said. "But we will never be able to disarm this country. You could try by conducting searches and confiscating what has been found, but we could never find all the weapons. And if weapons then appeared, we would be blamed."

This was the same understanding we had worked out for Haiti. Searching for weapons and trying to enforce disarmament was a matter for police.

"But we could define a zone that we could keep forces out of, and in the small zone, we could specify no weapons, couldn't we, sir? This would actually be a force protection measure for us. It could be like a demilitarized zone."

"Yes," he said, "that's OK, so long as our forces actually have the capacity to secure and enforce the requirements in this demilitarized zone." At the suggestion of Lieutenant General Walt Kross, the Director of the Joint Staff, we decided to call this weapons-free zone the Zone of Separation.

And so we worked our way through the coordination of the emerging military requirements for the peace agreement. First, in consultation with Joulwan, I established enough of a concept to gain support of the U.S. military authorities. Then we began to work the ideas within the U.S. government. The next step was to coordinate with our NATO Allies, and then with the contending parties themselves, who listened but said little. The Bosnian Muslims wanted the NATO force to do as much as possible; the Serbs wanted it to do as little as possible.

At one point in shuttle diplomacy, over a dinner in his palace, Milosevic was reflecting on the ideas I had presented and said, "General Clark, how soon will NATO forces come after there is agreement? It would be better if it were not soon. Serb people are proud, and it will take time to accustom them to outside force."

"Mr. President, the forces will come almost immediately after the agreement goes into effect. They will be here very soon," I answered.

"Then it would be best if they would come in small numbers," he replied.

"Well, they will come in large numbers, Mr. President, and they will come soon. It is the way it has to be done. That way there will be no doubt about their capabilities. And the agreement will thus be respected." General Shalikashvili, General Joulwan, and I had determined to push the principle of decisive force, not in conventional war, but in this precedent-setting peace enforcement operation, and NATO was apparently going to accept it implicitly.

Milosevic grunted and turned back to his plate. He wasn't happy, but he couldn't make too large an issue of this, since there were so many other matters to be worked.

We also used the emerging military plans to court the Russians. We had consulted with them early on, and had promised to bring them into the agreement as it developed. In early October I went with Deputy Secretary of State Strobe Talbott to meet with the Russian military and foreign ministry staffs in Moscow. It was dark and gloomy in Moscow in the short October afternoon, but the atmosphere was cordial in the foreign ministry. At the brief reception following the talks, my counterpart from the Russian General Staff approached me with his interpreter. Colonel General Viktor Barynkin was the consummate insider within the Russian military establishment. As Director of the Main Operations Directorate with a complement of about sixty generals and over 600 officers, he planned all Russian operations and was responsible for headquarters functioning, communications, and nuclear matters. He was also responsible for Russian military doctrine. Barynkin was about my age, fit-looking and gray, and a veteran of two years' combat in Afghanistan. He had established a reputation as an aggressive and innovative division commander and earned his promotion to general officer on the battlefield. I looked on him as a serious and effective colleague.

"General Clark, we know what you Americans are up to," he began. "You are coming into Bosnia because it's in our part of Europe and you want to be there. And you say you will be gone in a year, but you won't be; you will stay."

I began to protest. "No, Viktor Andreyevich, we are coming only to help bring peace. And the President has said we will be gone in a year."

"Please, please," he cut in on me. "Do not be offended. We Russians understand you. And if we were in your position, we would be doing the same thing!"

This, then, was the insider view among the Russians in high military positions. They saw the peace plan in Cold War terms, more "geostrategic competition" to establish spheres of influence. It was an opening to the Russian attitude that I would see again and again in the years ahead.

A few days later I accompanied Secretary Perry to meet Defense Minister Pavel Grachev to arrange the details of Russian participation. The trick was to bring the Russians in and under unified command and control without requiring the Russians to work under the control of NATO. They had no problem working under the Americans, just not under NATO. In time we sketched out a concept under which the Russians would be there, part of the Western effort at our invitation, despite their suspicions, and operating on their own Cold War–style agenda. Joulwan and Grachev later concluded the arrangements.

As the Holbrooke team moved closer to face-to-face negotiations, my colleagues and I realized we had to bring the whole package into the U.S. government for a serious and comprehensive review before proceeding forward. There was an interagency review, which generally approved of the muscular military enforcement that we had written into the agreement.

Then the top leadership of the State Department gathered at Airlie House, in rural Virginia, before the negotiations commenced, for one last look. With Secretary of State Warren Christopher, U.N. Ambassador Madeleine Albright, and Undersecretary of State Peter Tarnoff, we went through the draft military text. I knew all three from work within the interagency process, including Ambassador Albright. As the J-5 I was designated her point of contact in the Joint Staff, and I had worked with her in New York helping to arrange U.N. support for the U.S. intervention into Haiti in 1994.

"Wes, could I just suggest that something's missing here, regarding the authority of the commander of the Implementation Force," said Tarnoff. "You've listed what his authorities are, you've specified all the key things that he has to do, and you've empowered him to use military force to accomplish these if necessary. But you can't anticipate everything. What if something else goes wrong?"

"Yes," said Ambassador Albright. "Why don't you just give the commander the authority to use force whenever he feels it's necessary to do so?"

The agreement was robust aready. Holbrooke and I knew this would be essential, and the military supported us. But these comments were the crucial, final insight that enabled us to provide the military the authorities needed for success. We took the thought and turned it into what became known as the "silver bullet" clause: "IFOR has the right and is authorized to (a) compel from any location in Bosnia Herzegovina the removal, withdrawal, or relocation of forces or weapons and (b) compel the cessation of any activities that IFOR deems a threat or potential threat to itself or its mission, or to another

Party. Forces resisting IFOR action in these regards shall be subject to the use of necessary force by IFOR." With this clause we had stood the weakness of UNPROFOR exactly on its head. Under UNPROFOR, the obligations of the force had been unlimited—protect civilians, assist aid deliveries, secure safe zones, and so on—but its authority was very limited. Under our agreement, we were seeking to limit the obligations of the military—you can't do everything with military forces—but to give the commander unlimited authority to accomplish these limited obligations.

Not everyone recognized the virtue of this formulation. There were continuing concerns from the U.S. Congress about the possibilities of "mission creep." Drawing on the U.S. experiences in Somalia in 1993, senators and representatives feared that the military mission would tend to expand its responsibilities beyond approved limits and available capabilities and cause the mission to fail. However, we believed the first priority was to ensure that the military commander had the necessary legal authority to fulfill his limited and clearly specified responsibilities. Sound military judgment and political guidance would have to serve to avoid a repeat of the Somalia experience.

Ambassador Holbrooke realized early that one key to the success of the negotiations would be to prevent Milosevic and Izetbegovic from playing off the Europeans against each other, or against us. It had been agreed that our American team would be the sole interlocutors with the parties, and that we would keep the Europeans informed through the mechanism of the Contact Group and direct consultations. This was a hard tactic for the experienced, proud Europeans to accept. After several years of leading the efforts to find a solution, they were now in a supporting role.

As we moved from shuttle diplomacy into the make-or-break on-site discussions at Wright-Patterson Air Force Base near Dayton, Ohio, the Europeans joined us. They were led by the European Union negotiator, former Swedish Prime Minister Carl Bildt. He was accompanied by Pauline Neville-Jones, the political director at the British Foreign and Commonwealth Office; Jacques Blot, the former French ambassador to NATO and now political director at the Quai d'Orsay; and Wolfgang Ischinger, the political director from the German Ministry of Foreign Affairs. Completing the representation from the Contact Group was the Russian deputy foreign minister, Igor Ivanov. They came prepared to be involved in the discussions if necessary and to represent their governments. They seemed to bring a certain wariness of the American methods, and in particular, of Dick Holbrooke's effectiveness with the press.

In fact, nothing had captured the popular imagination more in the weeks leading up to Dayton than Holbrooke's dominance of the media, especially in Europe. From his dramatic pronouncements in Belgrade during the bombing through his careful manipulations after almost every meeting in the following days and weeks, Holbrooke harrassed the media to help drive the diplomacy. In the process he had become the model of the modern, globe-trotting diplomat and troubleshooter. His energy seemed to leave other governments gasping.

There was a clear method to the masterful way that he handled the media, for he knew that all sides were watching his brief CNN statements. As he went from meeting to meeting, he had to convey a sense of what had happened in the previous sessions to the participants. Milosevic would often say, as Holbrooke would begin to describe the latest meeting with the Croats or the Bosnian Muslims, "Yes, I saw your report on CNN." The media helped him build the momentum that would carry the negotiations to success. It was also the means to influence Milosevic. It was also critical for getting Washington policymakers on board. This was another of the key lessons I took from the experience with Holbrooke.

I had my own experience with the media, too. In the beginning of our travels, I had done my best to stay away from the cameras. I was seldom seen, and then only in the background, sometimes carrying my bag or a briefcase. But this had begun to rankle some in the Pentagon. On one of my returns to Washington, Walt Kross told me, "Wes, the Chairman and I have been watching you on TV. You're too much in the background. You look like one of Holbrooke's aides, rather than the J-5. We think you should stand up there with him in the TV shots."

Holbrooke agreed immediately when I approached him. It must have succeeded. A few weeks later, General Shalikashvili told me, "Wes, you are the most well-known general in Europe." And I had never said a word.

Despite the use of the media during the shuttle negotiations, however, at Dayton we cut the press out. The relative isolation and the great U.S. Air Force support made the base at Dayton the perfect location for the face-to-face negotiations. It was planned as a make-or-break event: bring them all there; keep them there until it's done; and if there's no deal, well, then we'd have to figure out what to do from there. All sides agreed that there would be no reports to the media as the talks were proceeding.

As the lead military officer I had the responsibility for the military annex, describing the military responsibilities and authorities, and for the military support to the map discussions regarding the division of territory. I also did as much as necessary in the other negotiations to protect what could be considered military "equities," anything that might involve the military or create situations in which security might be at risk or the use of the military might be necessary.

At the outset I was occupied with some of the top Europeans in a tense negotiation to revalidate the military annex before it was given to the parties for their examination. Because the annex gave so much authority to the commander, and because it was so totally opposite from the highly restricted military authorities that the Europeans had become familiar with, these foreign ministry representatives took a very critical look at what their own defense ministries and most of NATO had already informally approved. There were a few minor changes, but I stuck to my ground and defended the approach. It was a useful process.

Negotiating the military annex with the contending parties themselves proved relatively easy. Minister Susak liked it from first read. He returned it right away with virtually no requested changes. The Bosnian Muslims took a long time, each day promising me their thoughts, then apologizing for not being prepared. And for the Bosnian Serbs I gave a special briefing.

It was the first time I had met Momcilo Krajisnik, Karadzic's representative to the talks and himself the key political leader among the Bosnian Serb delegation. He spoke no English. And he had a maddeningly stubborn countenance, under thick, bushy eyebrows. "He's really something," warned Chris Hill before my first meeting with him. Jim Pardew, my colleague from the Defense Department, reported, "I tried to go over some map ideas with him, and he just kept shaking his head and saying no."

It was no better in the military briefing. Krajisnik listened impassively as I explained the concepts and some of the fine points of the military annex of the proposed agreement. I departed after an hour and very little discussion, and I left behind a copy of the military annex for his detailed consideration. "Indicate to me anything you have trouble with, and we can discuss this," I said, as I got up from the table and left.

Two days later I had the Bosnian Serb reply. The copy I had given them was returned, with huge sections lined out as unacceptable. They wanted to reduce the commander's authorities to those of the UNPROFOR commander. It was an absolute non-starter. I went to see Milosevic.

"Mr. President," I said, "the Bosnian members of your delegation have not cooperated in reviewing the military annex. They have just rejected large portions. Despite my explanations, and our discussions numerous times over the past two months, they are trying to make the Implementation Force a repeat of UNPROFOR. This is trouble for us." Milosevic had previously offered to help if there was any difficulty. Here was his chance.

"See Mr. Milutinovic," he said. "He will review it and help you."

That afternoon I gave the marked-up document and a fresh copy to the Serb foreign minister, Milan Milutinovic, and explained my concerns. I had become quite familiar with Milutinovic during the shuttle diplomacy leading to Dayton. He was a crafty diplomat and a Milosevic crony, concealing his insights under a disarming silliness and jocularity. Milutinovic promised to take care of the problem. The next day Milutinovic came to see me. He handed me the clean copy and said, "Don't worry about what they thought. They didn't understand. The document is accepted as written. There are just a couple of points we would like to see clarified." They were truly minor points. We had gotten it through the Serbs.

Then the Bosnian Muslims brought in their concerns. It was a replay of an attitude I had seen before—multiple requests to expand the responsibilities of the military into every matter in the negotiation. We would have been drawn heavily into the policing and regulation of their country. The Muslims brought in an American team of lawyers, including former Assistant Secretary of Defense Richard Perle, to argue their case. But in the end, they, too, agreed with the thrust of the military annex. They could see that it was going to create a strong commander with real authority in a limited area, they understood the concerns of the Congress about "mission creep" should we move into civilian matters, and they ultimately recognized the wisdom of the "silver bullet" clause. We had locked up the military annex. It was agreed and final.

There was still a great deal to do, however. For the U.S. military to limit its responsibility, we would need to arrange for some kind of police force. This was a major lesson from the Haiti operation of 1994. We knew we would have to get European agreement.

I helped draft the police annex, giving the international police expansive powers of search, records review, interrogation, and so on, but the Europeans insisted that the international police would only monitor; they couldn't possibly "enforce" because they didn't know the laws. For the French, in particular, this was the crucial problem. And, since the police would not enforce, they wouldn't be armed. After all, our Bobbies aren't armed, the British insisted. On this point the Europeans were hard. "Our governments would never accept it," they said. We failed to persuade the Europeans on these points, a failure I would come to regret very much in the years ahead.

We had another difficult issue with the Europeans on the issue of civil-military relations. One key lesson we took into the preparation of the agreement was the necessity for a clear military chain of command. We wanted no repeat of the UNPROFOR experience in which a diplomat could insert himself into the command chain and block military action. This meant the line of command had to run from the forces in Bosnia-Herzegovina through the NATO Supreme Allied Commander, Europe, and then into NATO headquarters in Brussels. While not disputing the need for international civilian authority on the ground in Bosnia to help implement the agreement, we believed he could have no authority over the military Implementation Force or its commander.

There were days of difficult discussions with the Contact Group members on this issue, and many phone calls to General Joulwan in Europe. I was doing my best to construct formulas for a clear chain of command, under American leadership, going up to NATO. Joulwan was working the same issue with his NATO military colleagues. But the

Europeans insisted that the European diplomat on the ground have authority over the force. Finally the issue came to a head.

"Wesley, what you are proposing is very difficult," said Jacques Blot, the French representative. "It may work in practice, but the question is, will it work in theory?"

I snickered. Surely this wasn't a serious question. But Blot wasn't smiling.

It was a stunning question, and very serious. It fully exposed the gulf separating the pragmatic Anglo-Saxon style from the more abstract and deductive French approach. I looked over to the British representative, Pauline Neville-Jones, for support. She had won high honors at Oxford as an undergraduate, and I felt she might be sympathetic to my approach.

She smiled at my problem and shrugged her shoulders, as if to say, You see what a difficult problem this is? But she stuck to the European position.

I tried another approach. "Look," I explained to Neville-Jones and Blot, "You are arguing against my position on military grounds. You say that your governments can't support my proposal because your military leaders won't support it. Suppose I ask General Joulwan to go to your military leaders and work this out with them. Would you then support it?"

They agreed to do so, and I called General Joulwan and explained the problem. He assured me the British and French military leaders would agree with the proposal. He promised to call back the next day.

After his call the next morning, I met with the Europeans again. "Well, it is all agreed," I said. "Your Chiefs of Defense agree with what we're suggesting."

"This is not possible," they countered.

"I assure you that it is," I said, recounting the details Joulwan had given me about his conversations with the British and French Chiefs of Defense.

"I don't believe it," the British representative shot back. "Besides, he doesn't understand what's at stake here. I am calling London right now."

The Frenchman held his ground, too. "The military does not run France," he said. "I will call the Elysée."

Despite the fireworks we did eventually agree on the distinctions between military and civilian lines of authority. It was a distinction that was the source of persistent unhappiness among the international civilians, but over time proved critical in ensuring the effectiveness of the military mission.

Another issue that had been raised from time to time was the arrest of those indicted for war crimes. The first indictments had been issued a few months earlier, with Karadzic and Mladic included among those cited. Holbrooke had raised the issue repeatedly with Milosevic, but always without success. Milosevic's answers varied, usually running along the lines of "Serb people will know who will bring peace; they will want change of leadership." Milosevic would do no more than agree with a formula that bound all parties "to cooperate with the International Criminal Tribunal," implying that he would act upon the orders of the Tribunal, but without sufficient specificity to compel his action. This was an aspect of the agreement that would cause many difficulties in the years ahead.

We were also conscious of the problem of Kosovo. During the shuttle discussions and at Dayton, Dick Holbrooke and Chris Hill tried several times to raise the issue of Kosovo with Milosevic. No deal. "This is internal matter for Serb people and Albanians," Milosevic said. He stood his ground. We could get no "traction" to move the issue at Dayton, though Milosevic did agree eventually to allow some visits and to permit the opening of a U.S. embassy information office in the capital city of Pristina.

It was a mark of Holbrooke's leadership of the team that he encouraged discussion of the issues on a minute-by-minute basis and respected differences of opinion. He badly wanted to get an agreement. He also knew the depth of resistance in the Pentagon to an open-ended involvement in the region. About 2:30 one morning, it finally came out in a personal discussion in his room. "Wes, what's wrong with the Pentagon?" he asked. "Don't they understand they have to participate? The President has said he wants an agreement. What's happened to the military since Vietnam?"

I tried to explain the current climate, the impact of Somalia and Haiti, as well as the new role given to the Chairman of the Joint Chiefs of Staff under the Goldwater-Nichols legislation adopted in 1986. "He is the military adviser to the President and the National Security Council by law," I explained. "This isn't Vietnam. And no one is going to go behind his back or around him."

Holbrooke listened, but he was frustrated. "Wes, do you understand that there are members of the Joint Chiefs who want our effort to fail, and they probably won't even admit it to themselves?"

But not Shali. It was a heated discussion, and my aide, Dan Gerstein, overheard it outside the door in the narrow hallway of the dormitory. "You really gave it back to him, sir," Gerstein said. He saw it in terms of civilian versus military, and he was loyal to what we'd been working for.

Maybe so, I thought, but I sensed a lot of truth in what Holbrooke was saying.

Holbrooke and I had also brought slightly different perspectives into the negotiations. Although I was committed to the effort, I wasn't the President's emissary. Holbrooke was. He felt his responsibilities very strongly, he wanted the agreement. As he once remarked, it was sometimes unclear whether we were negotiating or mediating, but he felt that all sides had to give to get the agreement, and that at this point, it was just a matter of pushing all sides to closure.

I had concerns about the workability of any agreement for the military. And I felt that Milosevic had more to give, and should. I saw him as a supremely manipulative liar and bully. We needed every advantage on our side before we put our troops in.

As we ploughed through day after day of negotiations, we slowly closed the gap on the open issues. Finally, all was resolved, except the status of Sarajevo, the division of northwest Bosnia, and making sure everything added up to the 51 percent–49 percent division that all sides had been promised. Milosevic made a key concession, agreeing to Muslim control of the city. It seemed we were done. Then, after Silajdic had accepted the deal, Izetbegovic and Granic rejected it. There was a daylong scramble, and at the end Izetbegovic decided that the city of Brcko, which sat within the Serb area, must be addressed. The negotiation continued that night and appeared to break down around midnight. Holbrooke sent Hill, Pardew, Kerrick, and me over for one last try with Milosevic. Our persuasion ran the gamut from blandishments to warnings and dire predictions. It was a style that stuck, as I reflected later on our success. At the time, though, we left, unsure of our impact. The next morning I awoke to the sound of moving boxes being shuffled in the hallways and sad goodbyes. It was over, a failure. I found myself thinking that at least the failure meant that our military wouldn't have to wrestle with the stresses and strains of ground operations in Bosnia. There would be struggles of ambition and authority from such a commitment and significant risks to the Army in particular. The full impact of failing to secure an agreement hadn't really sunk in.

Then, suddenly, the breakthrough came. The word flashed through the hallways of the dormitory: "There's been an agreement. The initialing ceremony is back on for 11:00 A.M." Several efforts, including our post-midnight pressure, had worked.

Holbrooke rushed by. "Wes, it's been agreed to arbitrate the Brcko area, after one year. Put it into the map."

So, we had succeeded. The agreement was initialled that afternoon.

The plan after Dayton was to allow the leaders of each of the factions and countries to return home, explain the agreement, and, as necessary, gain support from their constituents. Then the participants and other leaders would gather in Paris for the formal signing, which would put the agreement into effect. For the Europeans, having an agreement that was hammered out in the United States was a humiliation. The Paris ceremony was important in anchoring the agreement in Europe, and perhaps salving some wounded pride there. But the European reaction should also have been a clear warning of future transatlantic stresses.

Before the signing ceremony, Holbrooke took us back through the region to see how the agreement was being received. In Belgrade, at a last lunch with Milosevic, in a moment of candor, I learned a great deal. Milosevic was hosting our discussions over a rich, heavy meal in the presidential palace. The mood was upbeat.

Then Milosevic turned to me at his right to open a new conversation. "Well, General Clark, you must be pleased that NATO won this war," referring to the last round of fighting in Bosnia, which the agreement at Dayton was ending.

"Mr. President," I replied, "NATO didn't even fight this war. You lost it to the Croats and Muslims."

"No. It was your NATO, your bombs and missiles, your high technology that defeated us." He continued his lament, "We Serbs never had a chance against you."

Was it flattery? An excuse, the Serb penchant for blaming their problems on some superior outside power? Or a frank admission of vulnerability and weakness? I replayed the conversation in my mind for some time afterward, and three years later, retold it again and again as events were spiraling toward conflict in Kosovo. I had learned his fear.

And throughout the process of negotiation, I had learned the region and its personalities, the acute sensitivity to military power, the self-interest and corruption of some of the leaders. Above all, I recognized that fundamentally, quarrels in the region were not really about age old religious differences but rather the result of many unscrupulous and manipulative leaders seeking their own power and wealth at the expense of ordinary people in their countries.

After the signing ceremony in Paris, the key responsibilities in Bosnia fell onto NATO and the U.S. European Command, under General Joulwan. For me, it was time to return to the Pentagon and finish my duties as J-5.

Under the Army system, promotion to three stars starts the clock ticking. Three-star jobs are for two years, with the understanding that the Army can ask you to stay for a third year or take another job. But you sign and submit your retirement letter in advance, just as you are receiving congratulations on your promotion and bright future.

My two years would be up in April 1996. It was time to seek outside employment, unless I was either retained in position or offered another job. I heard that the Army Chief of Staff, General Dennis Reimer, was against giving me a four-star assignment, though as might be expected, no specific reason was given.

Nevertheless, in March 1996, I received official word that I would in fact be nominated for a fourth star, and the position of Commander in Chief, U.S. Southern Command. It seemed that the Army's pick for the job hadn't been accepted for some reason. In late June, after Congressional confirmation, General Shalikashvili promoted me.

I departed Washington a few days later and turned my attention to Latin America and the Caribbean. Secretary Perry warned me upon my departure that he had two questions about this small command:

whether the counter-drug mission was worthwhile, and what should happen to the Command if Panama didn't ask us to remain in the country when we turned over the Canal on December 31, 1999.

It was an ideal charge with which to learn the duties of a regional commander in chief. Come back often to Washington, the Deputy Secretary of Defense told me. You must represent the needs of your command around town, across the river and on the Hill, General Shalikashvili coached. I learned to speak Spanish, traveled extensively in the region, and reported faithfully on the key events and concerns. I also tried to strengthen relations with the Army Chief. General Reimer and I both understood that as a regional commander in chief, or CINC, I would be reporting not to him but to the Secretary of Defense, through the Chairman of the Joint Chiefs of Staff. Still, as an Army four-star I was part of the Army, and there was a sizeable Army contingent in the Southern Command. I would need General Reimer's support.

During my time in the Southern Command, I saw how the Services' interests often conflicted with the interests of the CINC. One instance was particularly gnawing. The U.S. Army headquarters in Panama, U.S. Army South, had to move somewhere, in preparation for the Canal turnover. My headquarters, U.S. Southern Command, was moving to Miami, but there was no room to accommodate the Army component there. The Governor of Puerto Rico expressed interest in hosting the Army headquarters at Fort Buchanan. General Reimer agreed to support my exploration of the concept. But as the months went by, the Army raised objection after objection. First, it would cost too much. We reduced the cost. Then, the quality of life was too poor. A team was formed that refuted the concern. Then, the crime rate in Puerto Rico was too high; investigation showed it not dissimilar to that of Atlanta or the areas around Fort Hood, Texas.

After six months General Shalikashvili asked me to make a decision. I explained to him my problem with the Army leadership. He arranged a meeting between Reimer and me. "Wes, what do you want?" Shali asked.

I laid out the case for moving the headquarters to Puerto Rico. It had to do with the Southern Command's ability to accomplish its mission in Latin America and the Caribbean.

Then he turned to General Reimer. "Denny, what do you want?"

"Well," he said, "we have empty barracks at Fort Gillem in Atlanta, and I want to fill them."

These were competing requirements. For the Army, the priority was to save money by relocating the Army component headquarters to existing buildings in the United States. For me, the priority was to have the Army headquarters located in the region, in a Spanish-speaking area where it could host visiting militaries and be closer to the advisory and assistance role it was to play. Indirectly, of course, this relocation to Puerto Rico would also help the Army to retain its status as the major player in the Southern Command, and the resources that would come with the mission. But when there were conflicting demands, the Services, and especially the Army, seemed to work too often for their own priorities even at the expense of "accomplishing the mission" for the CINC. Comparing notes with other colleagues, I knew I wasn't alone in this perception. There was a built-in tension between the Services and the CINCs.

"All right," General Shalikashvili said, " We'll go ahead and move the headquarters to Puerto Rico."

And so it was decided. Unfortunately it wasn't the last conflict I would have with the Army or with Reimer. And, subsequently, the Army staff fought a stubborn but unsuccessful rear-guard action to kill the move to Puerto Rico.

By the spring of 1997, the Pentagon was in a full effort to review and update the basic military requirement and the strategy that we had developed some three years earlier. Defense legislation in 1996 had mandated a study of the strategy and resource requirements for the Department of Defense, called the Quadrennial Defense Review (QDR). The process was ideally suited to help the new Secretary of Defense, William S. Cohen, as he took charge of his vast responsibilities. As one of his regional CINCs, I participated in the process as the draft papers and ideas moved forward. What I saw was a gradual and comfortable evolution in Pentagon thinking.

Under Secretary Perry, the Department had participated vigorously in a variety of military activities abroad that we called engagement. We were making use of the military forces and forward presence left over from the Cold War in an effort to help head off problems in the post-Cold War period. It was a process of conducting visits, using international military education and training, conducting exercises, and showing the flag that gained us influence with foreign leaders in peacetime and early warning of crises. In case of trouble, we would already have the relationships in place to help us deal smoothly with the personalities and issues. And the presence of our forces would not only reassure Allies and friends but also help deter potential adversaries. I vigorously defended our activities and the continued retention of forces abroad. Engagement was retained and supported in the new QDR process, though it was now to be called "shaping" the international environment.

Another evolutionary transition was the idea of responding to crises. Although the Bottom-Up Review remained part of the foundation for Defense Department thinking, it was decided to focus particularly on the two most demanding contingencies, potential operations in Korea and the Persian Gulf. In practice, the requirements that we had been detailing in our Joint Monthly Readiness Reviews pointed to the need for additional preparatory investment for dealing effectively with potential crises in these two areas. Additional force pre-positioning was needed to reduce reaction time. And the added forces required additional logistics such as ammunition, too. Force protection enhancements were required, as well. The tragic deaths of nineteen service members at Khobar Towers in Saudi Arabia in July 1996 had demonstrated our vulnerability to terrorists. Thus it was perhaps natural that the terminology shifted to two Major Theaters of War, rather than two Major Regional Contingencies.

I didn't fully appreciate the significance of the change in terminology at the time, but the continuing turnover of officers in the key staff billets seemed to tighten our focus on only Korea and the Persian Gulf. This attitude would prove to be extraordinarily troublesome as we approached conflict in Kosovo.

A third evolutionary adaptation in the QDR had to do with resource requirements. In fact, the Department had been struggling with the resourcing issues for some time. The forces were downsizing. Personnel strength, aircraft, ships, and Army divisions were cut, but the Armed Forces were having difficulty surviving within their budgets. Procurement and research and development had slid. Under the Budget Agreement of 1996, not much could be expected in the way of increased defense funding. This was the context in which the QDR strategy of "Shape, Respond, Prepare" emerged. "Shaping" was already under way, but no more resources were likely to be made available for this. Any "Responding" would draw more resources away from the research, development, and procurement accounts, further jeopardizing the future of the Armed Forces. So it was logical that the Defense Department should include "Prepare" in the strategy, and work to shift resources into research, development, and procurement. It was a departmental outlook that was to pose extraordinary difficulties for me in dealing with my future responsibilities.

In March 1997, I was interviewed by Secretary Cohen for a new position. General George Joulwan had announced his retirement as Supreme Allied Commander, Europe, to take effect in the summer, and a replacement was needed. Each of the Services had nominated candidates, and I had been thrown into the pot as an add-on, as someone very familiar with the situation in the region but not as a recommendation by the Army.

I hadn't known Secretary Cohen before he came to the Pentagon, though he was well thought of within the military for his service as a congressman and as a U.S. senator and for his courageous stand during the Watergate hearings in the early 1970s, when he was one of the few Republicans on the House Judiciary Committee to vote in favor of President Nixon's impeachment. I was escorted into the Secretary's third floor E-ring office by his military assistant, Marine Lieutenant General Jim Jones. The tight group gathered around the table for a lunchtime interview included the Secretary, his policy adviser, James Bodner, and his chief of staff, Robert Tyrer, as well as Jones. Secretary Cohen led a substantive discussion, with issues ranging from weapons sales to Turkey through the situation in the Balkans.

During the meal he made his own position clear: we were going to withdraw from the mission in Bosnia soon, not later than December 1997. I had the impression that we would withdraw regardless of whether the mission was completed or not. He had had to announce it publicly, he explained, in order to set public and executive branch expectations. During his time as a senator, Cohen had never been among those eager to see American involvement to stop the fighting in Bosnia and had, in fact, appeared inclined to oppose the Dayton Agreement. Now, as Secretary he was also saddled with the need to meet our budget limits and to do so by reducing expenditures abroad. I respected his courageous stand on the mission; it wasn't going to be my call, in any case, whether I was picked for the new job or not.

The interview went well, and he selected me to replace General Joulwan, subject to Presidential nomination and to Senate confirmation.

I was very pleased by the opportunity to go to Europe, returning to Supreme Headquarters as a four-star, eighteen years after I had left as a major. I would also have the responsibilities for overall command of the NATO force in the Balkans. It was like a dream come true. But sometimes dreams turn into nightmares. A few days before I departed I had a strong premonition of what was to come.

As my wife, Gert, and I were vacationing at Virginia Beach, General Shalikashvili called. "Wes, there is an operation which may be occurring as you take command that you need to know about," he said. He told me that several Serbs indicted for war crimes by the International Criminal Tribunal in The Hague might be seized by British forces in the next few days. The timing was uncertain.

"But, sir, I thought we were opposed to seizing war criminals. What happened to make us do this? What about the risks?" I asked.

I knew that Shalikashvili and virtually all of the NATO military leaders had been cautious about dealing with the war criminal issue. They had wanted a "clean" mission and were proud of the rapport and trust they had established with the local population throughout Bosnia. Arresting war criminals might mean taking sides and assuming additional risks, though personally, I had always believed that these risks were exaggerated. In any case, the military answer was always that detaining the indicted war criminals was the responsibility of local leaders themselves, and especially the responsibility of Milosevic. He had promised cooperation but had not delivered.

"There's been a change at political levels," Shali said, and mentioned the new British government of Tony Blair. "You'll have to deal with the full program after you take command, but I wanted you to be aware that there is the possibility that this action may take place around the time you arrive."

At Mass that Sunday, I noticed the statue of St. Michael recessed in an alcove above an archway as I prayed. I had worn a St. Michael's medal around my neck in Vietnam. As I thought about the statue, I had a strong premonition that in taking command in Europe, I would be heading into war. It seemed a far-fetched idea at the time.

PART II

THE ROAD TO WAR

FOUR

WEARING TWO HATS

ARRIVED IN EUROPE on the morning of July 10, 1997, fifteen minutes late for the change of command ceremony for the U.S. European Command in Stuttgart, Germany. This was the top command in the Armed Forces, I figured, and had been since the days of Eisenhower. My position was what they called "double-hatted": I was to be Commander in Chief, U.S. European Command, abbreviated as CINCEUR, and simultaneously I would be serving at NATO in the position of Supreme Allied Commander, Europe, or SACEUR. That second change of command ceremony would occur the following day in Mons, Belgium.

It had been a long overnight flight from Washington following the Senate hearing and confirmation the day before, and General George Joulwan was ready to get on with the ceremony. Joulwan was completing almost four years of command, following a three-year tour of command in the U.S. Southern Command in Panama. He had earned a fine reputation among the U.S. leadership as a strategic commander, and I had appreciated his confidence in me during the Dayton negotiations. It was an honor to follow him in command.

In the military tradition, the actual changeover was conducted on a parade field, with a representative number of troops, several hundred spectators, and a band. General Shalikashvili was on hand to transfer the flag of the command, and with it the responsibilities for the 109,000 American servicemen and -women, about 50,000 civilians, and another 150,000 family members. Most of them were in Germany, but there was a substantial group in southern Europe as well, including about 10,000 U.S. troops in Bosnia. I would be responsible for U.S. activities in a region running from Norway through Europe, most of Africa, and Israel, Syria, and Lebanon.

The ceremony flashed past, anticlimactic after the rush through congressional confirmation. But there was a brief instant, as I took the flag from Shali, when I felt the weight of command responsibility descend. Then it was off to the reception for two hours of hand-shaking with local notables and the staff.

Late that afternoon, I flew to Belgium, to consult with Joulwan and prepare for the next change of command the following morning. This would put me in charge of all NATO forces and military activities in Europe. Gert and I had a walk around the nineteenth-century Chateau Gendebien in Mons that would be our new home. It was a magnificent Flemish-style chateau, provided by the Belgian government, set on twenty-three acres with a wide lawn, circular drive, several two-hundred-year-old trees, three greenhouses, five gardeners, a tennis court, and newly renovated interior fixtures.

The accessories of the office matched the scale of the house. As SACEUR, I would have my own aircraft, a converted DC-9 of early '70s vintage, in pristine condition and equipped with modern communications. There were two Blackhawk UH60 helicopters for shorter journeys. For security purposes, there were two armored Mercedes staff cars. We had our own airfield some eighteen miles away at Chievres. For personal staff, I would have a brigadier general as executive officer, two aides-de-camp, and a personal office staff of about one hundred people, in addition to the staff at the chateau. Having been one of those one hundred people when General Alexander Haig was the SACEUR, I knew that these were not just "perks"; they were the essentials to be able to operate effectively in this high-tempo position.

Joulwan and I talked a lot about personalities of the staff, and particular concerns of the command. I listened to his long and detailed telephone conversations with his subordinate commander on the ground in Bosnia, U.S. Army General Bill Crouch. They were really down into the fine points, I reflected. Joulwan was still the NATO commander until the flag was passed the next morning, and with the rising international pressure for more vigorous NATO actions in Bosnia-Herzegovina, he knew he was departing at a critical time.

One action, which he concluded the next morning, was a long effort to have the Stabilization Force in Bosnia, or SFOR (the name had been changed from Implementation Force to Stabilization Force a few months earlier), assume responsibility for the Ministerial Special-ist Police—the bad apples who had been at the center of the Serb eth-nic cleansing efforts. Inexplicably, this had fallen between the cracks during the previous eighteen months, with the military insisting they were police (and therefore not the military's responsibility) and the international civilians insisting it was beyond their means to monitor them. In the Dayton Agreement, thanks to State Department lawyers, they were clearly listed among "forces," and therefore subject to mili-tary jurisdiction. Joulwan signed the implementing order that morn-ing, as I looked on.

As we prepared to leave the office to move to the front of the head-quarters for the change of command, I noticed that the news headlines were reporting yesterday's action to capture indicted war criminals. The British had conducted NATO's first operation. One had been taken, another killed while resisting arrest. A British soldier had been wounded. This was a significant departure from past practices by NATO. The reaction in the international press was positive.

Prior to this action NATO forces had been criticized for a kind of studied passivity. Perhaps it was the carryover effect from UNPRO-FOR, where many of the Allied troops and leaders had previously served. Or maybe it was the influence of the very strong tradition of U.N. peacekeeping in Cyprus, the Golan Heights and elsewhere. For whatever reasons, the force in Bosnia had done its best to preserve its neutrality between the two sides. Its leaders did not want to take unnecessary risks by angering the Serbs. And, reflecting strong con-cerns about mission creep, it strived not to accept additional require-ments, clinging instead to the exact description of duties listed in the military annex of the Dayton agreement. Going after the war criminals had materially changed the situation. This wasn't the only change, however, as I learned a few days later, when I traveled to NATO headquarters in Brussels at the invitation of Secretary General Solana.

I had been to NATO headquarters before. In addition to my work with General Haig, I had met with the ambassadors who made up the North Atlantic Council several times during the Bosnia negotiations in 1995. But this was different. I was coming in to see the Secretary General, to receive my instructions.

I had received one piece of guidance from every previous SACEUR whom I'd consulted. Work closely with the NATO Secretary General, they all said. Don't be at odds with him. You can expect some divergence of views with Washington, but don't allow disagreements to develop with the SecGen. You have direct access to him for operational purposes. Use it wisely.

When I arrived, Solana was open and friendly but came to the point quickly. "Wes, you must make the NATO mission in Bosnia successful. It is the only operation NATO has done, and it must succeed."

I was confident. I knew the mission, the region, and its leaders. "Of course we're going to succeed, Secretary General," I said.

"Yes, but understand that NATO cannot succeed with its mission if the international mission as a whole is not successful. This is not a matter of simply protecting your forces. You must actively help the civilians succeed. You have to stay within the limits of the military mission you have been given, but within that mission, you are going to have to do more to help the overall Dayton implementation succeed."

It was a heavy charge. It struck at the heart of what some of the military leaders had been attempting to do, namely, to restrict their involvement in assisting the civilian aspects of implementing the Dayton agreement. Solana was asking me to push the NATO military into a more active role in assisting the international civilian authorities. It raised all the flags of mission creep and of involving the military in police work, which we had labored at Dayton to avoid. "I see what you're directing. I'll do the very best we can, and we will succeed," I told him.

After a few more minor matters, the office call was over. "And call me Javier," he directed as I left the office. But I knew I would have to think through Solana's charge to me. I had to stay within the mission limitations, but I also would need an active strategy. I later learned that there had been an international meeting in June in which all of the nations contributing military forces had agreed to act more forcefully to provide military support to the international civilian authorities in Bosnia. I would have international support, and support from the U.S. government, to push the boundaries of the mission. I had been directed to do so. It wasn't mission creep.

The Serbs wasted little time in showing their displeasure with the British effort to capture the indicted war criminals. Small bombs were exploded at various locations, unarmed members of the international community were threatened, and an occupied car belonging to the United Nations was burned. It was a sustained campaign, accompanied by various warnings and threats. It had to be answered.

Within a few days I was back in Bosnia, meeting with the leaders I had come to know at Dayton. Representing the Bosnian Muslims was President Alija Izetbegovic. The Bosnian Serbs were represented by a lower representative as their member of the Tri-Presidency, Momcilo Krajisnik, the hard-line Karadzic associate, who showed his displeasure with the British action by refusing to attend the meeting. The Bosnian Croats were represented by their president, Krecmir Zubak, who had played third fiddle at Dayton to President Tudjman and the strong Croatian defense minister, Goyko Susak. Around the table, it was like old times. Each leader seemed to blame the others for lack of progress. Their relatively polite demeanors masked passionate disagreements.

My service in Latin America seemed a dream from a long time ago; I slipped back into the memories and mindset of Dayton almost instantly. Toughness, firmness, and determination were required here. And, drawing on lessons from Holbrooke, I made our position clear to the media in Sarajevo. NATO will not be intimidated.

Then I flew on to Belgrade to visit President Milosevic to convey a strong impression, and to renew our acquaintance. I wanted to find out first-hand whether I could use my experience at Dayton to bring him into a more supportive role, or whether he would become an adversary.

I took Milosevic through the progress achieved in Dayton implementation and the problems. Although the military implementation had gone well, the progress in implementing civilian aspects had been somewhat disappointing, especially the slow work on the police restructuring. Serb hard-liners in positions of power were frustrating Dayton implementation. Especially worrisome was the role that Radovan Karadzic, now an indicted war criminal, continued to play behind the scenes. I explained my belief that progress was the responsibility of the parties themselves. Then Milosevic issued a warning to me.

"General Clark," he said, speaking very directly and conversationally, "it would not be good if more actions were taken against Serbs. Trying to seize these 'war criminals' is like holding lighted match over bucket of gasoline."

He paused and looked at me to let it sink in, then continued, "Besides, I told you at Dayton, what was magic word. Do you remember?"

"I do, Mr. President," I responded. "You advised that we must be even-handed. And we have been even-handed. And you promised at Dayton to cooperate with the International Criminal Tribunal."

"General Clark, please believe me. You must not continue actions like this or Serb people will view you as army of occupation. And occupying armies have not done well historically." It was a threat.

"Mr. President, I understand what you're saying. But I am a soldier. I follow orders, and what they tell me to do, I will do." I wanted to stand my ground without making it appear that I was initiating things. I thought it would be important to keep open the channels of communication.

We left it at that in our first meeting. We had each warned the other.

At one point Joe Ralston called from Washington to inquire about the possibility of launching limited retaliatory strikes against the Serbs, an idea he attributed to Joulwan. Ralston was an Air Force general and had become Vice Chairman of the Joint Chiefs of Staff in 1996. We had first met in 1991, when we were both in two-star positions, participating in a series of meetings on development priorities. He was the kind of officer you didn't forget. I remembered thinking at the time that he certainly knew how to round off the rough edges of an issue. I knew he had the ear of the Secretary of Defense, as well as the Chairman. "Airstrikes are being talked about here," he said, referring to the problem of responding to Serb actions after the seizure of the war criminals. "And your predecessor has mentioned that he would consider doing it."

"We're looking at it," I said, "but right now I can't see the point. What would we bomb? If we want to destroy something, we own the ground. We could just go into any weapons cantonment area and seize things. Or destroy them with pinpoint hits by an Apache," I said, referring to our combat helicopters with their pinpoint-precise Hellfire missiles.

General Bill Crouch, the American four-star general on the ground in Bosnia, and I were talking daily. He was keeping the pressure on the Serbs. Neither of us believed there was a need to bomb, and soon Washington's interest in the bombing option faded. My superiors supported standing firm, but wanted to avoid an overreaction that could further inflame the situation. After all, the Serb response had carefully avoided serious harm to any members of the international community. In time, the violence in Bosnia tapered off.

But I was unable to get General Joulwan's final order on the Ministerial Specialist Police implemented by SFOR. Day after day, there was always something more important, some new consideration or objection, or someone else that Bill Crouch needed to coordinate with. I came to see the difficulties of Supreme Command—and the challenges facing my subordinate in Sarajevo, too.

In late July, Crouch departed, and a new commander, newly promoted General Eric Shinseki, reported into the command. Like Crouch he also would be "double-hatted," commanding both the NATO mission in Bosnia from a headquarters in Sarajevo as COMSFOR and all U.S. Army forces in Europe as Commanding General, U.S. Army, Europe, from a headquarters in Germany. It was a tough and demanding assignment.

I had remembered Shinseki as an upperclassman at West Point, where he was a year ahead of me. During the course of our careers, I had been promoted a little faster, even though he was himself a very effective commander. In fact, he had replaced me as commander of the First Cavalry Division when I left to become J-5 in Washington. Although he had no previous experience with the Balkans, he was coming from a key job in the Army staff, where he often participated in the Pentagon policy reviews and discussions. I gave Shinseki the mission of taking charge of the Ministerial Specialist Police, as well as a clear set of guidelines and tasks.

The strategy I was adopting for the mission was to use our forces to discredit the Bosnian Serb hard-liners, the most ardent opponents of the Dayton Agreement, by taking away the instruments of their power and embarrassing them in front of their own people. We could do this by shutting down the specialist police. We could also do it by continuing to split the Serbs politically by supporting the relatively moderate Bosnian Serb President of Republika Srpska, Biljana Plavsic, at the expense of the hard-liner Serb member of the Bosnia-Herzegovina Tri-Presidency, Momcilo Krajisnik. In fact, anything we did legally and within our authority that could push or restrict the Serb hard-liners would contribute to our aim. While the Serbs weren't the only ones resisting aspects of the Dayton Agreement, their resistance was the most visible and obstructive to our overall efforts.

The place to begin was to take responsibility for the Serbs' specialist police, inspect them, determine their activities and sources of support, and then shut them down, if, as we suspected, they were behind a lot of the trouble. Shinseki immediately ran into the same stumbling blocks from his staff that I had already received. More study, more coordination, more concern. He'd been in command in Bosnia a few days when I spoke to him face to face at his Army headquarters in Germany. "Ric, please, we've got to stop studying the issue. It's been more than a month. Just do it." I knew how I felt my first few days in command, and I knew both NATO and the region. Shinseki knew neither, so I could imagine the care with which he wanted to move forward. But there wasn't time. The strategy was my responsibility. I had to push a little.

He nodded, "Yes, sir." And he put out the order. He was in a delicate situation, though, for he had to gain control of a multinational headquarters where his key subordinates came from different nations, bringing their different national perspectives, at a time when expectations for NATO action were rising and NATO military remained reluctant to accept risks.

His British deputy, Lieutenant General Roderick Cordy-Simpson, began the discussion with the head of the specialist police. More problems arose. "They are insisting on keeping their weapons personally, like other police," Shinseki explained, "and Roddy believes that if we give the order for them to turn in their personal weapons, they'll go underground and cause more trouble."

Does this make sense? I thought. They're already causing trouble, we don't know who they are, many of their activities are already underground, and they aren't like other police—they are considered "forces" under the Dayton Agreement. No other "forces" were keeping their personal weapons. Requiring the specialist police to give up their weapons would be a dramatic sign that we were moving ahead to implement Dayton.

"Ric," I said, "let's just take the chance. Tell 'em to turn in their weapons." We worked out a measure to explain that if and when they were re-certified as police, they could apply to keep their weapons. And they didn't break off the negotiations. It was the second of several occasions on which I had to push to override the concerns of the force on the ground in Bosnia in order to get things done. There was a reluctance to act among the leaders, especially among those who had participated in the U.N. mission, that required constant effort to overcome.

Nevertheless, the troops were capable of brave and bold action. In mid-August, after a threat and rumors of coup attempts directed at Republika Srpska President Biljana Plavsic from the specialist police station in Banja Luka, British troops, on Shinseki's orders, surrounded the police station at dawn, with armored vehicles' cannons pointing at the building. A lone sergeant major reportedly walked to the door and announced grandly that the Serb police had thirty minutes to depart the premises. "They came streaming out barefooted and in pajamas," Shinseki told me. "And we've closed the station."

I remained deeply involved in the Bosnia mission, because every day's activities had strategic impact. This wasn't like some textbook campaign, where the top commander waves his hand over a map and then sits back patiently for a few days to await results. The way I saw it, each action or decision involved four elements: the political, the strategic, the operational, and the tactical. This was a function of modern communications and the media—actions that were relatively small could have potentially large political impact, and therefore affect the course of an entire campaign. Such an incident had occurred in the Gulf War, when our aircraft struck a command bunker that was being used as a bomb shelter by families. The lesson wasn't lost on us: watch the political impact of every decision and event.

In military doctrine, we recognized that the strategic, operational, and tactical levels of war had been compressed, and their distinctions blurred. High-level commanders were involved in day-to-day decisionmaking and had to have a strong grasp of detail. Lower-level units had to pay close attention to the political overtones of seemingly insignificant actions. And all levels had to communicate, exchanging information, and receiving guidance, with an intensity not previously required.

Of course, we weren't at war. But we were deploying our forces, and by presence, movement, and observation causing intimidation, and influencing events on the ground. We were using forces, not force; we were doing everything but actually shooting. We collected intelligence, tried to maintain operational security, issued orders and communicated, maneuvered, prepared routes and positions, maintained our equipment. And so, we still had to follow the principles of any military operation.

In late August, Shinseki called to report that a moderate police captain aligned with Plavsic was going to attempt a takeover of the Serb hard-liners' police station in Brcko. He had already talked to the U.S. forces in the vicinity, and Major General Dave Grange, the local U.S. commander, was fully informed. The Serb police captain had asked us to do nothing until he notified us.

As so often can happen in such cases, the takeover misfired. Inside the police station, there was a face-to-face discussion between the two opposing police leaders, and Plavsic's man apparently lacked the forcefulness to disarm and arrest his adversary. There was a long standoff, followed by his surrender to the hard-liners.

Outside, the hard-line Serbs reacted quickly. A large siren sounded in the city, and a mob of angry Serbs, including some paramilitaries in civilian clothing, filled the streets. U.S. forces succeeded in extracting endangered international civilians, but the Serb crowd got out of control. By mid-morning they had burned several cars, and run the international staff out of Brcko. The American troups held their positions in the concertina-wire protected checkpoint at the bridge along the Sava River. The Serbs were brandishing lumber, sticks, and bricks.

We replied to the crowd with tear gas, and restraint. Grange used his helicopter to blow down the antenna of the local Serb radio station, which was inciting people to violence. We had reinforcements and the capacity to defend ourselves with deadly force, if required.

Then, almost as suddenly as the violence had begun, a man appeared near the back of the crowd and told it to disperse. It was over.

But the events created some ugly scenes for the media, giving the impression that we were being pushed around by the Serbs—the stories played up the angry Serbs, not their later dispersal—and eroded the momentum we had developed. As I had learned from Dick Holbrooke, in order to maintain momentum, you have to have favorable images on TV—not images like these.

The Secretary of Defense also gave me some guidance. "Don't let our troops be forced off the field of battle," he told me.

I flew down to Sarajevo the next day to meet with Shinseki and review the action. What happened, and what could we have done to improve the outcome? I asked. Shinseki talked me through the sequence of events as we knew them. Our troops had done well. They had not instigated trouble, but had protected international civilians and acted with restraint and discipline in confronting the mob. Under the circumstances we couldn't have done more, but maybe next time we could alter the circumstances. I was hopeful that this wouldn't be the end of Serb moderate resistance to the hard-liners, but I knew this would frighten the moderates.

Then I updated Shinseki on refinements to my thinking. I explained my interpretation of the four components of every action: political, strategic, operational, and tactical. The political and strategic components were of necessity problems for my headquarters, and we had to communicate on operational and tactical matters which carried larger political or strategic impact. And I emphasized the increasing interest at NATO headquarters in helping the international civilians to deal with the antagonistic and provocative Serb media.

Shinseki took it all in, then focused on the immediate. "Grange has come to me requesting permission to remove the checkpoint at Brcko Bridge. It ties up a whole company. He says he can do a much better job providing security for the town by active patrolling. And we won't be vulnerable to the kind of surprise that happened yesterday. Is this the kind of tactical move that I should clear with you?"

"Yes, it probably is," I said, "but it seems like there are very good reasons for doing this. Go ahead. I'll take responsibility if there's any question at NATO."

It may have been the right thing tactically but it was my mistake politically. The international and local press read the shift to mobile patrols as a withdrawal. According to them, we had been forced off the bridge, imperiling what little progress had been made in Brcko. I had to make a number of telephone calls, but I couldn't correct the erroneous perception. It was another lesson to be learned.

That evening Shinseki reported in on a very strange occurrence in his Friday afternoon meeting with Krajisnik. As the meeting was ending, he said, Krajisnik suddenly demanded, "Give us back our television tower."

As Shinseki explained it, he was dumbfounded. "What TV tower?" he asked.

Krajisnik apparently believed that we had occupied a key television relay site in northwest Bosnia, but we knew nothing about it at the time. Subsequently, Shinseki reported, he learned that some of Grange's troops had in fact moved up to the hilltop on which the television relay antenna was located, in order to block more Serb troublemakers from entering Brcko during the riots yesterday. And they were still there as a force protection measure.

We had inadvertently occupied a key Serb site, one that we saw could help further NATO's aim of restraining the Serb media. We said that we might somehow, at a later time, be able to leverage a deal that the Serbs would restrain the media in return for our leaving the hilltop. Shinseki and I agreed we would leave the troops in position for now.

I could hardly wait to share the good news with Solana and General Shalikashvili. Now we had leverage, I thought. Both headquarters were appreciative. Two days later I departed for a commanders' conference in Washington in a good mood.

On Monday I received a call from Shinseki. A large crowd of Serbs in civilian clothing had moved to the top of the hill and was threatening our troops. We were outnumbered, and though we'd erected concertina wire, the Serbs had their hands on it, trying to pull it out. We were prepared to shoot to defend ourselves if necessary.

I called Milosevic through the State Department Operations Center. "Mr. President," I said, "your troops in civilian clothes are menacing my soldiers on top of the hill near the TV site. You order them to pull back, or we'll use force against you. We will defend ourselves. And we're not police; we use military weapons." I made a clear and direct threat.

"Please, General Clark, this is political," he said, as though we wouldn't want to use force on such a minor "political" matter.

"No, it isn't," I insisted. "We don't have non-lethal weapons. And we are going to protect ourselves. So you order those men to pull back."

"I will see what can be done," he said.

From Shinseki I heard that a few moments later the pressure had slackened off.

Then more phone calls started coming in from Europe. Somehow the U.N. Deputy High Representative, one of the three top-ranking international civilians, had gotten involved. He had taken the idea that Shinseki and I had discussed earlier—an agreement using our occupation of the TV site as leverage to gain control over the Serb media. But he had worked an informal arrangement with Krajisnik that if Krajisnik would pull the Serbs back, then the United States would pull its troops off the hill. Shinseki had told Grange, who was near the site, to prepare the agreement. For good measure the Serbs would offer some general comments about good behavior in the use of the television. But in these circumstances, the proposed agreement sounded backwards, as though the Serbs were forcing us off the hill top.

I checked political signals with Ambassador Robert Gelbard, the State Department's coordinator of Bosnia policy. Gelbard had been Ambassador to Bolivia in the 1980s and had recently worked international law-enforcement issues at the State Department. He was an advocate for tough action to enforce the Dayton Agreement. I described what I knew of the proposal. "Bob, will it look like we're pulling off the top of that hill in response to a Serb mob?" I asked. I had worked with Gelbard on our planning for Haiti in 1994, and we had compared notes a few times on Bosnia. Gelbard had a good nose for the politics of the situation, and though I was careful not to take instructions from him—he was not in my chain of command and my orders had to come from the Secretary of Defense through the Chairman of the Joint Chiefs—I spoke to him when he visited Europe and occasionally exchanged perspectives with him.

He didn't mince words. "Wes, this is a disaster," he said.

Gelbard's view confirmed my own. This would also violate the Secretary of Defense's guidance about not getting pushed off the field of battle. Somehow this had gotten out of hand. More importantly, what could we do to fix the situation now?

It seemed that Grange and the Serbs had already made an agreement in writing. Worse, Krajisnik had called Shinseki to ask him whether, on his word as a general, he would support the agreement. And Shinseki had given his word, apparently believing the agreement would give us greater legal and political leverage over the Serbs. But he didn't have a copy of the agreement.

Trying to work our way out of this situation proved difficult. Shinseki felt that he couldn't withdraw his support from the agreement. If I ordered him to do that, he would have to resign, he said. But couldn't he simply say that I, as his superior officer, disapproved of the agreement? Didn't I have the authority to do this? I asked. Not without compromising his integrity or so damaging his authority that he would have to be replaced, he felt.

Of course he had to protect his credibility, but I asked, are you so bound by your word to a Serb hard-liner, a man whom we know lies with impunity at any time, that you can't even defer to higher authority? How can we get out of this without either requiring you to breach your integrity or placing NATO into an agreement where it will be discredited? We talked for some time. Shinseki was adamant. We would have to pull off the hill. We had a real problem.

Meanwhile, Shinseki arranged to see the agreement. After several hours, contrary to what he had heard, he told me, we were not obligated to pull off the top of the hill, we were just going to pull fifty or one hundred meters away from the television tower itself. Would that help us? Yes, I said, this is a significant distinction. We would still control access to the television station.

The way out was to talk to Krajisnik myself, explaining that we weren't leaving the hill and telling him again to pull back the Serbs. I arranged for an interpreter to come over and made the call. We talked for some time, with sequential translation. It was morning in Bosnia by this time. We did not give up the hill.

With that the first crisis in my command was over. We reinforced the necessity for close coordination between events in Bosnia and the higher chain of command. Despite the friction, we succeeded in getting the Serbs to commit in writing that they would not be provocative in their media. Since we retained the high ground around the television station, we still held our leverage and could shut it down on a moment's notice if the Serbs violated the agreement.

The press was less kind. They still saw the agreement as a sign of NATO weakness.

At the direction of the Department of Defense I held a press conference in the Pentagon the next day. "We will not be intimidated by threats to our troops," I said. It was a strong statement, just as I had been making locally in Bosnia on each of my visits there. Several people told me, this is exactly what was needed. The next day I was summoned to see the Secretary of Defense.

I had had several previous meetings with Secretary Cohen and had spoken to him by telephone once or twice. I wanted to be sure he knew everything that was happening and had the opportunity to give me guidance. In this case, he was mostly concerned about the press conference. "Wes, you have to be careful what you say," he cautioned. "You may find yourself getting committed to something that we can't or don't want to do."

I was beginning to see that I was caught between two different American perspectives. The State Department and the White House were clearly interested in the success of the mission, in terms similar to those imparted to me by Javier Solana. The Pentagon wanted success, too, but sought to keep the mission as limited and as risk-free as possible. Secretary Cohen wasn't comfortable with my making the kind of statement that I believed was required to warn off Milosevic and his thugs. These were differences that would bedevil my command for the next three years.

At this time, however, there was concurrence in Washington that NATO must make more clear that its actions were directed not at arbitrating between the competing sides on the ground, but at the implementation of the Dayton Agreement, including the use of military power to enforce compliance, if necessary. The previous policy of "even-handedness," or as it was sometimes mistakenly called, "neutrality," received an important corollary. NATO, it was stated, would support those who supported implementing the Dayton Agreement and oppose those who opposed it. The words were crafted in the White House and approved and published by NATO. They provided crucial "policy-backing" for the actions we were taking in Bosnia-Herzegovina.

This clarification was vital, because we weren't yet through with trouble in Bosnia. The first round of local elections were to be held in Bosnia on September 10. The hard-liners were determined to hold on to their control of the municipal governments. There was authority, and probably illegal funds, available to the winners, as well as the power to obstruct the further implementation of some of the key provisions of Dayton.

In early September I returned to Belgrade for another go at Milosevic. At Dayton Milosevic had guaranteed the safety of our troops to General Shalikashvili, and I intended to remind him of that pledge.

But Milosevic had other plans. The discussion was a repeat of my first visit, until I got up to leave. "General Clark, I don't like that you are trying to split Serbs."

"Excuse me, Mr. President? I don't remember even discussing anything like that."

"Yes, and also, I warned you last time not to go after Serb 'war criminals.' Yet you still talk about this. It is dangerous." He was smug, threatening.

"Mr. President, I don't remember saying anything about war criminals. Where did I say this?" I had been careful simply to restate publicly the agreement that we'd made more than a year earlier with the International Criminal Tribunal, that if we encountered the suspects, tactical situations permitting, we would detain them. It was felt that to say more, acknowledging our determination to capture the war criminals, might raise our risks by encouraging the Serbs to target us.

Milosevic reached into the pocket of his suit and took out a folded sheet of paper. "In your letter, here, you say 'split Serbs' and 'be prepared for more detentions of—.'"

"What letter? May I see that, please, Mr. President?" The words sounded familiar.

He held out the paper but didn't release it. I looked in dismay—it was a copy of the personal and private memorandum I had given to General Shinseki in his office in Sarajevo on the day a few weeks earlier when he had taken command.

"Mr. President," I said, attempting to keep it cool, "this was a private letter. It wasn't meant for you. How did you get it?"

Milosevic was gloating, "Let us say that we have many friends, General Clark."

This was a stark warning about the effectiveness of the Serb intelligence system. We investigated the loss at my headquarters and in Sarajevo. I had handed Shinseki the letter in a small meeting, attended only by the two of us and Javier Solana. Only one duplicate was prepared, and it was returned to my office. Shinseki's original was locked in the safe in his office. He was reasonably confident that it had not left U.S. military control. Mine was filed, but had been inadvertently sent outside my immediate office and into the large staff system, with copies provided to each National Military Representative at SHAPE. It may have been sent to every government in NATO, and reproduced in dozens of copies, one of which may have found its way to the Serbs. It was a sorry way to begin.

On Friday, September 5, Shinseki warned me that Krajisnik had called for a nationwide rally of Serbs to be held in Banja Luka the following Monday evening. Banja Luka was Plavsic's town, and for Krajisnik to go there meant trouble. The Serb plan called for some 250 large buses full of demonstrators, we had heard, and the advertisements were calling for "All Intelligent and Courageous Serbs" to attend. This was a formula for violence. There could be more than 10,000 Serb demonstrators—mercenaries, really—who were said to be offered up to $250 each for participating in the day's trouble. Shinseki said that about all his forces could do was to search the buses to keep weapons out of Banja Luka.

Later that day, I learned that some of our British troops had discovered a cache of weapons and police uniforms hidden in wait for the rally. Perhaps, we speculated, there was to be an effort to infiltrate Plavsic's headquarters to threaten or capture her and end the split that was emerging among the Serbs.

By Sunday Washington was alarmed. That afternoon Gelbard

called me to see what I knew. Did I have any suggestions? What was the worst that could happen? Gelbard's call caused me to review our options again. Commanders had to have plans and create options.

Late that evening I called Gelbard back. "Why don't you just ask Mrs. Plavsic to declare the rally illegal," I asked. "That way it won't happen. And if it does, then we can take action to block it."

"All right," he said, "I'll call Mrs. Plavsic and ask her to do it."

I went to bed feeling pleased and confident. This was the way it had to be done—use their own laws and authority against them.

The next morning I was at my desk, reading the latest intelligence reports, when the phone buzzed. It was Gelbard. As I lifted the receiver, it crossed my mind that it was 2 A.M. in Washington.

"You …! You've caused me to ruin my reputation. What the hell are you doing?" He was upset. But I had worked with Gelbard off and on for three years. I'd heard his temper many times. Usually it was an outburst that quickly passed.

"Bob, what's the matter?" I said, calmly. I wanted him to drop the emotional level and get to the issue.

"After I had Mrs. Plavsic declare that the rally was illegal, your people now have refused to enforce the ban. You've ruined my credibility with her. How can you do this to me?"

I called Shinseki right away. He said that the High Representative and his team were under the belief that because rallies were normal in democracies, that they had no right to allow Plavsic to interfere with this one. The key decision had been made by the Deputy High Representative, Jacques Klein, who was an American. He was trapped by the precedents set, and by the way the High Representative's office was looking at the problem. The NATO force couldn't block the buses until Klein or his boss, the High Representative, Carlos Westendoerp, supported Plavsic's declaration that the rally was illegal. I called Gelbard and explained what had happened.

"I'll fix it right now," Gelbard said.

Ten minutes later Jacques Klein called. He was highly upset. "Strobe Talbott just called me and he threatened me," Klein said. "He said I wasn't being supportive, but I had to let the rally proceed. This is what democracies do." I talked Klein through a different line of thinking. Isn't it possible that even in democracies, a permit is required for a rally? And if there is a high probability of trouble, would the permit be issued? Wouldn't you think that the police uniforms and weapons found Friday may indicate an intent to use the demonstrators as cover for something else, directed at Plavsic? And did you know that Krajisnik has already refused Shinseki's request that he relocate the rally from the square in front of Plavsic's headquarters to the stadium outside town? Anyway, if this election is about local governments, is it essential that Krajisnik assemble all his Serb supporters in one place?

Klein perked up on the telephone. "OK, I understand. I'll see Krajisnik and ask him to change the location, and if he doesn't do it, then we'll declare the rally illegal."

Meanwhile, the NATO force was doing all that it could to slow down the buses. They had started from all across Bosnia, picking up Serbs from dozens of small villages and towns and moving on multiple routes. Our troops had them under observation. Each bus was stopped once and searched for weapons. No firearms were found.

As the day wore on, we received continuing reports on the movements from our checkpoints and observation helicopters. A few buses broke down, but the delay was helped by the NATO actions while we waited for Jacques Klein and the international civilian leadership to declare the rally illegal.

In some cases the buses were preceded by NATO armored vehicles, barely moving, and holding up the convoy. Repeated checkpoints requested identification from the drivers. But by mid-afternoon there was no decision from Klein. Krajisnik, of course, was stalling. I was continuing to insist that we slow down the buses so that when the decision to call off the rally was finally made, we could keep most of the demonstrators away from Banja Luka.

At one point the British troops had placed "caltrops," the little spikes that puncture tires, across the bus route. As described to me later, a single British soldier stayed behind to pull the cord to spring the spikes as the first bus passed over them. Sure enough, the tires blew and the bus halted, blocking the narrow road. As the Serbs dismounted and recognized the trick, they grabbed their lumber and sticks from the baggage compartments of the buses and searched for the soldier in the brush. This was no game. Fortunately, he had already escaped. The caltrop maneuver was executed at least once more.

As the buses approached Banja Luka, still with no decision from the international civilians, the British troops escorted Plavsic's local Banja Luka police out to block the roads. They backed the local police up with their own forces with riot control gear. Artillery was positioned to fire illuminating rounds overhead if required.

By this time I had left the office in Belgium and was aboard my aircraft, with some of my key staff, en route to Canada for meetings with the NATO Chiefs of Defense. These meetings occurred three or four times each year and were critical in retaining teamwork and consensus among the nations. It wasn't wise, or really even possible, to miss these meetings. They were essential to my effectiveness as SACEUR.

Somewhere near Iceland I got the call from Ric Shinseki that Jacques Klein had at last declared the rally illegal. We had most of the buses under control and were turning them around, he said. We had done it legally, and without bloodshed. It was a near thing, but successful. But the best was yet to come.

Later that evening I received a report that Krajisnik had made it into Banja Luka after all, had held the rally with only some 400 supporters, and had been hooted off the platform by a larger crowd loyal to Plavsic. I landed in Ottawa pleased and ready to move on to other issues. It had been a long day.

Early the next morning there was a phone call from Serbia. It was Milosevic's man, Milan Milutinovic, now President of Serbia. "General, I am calling to ask your help," he said. "Some of our people are trapped in the Hotel Bosna in Banja Luka, and they may be in danger."

"Tell me what happened, please," I asked.

"Well, you see," began the explanation, "some of our people were in the hotel when Mr. Krajisnik fled there to escape the crowd in Banja Luka. And now this crowd has the hotel surrounded, and they are calling for Mr. Krajisnik to come out. And this is very dangerous. And they may mistake our people as part of the team around Krajisnik."

"But who are your people, and what were they doing in the hotel?" Actually, I had a very good idea who they were and why they were there.

"They were just businessmen," he insisted. "They became confused, they stayed there and now they are in danger."

Sure. And the Belgrade leaders just happened to have real-time situational awareness, too. I suspected it was a little more than this. Then

Milosevic came on the phone. He could tell Milutinovic was having trouble explaining the situation. "General Clark, you must help President Krajisnik," he pleaded. "He is in danger, and he is president." Milosevic expected that, as a soldier, I would be especially respectful of the civil authority that Krajisnik represented.

I explained what I knew about how he came to be trapped inside the Hotel Bosna. And I assured him our troops were there to provide assistance; all Krajisnik had to do was ask NATO for help. But for Krajisnik this would have been an admission of defeat.

Milosevic continued to make the case, "Please, General Clark, Krajisnik is Serb President. You must help him be released. He must not be harmed."

Shinseki and the local British commander had assured me that no harm would come to the group surrounded in the hotel. But this was the key opportunity to continue the strategy of destroying the authority of the hard-liners. And perhaps there were war criminals with Krajisnik as well. I knew that the media would learn of this as soon as we did, and if we had let them escape, we'd be pummeled again in the local papers.

"All right, Mr. President, you tell Mr. Krajisnik that all he has to do is walk out of the hotel. We will put him and his group in armored vehicles for their safety, escort them to our military base, and, after we identify them, look for weapons and so forth, they can be released if they've done nothing wrong. They don't have weapons in that group, do they?"

"Please, General Clark, they are armed. This is normal. Krajisnik is president. You must treat with respect."

While a number of those inside the hotel eventually turned themselves in to the British troops, Krajisnik rushed for a waiting limousine and jumped in. As he was leaving, however, one of Plavsic's supporters smashed the windshield with a large rock.

For Krajisnik it was a narrow and humiliating escape, well reported in all the local papers. For the Bosnian Serb hard-liners, it was one of their most punishing defeats, especially because it was dealt by another group of Serbs. It cleared the way for a successful round of local elections. And for the NATO-led Stabilization Force, it was an astonishing victory, turning a probable coup attempt into a crushing defeat for the hard-liners.

No shots were fired, but this was a modern way of war—intelligence, maneuver, operations security, surprise, superior communications, Allied teamwork with air and ground forces of different nations, all in close coordination with civil authority. Troop morale was high. The officers and soldiers understood what they'd achieved and were proud of it. In fact, troop morale had risen with each successive "action" over the last few weeks. The troops liked the new sense of activity, they could sense that they were having an impact, and they were proud of it.

NATO was pleased as well. Solana was supportive, and General Klaus Naumann, the Chairman of the NATO Military Committee, was effusive. There was a feeling that we had turned an important corner in our overall efforts in Bosnia.

Of course, I had kept Washington informed step-by-step throughout the process, especially when there was a chance of trouble from some action. I reported to the Chairman or Vice Chairman of the Joint Chiefs of Staff, and occasionally talked to some of the top people in the Office of the Secretary of Defense, including Walt Slocombe. Bob Gelbard was usually kept informed by one of the Joint Staff officers, but we also spoke by telephone occasionally.

In fact, I was operating under two lines of authority, one from the Secretary of Defense and one from the NATO Secretary General. I always kept the other informed of what I had been instructed to do, and this seemed to be working well. But as I briefed Secretary Cohen on my next trip to Washington in mid-September, I ran into problems with the more active strategy we were pursuing.

We were gathered around the small, round table in his office, with a few of his key personal staff looking on. I flipped through the briefing charts that I had prepared outlining the situation on the ground and our strategy. I was explaining that in July, it had been clear that we were much further along in the military implementation of the Dayton agreement than in the civil implementation.

As I was recounting what we came to call the battle of the buses around Banja Luka and how we would continue to pressure those who weren't supporting implementation of the agreement, the Secretary's body language shifted abruptly. It was startling. I paused in the briefing.

"Sir, I am within your intent, aren't I?" I asked. I knew he didn't want any casualties or problems, of course, but he also had directed that I not allow American soldiers to be pushed around. And the U.S. policy was to support those who supported the Dayton Agreement and oppose those who opposed it. "Just barely," he said, looking at me piercingly.

I paused, expecting more guidance, but there was no elaboration. Instead, I found myself on the defensive, trying to explain how we would minimize the risks and stay within our mandate and capabilities. His concern took the enthusiasm out of my briefing as I continued.

It seemed clear that there was going to be little Defense Department backing for pursuing a more active strategy—even though the nations had approved this earlier that summer—but perhaps Cohen didn't want to tell me so directly. I was going to be on my own.

The next day, still in Washington, I was asked to stop by the Vice Chairman's office. Joe Ralston was always cordial and hospitable. "Wes," he said, coming quickly to the point, "the Secretary was uncomfortable with your briefing yesterday."

"I know he was concerned," I replied, "but I didn't get any guidance to change direction. This is working, and I don't see any real alternative to this approach if we want to be successful." I also repeated the points on risks and mandate that I had presented the day before.

Ralston nodded and said he'd continue to work the issues within the Pentagon. But I left Washington with a sense of unease. I didn't want to be out of step with the Secretary but I couldn't see quite how to meet his concern and still have an effective strategy. Without this strategy, I thought, how were we going to be able to reduce U.S. forces on the ground?

Meanwhile, we were keeping up the pressure against the Bosnian Serbs, especially over their use of the media to undermine successful implementation of the civil aspects of the Dayton Agreement. High Representative Westendoerp repeatedly complained about the Serb media, which had been especially vitriolic recently, with images comparing NATO troops to Nazis and other incendiary efforts directed at undercutting implementation of the Dayton Agreement and inciting violence against our troops. Westendoerp requested that NATO be ready to help, and in response the North Atlantic Council had agreed on procedures by which NATO could act against the Bosnian Serb media by jamming communications, by occupying facilities to prevent their being used, or, as a last resort, by destroying facilities.

On September 28, the Serbs stepped over the line and broke their media pledge. A broadcast interview with an official of the International Criminal Tribunal was doctored to make it appear complimentary to Radovan Karadzic. When Westendoerp received the report of this, he called me in Washington.

I was at Fort Myer, attending the departure ceremony for General Shalikashvili and welcoming the new Chairman of the Joint Chiefs of Staff, General Hugh Shelton. It was my third trip to Washington that month. Like all changeovers, this would be stressful. Shali was a good soldier and leader, and he was also a brilliant policymaker. His deep understanding of international affairs, his clear, subtle thinking, and his real empathy with the Europeans made him a tremendous force within NATO. His replacement, General Shelton, was a man I liked and admired. He had outstanding field command credentials, but little Washington experience and no previous service with NATO.

Westendoerp called me just before the parade. He explained what the Serbs had done, and said, "I want SFOR to take over two Serb TV towers." It was an open line, and surely the Serbs or their friends were monitoring. I told him simply that I would get back to him.

Ric Shinseki and I had previously discussed how we might handle this situation, and an operations plan had been prepared. I called Shinseki and briefed him on what I knew. He was aware that Westendoerp was calling me, and he was concerned. There were complicating issues, he said, and wanted to discourage me from taking action, explaining that the High Representative's team was to blame because the Serbs had been given permission to shorten the taped interview. I told him that I would review the need to act, but that his job now was to make sure the plans were ready. It was already almost dark in Bosnia. If we acted, I wanted to act that very night, before the Serbs had time to prepare to resist us.

After I went back through the facts and spoke to Westendoerp and to Secretary General Solana again, it seemed that we could not dodge the request of the High Representative. This was a case that precisely captured Solana's early guidance to me: NATO had to act to make the entire mission a success. When the High Representative asked for help, we should provide it if it was within our mandate and we had the necessary resources and capabilities.

I consulted with General Shelton and Secretary Cohen and explained that we already had plans just to drive up to the television towers, invite the Serbs to leave, and move ourselves in. Secretary Cohen gave me the go-ahead to use the American forces. Of course, there was no guarantee that we wouldn't meet Serb resistance.

On the flight back to Europe that afternoon, I was in continuous communications working to set the operation. Finally, at 11:00 P.M. European time, I reported to Solana that we were ready to execute the mission at dawn. "Well, I guess we have no choice but to do this. Go ahead," he said. We agreed to meet the next morning just prior to the start of the defense ministers' meeting that we would be attending in the Netherlands.

Immediately, I gave Ric Shinseki the order to conduct the operation, talking to him from my aircraft by secure telephone. "General, I don't understand the purpose of this operation," he replied. "If you want me to do this, you'll have to put it in writing."

"You want it in writing, you'll get it," I said. I dictated a couple of paragraphs citing the need to "provide for new management," faxed it to Shinseki, and confirmed his receipt.

Four NATO units—one Spanish, one Italian, and two American—set off early the next morning and succeeded in taking over the four Serb television towers that Shinseki and his planners had decided on. There was no resistance, and by a little before 9:00 A.M., the Serbs were gone and we were in control. We then blocked the electronic retransmission of Serb television, just as the High Representative had requested. Despite their misgivings, Shinseki and his staff had done an outstanding job of coordinating the operations.

At 9:00 A.M. I went before the defense ministers of NATO, gathered in one of their three annual meetings, and briefed the details of our successful operation along with an overall appraisal of the NATO mission in Bosnia-Herzegovina. I could only imagine how awful it would have been to report to them that the operation had failed.

The action against the television towers was another example of using forces, without using force. No shooting. Just "presence." And we had done it smoothly, pulling together the operation overnight despite the geographic dispersion of the units. It took planning, but also solid communications and real interoperability. I was proud of the work done by the leaders and troops of SFOR.

The effect was all we had hoped. Hard-line Serb opinion was shaken, and Belgrade was complaining. The international press was impressed with NATO's firm response. It was clear that the seizure would advance Dayton implementation. Even Krajisnik, meeting later with General Shinseki in Sarajevo, confirmed that the seizure of the TV towers and disruption of Serb propaganda would cost him several seats in the parliamentary elections to be held in Bosnia in mid-November.

And that was the way it worked out. SFOR kept the pressure on the Serb hard-liners, becoming increasingly proactive as Shinseki built his experience and relationships within the command there. Krajisnik's Socialist party, the party of Karadzic and Milosevic, lost its majority in the November parliamentary elections. Despite multiple efforts to shake the moderate opposition, by mid-January 1998 a new government for the Serb entity within Bosnia, Republika Srpska, had been formed, supported by a combined Serb and Muslim coalition, and led by a more moderate Serb, Milorad Dodik. To obtain such a result would have seemed unimaginable in July.

From almost the time I took command, I knew that there was strong pressure from the Pentagon and from other NATO governments (particularly the British) to reduce the size of the U.S. and NATO forces in Bosnia. Secretary Cohen had withdrawn his opposition to continuing the mission, but he was still apparently hopeful to see the forces drawn down. General Shelton played it straight with us. He was intent on providing us what we needed to accomplish our mission and protect our troops.

A cardinal principle in discussions about forces was to avoid over-reaching and asking the forces on the ground to do more than was possible. The military would ask of its civilian leaders, "Tell us what you want us to do." Then the military would provide its estimate of the military forces required to achieve these goals. We called it "working the troop-to-task ratio." It usually resulted in a reduction of the tasks, since the "bill" for what the diplomats wanted done was often higher than what the NATO military establishments could afford to provide.

In the United States, an interagency team had prepared a set of four options, labeled A through D, describing the possible future missions of SFOR. Options A and B were essentially "throw-aways," calling for mission changes so drastic as to be quickly discarded. The real choice was between options C and D. In Option C, the military was supposed to take a limited role, providing selective assistance to international civil authorities in matters like organizing elections, controlling the media, or backing up the international police monitors. In Option D, the military was to provide more comprehensive support to civil implementation.

U.S. Option C was what we were currently doing. Apparently, the State Department had pushed to create Option D in an effort to draw more military support into civil implementation. This would seem to require us to increase the size of the U.S. forces in Bosnia. But we were doing well with the forces on hand, and I saw no prospect that we could get more done with additional forces anyway.

State and the Pentagon battled out the issues. I was occasionally asked my opinion, but this was a Washington fight. I kept my head down.

I was more concerned with creating options that could be used to shrink the force without changing the mission and tasks by reducing overhead or otherwise making the force more efficient. And in both the U.S. and NATO channels I was dealing with Ric Shinseki.

As the commander on the ground, Shinseki's opinions rightly carried significant weight with me. When it came to reducing forces, he was cautious. As I understood his views, it really wasn't a matter of "options" for supporting civil implementation. Because these support requirements were unpredictable, they couldn't be used as the basis for calculating troop strengths. What did drive force levels were military tasks and the protection of the force itself. The 10,000 American troops in the Multinational Division North sector had to secure their own positions and the critical location of Brcko. They also had a large zone extending around the nearby Russian brigade and up to the international border with Serbia. As Shinseki explained it to me, this required three battalions—just what he currently had. Perhaps there could be some adjustment of numbers at the margins, but not any reduction in the number of battalions. That was what the mission and force protection responsibilities demanded. With those forces, he could, on the margin and as additional duties, support civil implementation, just as he was doing.

I was passing these insights up to Hugh Shelton at the Pentagon in periodic phone calls, making the case that Option C, with three battalions, was the only realistic approach. We weren't proposing adding any forces, but there was no prospect for eliminating a battalion, either.

The situation became more complicated when the debate entered NATO. The State Department used its channels to introduce a package of options that were designed to parallel the U.S. options. So, there were the seemingly familiar Options A through D. But somehow, as the options went through NATO, they became subtly twisted. In the U.S. paper, Option C was what we were currently doing, Option D was an expansion in responsibilities. In the NATO paper, Option D was what we were doing, and Option C was a reduction, implying a reduction of forces, which I couldn't support.

And within the NATO headquarters in Brussels, the Pentagon and the State Department kept up their running struggle over the future of the mission. The Pentagon, working through the U.S. Military Representative to the NATO Military Committee, was reportedly arguing for a position slightly different and more restrictive than the State Department, which wanted to draw NATO more closely into the support of the international civil authorities. Several European delegates came to us in frustration to complain about the open inability of the Americans to agree on what they wanted.

Shortly after Christmas, I had to submit my recommendations on options to NATO, in my hat as SACEUR. Based on phone calls with Hugh Shelton, I thought I had the Americans in support: we would continue doing what we were doing, and we would maintain the present troop levels for the time being, which meant NATO Option D. But there was a misunderstanding.

On a Sunday evening I received a call from my executive officer, Brigadier General George Higgins. "Sir, do you know that the American military representative has received instructions from the Pentagon to announce at the Military Committee meeting tomorrow that your recommendations 'exceed your political guidance'?"

George Higgins had been my executive officer in Panama and had volunteered to come with me to SHAPE. A ramrod straight, forty-eight-year-old West Pointer who could have passed for someone ten years younger, he was one of those great Army officers who throws himself totally into a mission. Among his other assignments he had taught philosophy at West Point, and he was superb with conceptual issues, but at the same time he maintained excellent contacts within the Pentagon and had a keen nose for how things were lining up.

"No, I didn't know that. Are you sure? What are they talking about?" I couldn't fathom what the problem was. I couldn't imagine the U.S. military representative, a three-star general, leveling such a charge against an American four-star who was SACEUR. It would be foolish and incorrect. But it was reportedly the guidance that had come from the Pentagon to be given Monday morning in the meeting on the force structure paper. I called Hugh Shelton.

"Sir, I understand that the guidance cable to the Mil Rep instructs him to say—" I began, and went through what I had heard and explained the potential damage from any perception of daylight between Shelton and me. I also explained again the reasons for recommending NATO Option D, and how it was consistent with my positions that he had supported in the American channel. He acknowledged our previous discussions and said he knew about the guidance cable but he seemed vague about whether he had approved the language. "I'll look into it," he concluded, as though it were a staff error.

And yet the guidance cable was not corrected. Someone told me later that the Europeans twittered when they heard the Pentagon assertion that my recommendation exceeded my political guidance. Eventually NATO adopted the recommendation to retain the existing force structure and mission, but the incident reflected some lack of coordination within the American channel.

The episode caused me to review exactly where I stood with NATO and the Pentagon. Responding to guidance, I had adopted a somewhat more active strategy for using NATO forces to assist civil implementation during the last six months. And formulating a strategy wasn't enough—you had to push relentlessly to make it work, including, sometimes, pushing against the judgments of your own subordinate headquarters. Implementation of the Dayton Agreement was going better, despite dire predictions that a more active NATO force might prove dangerous for our troops. In fact, the opposite was the case: the more we pushed against the hard-line Serbs, the less they wanted to challenge us. We'd done a lot and still avoided any significant injuries to our troops. In fact, troop morale was higher. Furthermore we had achieved these results by working cooperatively with the High Representative and the other international civilians, as well as with our own State Department.

Relationships with NATO headquarters in Brussels, and with the Allies, couldn't have been better. Solana and Naumann could see the positive results on the ground. They were probably getting less pressure from the nations, including the United States. Personally, I sensed strong support, respect, and deepening friendships with the leaders in NATO.

Relationships with the Pentagon were more problematic, though. I could sense the impact on my support within the Pentagon as Cohen and Shelton focused more attention on the problem of Iraq. NATO wasn't as important now. The Pentagon was pushing for the Bosnia exit strategy. And the experience and dynamics of the new team were different, too. Without General Shalikashvili's deep sense for NATO, the tough issues seemed to be handled at lower levels of attention. The Vice Chairman, Joe Ralston, who had the full confidence of the Secretary of Defense, was much more engaged in the details of daily policy and coordination, now that Shalikashvili had departed. There were also indications of a deepening policy split in Washington between State and Defense, which put me in an awkward position, since success in NATO required me to work with both departments.

Moreover I had been unable to regain the spark of communication with Secretary Cohen that I had felt when he selected me for the job. I tried on several occasions, but something had changed—there was a distance, a reserve, a certain wariness that I didn't understand and was never able to resolve. Perhaps it was simply his style, or the fact that participating in the Dayton implementation was distracting the Pentagon from its preferred focus on the Persian Gulf and building up the procurement account.

Still, I had to rely on what I knew worked. Create and implement a strategic vision, as best you can within the mission and resources, play straight, work cooperatively, take care of the troops, and trust your superiors. Be persistent. It was command at the strategic level, but it was still command. I resolved, though, to try to work even more closely with the new team in the Pentagon.

FIVE

CARROTS AND STICKS

I N MARCH 1998, on a visit to review U.S. troops working with the U.N. Preventive Deployment Force (UNPREDEP) in Macedonia, I was invited to join U.S. Ambassador Chris Hill and Macedonian President Kiro Gligorov for a meeting in the President's office.

It was almost dark when we arrived. Gligorov and two of his ministers were congenial and candid. I had known Gligorov since the early days of the Dayton shuttle negotiations. He was the "grand old man" of Yugoslav politics, already over eighty years of age, with a full head of hair, a strong grip, and a keen mind. His most pronounced feature was the inch-deep round hole in his forehead, over one eye, the result of near-fatal injuries from a 1995 assassination attempt.

Gligorov always had interesting things to say about the region. He seemed to know all the Balkan leaders personally, and had been associated with the top leadership in Yugoslavia since the late 1940s. And he was no friend of Milosevic—he had seen him at work too often, and continued to feel the threat posed by the Serb troops along his northern border and by Milosevic's refusal to adjudicate the boundary. For him the small U.S. troop presence was critical, and I expected yet another entreaty to keep the troops there indefinitely.

But what was also on his mind was the situation north of the border, in the Serbian province of Kosovo, where the Albanian majority had been systematically repressed and abused under the domination of a Serb minority. The Serb military and police had recently attacked and wiped out some sixty members of a large Albanian family, the Jasharis, whose head was accused of leading the shadowy Kosovo Liberation Army. This action was going to provoke trouble, Gligorov warned. He knew the Albanians, because there was a sizable minority in his country, and they would call each other to arms for vengeance in this case. This was a conflict in the making, he said, thanks to Milosevic. The more the Serbian president tried to use force to repress the Albanians, the more he would radicalize them.

This was the same idea that Gelbard had been explaining to Milosevic a few days earlier in Belgrade, when he warned him that by attacking the civilian population in his efforts to eliminate the KLA, he was actually becoming their best recruiting agent. I had heard reports of Gelbard's visit and had followed news of the Serb action against the Jashari family, but Kosovo hadn't been at the top of my priorities. My visit to Gligorov changed that.

Milosevic, he said, may well seek to wipe out the KLA with his military. He likes to use military force. And, though he may say he will negotiate, he does this to complicate situations, so he can seek advantages for himself. In the end he respects only the threat of military force.

It was a clear warning of what was to come.

I spoke with Chris Hill on the way back to the airport. Are you going to report this to State? I asked. He assured me that he was, along with what he saw as the need to reinforce the so-called Christmas warning issued by President George Bush in December 1992, which stated, "in the event of conflict in Kosovo caused by Serbian action, the United States will be prepared to employ military force against the Serbians in Kosovo and in Serbia proper."

"I'll put something in, too," I said. "We can't let this get out of hand."

It was part of my job as CINCEUR, I reflected, to keep my ear to the ground, to provide early warning, and to offer policy suggestions to the Pentagon.

Flying back that evening I drafted a message and finished it up the next day, reporting on the meeting with Gligorov and recommending that we consider restating the Christmas warning, making it a NATO warning if possible, to provide the basis for diplomacy to head off the possibility of conflict. I advised that the sooner and more completely we could halt the growing Serb repression of the population, the greater the likelihood of a stable and low-cost solution. I tried to convey a sense of urgency.

I wanted to speak to Hugh Shelton directly, but he was traveling and I couldn't connect with him. So I decided, given the urgency of the situation, to go ahead with the text I had prepared, addressed to Shelton and to Secretary Cohen. In using the most expedient means possible, I sent my memo by fax for immediate delivery.

As I entered the office the next morning my executive officer, Brigadier General George Higgins, gave me a message to call Joe Ralston. "The Vice just called, said for you to call him regardless of the hour, very important."

It was 2:30 A.M. Washington time when I spoke to Ralston.

"Sir, I'm sorry to wake you. What's up?" I almost always called him "Sir." He was a year senior by date of rank to four stars, a year older, and was above me in the U.S. chain of command. And, from watching four-star relations at close hand as the J-5, I had found that four-star ego was a powerful and particularly dangerous force. Overfamiliarity was usually counterproductive.

"Wes, this message you sent in—the Secretary is really upset," he said.

Really upset? I could guess that the Secretary wouldn't be happy to hear about another problem, but I wasn't making it up—it was my responsibility to keep him and the Chairman informed.

"Look, Wes," Ralston continued, "we've got a lot on our plates back here. We've got our Defense bill to get through and NATO enlargement coming up in the Senate. We can't deal with any more problems. And," he continued, "the Secretary's concerned that Madeleine Albright might get a copy of this."

I was not surprised that they were otherwise occupied; it was precisely why I had sent the memo. "Well, I'm only trying to do my job of keeping you all informed of what's going on. Besides, I sent the message by fax—it wasn't info'ed to anyone and it should have gone only to the addressees."

Ralston finished his points: "And the Chairman is pretty upset that this got to the Secretary without his seeing it first. You better speak to him when he gets in." By law I reported to the Secretary of Defense. Normally, the channel of communications to the Secretary went through the Chairman of the Joint Chiefs of Staff. But previous CINCs and secretaries sometimes passed information and reports directly, keeping the chairman informed. In this case, I had addressed the memorandum to both and, since General Shelton was out of town, it had gone to Secretary Cohen without Shelton's commenting on it.

I was eager to speak with Hugh Shelton about what I had learned in Macedonia. I sensed that events in Kosovo were moving very quickly, and I knew Milosevic well, and how he liked to test the reactions of the international community to see how much he could get away with. He was preparing real trouble there. But when Shelton and I finally spoke, the conversation was more about channels of communication. I sensed that I hadn't succeeded in raising the priority of the Kosovo problem in the Pentagon. Instead I had raised my own profile and the differences between my concerns and those of the Pentagon.

A few days later Javier Solana and I discussed the situation in Kosovo. His reaction was entirely different. He had followed the Serb efforts in Kosovo with alarm. He was well aware of Milosevic's methods, from personal experience.

Solana and I had journeyed to Belgrade a few months earlier to put more pressure on Milosevic to keep his hands off Bosnia. "We know you have your secret police in there and are taking payoffs," Solana had warned him.

"I am not," said Milosevic, puffing furiously on a cigarette.

"You are," insisted Solana.

"You are calling me liar?" challenged Milosevic.

"Yes, you are lying," Solana said calmly.

"Who are you to call me liar," Milosevic said threateningly.

"Look into my eyes," Solana said evenly.

Milosevic leaned forward, glaring directly into Solana's face and scowling, red-faced with anger.

"Yes, you are lying," Solana said, with an air of detachment.

Milosevic quickly switched subjects. He couldn't intimidate Solana. In a later aside, he told Solana, "Yes, you are right, I was lying. But this is normal, everyone does this."

Javier Solana recognized the character of the man in Belgrade. He also recognized the difficult problem that Serb military action in Kosovo would pose for NATO. "Wes, what are we going to do about this?" he asked, as we sat in his office.

This was another in a series of such dilemmas. Did I give my honest opinion, or not? I believed I couldn't duck. As a U.S. commander I had given my warning and made my recommendation. Now I had to fulfill my responsibilities to NATO.

"Javier, we are going to be in trouble here, if we don't somehow persuade Milosevic that he can't get away with using force on his own people," I said.

"And you think he will do this?" Javier asked.

"Yes, I do."

Solana didn't need another "rock in his rucksack," but he took it anyway. We agreed to follow events closely and that he would consult with ministers from the various NATO countries. On a subsequent trip to Bosnia, Solana and I discussed the problem of Kosovo with Biljana Plavsic, the President of Republika Srpska. She moved us into another room and whispered, "The solution to the problem of Kosovo is democracy in Belgrade." Solana and I continued to reflect on her insight in the months ahead.

As the news of fighting and preparations for fighting continued to trickle out of Kosovo, it was becoming clear that the Serbs were making serious efforts to position forces, reinforce with heavy weapons, and prepare for military operations. European concern rose with each worsening report from Kosovo. So did the concern from the State Department.

At the NATO foreign ministers meeting a few weeks later in Luxembourg, Klaus Naumann and I briefed the situation in the Balkans and our NATO efforts. Subsequently, Secretary Albright and most of the foreign ministers spoke of the impending dangers in Kosovo. There was a common condemnation of Milosevic and his policies, but no call for any specific action. Robin Cook, the British foreign minister, called me aside for a discussion. Could Milosevic's policy of increasing repression be halted by the threat of airpower? He asked. I related my recollection of our experiences in 1995, and the conversation with Milosevic after the Dayton agreement. Yes, probably, I concluded. Cook and several others seemed determined that we would not allow another round of this Balkan tragedy.

When the session resumed, Klaus Kinkel, the German foreign minister, spoke as strongly as any. Since he represented Germany, he was listened to very carefully. He wanted to halt the campaign that we could all see unfolding. "A clear red line must be drawn," he said emphatically. I was impressed by the strength of his remarks. As he left the hall I jumped up from the side to walk out with him. "Mr. Minister, great statement," I said. "But let me ask you, what is the red line you have in mind?" I was concerned about the implications for our forces. The fact was, at that moment, there were no clear ideas on how to proceed. Policy was still unformed.

Richard Holbrooke was now an investment banker in New York, but he was still a consultant to the U.S. government, and he was asked to come to Europe to meet with Milosevic. General Shelton called to inform me of the mission and assure me that it was, in fact, sponsored by the U.S. government. Subsequently, I telephoned Holbrooke to make coordination for any support and to learn about the mission. I hoped he would take a strong approach to Milosevic. "I think he's in a difficult position," I said, "because the Army is probably resisting doing his dirty work in Kosovo and the KLA is getting stronger. You will have him at a disadvantage." I was offering my impression of the political situation Milosevic was facing, and building on one of my main conclusions from Dayton—that we hadn't pushed Milosevic hard enough.

To follow up the conversation, I forwarded to Holbrooke the Bosnian Muslims' assessment of the Kosovo situation and of Milosevic, which had been given to me by Mohammed Sacirbey, the Bosnian ambassador to the United Nations. Sacirbey and the Bosnian Muslim leader, Alija Izetbegovic, were not particularly sympathetic to the Kosovars and were more concerned about the diversion of interest from Bosnia. Nevertheless, I thought it was a useful background paper for Holbrooke to read, since he knew the Bosnian Muslims so well. As it turned out, I saw no evidence that my ideas had much influence on Holbrooke.

But my effort did make an impact in the Pentagon. A few days later I received an urgent call from General Shelton. You're in trouble again, was the message, for giving Holbrooke military advice. But I didn't, I protested. Of course, I had talked to him; you had told me he was coming into my Area of Responsibility. I assumed there was no problem contacting him, I explained, and summarized the discussion I had had with Holbrooke.

Then Secretary Cohen called. He came right to the point, reading from a text about the situation in Kosovo. "And does that sound familiar?" he asked. His voice was like ice. It wasn't a friendly question. The text did sound vaguely familiar.

"Well, sir, it sounds like something I might have seen," I ventured, unable to place exactly where I had read it.

"This is the paper you wrote and sent to Holbrooke," he shot back. "And I've told you before, you don't give military advice to Holbrooke." Of course, the Secretary wanted to preserve his authority, since giving U.S. "military advice" to anyone outside the Department of Defense was properly the legal responsibility of the Secretary of Defense and the Chairman of the Joint Chiefs of Staff. Ideas and opinions coming from within the Department of Defense could be used against him in the Washington interagency process. On the other hand, as a regional commander in chief I couldn't very well do my job without sometimes exchanging ideas with other members of the U.S. government traveling in my region.

"No, sir. I don't remember writing any paper," I said. I was stunned and puzzled, and then it hit me. This was Sacirbey's report. I explained to Secretary Cohen that this text was the product of the Bosnian Muslims. I wasn't giving military advice. I was trying to give useful background information to assist Holbrooke in his diplomatic dealings with Milosevic. Someone had apparently made a copy of the Bosnian Muslims' paper and sent it to Secretary Cohen, without knowing what it was. It was another reminder of the nature of relationships in Washington, and their impact on my activities in Europe. It was also an indicator that some in Washington really didn't understand the web of relationships and full array of policies that flowed through the SACEUR's position.

Being caught between the Pentagon's determination to resist deep-

ening engagement in the Balkans and my duty to provide warning of a
new problem, which could cause our mission in Bosnia to fail, generated enormous tension. But I believed the issue had to be faced. The
facts on the ground were unmistakable. European governments were
searching for an appropriate response. This was the moment for American leadership.

At the Chiefs of Defense meeting in Brussels in May, the Albanian
Chief of Defense, General Aleks Andoni, asked to see me. (Albania was
attending the meeting as a member of Partnership for Peace, a grouping of NATO-friendly states who sought closer relationships with the
Alliance.) The situation in Kosovo is very grave, he explained. From
our positions on the mountain ridges in northeast Albania, he said, "we
can see their artillery impacting on our families and relatives in
Kosovo." Andoni was calm and unemotional, but there was no mistak-
ing the earnest concern in his assessment.

The Albanian diplomats were also trying to convey their anxiety.
That spring they requested an opportunity for a "sixteen plus one"
consultation, a right accorded to member countries in Partnership for
Peace. Such a request could hardly be denied, but some NATO nations
were nervous. They didn't want the Albanians to ask for military assistance directly. "You can give them the consultation," one nation
reportedly told the NATO secretariat, "but they must agree in advance
not to ask us for a troop presence." A substantial Italian stability operation had only recently been completed in Albania. Still, such reservations would do nothing to deter Milosevic, and were symptomatic of
the difficulties NATO would face in gripping the situation in Kosovo.

Nevertheless by mid-May we were already receiving directions
from NATO headquarters to consider preventive deployments to
Albania, on the grounds that perhaps if we stacked troops around
Milosevic's border, he would be deterred from acting. Even though
there was no resolve to act, at least the nations were talking about
options. The planning system worked at the direction of the Military
Committee under the leadership of General Klaus Naumann. Various
nations' questions and issues were compiled and coordinated, national
approvals were obtained, and then specific planning tasks or issues
were given to me and my staff at SHAPE. After we had answered the
directive, the Military Committee would serve to coordinate national

evaluation of our proposals, and assure that the various foreign ministries understood the military answers given. This was to be essential work in generating a consensus of support behind our plans and operations over the next year.

The first questions arrived in the midst of the annual commanders' conference that we held each May at my headquarters in Mons: what about deploying some NATO troops to sit along the border in northeast Albania? I pulled the Deputy Supreme Allied Commander, General Sir Jeremy MacKenzie of the United Kingdom, and the SHAPE Chief of Staff, General Dieter Stockmann of Germany, into in my office to consider how to develop the answer. It was to be the start of a full summer and autumn of non-stop planning, as the Military Committee was driven by almost unending questions and suggestions from the nations.

Jeremy MacKenzie was a close colleague and friend. We were both armor officers, we socialized and played sports together, and we shared a certain bonhomie based on my years at Oxford and the special Anglo-American relationship. I had met him more than a decade earlier, in Germany, where I was giving a briefing to a conference of British officers. MacKenzie was a brigadier at the time, and had a strikingly charismatic manner. A former British Olympian in the biathlon, he was in his mid-fifties, with a keen and competitive mind and years of experience in NATO.

Dieter Stockmann was the epitome of the German professional soldier. Six feet tall, ramrod straight, with a ruddy complexion, firm grip, and piercing sincerity, he was one of the finest officers I had ever met. He had just joined my staff after four years in various NATO commands and was considered one of the top German officers of his age group. He would soon become a close friend and a key player within the top leadership of NATO.

Together, as we sat around the table in my office, MacKenzie, Stockmann, and I agreed on possible means of answering the request to evaluate a mission to Albania. One option was to assign the problem to AFSOUTH, the subordinate headquarters in Naples. Or we could just do a map assessment. Or we could send out a team led by Major General John Reith, commander of Allied Command Europe Mobile Force (Land), a small, immediate-reaction force.

Reith would be able to get in and look at the ground, I reasoned, and anyway, if we ended up with this mission, he would be a likely candidate to do it. So it was decided, and MacKenzie and Stockmann put the mission together. AFSOUTH would participate also, and we would read in Lieutenant General Mike Jackson, commander of the larger Allied Command Europe Rapid Reaction Corps. We had established the pattern that would carry us through the rest of the planning.

Another pattern emerged here, also: the lack of American participation. (Reith and Jackson were both British.) In my U.S. capacity I had plenty of assets that could help this NATO mission, including what we really lacked—helicopter transport. But it was Pentagon policy to have the Europeans take on an ever larger role. I approached the issue of helicopter support gingerly, running it up through U.S. staff channels, and mentioning it as a possibility to Hugh Shelton in a phone call. But, after checking, the answer was no, too risky to fly in northeast Albania.

MacKenzie then went to the Italians. No problem. We would have our choppers the next day. It was what I had come to expect from Italy. Albania, of course, is right across the Adriatic Sea from Italy, but the Italians were a truly surprising ally, with a capable military and a remarkable ability to make decisions and undertake commitments that others found impossible.

The evaluation mission was completed without incident within a few days, with Reith reporting that a preventative deployment to northeast Albania was a bad idea. Our answer began the long series of questions and issues that would occupy our planners for the entire summer. If not a deployment to northeast Albania, then what about a deployment to Albania and Macedonia? Or to central Albania? What about a peacekeeping force on the ground or a no-fly zone in the air? What about some exercises to suggest we could do more, but without actually doing it?

Meanwhile, I had been reflecting on Robin Cook's question about the threat of using airpower in Kosovo, and Milosevic's comment to me in December 1995 about how the Serbs had no chance against NATO airpower. I discussed the Kosovo situation frequently with Klaus Naumann and other European military leaders. We could see that NATO's involvement was practically inevitable. The questions were how and when this should take place. We reviewed all the military options under work, including the discussions about the use of NATO air assets, and the comparisons to the 1995 situation in Bosnia. Naumann noted a significant difference in Kosovo in 1998: there was nothing comparable to the Croats' ground campaign of 1995 that could threaten the Serbs with defeat. Relying on NATO airpower was a possibility but, we both recognized, it might ultimately need to be connected to the threat of further escalation. Airpower by itself offered no guarantee of success. As soldiers we knew that any threat meant, at the end of the day, the will to escalate and eventually to see it through. Klaus had made this point repeatedly to the ambassadors. But the key was not NATO force—it was to find a diplomatic solution.

In late May I drafted a message to Hugh Shelton, outlining how we could use a carrot-and-stick diplomatic approach to bring Milosevic to the point of negotiating a political solution to the emerging conflict. My staff and I worked it for a day or two, and then I put it aside to think, before I sent it. There had been already so much tension associated with forming a response to this issue that I wanted to be careful to move ahead in a constructive way. I discussed the concept with MacKenzie and Stockmann. Yes, it could work, we agreed, to promote speedy negotiations.

In early June I was back in Washington for another visit, and I arranged to brief Hugh Shelton and Secretary Cohen, as always. My first meeting was with Shelton. I updated him on the current situation in the region and laid out a dual strategy for Kosovo along the lines of the message that I had prepared (but had never transmitted)—establishing a comprehensive proposal as we had in the Dayton negotiations, including incentives for both sides, with NATO to provide military leverage to compel negotiations. There was no point in looking at NATO options unless they were linked to diplomacy. "Milosevic will pretend to negotiate but won't until he's under pressure," I explained. "The air threat will provide the crucial leverage for the diplomats to be able to achieve a meaningful agreement. And it's better to move forward with this policy now than let the situation continue to deteriorate. We need to put the diplomats out front." I was reporting to them as the U.S. theater commander, not as the SACEUR. I didn't want to use force, or even deploy forces—instead I believed we should push for an early, negotiated solution.

There had already been much discussion about NATO threats and deployments, and the Administration was trying to initiate some negotiations through Dick Holbrooke and Ambassador Chris Hill. But as yet I had seen no linkage between the military and diplomatic tracks. I proposed linking the two options in the way I had seen work in Bosnia—carrot and stick.

To my relief, Shelton bought the idea and agreed that I should see Sandy Berger at the White House and get him signed up as well.

Later I went to see Secretary Cohen. He nodded as I briefed him on the proposal. He seemed supportive; it put the diplomats out front, using the military to gain diplomatic leverage.

I also visited with Strobe Talbott at the State Department. Talbott had always been a friend, as well as a colleague with tremendous insight and intellectual powers. I had admired his clear thinking and forceful interventions in the interagency discussions during the time I was the J-5.

"So, how do you feel about the situation in the Balkans?" he asked, leaning back on the aging government sofa in the private sitting room behind his office.

"Well, I'm very concerned," I said. "Milosevic is building up his forces, and he is testing the West. He's always pushing against the high bar to see if we mean what we say." I continued through my view of the situation.

"So, if the negotiations don't work, what will happen?" he asked.

"Milosevic will use force. He'll try to take them out, and a lot of civilians besides," I said. I was very firm that Milosevic was the source of the problems in Kosovo, and Talbott agreed.

He also agreed with the need to provide incentives to move the negotiations forward, and he thought it was a good idea that I was going to see Sandy Berger about it.

I hadn't been to Berger's office for several months, but there was an old familiarity as I entered the West Wing basement. I recalled briefly the David Hume Kennerly photographs of President Gerald Ford, and his daughter, Susan, that used to hang on the walls in the entranceway behind the guard when I was a White House Fellow in 1975. There were photos of President and Mrs. Clinton now, updated since my last visit a few months earlier.

Berger was interested in the proposal and receptive. He saw the need for a more comprehensive approach. "And you think the air threat will deter him?" he asked as I concluded.

"Of course, there's no guarantee. But, yes," I said.

Berger nodded in assent. I walked out thinking there was a chance that we could use diplomacy backed by the threat of airpower to head off the looming crisis in Kosovo.

Joe Ralston called after I returned to Belgium. He was working his way through the policy ideas I had left behind. "Wes, what are we going to do if the air threat doesn't deter him?"

This wasn't an academic question. He was driving toward a conclusion.

"Well, it will work," I said. "I know him as well as anyone. And it gives the diplomats the leverage they need."

"OK, but let's just say it doesn't. What will we do?" he asked.

"Well, then we'll bomb. We'll have to follow through." I said.

"Right, but you know that there are real limitations on what the Air Force can do," he said. "And what if the bombing doesn't work?"

"I think that's unlikely, but in that event, I guess we'd have to do something on the ground, directed at Kosovo." Of course, everyone recoiled from the idea of a ground operation. But were we going to let our policy be paralyzed by the fear that it might go that way? Shouldn't we instead be asking ourselves what we could do to make sure the threat itself worked?

"And if that doesn't work?" he persisted.

"Well, then we keep going. But I think you have to work at the front end of the policy, on how to make it effective. Besides, I know Milosevic; he doesn't want to get bombed." The whole idea was to get diplomacy working to prevent a crisis, not wait for the crisis to happen.

But Ralston was reflecting what I had come to recognize was the military's innate conservatism. The top military officials wanted to protect their people and their resources. So did I. They were committed to the national military strategy, prioritized on the Persian Gulf and Northeast Asia. It was the approved strategy, and I had helped form it. They didn't want to step forward and take responsibility for difficult and dangerous actions in what they saw as a less vital region. Unfortunately, this reasonable logic left us with a mounting crisis in Europe.

Ralston and I had just talked through what was to become my strategy. I was prepared. Klaus Naumann and I had discussed for weeks the need to be able to escalate if we began to use airpower. The strategy couldn't have been any clearer. Nor could the Pentagon resistance.

At NATO we were busy trying to answer those same questions: Would it work? What if it didn't? How many troops? How soon? How much logistics?

By the time the NATO defense ministers met in mid June, the planning process was well under way, and some of the early answers were in. There was only slight interest in preventive deployments of ground troops. But there was interest in an air operation, relying on the experience coming from Bosnia. And there was a recognition that we had to do some examinations of a follow-on escalation to ground forces. The questions themselves were evidence of the success of the proposal. After the discussions concluded, Secretary Cohen pulled me aside on his way out of the conference room, and said, "Get an air exercise going, just as you described it in your briefing, and do it right away. How soon do you think?"

"Sir, we'll do it early next week," I said.

Operation Determined Falcon came off on schedule on June 16. Approximately one hundred NATO aircraft flew through Albania up to the Serbian border and then flew east, within Albanian and Macedonian airspace.

I was proud of Admiral Joe Lopez and Lieutenant General Mike Short, the NATO regional and air commanders, for the speed with which they gathered the forces and worked the flights. But in truth it was a whole NATO show, with my own staff at SHAPE heavily involved in drawing in the aircraft and coordinating airspace and overflight permissions.

It was just a one-day demonstration. But it showed how rapidly NATO could mass aircraft. And it lit up the Serbs' radar screens.

The NATO strategy had essentially been sketched out in the questions and the planning that was ordered. It was to be a step-by-step approach. Some NATO ambassadors took comfort from the planning itself, believing that as word of it was announced or leaked out, there might be some deterrent effect on Milosevic. The planning served another purpose, too, for it showed a path of escalatory options. Like stepping stones across a river, the next actions were visible ahead.

NATO's approach had the virtue of experience and logic. Our actions in Bosnia had set a pattern that could be applied again, despite the absence of the equivalent of the Croatian army with which to threaten the Serbs. Wasn't it also logical that NATO would simply ask all these questions, assemble the facts and the options, and then make decisions as necessary?

But this meant that the strategy was implicit, not explicit. By taking the first step we had started down a path that, as I was to discover, no government was prepared to acknowledge and for which no military was able fully to prepare. Moreover, the whole purpose of the NATO effort was to empower diplomacy—yet much of the energy was consumed in the arguments about the various military options.

By mid June the discussions were under way with the Serb leadership. Ambassador Chris Hill was the U.S. lead negotiator. He had forged a working relationship with Milosevic and was respected by both Americans and Europeans. Holbrooke was available as required to add emphasis and reinforce as necessary. And Bob Gelbard, the President's emissary, was in the process of initiating contacts with the Kosovo Liberation Army.

The quarrel in Kosovo was about the status of the province and the rights of its inhabitants. The Serbs, and Milosevic in particular, had made Kosovo the touchstone of their heritage and power. He wanted to retain and strengthen his grip on it, despite the fact that the vast majority of its population of nearly two million was Albanian. The Albanians, repressed by years of Serb domination, wanted independence, or at least self-government—and they were increasingly prepared to resort to violence to get it.

Since it was clear that the final status of the province was the principal issue, the diplomats saw an interim agreement as the key to peace. As I understood their logic, they believed it might be possible for the two sides to agree to a peaceful interim process, stretched over some years, during which they would compromise their differences in search of a peacefully obtained final status, even though both sides were well aware of their mutually incompatible aims. All involved acknowledged that it would be extraordinarily difficult. But this was the nature of the problem.

In late June, while I was travelling in California, Dick Holbrooke and Javier Solana asked me to call Milosevic. Holbrooke was in Kosovo, observing the ominous buildup and positioning of the Serb forces.

"Call him and let him know you're watching," Holbrooke said. "You know, he's always liked you. Just see if you can reinforce the message I've been giving."

It was a one-hour phone call. Milosevic was glad to hear from me. Why didn't I come for a visit? Ride horses? But the conversation turned serious when I asked him not to use his military against his own people.

"General Clark," he said, "these are all our people. I want them all to live together in peace, despite your threats."

OK, he'd gotten the point of the air exercise, I thought. I reported my conversation back to Brussels and Washington.

During my stay in California, I was scheduled to receive an update on the Air Operations planning effort. With some of my personal staff I went to the nearest military Video Teleconference facility for the air planning update. General John Jumper, the commander of the U.S. Air Forces in Europe, was leading the planning effort in Ramstein, Germany. I had known Jumper for almost ten years, ever since we had been brigadier generals working with our own services in the American desert, he at Nellis Air Force Base, and I at Fort Irwin. He was energetic, broad-gauged, and able.

I looked at the screen as Jumper described the plan. How bizarre, I thought, to be in California, connected to war planning going on in Europe, for what, if it was ever executed, would be a major war plan. The intent of the plan, as we wrote it, was to halt or degrade a systematic Serb campaign of ethnic cleansing in Kosovo. My intent was that the air strikes would be coercive in nature, following the Bosnia model, providing a strong incentive for Milosevic to halt operations.

Jumper and his staff went through their planning. It was familiar, doctrinally sound thinking. Unlike Bosnia, of course, there were significant Serb air defenses. So, this was to be a replay of the Desert Storm strike, with the first few days intensively planned to knock out air defenses and establish air superiority, then moving on to other targets. I liked what I heard about using Naval and Air Force assets simultaneously, and the detailed timing and synchronization of the manned aircraft behind the missiles. How long would it take to get through this first phase, I asked, or until we destroy Milosevic's air defense?

Hard to say, was the response. Could be a day or two, maybe six. Depended on the weather, and the effectiveness of his response. The best thing would be if they fought back. It would be tougher if they just hunkered down, the air planners said.

This was a purely American plan. We had to work through a number of issues yet, I said. It must be taken into NATO, and NATO is going to be sensitive about going after some targets. And you have to be able to strike at the Serb forces on the ground, I said.

"Sir, we're just not very good at plinking tanks," Jumper responded.

"I know, but we need to be able to go after his deployed heavy weapons in the first phase, before he deploys everything to the field. Then we will have a chance of deterring a wider conflict. The idea of the first phase should be that the materiel in the cantonment areas isn't struck—it's held hostage—but we strike the stuff in the field."

This was a key part of what I hoped to do with the plan, to embed in it powerful incentives for the Serbs to halt what they were doing, rather than to intensify their actions. "Intrawar deterrence" was what some of the nuclear strategists called the approach. And it perhaps could be achieved by using force strongly initially while simultaneously holding additional assets, forces, and fixed targets, at risk.

"Sir, we'll work on it, we'll do our best, but I can't promise you," Jumper said. He was a straight talker who would do his best to put my guidance into action.

I left the videoconference facility feeling comfortable. We were going to have a good plan. No half measures. No Vietnam. Some work to be done on striking any deployed Serb forces, and while we'd never hit them all, I thought we could arrange a workable system to strike at them. At a minimum, I knew, we could go back to the so-called "killbox" method the Air Force had used over the Iraqi forces in Kuwait: Just keep sending the same pilots back over a designated area day after day—as they scan it, they'll pick up changes and really control movements and repositioning from the air. We also had some new assets, like the Predator unmanned aerial vehicle, which could orbit overhead and target enemy forces. We had been using the Predators over Bosnia and received excellent information with their color television capability.

Still, I recognized, the plan would be fundamentally coercive in intent. Milosevic would have to give in to the overall weight of his losses, because there wasn't any way to block all Serb military and police efforts on the ground. We knew, despite brave talk in American circles about precision strike and the so-called Revolution in Military Affairs, that in terms of air attack against ground forces, the promises of the new technologies required hardware and systems that hadn't been developed or deployed. We should be able, eventually, to destroy much of his force from the air, but it would be a long slog if it were dispersed and hidden.

Besides the air effort, we were still working our way through other tasks given us by the Military Committee. Concepts for ground intervention in Kosovo and, should that prove insufficient, for continuing into Yugoslavia itself were under development for forwarding to NATO Headquarters.

When we submitted the air plan to NATO in July, there was some grumbling. The air operation sounded too large, too threatening. The diplomats in Brussels were asking whether there wasn't a way to begin in a more limited fashion. There was resistence to strikes around Belgrade. Jeremy MacKenzie then came in to report the response from London.

"SACEUR, what they're asking for is just something more measured. Charles Guthrie [the British Chief of Defense] will support whatever you say, but he has to know that you've considered a more limited option." MacKenzie was looking for an answer, not necessarily a positive reply.

"Absolutely not," I said. "We're not going to put our pilots in there until we've taken out the air defense system, and we're not going to be able to do that unless we fly the length and breadth of the country." This was something John Jumper and I had agreed on. And it was satisfying to stand on military principles against the inevitable weakening of plans that the diplomats always seemed to suggest.

MacKenzie dutifully reported the answer to London, but I began to have second thoughts of my own. I discussed the problem with Hugh Shelton and with the officers in my command. The logical hole in my firm stand was that it wasn't necessary to expose our pilots to their air defenses in a limited strike. We could just use missiles. We could take some of the firepower planned for the first night of the major air operation and use it without risking any pilots or aircraft. What was wrong with that? I asked myself.

Well, for one thing, it was a poor use of assets. It takes a lot of mass to achieve effects from airpower. How many missiles would be expended? A few missiles would make a political statement, but that was all. Then, too, a missiles-only approach couldn't hope to hit all the right targets. To me it didn't seem a wise way to proceed. On the other hand, such a strategy wasn't illegal or unethical. If nations wanted to fire a few cruise missiles to make a political statement, did I have the right to say they couldn't? I might argue against it, but there was no reasonable argument against just looking at a limited option.

So, despite my reservations, I notified the Secretary General that we would accept a tasking to create a Limited Air Option, but using only missiles—no manned aircraft. Solana was delighted.

In part, one of NATO's problems was that the initial step into using force was too high. It was also true that some European nations were having difficulty with the idea of threatening to use force at all. Here, the problem seemed to be legal, not the nature of the strikes themselves. Throughout July there was a rumble of statements from French and German sources, in particular, that force could not be threatened or used against Milosevic unless specifically authorized by the United Nations. This was a principled stand, and, no doubt, an earnest attempt by some governments to undercut domestic political opposition by wrapping hypothetical NATO actions in the unchallengeable mantle of the United Nations.

But it took very little imagination to picture, amidst the coming and going of diplomats and emissaries between Moscow and Belgrade, that the Russians might well have assured Milosevic that there would be no Security Council Resolution explicitly authorizing NATO to use force against him.

No amount of NATO planning, training exercises, or public discussions of plans and exercises could overcome the corrosive effect of governmental indecision in the West and Russia's steadfast determination to preclude another NATO action in southeastern Europe.

Moreover, convincing European governments to become more serious about threatening the use of force was made more difficult when the American and European diplomats responsible for the discussions between the Albanians and the Serbs were announcing periodically that they were making some "progress." This may have been straight reporting or an attempt to emulate Holbrooke's use of the media in 1995, but it lulled Western governments into postponing the tough decisions before them.

An additional complication emerged with Western determination to place unarmed observers on the ground in Kosovo. Holbrooke persuaded Milosevic to accept a multinational group of about one hundred which became known as the Kosovo Diplomatic Observer Mission. On the one hand, members of the mission would provide information from personal observation. On the other hand, they would be subject to harassment and intimidation—and they could be taken hostage. I understood the value of the mission in providing information, but their presence inside Kosovo also vitiated the implicit NATO threat against Milosevic or his forces.

Meanwhile, in late July I carried the limited air operation plan, which involved only American assets, back to Washington to show it to Hugh Shelton and the leadership in the Pentagon. Once it was approved in U.S. channels, I would be able to submit a NATO version to Brussels.

Unfortunately, Shelton wasn't available to see me the day I arrived. But, through prior coordination, I had given notification that I would visit the State Department to compare our assessments of events and actions in the Balkans with Bob Gelbard. We talked about Bosnia and Kosovo, and I gave Gelbard an update on the status of NATO planning, without disclosing any sensitive details. Then Gelbard was notified that he was late for a meeting with Jim Steinberg, the deputy national security adviser. "Come with me," he said, "and we'll continue our discussion there."

It was difficult for me to imagine that, as a four-star in a highly responsible position, authorized by my NATO instructions to speak to any level of official in any country, I should not accompany Gelbard on a visit to the West Wing of the White House. I had been going there for years, and I knew what to say and what not to say.

We were in Steinberg's office, little more than a cramped closet with a window, as Gelbard was explaining his assessment of the situation in the Balkans. Steinberg was keenly engaged but harried, as always, with a dozen pressing issues. Then Gelbard turned to the issue of NATO planning. "Wes says that he's finished the Limited Air Operation plan," he announced.

Steinberg looked up from his notes, curious, "Oh, you have? What's it look like?" he asked.

"Well, I've completed my draft, Jim, but I have to run it by Hugh Shelton. It's really not appropriate for me to discuss any of the specifics until it's been through the Pentagon," I said.

Steinberg respected that and asked me no further questions. But later in the afternoon, seeing Shelton at a White House meeting, someone apparently commented to Shelton something about my work on the Limited Air Plan. It was not long before my phone rang. One of my special assistants was on the line with an urgent message.

"Sir, the Vice just came out of the Chairman's office after he had returned from the White House, and the Chairman was really steamed at you. The Vice's Exec just called to tell me to warn you. He said Shelton was really angry that you had showed the Limited Air Option to Steinberg before he had seen it. The Chairman was saying something like 'you had one foot on a banana peel and one foot in the grave.'"

The Chairman was determined to protect his role in giving military advice to the White House, and I agreed with him. As I had learned on the Joint Staff, you couldn't have every four-star coming in individually and saying whatever he thought in Washington without clearing it through the Chairman. It was important that Shelton know my schedule and my recommendations if I went across the Potomac to the White House or the State Department and that was the rule I operated under.

But I wasn't guilty of giving away any information without coordination. It was well known that I was working on the Limited Air Option and that it was due in the Pentagon.

I tried to call Ralston, but couldn't get him. When I saw him early the next morning, he downplayed the Chairman's reaction as I explained what had happened. And when I got in to see the Chairman and discussed the plan with him, he denied having been upset at all. Maybe he had realized that he'd just misunderstood and overreacted, I thought. There was a lot of pressure in the interagency process in Washington.

Meanwhile, Milosevic was proving that he hadn't heard our message. Disregarding the NATO discussions, the rumors of NATO planning, the warnings from Holbrooke, and my warning call from California, he had begun a village-busting campaign in July. He systematically maneuvered his forces against the many small villages in western Kosovo, looking for the Kosovo Liberation Army, and began driving the Albanian residents from their homes.

For months it had been clear that a fundamental problem in Kosovo was Milosevic himself, though there was still an effort to rely on him as a legitimate negotiating partner. I kept returning to the formulation of Biljana Plavsic, president of Republika Srpska: "What is required to resolve the situation is democracy in Belgrade." With a democratic government there, peaceful arrangements could be made to address the Albanians' concerns. With Milosevic in power, I feared, a solution would never be possible. The negotiations needed to be refocused on regaining democracy in Belgrade.

In early August, I took one more trip back to Washington. Secretary of State Albright's staff had called, requesting that I meet with her, and, with Shelton's acquiescence, I carried to her my ideas on diplomacy. "We have to somehow ensnare conditions in Serbia in the negotiations, push democracy in Belgrade in the discussions," I urged. "As long as Milosevic exercises the kind of power he does, we'll continue to have troubles in the region." She seemed to agree with me. See Jim O'Brien, she said. He and Chris Hill are handling this.

I knew O'Brien from Dayton, when he was one of the leading State Department lawyers who drafted much of the agreement. I explained my ideas to him. He didn't disagree but insisted that the negotiations were already directed at conditions in Serbia. I couldn't seem to explain adequately that we needed subtly to embed in the negotiations measures to promote the return of democracy to Serbia. Positive incentives would be needed. Milosevic, I figured, was more likely to be dissuaded from violence by the prospect of something positive for himself than by focusing all the attention on Kosovo. O'Brien and I worked it and exchanged views. I hoped it would have an effect on the negotiations.

I had another shot at the White House, too, with Pentagon permission. Sandy Berger was tied up, but I had thirty minutes scheduled with Jim Steinberg. However, the meeting began almost twenty minutes late. I made my plea to focus the negotiations on enhancing democracy in Serbia. The problem wasn't really in Kosovo, I said. The problem was in Belgrade—the lack of democracy there. "Wes, I hear what you're saying, but we don't have any leverage to persuade Milosevic to accept more democracy in Belgrade," he said.

"Of course we do, Jim. We're discussing bombing, and we can also look at creating some positive incentives—."

"Wes, I'm sorry," he said. He had to rush out. I left the meeting with an empty feeling. I knew I hadn't delivered my point.

By late August, there were more than 200,000 Kosovar Albanians homeless, driven from the villages by Serb military and police operations, according to press reports.

After returning to Europe, I briefed a top-ranking group of U.S. senators on the situation in the Balkans, and on NATO planning. What is happening? they asked. What does NATO plan to do? Is it true that one of the plans calls for 200,000 ground troops? What should we do there?

It was an excellent session, I thought. It was always critical to insure that congressional leaders were well informed. Senator Ted Stevens, who led the delegation, was an extraordinarily powerful member of Congress on military matters. An Air Force officer in World War II, he now represented Alaska and served as the chairman of the Senate Appropriations Committee. He was the key man in supporting the Pentagon budget.

Later, Joe Ralston confirmed my sense of the session. "You really impressed him," he said. "He especially liked the fact that you said, 'No NATO troops for Kosovo.'"

"But Joe, I didn't say that. I said, 'No troops to Albania or Kosovo at this time.'" Senator Stevens's misunderstanding was corrected, apparently, but it was a signal warning of prevailing attitudes in Congress and the Pentagon.

The summer of 1998 was ending on a bad note all over the Balkans. In Bosnia, the progress in implementing the Dayton Agreements had stalled, as the hard-liners of all ethnic groups saw the international community, and especially NATO, stymied in dealing with the situation in Kosovo. Despite strong complaints about Milosevic using force, he continued to do so. The international civilians on the ground in Bosnia were discouraged by the continuing talk of troop withdrawals from Bosnia and the attention directed at Kosovo. And much of the NATO military leadership was worn down by its months-long intensive planning for potential operations in Yugoslavia, which was still ongoing.

My visit to Estonia on September 4 brought my concerns to a high level. I had met the Estonian president, Lennart Meri, at a NATO conference a few months earlier. Estonia was hoping to be considered for eventual NATO membership. Meri was a real institution in his country, an intellectual and a dissident film producer whose affection for Estonian culture had established him as a popular leader. He had long experience with Eastern Europe and the Russians and was thoughtful and reflective. You must come for a visit now, he suggested.

At the president's seaside villa, Meri had a grim message to deliver. "NATO is failing in the Balkans," he said. "With each passing day you lose credibility." He spoke in a whisper, barely audible. But it was a loud message.

SIX

DIPLOMACY BACKED BY THREAT

RETURNED TO WASHINGTON in September, but I didn't find a great deal of concern in the Pentagon about the situation in Europe. The big item on the Chiefs' minds was the September 15 meeting with President Clinton scheduled for the National Defense University. All regional Commanders in Chief were to attend, and each of us was to tell the President about "readiness." These conferences were always useful. We heard the Washington view, and the Chiefs could hear from the CINCs. But this one, in particular, clearly exposed the weak positions of the regional CINCs and illustrated the pressing concerns and orientation of the Pentagon, which centered on long-term funding.

This conference was an effort to get everyone on the same side, a collective effort to lay out for the President the views of his commanders and to gain his support for increased defense resources. In the moments before he arrived, we each gave a shortened version of what we would say. The comments were harmonious, reinforcing, and balanced. Anyone would understand that we needed more money.

After the rehearsal I approached the Army Chief, General Dennis Reimer, to raise one suggestion: "Chief, in addition to talking about the shortage of Apache helicopter crewmen, intelligence specialists, and communications personnel, do you think I should just put in a plug for a larger Army overall? This might be an opportunity to help lay the case for more troops." Some members of Congress had continued to chastise the Army for not making its case for additional resources and troops more strongly and had even asked me to help push for a more forward approach; I thought maybe I could help the Army here.

Reimer was thoughtful but cautious. "No, I don't think so," he said.

As the President came in, we stood in place and he worked his way around the outside of the table, chatting briefly as each of the four-stars introduced himself. As he came by to shake hands, he touched my shoulder and said, "You'll be ready to take care of the Kosovars, won't you?"

"Yes, sir," I said. It was his way of showing he knew what was on my mind. And I hoped it was on his mind, too.

Then we began. For well over an hour, one by one, the top leaders in the U.S. Armed Forces cited their problems. The President listened impassively as I described the manning shortfalls in Europe: "Sir, troop morale is good, our forces are well trained and capable, but we are short manpower. There are 144 Apache helicopters assigned in Europe, but fewer than 100 are fully crewed. We're short intelligence specialists and communicators. One of my key intelligence outfits is below 60 percent strength...." Then it was on to the next commander.

This wasn't a good-news session. When it was over, the President thanked us and left. We learned that he would support additional funding for the Armed Forces, but that, with his hands tied by the funding agreements with Congress, it was going to be up to the Armed Forces to gain Congressional support to modify the funding cap. It was months later that I realized the full difficulties of our position. Wasn't the Commander in Chief more or less asking his Pentagon to fend for itself on the Hill, with the opposition party controlling the Congress, many of whose members had been openly disdainful of the President's skill in foreign and security policy? And didn't this further weaken the position of the regional commanders in chief, who were more interested in near-term activities rather than longer-term issues? I knew I would have to push hard for the strategy I thought we needed.

I had my opportunity on the same trip. I visited privately with Hugh Shelton and told him of my growing concern with NATO's visible failure to prevent the heavy handed Serb military and police operations which were destroying village after village in Kosovo. He agreed with me.

Next I went to see Walt Slocombe and ran the same concerns by him. "Walt, I think the U.S. has to take the lead in calling for this to stop," I said. "And if we don't do it soon, it will be too late. Milosevic needs to receive an ultimatum. There's a NATO defense ministerial meeting coming up in Portugal; it's going to be the key time for us to affect the Europeans."

Slocombe was one of my oldest friends in the Pentagon. A graduate of Princeton, Oxford, and Harvard Law School, he had a "judicial temperament"—he didn't exaggerate or make snap judgments—and one of the sharpest minds in town. I had always carried the highest regard for him. "Personally, I agree with you," he said, and together we went in to see Secretary Cohen. Despite the sometimes rocky road of my relationship with the Secretary, I was always hopeful when I went into see him. I laid out my considerations and conclusions. I followed right through on the theme I had developed with Slocombe an hour earlier.

Cohen's skepticism appeared to be softening as I proceeded, and I moved into the conclusion. "Mr. Secretary, we're running out of time to save NATO and our credibility. It will be all over in Kosovo by mid-October, Milosevic will have used force, made 350,000 homeless and killed who knows how many, and we will have stood by and done nothing but posture. Sir, we need to stop him. You need to help us get an ultimatum to Milosevic."

Without a break in the rhythm, Slocombe joined in, "Mr. Secretary, I agree with Wes."

Cohen snapped back, "I'll give an ultimatum all right." But, as he continued, he was as concerned about the Europeans, too. He was angry and wary, doubting that they would support his call for a strong threat against Milosevic. As far as he was concerned, this was their "last chance." It was a sharp retort, and I had the sense that some of the sharpness was a reaction to being pushed a little. But it also reflected underlying transatlantic tensions and Pentagon skepticism about the Europeans that would later become much more pronounced.

We concluded the meeting, discussing the timing of our diplomatic efforts and the importance of an interagency diplomatic team like the one we had in Dayton. I walked out enormously relieved. I understood that Secretary Cohen wouldn't welcome a deeper engagement in the Balkans. But, as Slocombe confided, "I've never seen him shift positions like that in a meeting."

I could hardly wait to assure Solana of the new, more determined American attitude. I returned to Europe and intensified our NATO planning effort.

Secretary Cohen delivered. The U.S. interagency effort moved forward, helping to arrange a U.N. resolution adopted finally on September 23, calling for a halt to hostilities and demanding immediate steps "to avert the impending humanitarian catastrophe" in Kosovo. It also sought a political solution to the situation in Kosovo and the withdrawal of security units used for civilian repression. And all U.N. member states were called on to provide adequate resources for humanitarian assistance. Resolution 1199 was adopted under Chapter VII of the U.N. Charter, authorizing member nations to use "all available means" to enforce it. While not explicit, this was U.N. code for the use of force if necessary. NATO planning moved forward, with nations being asked to consider how many aircraft they would provide for the air operations plans.

That same day, the NATO defense ministers assembled in Villa Mora, Portugal, for their annual "informal" meeting. If the threat was to be made real, and Milosevic was to be stopped, the decisions would have to be taken here. The fact that these were "informals" was to our advantage. It meant that there was no communiqué agreed on ahead of time. And there would be adequate time for discussion. However, if we left the meeting with no agreement on the way ahead, our indecision would be exposed for all to see.

At these meetings, Solana would speak first, followed by General Naumann and me, before the Defense Ministers joined in to respond or lay out their own concerns. In this case, Javier couldn't have been more clear. He was determined to save NATO's reputation in the region and its credibility. Milosevic, he noted, was playing a game with us. "His motto is, 'A village a day keeps NATO away,'" Solana said. He was obviously trying to goad the defense ministers into action.

As always, I was introduced by Naumann, who made his own view clear in his introduction: the outlook for Kosovo was bleak; the KLA would be defeated initially but more fighting could be expected in the spring. I then gave my appraisal of the operations. In this case I laid out the Serb's blatant disregard for NATO's efforts over the summer, and then briefed the results of our planning. We had about a dozen plans completed or underway at this point, all in response to political guidance from NATO headquarters.

After my briefing the defense ministers began to speak. There was no particular order. The first speakers congratulated themselves on the successful completion of some of the NATO plans, including the pending adoption of ACTWARN for the Phased Air Operation and for the Limited Air Operation. ACTWARN was a specific authorization to be provided to me to ask governments to identify the types and numbers of aircraft that they would provide for these operations. This was to be the first time that NATO would move forward to ACTWARN without an explicit U.N. Security Council Resolution. The first ministers to speak were seeing ACTWARN as the end of the planning process, so that the plans could now be put on the shelf.

But ACTWARN didn't bind governments. Without a legal commitment to proceed, it would not be perceived as a threat. Secretary Cohen, building on our conversation in Washington, called for moving ahead, going to legally binding commitments, the so-called ACTREQ, and putting immediate pressure on the Serbs to stop. It wasn't exactly a call for an ultimatum, but it was the firmest call for action I had heard in my year-plus with NATO.

Perhaps caught off-balance by U.S. determination, many of the following speakers hedged and measured their words. Only one nation gave unequivocal support, but even the British defense minister, George Robertson, was cautious. The majority expressed doubts about ACTREQ. A few countries were firm: they would approve no threat without a U.N. resolution, and ACTREQ would be seen as a threat. Secretary Cohen's remarks had clearly exceeded most national policies.

That evening the contentious dialogue continued over dinner. Several ambassadors approached me to complain that we were pushing too hard. Sure, they knew Milosevic, but there was international law to consider. I pushed back. I could see Solana, Cohen, and Naumann engaged similarly. There were earnest discussions and "pull-asides," hurried phone calls back home. NATO's strong sense of corporate commitment asserted itself. The weight of opinion shifted. By the next afternoon it was as though an early autumn thunderstorm had passed. Ministers now began to say, well, of course ACTWARN was only the beginning of the force commitment process. Certainly, governments must continue the planning through to achieve ACTREQ, the meeting concluded.

In the press conferences, Solana described the decision to authorize ACTWARN as another step in NATO's preparations to use force. Secretary Cohen called on Milosevic to stop the killing and destruction in Kosovo.

I returned to Mons to continue intensive planning. There were details to be worked on both the air threats and the potential ground options if NATO should be requested to enter on the ground. We had some targets identified, but we were scrambling to identify more.

NATO would need to hear the details on the planning for the air operations, but how many details? I thought about my letter to Shinseki, which had found its way to Milosevic—confirmation of the strength of Serb intelligence. I was wary of saying too much.

I conferred with Hugh Shelton and worked out what we believed would be the right system. I would describe the approximate number of targets by target categories, and perhaps an example or two if needed but would not disclose the exact targets we had selected at the North Atlantic Council meetings. The United States would support my position.

I received a call from the NSC staff, to consider the next steps. How were we going to actually use the NATO threat to cause Milosevic to halt his operations? Public announcements weren't enough. I recommended sending Ambassador Richard Holbrooke to carry the threat personally to Milosevic. Chris Hill was up to his eyeballs in his ongoing negotiations. Holbrooke would have to lower the hammer and use the threat of airpower to halt the Serb campaign.

Meanwhile, the pace of planning both the air operations and the diplomacy was frantic. Over the weekend of October 3 and 4 we had multiple planning conferences and calls within NATO and Washington. The Pentagon wanted to know in detail the targets we would strike, and our plan was still being assembled. We were also concerned about the three hundred fifty American soldiers deployed in Macedonia, along the border with Serbia. Ric Shinseki wanted to reinforce them before we struck, just as a matter of force protection. And we were also anxious about the end results of the possible Holbrooke mission. If Milosevic agreed to halt his operations, then what? I knew the Pentagon was strongly opposed to a U.S. troop presence inside Kosovo, even if Milosevic would agree to it. And in our planning, we judged that inserting NATO troops between the Serb forces and the KLA inside Kosovo would be a really difficult mission. But, without an armed troop presence inside Kosovo, would any cease fire achieved have a chance to succeed?

In U.S. channels we considered the possibility of imposing a no-fly zone, or perhaps a NATO air surveillance mission over Kosovo. A no-fly zone was part of the Phased Air Operation plan. I discussed the idea with the Pentagon. They seemed cool to putting aircraft over Yugoslavia, but I succeeded in getting Joe Ralston to agree that he would "put the issue before the Deputies" in the meeting on Sunday. There was also a report that the Pentagon was questioning whether Holbrooke should come at this point. "Of course he must come," I pleaded to Ralston.

Holbrooke arrived in Brussels on Monday morning, October 5, after an overnight flight from the States. I provided an aircraft from the European Command for his use and sent an officer with him to represent me in my U.S. capacity in the negotiations. I met Holbrooke in Brussels in the office of Sandy Vershbow, the U.S. ambassador to NATO to confirm arrangements.

Holbrooke went through his guidance in general terms: Get Milosevic to agree to cease fire, to halt the fighting, and to comply with the terms of Security Council Resolution 1199. In this resolution was the requirement that the Serbs withdraw the additional forces that had moved into Kosovo after February 1998. And, Holbrooke complained to me, "Your Secretary of Defense warned me that under no circumstances was I to offer NATO ground troops as peacekeepers." I was not surprised that the Secretary was firmly against U.S. troops—

the Congress would have been extremely skeptical, and it would have become an immediate and divisive issue in the midterm elections in November.

"Now, what I need to know is, what are the targets? And how long is the time between the order to execute and the first strikes?" Holbrooke wanted the details in order to have leverage in his forthcoming dialogue with Milosevic. But I wasn't able to release a list of targets—this had to stay within military channels. I gave him some representative targets, instead. Then he and Vershbow and I went in to see Solana.

Holbrooke reviewed the timing of what he was trying to do, sensing the need to understand the "mechanics" of how NATO would proceed to bring its threat to a head. There was little discussion of what he would actually say to Milosevic or how he would proceed. Knowing Holbrooke, I figured he would feel his way in the first sessions. He usually didn't operate off a formal road map.

Then he was off. About 2:00 a.m. I was awakened by a call from U.S. Brigadier General Alan W. "Bud" Thrasher, my representative accompanying Holbrooke. "Sir, the Ambassador has the agreement almost completely worked out," he said. "President Milosevic has agreed to accept what Holbrooke is calling unarmed "verifiers" on the ground to observe Serb compliance with the U.N. resolution. It'll be done by the OSCE [the Organization for Security and Cooperation in Europe]. Really about the only thing left is to agree on how many "verifiers" there will be. Milosevic says he's willing to take three hundred, and Holbrooke wants maybe one to two thousand."

As Thrasher talked, I realized that I had not seen Holbrooke's actual guidance, though in talking to the Pentagon I thought I knew what was expected from the mission. Holbrooke hadn't disclosed these ideas on his trip through Belgium the day before. How could he have gotten an agreement so quickly? And what did it mean? We'd had a small number of observers in Kosovo since June, who provided information on activities on the ground and corroborated news reports. Holbrooke had been a proponent of this group, but it worried me, because in the event of any trouble, the observers would be vulnerable in case the Serbs needed Western hostages. More potential hostages reduced the credibility of the NATO hammer. OSCE had no standing capability to do this; everything done by OSCE was piecemeal, slow, and politically brokered. Where would all these people come from? And what were they going to verify, exactly? Had Milosevic committed to withdrawing his forces? Thrasher wasn't sure. It did not add up. I had expected some back and forth over a period of days, not a final agreement. I couldn't reach Holbrooke.

After another try with Thrasher, I called Mike Durkee, my political adviser, and Ambassador Vershbow, waking them to give them the news. It was almost over, but did it make sense? The emotion in their voices was clear: they were bewildered. Was this some kind of a Milosevic trap? How could this have happened like this? After all we had put NATO through, was this the most we could hope for? Would it be enough? Vershbow thought that he had received the terms of reference from Washington, but they didn't suggest this kind of an arrangement.

We believed we had just this one chance to use the NATO threat as leverage against Milosevic and I knew Holbrooke felt the same way. He had been highly frustrated that we could not get NATO troops on the ground. Nevertheless we knew we had to come out of this with substantive achievements. We also recognized how artful Milosevic could be in twisting and manipulating agreements.

Durkee and I continued to talk during the night, with the last call around 4:00 A.M. I was concerned by the pace and finality of the discussions in Belgrade. NATO was going to be shut out of any role, it appeared. We were so concerned that we had forgotten to engage the "secure mode" on our telephones. When I noticed this, I broke off the call.

About 9:00 Tuesday morning, Solana called me. He had heard something about last night. "Wes, I hear that it's almost finished. What do you know about it?"

I explained what I knew about the unarmed verifiers, trying to present it in a balanced way. But Solana saw through the balance immediately.

"This won't work. And it means that NATO will have no role. This is terrible. You must fix this."

"Javier, I'll try. I have an idea." I discussed the idea I had discussed in U.S. channels: put NATO aircraft over Kosovo. They could work in concert with OSCE to verify Serb compliance. I trusted NATO to report factually, without political pressures to shade the information. By giving us our own independent voice in interpreting Serb compliance, the NATO verification mission would help us avoid the kind of "dual-key" that had hobbled NATO support of UNPROFOR in Bosnia.

"Do whatever you have to," Solana said.

I finally connected with Holbrooke shortly before 1:00 P.M. I hammered away at all the problems with OSCE. Have you seen how limited OSCE is in Bosnia? Don't you understand that SFOR has had to run the elections' logistics for them? What is this really going to achieve? Don't you see how this is going to be viewed? Holbrooke was just as emotional back: your Secretary Cohen wouldn't let me offer NATO troops; this was the best I could do. OSCE can be made to work. We'll have Americans with it. Milosevic understands that there will be military officers as part of OSCE, and they will have broad powers to observe and investigate. It will make a difference. Besides, do you really want to use those missiles?

There has to be more, I said. What about the concept of an air verification system by NATO as an adjunct to, but separate from, the OSCE mission. There has to be verification—why not by air, too? Holbrooke made no commitment to this approach, but seemed to factor it in.

Perhaps he had already considered it or worked it informally with someone in Washington. We were on an open telephone line. He couldn't say more. I knew that he was without sleep for two nights and deep in the negotiations. He was incredibly intense, determined, and alert to every opening and possibility. I had enough to move forward with the NATO air idea.

I went immediately to the Joint Staff, to Brigadier General George Casey in J-5, to explain the idea to him and enlist his backing. Casey saw the logic, and we began to discuss how we would structure the mission. And I called Hugh Shelton, to give him my appraisal and run the idea past him. He didn't say no, either.

Then I brought in Jeremy MacKenzie and Dieter Stockmann to consider how we were going to organize this. They went to work.

The meetings were continuing in Belgrade but I couldn't tell whether there was any change in the status of the discussions. I called Thrasher and asked him to work the NATO air verification mission into the discussions inside the team. Now it seemed that the negotiations were much further from producing an agreement. He was positive and sensed that Holbrooke, seeking a way to get NATO engaged, would be supportive.

Joe Ralston called from Washington later that afternoon. "Wes, George Casey's in here talking to me about this air verification mission, and I am just not sure about it."

I had expected the call. "Well, if we don't keep NATO engaged in some way ...," I began, and I went through the arguments.

"Wes, I understand all that, but these aircraft won't see anything from high altitude. You're talking about U-2's? And then what happens in bad weather? I just don't want to see us build up expectations that we can't deliver on. And how much can the Allies do in any of this? They don't have any U-2's." Ralston was reasonable, prudent, and conservative in committing resources. It was part of his duties as Vice, to be sure. But it also seemed something more, part of the ongoing dynamics among the top three people in the Pentagon, of sorting the CINC's interest against the Services, and perhaps the Pentagon against the State Department. It was part of what I was working through on a daily basis, I reflected, but it was jarring. When you were a CINC, you were supposed to be able to call on the Vice and the Chairman for support in accomplishing your missions. But in this case, I knew, there was going to be a concern about the overall allocation of resources to support this mission, since we were not a priority—priority would be given to the missions required in one of the two Major Theaters of War that the Pentagon planning had postulated.

The conversation ended inconclusively. I knew I hadn't answered every issue to his satisfaction, but he hadn't said no, either. And George Casey was still shopping the concept around the building and in the interagency. So far, so good. I knew Solana and Vershbow were also pressing Washington for a NATO role.

On Thursday, the deal still wasn't closed. Thrasher reported that Holbrooke was supportive of the NATO mission, but the agreement hadn't been reached with Milosevic yet. According to Thrasher, Milosevic was categorical: no NATO anywhere. Holbrooke was going to go to London to link up with the Contact Group representatives. But on the way, he was stopping by NATO to have lunch with Solana and with Secretary of State Albright at Ambassador Vershbow's residence in Brussels. I was invited, too.

As we sat down at the long dining room table, elegantly set with fine china and crystal, Holbrooke began to lay out his results thus far. He described the idea of using OSCE and indicated that he had already heard from the Russian foreign minister, Igor Ivanov, that Russia could support this.

Solana jumped in, one of the few times I had seen him interrupt. "Of course Russia will support it," he said, "It is their plan, what they offered to Milosevic a few days ago." Perhaps in Holbrooke's view, that was the genius of it.

Secretary Albright was listening to the discussion, not saying much.

After Holbrooke finished his presentation, I raised the issue of the air verification mission. NATO had to be engaged to ensure continuing restraint on Milosevic, I contended. There were nods around the table as I explained the air verification mission, though Holbrooke was uncertain whether it could be made acceptable to Milosevic or not. I couldn't seem to get him to commit at this point. So far as I knew, we didn't have Washington approval yet, either. There had been continuing questions from the Pentagon about the relationship between NATO and OSCE, and whether there could be a NATO ground force without United States participation. Although I was the senior U.S. military commander in the theater, I wasn't privy to all the nuances of direction and authority that Holbrooke may have been under. He maintained many lines of communication, I suspected, and the nuances and opportunities could change so fast in the negotiations that it was difficult to stay abreast from the outside, even with the assistance of Thrasher.

As we left the table, I approached Secretary Albright. She saw Milosevic's challenge very clearly and had been among the first that spring to warn about what he was trying to do in Kosovo. "We've got to have NATO engaged," I said.

"I understand. I'll try," she said.

Since we still weren't assured of the mission, we continued to press Holbrooke and touch base with the military and political advisor channels back to Washington. Moreover, even if we got the NATO mission, the relationship with the OSCE would have to be clarified—we didn't want to pass NATO information to OSCE for their assessment. Rather, we wanted an independent NATO voice in assessing compliance.

After his meeting in London, Holbrooke and the team headed back to Belgrade to resume discussions with Milosevic. We had gained Contact Group approval to introduce the NATO Air Verification mission into the talks, as well as the rest of the package that Holbrooke had worked. Washington was still fussing over the relationship of NATO to the OSCE, with someone there continuing to resist the idea of NATO leading the air monitoring effort, while we were pushing for the OSCE ground presence to support NATO's queries from the air. But these issues would have to be worked out in parallel with Holbrooke's discussions in Belgrade.

To carry this new task forward, Holbrooke asked for a senior airman to return with him. I sent Lieutentant General Mike Short, the NATO Air South Commander, to join the Holbrooke team. He was the man who would actually prepare the plans and orders for whatever strikes might be required.

In the midst of this, we were changing commanders in the NATO and U.S. Navy chains of command. Admiral Joe Lopez, the Commander in Chief of U.S. Naval Forces in Europe and also the Commander of the NATO Allied Forces Southern Europe command in Naples, was retiring. His replacement was newly promoted Admiral Jim Ellis, a naval aviator coming from the Navy staff in Washington. Ellis had no recent experience in the theater, but he had participated in some of the policy discussions in the Pentagon in his previous position. He had a Navy-wide reputation as a "quick-study" and a real "comer." His brilliant analytical skills came through from our first meeting.

The three of us were joined on the platform in front of the Bagnoli complex by Admiral Jay Johnson, the U.S. Chief of Naval Operations. The flags were flying, and the various troops of the command were smartly outfitted standing in front. The Italian carabineri, with their colorful plumes, were the stars of the show, as always. But what was on the minds of the press and the military leaders in attendance was the continuing crisis in the Balkans. It was a crucial moment, and in my remarks I warned Milosevic that NATO was there, observing, and ready.

But it was also a foretaste of things to come, when, afterwards, I was approached by several of the European officers with complaints that Admiral Johnson had been on the platform with us. "This was a NATO ceremony," they said. "He is just a service chief. What was he doing up there?" The American Navy had acquired a certain reputation for ownership of the command that some found overbearing, and Johnson, with the best of intentions, had reinforced their concern.

Meanwhile, Holbrooke and his team, including General Short, had arrived back in Belgrade. Short had experience in the region and was an extraordinarily well-qualified airman. He brought along the kind of gruff humor, with an edge, that made him a strong leader and a forceful personality, and in no time, with Holbrooke's coaching, he seemed to bludgeon Milosevic into accepting the air mission. Then he went into discussions of the details with the Serb generals. We had gone over what he should propose in advance, but when he forwarded up his first draft for review, the document was disturbing. For one thing, he had incorporated, just for discussion, a Serb proposal to restrict the overflights to photographic missions only, making us vulnerable to exactly the charge Joe Ralston had expressed—no "take" when it's cloudy. We had pulled Short in because Holbrooke wanted a "blue-suited" general to impress Milosevic and handle the "air" details, but Short and I hadn't had enough time to work through all the wrinkles that he would face or the procedures he should use in developing an agreement. Improvising, we set up a "backstopping" system, so that the drafts could be reviewed at my level, with George Higgins and Mike Durkee helping me.

It was over in a couple of days, and Holbrooke returned to Brussels to explain the agreement to NATO. We had now achieved ACTREQ in our force planning process, meaning that the forces were committed legally, but as Holbrooke left Belgrade there was a flurry of discussion in the U.S. channels. Had he gotten enough? Should we trust Milosevic at this point? Was he actually committed to pulling back his forces, and if so, when? I had tried to get the answer to this last question, but I couldn't seem to understand the answer that Milosevic reportedly was giving. It wasn't exactly a yes or a no. As Holbrooke explained it in a phone call, it was "complicated," though Holbrooke seemed confident that he had achieved concrete results. It was decided in the U.S. channels to seek NATO ACTORD, the third and final step in the force authorization process, as a kind of insurance policy against Milosevic. This would actually cock the hammer and pull the trigger on the airstrikes unless it were later suspended.

That evening, October 12, the North Atlantic Council met, and Holbrooke briefed the ambassadors on the results of his negotiations. However, there was no timetable for the Serb compliance, including troop withdrawals, and there could be difficulties in organizing the unarmed verification mission. So the Council authorized ACTORD, the next step. This directed air strikes after ninety-six hours, with the understanding that any further suspension would have to be voted by the Council. With most of the strike aircraft already assembled in Italy, it was an unmistakable signal to Milosevic: NATO was resolved to act, on short notice.

To much of the media, it was over; the agreement was done. OSCE would go to Belgrade to sign its part of the agreement and NATO would do the same. But some of us saw another problem: there had been no pullback of the additional Serb forces from Kosovo, which was part of the agreement Holbrooke had arranged. And so when Solana, Naumann, and I flew to Belgrade on October 15 to sign the agreement authorizing NATO overflight and verification, I was also armed with intelligence on the disposition of Serb forces. We were resolved to force the issue with Milosevic.

We met at Belli Dvor, the White Palace. It was the same entry routine, with the TV cameras and lights, and the smiling president shaking hands with his visitors. We sat down to refreshments, and some light conversation. Milosevic had not met Naumann, the German general, before, and, in his usual manner he probed Naumann's receptivity to blandishment.

"So, General Neuman"—he got the name wrong—"you are German. Germany is wealthy country," he said. It was no doubt meant to compliment, but was there a slight trace of resentment in the comment, that Germany, one of the losers in World War II had done so well, while his Yugoslavia had fared poorly? I couldn't be sure. Naumann sat firm, responding minimally.

Quickly, the NATO agreement was brought forward and signed. Good wishes were expressed, and then the discussion ensued.

Milosevic began. He was uncomfortable about the NATO air threat. There was no doubt it was generating leverage against him. "So when will you get rid of this NATO ACTORD, Mr. Solana?" he asked pointedly.

Solana leaned forward on the couch, "You must do something first," he said.

"And what is that?" Milosevic asked.

"You must withdraw the additional military and forces you have deployed into Kosovo since February."

"No, Holbrooke said if I signed and agreed to NATO mission and OSCE, there would be no threat."

Solana stood firm. "No, you agreed to comply with the U.N. Resolution, so you must pull forces back now."

"There was no such agreement. Call your Mr. Holbrooke. He will tell you this."

"We know what was agreed, and you must pull back those extra forces." Solana wasn't giving in on this.

Milosevic pouted. Then he switched arguments. "That will happen when all OSCE verifiers have arrived and mission is operational," he said.

"No, it must happen now," insisted Solana. He was really being tough.

Milosevic paused, considering how to move forward. He switched his argument again. "There are no additional forces in Kosovo."

Solana paused. It was the signal for me to cut in. "Mr. President, have you ever heard of the 211th Armored Brigade?" I asked.

"No, I have not heard of such unit," he said sharply. He looked to his left where the Yugoslav Military Chief, General Momcilo Perisic, was sitting. They spoke briefly in Serbian. Milosevic was not pleased.

"Yes," he said. "There is such unit."

"Well, you must pull it back out of Kosovo."

"OK, it will be done. And then you will remove this ACTORD?" Milosevic looked back at Solana.

"No," Solana said, "You must comply fully with the U.N. Security Council Resolution. You must pull back all additional forces."

Milosevic was going to be stubborn here. I joined in again, "Mr. President, have you ever heard of the Third Military Police Battalion?"

It was going to be a repeat. "No," he said, and turned again to Perisic.

"OK, it will be withdrawn. Now will you remove the threat against my country?" he pressed. He really didn't like the NATO threat.

We went through a couple of more units: I would mention their designation, Milosevic would deny his awareness, and Perisic would then confirm our information. I could tell Perisic was walking a dangerous line. But we were beating down Milosevic's resistance.

I then turned to his special police units. "And what about the Twenty-fourth Police Battalion?"

Again, "There is no such unit." Perisic couldn't or wouldn't respond. Milosevic continued, "General Clark, there are no military police units. These are precinct numbers, not units."

"Well, Mr. President, our information says that you have brought in additional police. If they aren't in units, then you must explain their numbers. We aren't going to want to go out and count noses individually."

Milosevic took it. "OK, we will provide information to you. You can see then. And then you will remove this ACTORD?" He was getting angrier and more frustrated as he looked at Solana.

"President Milosevic, the ACTORD is NATO's. I cannot say what the nations will do." Solana was holding on to the ACTORD option. And in truth it wasn't his to give away.

Now Milosevic was steaming, "Then what is your expectation on this ACTORD?" Milosevic practically spit the words at Solana.

"I have no expectation," Solana said, standing his ground firmly.

Milosevic slumped back in utter frustration and anger. Perhaps he had always felt superior to many European diplomats. Trying to outmaneuver Solana was a different and unpleasant experience.

It was the end of the meeting. We left with the understanding that I would receive the police information and might return to clarify this with the Serbs.

The next morning, Milosevic called in Chris Hill, who was negotiating the interim agreement on Kosovo, to complain. As Hill related the story, Milosevic said, "General Clark and General Naumann are good men, but why do I have to take orders from that Spanish Communist Solana?"

NATO extended the suspension of the ACTORD to give Milosevic ten days to comply or else. After we examined the Serb police data, I returned to Belgrade on October 20 to discuss the data and apply further pressure for withdrawal of the excess security units, this time with the authority from Washington to actually deliver the threat personally if Milosevic was uncooperative.

Milosevic opened the meeting by hanging tough. Yes, he would pull out the units I had named previously, but everything else would stay in place. The Albanians were a threat, and he had responsibilities to protect Serbia from this threat.

"Mr. President, can I speak to you alone, please?" I asked. I wanted to get him away from the usual retinue of supporters. We both got up and walked into an adjoining room. We stood face to face.

"Mr. President, you are going to have to withdraw all your excess forces. Let's stop fencing about this. If you don't withdraw, Washington is going to tell me to bomb you, and I'm going to bomb you good."

Milosevic tried to appear blasé. "Well, General Clark, NATO will do what it must do," he said. This was his tough guy approach. I'd seen it at Dayton.

"Get real, Mr. President. You don't want to be bombed."

Now he was thoughtful. "No, General Clark, I don't."

"Then you tell your generals to be cooperative and work out a way to get all those excess forces out of Kosovo."

"OK, I will tell them. We will see what can be done."

The Serb military and police generals gathered in another room. A map was brought in. Colonel-General Djordjevic, the overall police commander, talked me through the map, pointing out to me the exact locations of the KLA as he knew them.

I added the total; it came to 410. "So, you were going to destroy this province to try to capture 410 people? And in the process, you'll generate 4,000 more who hate you enough to fight. This just doesn't make sense," I said.

"We were within two weeks of killing them all, when you stopped us," he said. "Why did you stop us?"

"Because you were targeting the civilian population and creating a humanitarian catastrophe for your own people," I said. "Don't you understand you can't stop something like this by using force and especially not against civilians?"

But they didn't. The military then showed me their dispositions, with General Perisic pointing at the map and explaining routes, garrisons, and key terrain.

Then the Army and the police began to formulate a way to pull forces out of the area. After several hours of discussion, what emerged was a two-phased proposal in which the first phase would see a pullback from the Pagarusa valley and the area southwest of Pristina, with a second stage to be defined. We never succeeded in completely accounting for the police locations, but the numbers suggested that there were some 4,000 excess police in the province, brought in since February.

I departed Belgrade telling the Serbs I would carry their proposal back to NATO, but that there was no guarantee that NATO would accept it. However, I did not want to reject it myself while I was there. It was movement in the right direction. And I was gaining a lot of useful information. How many commanders, I wondered, ever got to sit down with their adversaries after a crisis and probe their minds?

Sure enough, back at NATO the diplomats weren't impressed. This partial plan was inadequate, and there was no assurance it would lead to the full pullback of the additional forces that the U.N. resolution directed. And I hadn't been authorized to bring back such a plan, anyway. I arranged for General Naumann to accompany me back to Belgrade for a third visit before the ACTORD period expired.

Naumann and I arrived on Saturday afternoon, October 24. We were taken right in to see Milosevic. I reminded Milosevic that we had everything riding on this meeting, and as we left to meet the generals, I reminded him of my warning to him at the last meeting.

"I have not forgotten," he said.

Our intent was to try to strengthen the Serb pullback arrangement, building on what they had offered. We went to see Perisic. He was reasonably open, calling his Army the last "democratic" institution in Serbia, and asking us not to destroy it. After talking to him, we saw that what made the most sense was a Serb military withdrawal that left only three company-sized military units deployed outside their cantonment areas in Kosovo. But Perisic could not agree to anything. As he put it, it was Milosevic and no one else who could change things.

When we saw the police generals, there was no give. They went back to the unacceptable scheme of pulling forces back from around Malisevo. It was a stall for time. By 8:00 p.m., it was clear that we weren't going to achieve a full pullback. We asked to see Milosevic again.

I explained to Milosevic that the generals weren't able to cooperate fully; they felt that he would not support them. Naumann and I put on pressure. "Look, Mr. President," I said, "General Naumann has an idea." We had agreed to go after him directly if necessary. I turned to Naumann.

"Mr. President, you must simply pull back the excess police, all of them. This is what has to be done, and within the next two days." Naumann was polite but firm and forceful. He spoke with confidence and authority.

"Ugh," Milosevic exclaimed, scowling. He looked like he'd been hit. Then he recovered and began to argue.

We pushed back, alternating from the positive to the negative. You have to turn the table on the Albanians to restore Serbia's reputation, I argued; pull back so that the agreement can work. Naumann warned Milosevic that he was risking going down in his country's history as the man who ruined and lost Serbia. Milosevic shook his head. We continued to press. Soon it was over.

"Let me talk to my generals," Milosevic said. They stood up and moved to another room.

A few minutes later Milosevic walked back in, followed by his generals, along with Milan Milutinovic, now the president of Serbia, and Nicola Sainovic, the special minister for dealing with Kosovo. "OK," he said grandly. "It will be done."

We were waiting for this. "Good, but you understand that the police pullback is not enough?" I went through the Army pullback, the withdrawal of heavy weapons from the police, and so forth.

Milosevic listened, grunted grudging assent, and then said we should go work the details with Milutinovic. Naumann and I and our team were driven back over to the Serb Ministry of Defense headquarters and taken upstairs to the conference room. It was a large gloomy building, and the low lighting and eerie effects of being stuck there on a Saturday night made it seem surreal.

The arguments and discussions ran back and forth, as we played a game that Milosevic had set for us. We had learned at Dayton, Milosevic would concede in general terms on any given point, but his lieutenants might hammer away at the details to try to take back the concession. However, Naumann and I used the Serbs' fatigue in the early morning hours against them. At last we had the Serbs' concessions in writing.

General Naumann and I left at 5:00 A.M. to return to the Hyatt hotel. We had a draft document, and we had arranged to give it to Milosevic for signature at 9:00 A.M. Sunday. But first I needed to check it and also make sure I didn't have problems from Washington. The Pentagon had no problem. I spoke with Holbrooke, and then passed it to the White House.

After extensive discussion, we went back to Belli Dvor at 10:00. Milosevic welcomed us, and we got right down to business. He wanted changes. So did we, but we let him play his cards first. They were relatively minor wordsmithing, and he wanted to be sure that he reserved for himself and his forces the right of self-defense. Of course, unless we were going to be there to protect the Serbs, as we were in Bosnia, we couldn't take away their right of self-defense.

Then it was our turn. "Mr. President, I'm sorry to tell you that we made a mistake in the numbers last night, and we must correct them," I said.

"What is that?"

"Well, when we said you had to pull 3,000 police out, the number is really 4,000."

"Why is this? We had agreement—"

"Mr. President, this comes from the numbers you gave us; they clearly show that you have 4,000 police too many."

He studied the paper I handed him, a translation of his own document. He was trapped, and he knew it. "OK," he said at last.

"And all of this has to be done in the next thirty-six hours," I reminded him.

And so the paper was completed. These were to be his "promises" to NATO, which we said ought to be adequate to prevent the launching of the air attack, though of course we could make no guarantees. It just remained to correct the typing and sign them.

Milosevic brought in brandy for himself, Milutinovic, Naumann and me, and for once I joined him. He grew philosophical, as he began to discuss the economic future of Serbia. Then, as though a railroad engine had jumped its tracks, he abruptly switched subjects.

"You know, General Clark, that we know how to handle these Albanians, these murderers, these rapists, these killers-of-their-own-kind.

We have taken care of them before." His face turned red, and his voice rose in strength as he condemned them. This was a paragraph out of some public statement. He wasn't really speaking to us, I thought.

"In Drenica, in 1946, we killed them. We killed them all." Naumann and I were just staring at him.

He must have thought we didn't believe him, so he began to qualify the accomplishment. "Oh, it took several years, but we eventually killed them all." He was smug, satisfied, and looking as though he was expecting our approval.

We were stunned by the outburst. "Mr. President, we weren't even discussing the Kosovars, we were talking about the economic development of Serbia." But we knew then and there that the chances for a peaceful end to all of this were slight.

A few minutes later the retyped agreement was brought back in. Mike Durkee laid it in front of me for signature. I noticed that General Naumann and I were both expected to sign, but that Sainovic and General Djeordjevic would sign for Yugoslavia. I had seen enough diplomacy in the Balkans to smell a rat.

"Mr. President, your name is not on here for signature," I said, "And neither is Milutinovic's. Why not?"

"Is not necessary. General Djeordjevic and Mr. Sainovic are authorized to sign."

Sure, but then when he wanted to break the agreement, he could claim it wasn't his. I let him have it. "Mr. President, when General Naumann and I travel in Europe, we see the top people in every country. When we go to Denmark, we have lunch with the Queen. And we came here to deal with you. You have to sign this document."

It came out as an order. Milosevic pulled out his pen, almost meekly, and signed. He then offered us the pen.

I deferred the offer to Naumann. It looked like an expensive gold fountain pen, with a golf club and flag on it.

"Regulations prevent me from accepting this," General Naumann explained. And I certainly wasn't going to take it.

Then we were on our way. It only remained for the Serbs to implement the agreement, which, we had made clear, must commence immediately.

The next morning, I checked intel—nothing was moving—and I

spoke with Ambassador Dick Miles, our chargé in Belgrade, on an open telephone line. Surely the Serbs were listening.

"If they don't start moving by noon," I said, "I'm going to call Solana and ask for authorization to proceed with the strikes."

Within a few hours the Serbs began moving. This was diplomacy backed by threat. The air threat helped to halt the Serb campaign in Kosovo, just as I had expected. Milosevic was intimidated by NATO airpower, even in the absence of a significant ground threat. We wouldn't have been able to stop the Serb campaign without the air threat—that was clear from the "heavy lifting" we'd done since Holbrooke returned from Belgrade and reported to the Council. Solana, Naumann, and I were relieved, and enormously proud of NATO. Our credibility had been salvaged. With NATO watching from the air, and the ACTORD still held in abeyance, we believed we had some measure of control over what came next in Kosovo. It had been a long six months since my visit with President Gligorov in Macedonia, but NATO had proved its credibility in backing diplomacy to halt the Serb attacks on the Kosovars. We reckoned that Holbrooke's mission and our follow-up had saved perhaps thousands from freezing to death in the mountains that winter. But we worried about what would happen in the spring.

Jeremy MacKenzie and Dieter Stockmann hustled to establish the air verification structure, with the Brits providing a very capable brigadier, David Montgomery, to lead the effort. It was a buildup from scratch of a verification center on the ground. Working with the government of Macedonia, Montgomery arranged for his team to move into the old Yugoslav army headquarters in Kumanovo. There he would set up an information exchange center, providing air-collected intelligence to the OSCE, and taking from the OSCE information of happenings on the ground. If we developed it right, we believed, we might even be able to do real-time response to OSCE requests for aerial intelligence. And Montgomery would give NATO an unvarnished read of the situation.

As part of the verification agreement, we also established liaison with the Serb Air Force in Belgrade. We put three people there, working out of the headquarters in Belgrade, and the Serbs gave us a three-man team to be based with us in Aviano, Italy.

I had no illusions about the long term impact of what had been achieved, however. I wrote a detailed message to Shelton and Cohen warning that we had done no more than buy a pause in which diplomacy had to work. If it didn't, we would be facing conflict again within a few months.

Meanwhile, we had another complicated issue within NATO. Dick Holbrooke seldom let go of an idea, I had learned, and in this case, from the outset of the talks in Belgrade, he had wanted some armed Western, if not NATO, military forces on the ground in Macedonia, if not Kosovo, so they could intervene quickly if need be. He saw the forces as an additional factor for stability in Macedonia, too. Holbrooke had not managed to arrange for this in any formal agreement with Milosevic, but he had persuaded France to sponsor the effort.

This was the so-called French-led extraction force. It aimed to become a force of some 2,000, comprised of reinforced British, French, German, and Italian companies, with the French providing the commander, the logistics, and communications. They would share the NATO air verification headquarters in Kumanovo, just south of the border with Serbia. The commander would report to NATO, through SHAPE.

Washington insisted that no U.S. personnel would participate in the extraction force. It was to be European only, as part of the effort to persuade Congress that the American military was attempting to limit its role and place more of the burden on the Europeans. But this placed me in an awkward position. I was the overall commander, but I represented a nation that didn't want to participate.

NATO wasn't supposed to work that way. Going back to the days of General Eisenhower and Field Marshall Montgomery in World War II, Allied commands were distributed on the basis of who provided the troops. It wasn't a "beauty contest" between potential commanders; rather, the nation that contributed the most forces usually got the most significant positions. There was a sound logic to this, because the nation that contributes the most has the most to lose. And commandership is about not only accomplishing the mission but also managing risks. Of course, it could be argued that the United States was leading the mission in Bosnia, and we would supply the bulk of the air verification system over Kosovo. All true. But when I looked French Brigadier

General Marcel Valentin in the eye, I knew I wasn't speaking with the usual moral authority. The United States didn't need to be the largest contributor to the extraction force, but we needed to participate somehow. Instead, we had insisted on putting no "chips in the pot" on the ground, where the greatest risks would be.

As we sorted through these organization issues, NATO began to ask some tough questions about how this extraction force might be used. It was clear that this 2,000-person force was extremely limited. It could only go in if the Serbs gave it permission, and no one wanted to go to the Serbs and try to wheedle for that at this point. Klaus Naumann and I reckoned that we would need to look at the full requirements of extraction, and perhaps work out a more capable force. So we placed Lieutenant General Mike Jackson into the problem to back up the French-led force with a NATO Corps-sized headquarters.

After three weeks, it was clear that despite Serb compliance with the U.N. Resolution, and the efforts of the U.S. negotiator, Ambassador Chris Hill, little was moving on the diplomatic front to head off conflict in Kosovo. I was worried. We were in trouble. I talked with Hill, Hugh Shelton, Javier Solana, and Klaus Naumann, and I briefed the situation at the full NATO meetings—Chiefs of Defense, defense ministers, and foreign ministers—in November and December. To each I gave the same message: "We have only two to four months before fighting erupts again. This wasn't a settlement, only a pause. We have to use this time to make the negotiations work. If they don't work, we're looking at either a humanitarian disaster or a long-term NATO occupation force on the ground." Naumann was briefing along the same lines to the NATO ambassadors almost daily.

Given the governments' strong desires to reduce the levels of forces in the Balkans, I hoped this analysis would spur a greater effort in diplomacy.

In the meantime, we had declared the NATO missions, Verification and Extraction, operational on December 1, as planned. OSCE was also on the ground and working furiously to organize itself in Pristina and some of the other towns in Kosovo.

At the beginning of December, we bid farewell to Jeremy MacKenzie, who had completed four years as Deputy Supreme Allied Commander. MacKenzie's tour had spanned the entire period of NATO actions in the Balkans. He had created the system for "generating" forces, pulling them out from national authorities and assigning them to NATO. And he was a solid connection with both the British elements in the field and with London, and especially with the British Chief of Defense. NATO lost a great soldier..

The next Monday his replacement, General Sir Rupert Smith, arrived. Smith had come from command in Northern Ireland. Before that he had served as the final commander of UNPROFOR in Bosnia. He was a paratrooper who had commanded an armored division in the Gulf War, and he was well known to the Americans as well as the Europeans. I especially valued his experience and courage, demonstrated by his command in Bosnia in 1995. Though he had no previous experience in NATO, he was my pick to succeed MacKenzie.

Meanwhile, all the signs on the ground were bad. The KLA—and I suspected there were more than the 410 cited by the Serbs—had pushed right back into the areas the Serbs had vacated, despite entreaties by the international observers. The Serbs hadn't followed through with the withdrawal of heavy weapons from the police, as they had promised. General Perisic was removed, confirming long-held suspicions that he really was opposed to Milosevic. By late December, Serb forces were resuming their offensive actions in Kosovo, despite the promises to NATO.

I flew into Belgrade on December 20 to meet the new Serb military chief, Colonel-General Dragojub Ojdanic, and to encourage him to respect the promises that Milosevic had made to NATO on October 25. We met in a new building, where the Ministerial Specialist Police were headquartered. Sainovic, the civilian minister in charge of Serb activities in Kosovo, insisted on being present for the entire meeting. I figured that the Serbs didn't quite trust Ojdanic, and especially not in a room with me.

After the pleasantries, I got down to business. "We've seen your tanks north of Pristina, near Podujevo. That's not an authorized location. You're violating the promises that Milosevic and your predecessor gave to NATO," I said.

Mrs. Djankovic, the chain-smoking interpreter, was translating. As Ojdanic listened to her, he appeared confused. Sainovic spoke to him in Serbian. Then Mrs. Djankovic translated his reply, "It is permitted for these forces to be there, because they are on a training mission."

"No," I said, "it is not permitted, because you did not first give notice to OSCE that you were going to conduct the training mission. This is in the agreement."

Again the pause for translation, and the confused appearance by Ojdanic, with Sainovic offering more explanations. Mrs. Djankovic translated, "OSCE was notified today."

"Too late," I answered. "These are supposed to be advance notifications. And OSCE is supposed to be able to advise you on where to go." Of course we knew that these were the kind of training missions where the Serbs were searching for "training aids" who would shoot back. They were moving against the Albanian villages, looking for resistance and then using their machine guns and heavy weapons when they found it.

I went back through the entire set of promises that we had extracted from Milosevic on October 25, line by line. I wanted to be certain that there was no way he could be said to have misunderstood. But I realized, as the dialogue continued, that I was talking to a placeholder, someone who was ambitious enough to want the job, and maybe not smart enough to ask too many of the hard questions that had gotten Perisic in trouble. This was worrisome.

NATO's credibility was again at risk. It had been not quite two months since Milosevic had promised not to do this. Now what were we going to do? Solana and I realized we could do nothing during the Christmas holidays.

In early January I made another round of calls to leaders in NATO and Europe, warning that Milosevic was violating his promises to NATO. By this point there were only three possibilities if fighting broke out: first, Serb use of force, leading to a humanitarian catastrophe if NATO did nothing; second, Serb use of force followed by a NATO air campaign, after which the Serbs would concede and permit NATO to enter on the ground and face a long-term occupation; or, third, Serb use of force followed by a NATO air campaign and then, if the Serbs refused to admit NATO, a NATO ground intervention, that would end up destroying enough of the Serb military to force Milosevic from power. None of these was a good alternative. Therefore, diplomacy had to work.

As soon as possible I returned to Washington, with Solana's blessing, to propose a different approach to the negotiations. We would dangle the possibility of initiating a process which, if it returned democracy to Belgrade, could lead to Yugoslavia's return to OSCE membership. We knew Milosevic wanted this, and would gamble that he could enter into the process, confound Western efforts to reduce his power in Serbia, continue the repression in Kosovo, and eventually return to the OSCE. But, this would give us the opportunity to promote democratization in Serbia, tighten international presence in Kosovo to prevent repression, and keep Milosevic struggling to regain OSCE membership. It was heard with interest in Washington, but it was not adopted.

We knew we were running out of time but didn't realize how short our time was until Ambassador Bill Walker, the American diplomat who was the head of the OSCE mission, called me from near the village of Racak on January 16. "Wes, we've got trouble here," he began. "I know a massacre when I see one. I've seen them before, when I was in Central America. And I'm looking at a massacre now.... There are about forty of them in the ditch, maybe more. These aren't fighters, they're farmers, you can tell by looking at their hands and their clothes. And they've been shot at close range."

I knew Walker from previous work together in Latin America. He was experienced, and not prone to exaggeration. I reached Javier Solana by telephone in Spain almost immediately and described to him the news Walker had given me. Solana understood the significance immediately. He still had the trigger authority for the NATO airstrikes. He would have to consult with the nations, but no formal Council procedure would be necessary, "What should we do?" he asked. Solana was always a consensus leader; he liked to have your ideas before he made his own decision.

"Javier, I think you need to call the Council together, as soon as possible, tonight if you can, and lay out what's happened."

The Council convened Sunday night. Naumann and I briefed the ambassadors the latest on the situation as we knew it. Of course, by now, the massacre at Racak was public news, as was the NATO meeting. But there was no inclination to strike immediately against the Serbs, despite the authorization held by Solana. This case, after all, was precisely why the Limited Air Option had been created the previous summer. But the nations were not ready to act. There were charges and countercharges, as well as nearly 1,000 unarmed OSCE verifiers inside Kosovo who could be hurt by the Serbs if NATO struck. It was the kind of situation that rendered an immediate air threat meaningless. And both the Serbs and NATO knew it. But the Council had to make some response. NATO issued a press statement and determined that a fact-finding team should visit Milosevic as soon as possible and convey NATO's interest in what had happened.

NATO, of course, is a military organization; it doesn't have traveling squads of diplomats. And, as the discussion proceeded around the table, it was also determined that Solana was too senior to go. They agreed to send Klaus Naumann and me, over Naumann's objections. We were to go as soon as possible—tomorrow—and with no special instructions or threat to convey.

Naumann and I were seated next to each other at the Council table. We looked at each other. Something was wrong with this. First, we were going "weaponless." The Council hadn't authorized any threats or specific warnings. Also, we knew we were playing into Milosevic's hands by asking to come "as soon as possible." But there was no way to reverse direction; the Council's attention had already shifted to the proposed press statement. We were heading back into an almost certain failure, I reckoned.

Holbrooke phoned the next day. "You must do everything possible," he said. "Draw it out and work him over." Holbrooke didn't call routinely, and I always listened to what he said. But, of course, I didn't take orders from him.

On Tuesday, Naumann and I made the familiar trip to Belgrade aboard my aircraft. Ambassador Dick Miles was on hand to greet us when we landed. "He's in a foul mood," Miles said. "You'll find him really hard."

We used the NATO press statement as the guide to our discussion. We had three points to work—investigate the massacre, retain Ambassador Walker in Yugoslavia, and comply with the October promises to NATO. Our aim was acceptance of each point from Milosevic. After the pleasantries, we sat down at our places at the sofa and began:

"Mr. President, the Chief Prosecutor of the International Criminal Tribunal on Yugoslavia, Louise Arbour, would like to come here to investigate the massacre at Racak. May she come?" I asked directly.

"Well, General Clark," Milosevic began patronizingly, "as you know, we do not recognize jurisdiction of Tribunal here."

Of course we knew this. We had gone over it endlessly at Dayton and since. "Yes, but she would like to investigate, all the same. May she do that?" I pressed.

"General Clark, there was no massacre. Serb police are conducting investigation themselves. It is law here. But we know these police. They would not do this thing. Investigation will show this."

"But may she come also to investigate? You know, she could bring credibility to your work. And if it didn't happen, then everyone would know."

There was a two-hour long discussion on the matter of Louise Arbour. First, she could only come as a tourist, but could not go to Kosovo. Then she could visit Kosovo but only under the escort of the Justice Minister. She could not investigate but she could look at some bodies. No autopsies. She could question some witnesses but not alone. With each nuance I called Arbour and asked, is this enough? The answer was no, not enough.

This seemed to be an effort by Milosevic to play for time, to concoct a means of getting her in and implicating her in a cover-up of the facts. It was a standard ploy, used over and over again in the region by the Serbs. Arbour knew not to come in unless she had a free hand to investigate.

Second was the matter of Ambassador Walker. Milosevic believed he had acted prematurely in condemning Racak as a massacre, so Walker must leave.

"So, you will not allow him to stay?" I asked.

"No, he must leave. Is will of Serb government."

This led to a long, fruitless discussion of the obligations of diplomats to their host country. But Milosevic insisted Walker had to go, as it was the "will of Serb government." Then during a break, Milutinovic assured me that Milosevic might be willing to compromise on this later. Sure, that's why he was referring to the will of the government rather than his own view. This was a possible acorn for us to carry back to NATO, but he hadn't decided to give it to us yet. We would have to earn it, fawn a little, and play along with his charade.

Finally, there was the matter of the promises to NATO, withdrawing troops and refraining from using heavy weapons. "Will you comply with the promises you have made to NATO, Mr. President?"

"I told you, General Clark, that we must have right to defend ourselves."

After five hours of discussion, Naumann and I moved to wrap up the discussion. The difficulty was that there was no remorse, no remedial action, and, really, no resolution. The third issue—his promises to NATO—was the most crucial. We'd hit bottom. NATO's credibility was on the line here.

"So, Mr. President, you are telling us the answer to NATO is three 'no's; no to Louise Arbour, no to keeping Bill Walker, and no to the promises you made in October."

Milosevic was wary of how this sounded, but still uncompromising. This was going to be yet another rehash of the same game. Perhaps it was to wear us down, or convince us to carry back some meaningless "clarification" and continue this kind of dialogue. It was time for greater pressure.

"Please understand, Mr. President," I said, "that if we carry back your answers to NATO, they are going to tell us to start moving aircraft. They are going to ask, who is this man who is destroying his own country, who has crushed democracy, taken a vibrant economy and wrecked it, forced university professors to sign loyalty oaths." I continued to summarize the impressions and criticisms prevalent in Europe. I said it softly, conversationally, attempting to reason and persuade. Then I concluded, "Please don't leave it this way. Make a new start, move forward."

General Naumann reinforced with his thoughts along similar lines. Your country is the pariah of Europe, and you will end up sitting on the ruins of a destroyed Serbia if you don't comply, he warned.

Milosevic erupted. Red-faced, spitting out his words. This was the same man I had seen threatening Holbrooke at Dayton; this was the other side of the hospitable Godfather. "Who are you to accuse us— These are lies—Serbia is democracy—there are no loyalty oaths—You are threatening—You are war criminal."

After the outburst, we worked to settle him down. And we went through the issues for another two hours, but it was no use. At the end we shook hands, and I said goodbye. "I'm sorry it's worked out this way, Mr. President," I said. He looked indifferent as we departed.

SEVEN

THE THREE-RING CIRCUS

MILOSEVIC'S INTRANSIGENCE set many wheels in motion at NATO. On the diplomatic front, the Europeans still hoped to head off a military confrontation, and toward that end a new round of negotiations was begun at a French palace in the village of Rambouillet, outside Paris. The negotiations were to encompass all that had been discussed to date, with the aim of creating a comprehensive package that would end the repression, promote democratic standards, and establish the basis for a political solution in Kosovo. The Western nations, and even the United States, had come to recognize that a NATO force on the ground was essential in precluding a renewed outbreak of fighting in Kosovo, but they also knew that it would require Serb permission to place such a force there. The diplomats once again adopted a "carrot-and-stick" approach, warning the Serbs that if they didn't negotiate and accept the proposed agreement, and the NATO-led force along with it, then they would be hit by NATO airstrikes.

My staff and I were involved in drafting the military agreements for the Rambouillet negotiations, for which we used the Military Annex from the Dayton Agreements as a model, but we were simultaneously participating in three other rings in the "political-military circus." In the first "ring" we were completing the planning for the so-called Tier III extraction force, a more capable version of the approximately 2,000-person "Tier I" force currently under French command. We were also planning to deploy ground forces, should we be called upon to move into Kosovo directly on a peace support operation. This was the plan that had been approved in late autumn for a non-forced entry of 25,000 to 30,000 NATO troops into Kosovo after a peace settlement was achieved. British Lieutenant General Mike Jackson and the Allied Command Europe Rapid Reaction Corps (ARRC) were placed in charge of the detailed planning for this task.

However, there were a few items that had to be worked at my level. Assigning national sectors in Kosovo, I recognized, was a strategic and, even, political task. It was a matter for negotiation with the NATO Chiefs of Defense. The British Chief, General Sir Charles Guthrie, had first choice, since the United Kingdom had committed the largest force. Guthrie wanted the capital, Pristina. The Italians and the French were flexible, but the Germans, concerned about backlash from World War II (when the Serbs had been among their enemies) wanted a sector that had the fewest Serbs. This meant that they would take the southwest sector, including Prizren. The northern sector, at Mitrovica, was going to be the most sensitive, since it bordered directly on Serbia proper, and I thought the United States could take the critical position there, as we had done at Brcko, in Bosnia.

But the Americans refused the Mitrovica sector. The Pentagon wanted the quietest and what appeared to be the easiest sector, in the southeast, controlling the road to Macedonia. "That way," one of our senior officers revealed to me, "we can withdraw early, and leave it to the Europeans." This motivation wasn't lost on the Europeans. Ultimately, though, the Americans got their way, the French volunteered for the tough duty at Mitrovica, and the Italians took the northwest sector. With this planning for the most hopeful outcome done, it was now clear that no matter what happened at Rambouillet, there would be a long-term NATO troop presence in Kosovo.

About the same time, however, the refinement of the air plans was under way. This was the second "ring" of the circus. NATO's plans, approved in the late summer and activated in October, were on the shelf. Most of the aircraft that had flown to Italy in October had returned to their home nations. But Washington had begun asking the right questions. What if the negotiations don't work? What if the Serbs follow through on threats to take revenge against Albanian civilians? What if the Serbs strike our forces in Bosnia? What targets would we strike, and when? We took the previous target list, added more categories of targets, and parsed it into various packages to be used if the Serbs went after civilians in Kosovo, or after our forces in the region.

This was an all-American process, with collaboration between the targeting team on the Joint Staff, my EUCOM headquarters, Air Force General John Jumper and his team in Ramstein, Germany, and the men and women on Jim Ellis's and Mike Short's teams in Italy. We reviewed intelligence, looked at photographic imagery, picked what looked appropriate, and passed our views to Washington.

In mid February, I noticed one crack in our list of targets: not enough focus on the top level command and control. Where are Milosevic's key headquarters? Where are his key lieutenants operating? I wanted a rock 'em-sock 'em capability to go after high-value targets associated with Milosevic's means of power and control. But we didn't yet seem to have the targets we needed. And, as it was explained to me by the Joint Staff, the targets were being taken to the White House for examination and approval; there might be a little discomfort there about the high-level command and control targets.

To me, much of this targeting work fell into the category of repackaging. After the haste of the crisis in October, Washington was reassessing how it might actually want to conduct the air campaign, so far as I could tell. I was fully supportive of Washington's interest, but it wasn't going to impact the NATO plan unless we carried these new packages back through the Military Committee and the NATO approval process. And there was no appetite in Washington for that.

In fact, there was little appetite in the Pentagon for any serious preparations for Kosovo so far as I could determine. In December 1998 I had warned General Reimer, the Army Chief, that we might well be facing a war situation in Kosovo rather soon, and I recommended that he ask for the additional resources to prepare for it.

"But we don't want to fight there," he said.

"Of course we don't, Chief, but do we really want to fight in Iraq or North Korea, either?" He said he would take a look at whether he should ask for more resources.

In February I heard that in late January, the Joint Chiefs of Staff or their operations deputies had met privately to consider what could be done in Kosovo. Perhaps this was in response to my warning, but the reported results were disturbing. The Services were against any commitment there—never mind that we already had a commitment—because it wasn't in our "national interest." And any use of forces there would be bad for "readiness," which to them meant only readiness for the two Major Regional Contingencies.

I hadn't been asked to attend this meeting or even informed of its occurrence. I had been to Washington twice in January and talked with the top Pentagon people on both occasions. I spoke with Shelton almost every day, sharing my perspectives and trying to keep him apprised of the problems as I saw them. In retrospect, it seemed that a regional commander in chief would be asked to come in and present his war plans or at least his assessment of the theater. But in this case, the discussions were more preliminary: whether there should be any preparations. Different Services brought different perspectives to bear, of course. Later I heard rumors that some of the Chiefs had sought a formal process for ground invasion planning, perhaps with the intent of underscoring the high costs of taking action. This did not bode well, I realized, for Pentagon support as NATO moved forward, but I had faith in the people and procedures I knew well.

The evolving situation on the ground was worrisome, as the Serb military continued to move into Kosovo. The Pristina Corps had been reinforced with reserves, elite light infantry and helicopters, heavy artillery and first class armored units from northern Serbia. I estimated the force had been doubled in strength. I continued to warn Solana about the Serb buildup, and the dangers that the delay of the negotiations posed both to the Kosovars and to our air campaign. The greater the Serb strength and preparations on the ground, the less military impact we could expect from air strikes against the forces in Kosovo.

In early March, Solana directed me to call General Ojdanic, the Serb military leader, and ask him to stop bringing in his troops. I got the general on the phone and came right to the point. "General," I said, "why are you continuing to bring your Army forces into Kosovo in violation of the promises you made to me in December?"

"We are preparing to defend ourselves from you," he replied. "You are preparing to invade us."

"We are not going to invade you. Why do you think we are?" I pressed.

"We see your forces coming into Macedonia; your so-called extraction force is an invasion force." Ojdanic explained.

I tried to talk it through, including the fact that NATO had stated that it would not enter Kosovo without Serb permission, but he stuck to his position. After about a half hour, I broke off the call. From the Serb perspective the buildup of his forces made perfect sense. But it was also a great pretext for building up forces against the Albanians, too.

This was another dilemma of NATO's strategy as it had emerged. We were preparing for a peace support operation, to begin only if the Serbs invited us, and, simultaneously, we were threatening and preparing to bomb Serbia. It was perfectly logical, but it wasn't easy. It provided an opportunity for the Serbs and others to attack the strategy as confused and misguided. And the delay for the negotiations enabled intensive Serb preparations to deal with the air plan itself.

Klaus Naumann and I also worried about the nature of the military action. Klaus was a strong advocate for working the problem through to its conclusion. He knew that a ground option might well be needed to persuade the Serbs, but he had been unable to convince Solana to raise this issue to the Council. When I approached Solana on this issue, I had gotten a similar response. "Wes," he said, "you know the nations cannot deal with this issue at this time." Solana saw no chance of maintaining NATO cohesion if the divisive issue of ground intervention was introduced at this point. In fact, Secretary Cohen and influential German leaders had been speaking in conferences ruling out a ground threat. Lost was the basic recipe for NATO's success during the Cold War: preserve uncertainty in the mind of your opponent.

Javier Solana had an extraordinary touch for managing the delicate work of moving the Alliance forward. I recognized the wisdom of what he was saying. There was an important distinction between keeping the final requirements in view and pushing so hard that the initial options couldn't be executed. I couldn't be sure that an air campaign wouldn't work; it might. More important, it certainly didn't preclude a later decision to deploy a ground force. But if we pushed too hard for an immediate commitment to go in on the ground, we jeopardized our ability to take action at all.

This is always the agonizing point for the military. In Clausewitz's *On War*, there is a crucial passage in which Clausewitz writes that "No one in his right mind would, or ought to, begin a war if he didn't know how to finish it." This had been one of the favorite Vietnam critiques among the captains and majors at the Army Command and Staff College at Fort Leavenworth. But in practice, this proved to be an unreasonable standard. In dealing with complex military-diplomatic situations, the assertion of power itself changed the options. And trying to think through the problem to its conclusions in military terms always drove one to "worst-case" analysis. Had we done this in Bosnia, we could well have talked ourselves out of participating in any agreement. No doubt, I thought, someone could easily imagine the situation in Kosovo turning into a military quagmire like Vietnam—all one had to do was to assume the worst at every step along the way. While it was well to see the risks, some of the risks would have to be discounted by common sense. Others would have to be faced if they became more likely.

The third "ring" in the NATO and international circus was active in Bosnia. The long-deferred issue of the status of Brcko had come due. This had been the sticking point that had almost doomed the Dayton Agreement, until Milosevic agreed to submit the awarding of the disputed territory to arbitration. If the district were awarded to the Muslims, it would split the Republika Srpska. There were angry Serb threats about that possibility. If the district were given to the Serbs, then there would be no more leverage over them, and we would essentially be rewarding their recalcitrance. But I brought a new argument to bear: if we wanted to withdraw any more troops, then we had to resolve this issue. The time was now.

Bob Gelbard and Roberts Owen, the U.S. arbitrator, had discussed how the issue might be resolved. "Don't give it to either side," they considered, "and you can avoid the worst alternatives and set a basis for a new, more harmonious approach to the entire country." Of course. I pressed for its adoption as soon as possible. The Brcko problem needed to be resolved before we had to face the consequences of the negotiations at Rambouillet.

But the new president of Republika Srpska, the hard-line radical Nicola Polplasen, was continuing to defy the international authorities, creating a complication that played to the hard-line Serbs' advantage. So we actually faced two interrelated problems in Bosnia. And I knew that we would be faced with much worse in Bosnia if Milosevic had his way in Kosovo. Serb military success in Bosnia would immediately supercharge hard-line resistance to NATO and the international community in Bosnia.

I was fully engaged in all the "circus rings" under way in Europe. I also was busy with two other sets of activities that were to prove important to the outcome of the operation. One involved Congress. From the beginning of my tour of duty, I had made it a practice to try to see every visiting congressional delegation, usually by flying in to link up with them wherever they were, and to convey my personal view of the problems and progress in the theater. While I had complete confidence in my commanders at each location, none had the personal engagement with the leaders in Europe that I did. The Congress, I had found, depended heavily on personal relationships. You built those relationships with detailed information, candor, and attention, to the extent permitted by your superiors, so that in a crisis, the senators and congressmen had the information they needed and had confidence in its source. Like other senior military officers, I was often asked to visit many of the senators and congressmen in their Washington offices. Through these visits I learned their interests and concerns, and I was able to discuss NATO issues in great depth with many of them.

In late January, with Pentagon approval, I was asked to attend a private meeting with several senators, including Richard Lugar of Indiana and Chuck Hagel of Nebraska, to look in detail at the prospects in the Balkans. It was candid discussion as I reviewed recent events and restated my assessment that war was likely in six to eight weeks, starting with an air campaign. And if the air campaign doesn't succeed? I was asked. I said, "Of course, if the air campaign doesn't succeed, then we have to be prepared to follow up with ground troops." Once you engage, you're bound to follow through to success. This wasn't "policy." It was just common sense. How many? "Up to maybe 200,000 combat troops," I said. This estimate was well known by insiders, including several other senators. But these senators obviously hadn't been informed or consulted.

The senators clearly appreciated the information. However, that afternoon I received word that Secretary Cohen, who had approved my visit there, was upset about the discussion of possible ground action. I explained the difficulty of dodging those kinds of questions once they were asked. In answering, I was simply giving personal opinion, not approved policy, in response.

I had also learned from Holbrooke that a little information offered up front to the journalists, and a little personal attention before a story broke, meant that you at least would have a chance to be heard in a crisis. It wasn't a matter of giving out sensitive information and certainly not of leaking classified material. Instead, it was just personal courtesy, returning phone calls, and taking time to explain positions and interpretations.

I usually made myself available at least once a month for interviews in Europe. In the States I stayed in touch with the Pentagon and Defense press, as well as some of the diplomatic correspondents. I was determined that as we approached a crisis, at least the members of the press would understand the issues and facts insofar as I could share them.

Working these multiple areas, the time flew past, but the negotiations at Rambouillet were producing nothing close to an agreement between the Albanians and the Serbs. Klaus Naumann and I had been pressing to get NATO into the discussions, as well as the military arrangements, just as we did successfully at Dayton in 1995. But the diplomats wanted to avoid raising the issue of NATO, perhaps fearing to offend Russia or the Serbs. Toward the end of the first session in mid February, the American diplomats succeeded in pushing the idea of my visiting as SACEUR, just as General George Joulwan had done at Dayton in 1995. I would have preferred to visit both delegations, working again to bring the Serbs around. But I was going to be granted the opportunity to meet only the Albanian delegation at a French air base near Rambouillet. My intent was to assure the Albanians that NATO would be there to help, in order to break down their resistance to signing the agreement on the table.

Joe Ralston called from Washington. "The Secretary of Defense doesn't want you there," he said. "It would be a disaster to go without his permission."

I was surprised. It was hard to accept that he didn't see the advantage of a high-level NATO presence to reinforce the talks. Then Secretary Cohen called to give me personal guidance: I could go but do nothing more than explain the proposed military annex. Explanations only. No other discussions.

The Albanians were a fatigued and stone-faced group, listening impassively as I did my best to explain the agreement. Ambassador Jim Dobbins, a longtime veteran of crisis negotiations who was now the new Balkans coordinator at the Department of State, was on hand to answer questions or work the issues. But there was no discussion. I stood and moved to the door to shake hands with them on the way out. It was an emotional goodbye, as they gripped my arm and hung onto my hand. There was no deal. It was over, I felt. The Albanians didn't seem to understand their position and what the international community was offering—they couldn't, or they would be signing.

A few days later Strobe Talbott called me. "What do you think about the two sides?" he asked.

"Well, you'll have real trouble with the Albanians," I said. "They just don't get it. They are uninformed and incredibly stubborn." I recounted for him the meeting I had had with them.

"And the Serbs?" he asked.

"I can't believe that Milosevic won't sign, when the crunch comes. He always holds out. He has to be leaned on very hard. But he will come around," I said.

Talbott saw it the opposite way; he felt that we had an innate "in" with the Albanians. Conversely, he was increasingly concerned about the Serbs, with whom I hadn't been permitted to talk. Talbott, with the more direct information from the negotiations, was proved right.

A few days later, on Saturday, March 6, I was in London for a conference. Secretary of State Albright was there for a different set of meetings. She had been a firm proponent of using the threat of force to bring Milosevic to the bargaining table, and she asked me to brief her one-on-one about the situation.

I told her what was happening on the ground. "The continuing build-up and deployment of the Serb forces," I said, was occurring "in larger numbers than we anticipated. And, we've given them full warning of the possibility of air strikes, so we've probably lost the element of surprise."

If we commence the strikes, will the Serbs attack the population?

"Almost certainly they will attack the civilian population. This is what they are promising to do."

So what should we do? How can we prevent their striking the civilians?

"We can't. Despite our best efforts the civilians are going to be targeted by the Serbs. It will just be a race, our air strikes and the damage we cause them against what they can do on the ground. But in the short term, they can win the race."

So, what should we do? She was seeking my personal opinion.

"We will have to reinforce our capabilities. Ultimately, we can bring more to bear against them—we can overmatch anything they have—but it's not going to be pleasant." The Secretary did not seem surprised by my bleak assessment, even though it wasn't what she wanted to hear.

But you think we should go ahead?

"Yes, we have to." I had crossed the divide from forecasting to recommending. I was now responsible for the outcome, in a way I hadn't been before. I could feel the weight bear down on me as I continued. "We put NATO's credibility on the line. We have to follow through and make it work. There's no real alternative now."

"Yes, I think so, too," she said. These were policy matters. The leaders of governments would make these decisions.

I returned from London with the press of events in Kosovo heavy on my mind. The schedule was packed. Military Committee meetings were held on Tuesday and Wednesday, our annual SHAPE conference on Thursday and Friday, a visit to the French Institute of Higher Defense Studies on Saturday. And we were continuing to work the specific targets and methods of the air campaign. I was concerned when Admiral Jim Ellis and General John Jumper briefed me on their latest thoughts: they were focusing on the fixed Serb military infrastructure targets; they still hadn't worked in detail the techniques we would use to strike early against the Serb ground forces. "That's got to be done now," I said. They would get right on it, they said. And the planning has to stay within the already approved framework of the NATO Phased Air Operation, I reminded them.

The following week was just as busy. On Monday and Tuesday, we admitted Hungary, Poland, and the Czech Republic into NATO, and I hosted a dinner party Monday evening at the chateau for the Ministers of Defense and Chiefs of Defense of the three new members. At a small ceremony the next day, as the Chiefs of Defense and I stood together on the parade field, our thoughts were not on the future; instead, this was all about leaving behind the past, the past of the Cold War.

I returned to the States that week, where I testified before the Senate Armed Services Committee and met with Secretary Cohen and General Shelton. Once again I was in the Secretary's big office centered on the Pentagon river entrance, seated around the small circular table. I knew that Cohen and Shelton were both caught up in the problem of the air strikes, but I also sensed that they had no full appreciation of the overall NATO problem in the region, so I began to share some of my concerns.

"If we have to strike, Mr. Secretary," I began, "here are the other problems that will be facing us." I went through the disposition of allied forces in Macedonia—a real conglomerate, including our own 350 troops, intermingled with the U.N. contingent with no one really in charge; the considerations for the safety of the NATO personnel in Bosnia; the problems of the Yugoslav Navy in the Adriatic; the difficulties of moving additional NATO forces through Greece to reinforce our positions in Macedonia; and so on. Secretary Cohen listened closely, he seemed supportive, and when I left, I felt good about the meeting.

There was time for a quick visit to Macedonia, to see Mike Jackson at the headquarters he had established for the ARRC at a shoe factory in Skopje. Even more important was the opportunity to visit again with President Gligorov and his government. With each trip to Skopje I gained admiration for the tough man who was the Macedonian president. Gligorov was a courageous and canny survivor. We were counting on him, because it was obvious that the real weak point for NATO would be its dependence on Macedonia. Macedonia was our base. Without it, we would have no ground access into Kosovo. Without its airspace, we would have more restricted flight corridors into Serbia.

As we sat around Gligorov's conference table and discussed the issues, I wanted to convey firmness and confidence. He was attempting to show the same to me, and also keeping a wary eye on what might become of his country if things went awry for NATO. Fifty years from now, he was saying, Serbia will still be here, but will NATO? He was probing to determine our resolve. He would dole out Macedonian support based on what he saw as NATO's likelihood of success.

"I will not permit you, General Clark, to use the soil of Macedonia for attacks into Yugoslavia," he said. I could tell that his words were chosen deliberately and carefully. He was giving me permission to use the airspace any way I chose.

This removed one of my final concerns. I knew we would be able to come in over Albania and from the sea, but Macedonia gave that much wider access to the targets in Serbia that we wanted to be able to strike. It was enough for now.

Meanwhile, at Rambouillet, the negotiations had terminated and would not be resumed. The Albanians had signed, but the Serbs had refused. This set up the condition that called for the air strikes.

Now we had to face the reality on the ground in Kosovo. My first concern there was the safety of the more than one thousand unarmed "verifiers" operating under the aegis of the OSCE. If they attempted to leave, I wondered, would the Serbs permit their departure or take hostages? In that case, what were our capabilities to go in on the ground to rescue any of them?

There was no good answer for the problem of hostages. We had to hope that we weren't called—the forces available were simply inadequate for any task requiring a real "forced-entry" hostage rescue attempt. To help get things moving, I called the U.S. ambassador to the OSCE, who put me in touch with the OSCE Chairman in Office, Norwegian Foreign Minister Kurt Vollebaek. Minister Vollebaek then assured me that he was planning to withdraw the OSCE "verifiers" on Saturday, March 20. On that day, remarkably, the whole mission came out, with no hostages taken and no losses.

But as soon as the pullout began, the Serb military and police initiated their renewed ethnic cleansing of the Kosovar Albanians. By Saturday afternoon, March 20, the international TV networks were carrying video of Albanian refugees streaming barefooted from the village of Srbica.

Time had almost run out for diplomacy, and the final planning for the strikes was under way. The first problem was the readiness of the aircraft themselves. Most, but not all, of the aircraft had arrived at the predesignated bases. But the U.S. aircraft carrier that we had factored into our planning earlier had now been withdrawn, sent to a higher priority tasking in the Persian Gulf. We would make up the shortfall with land-based aircraft.

Then there was the matter of timing. We had been clear that we would need forty-eight hours from the decision to strike until strikes were to begin. This was required because some of the aircraft would have to fly across the Atlantic. We also wanted to strike only at night. This would give us several advantages. First, the Yugoslavs had limited capabilities to intercept our aircraft at night. Some of their antiaircraft weapons had no night firing capability. Second, the missiles that they might fire at us would be more visible, and hence more easily avoided if we flew at night. Observers on the ground might not be able to spot the aircraft and provide reports supplementing the air defense radars. Third, should we lose any aircraft, we stood a much better chance of recovering the aircrews safely at night than during daylight hours.

On the political level, the timing problem was different. Alliance leaders wanted to strike as soon as possible after giving the order, since the time for delay might undercut the authority of the strike and diminish its psychological impact. There was another political consideration—to ensure that the threat of the imminent strike would have the greatest possible coercive impact on Milosevic, perhaps achieving our objective without striking at all. The coercive impact of the strike, it was thought, would be greatest in the hours just before the first blow fell, or perhaps just after the first blow and before Milosevic had sustained so much damage that for reasons of national pride and his political authority he would have to continue the fight.

To the military, such an effort to wrest the maximum coercive value from the prospect of imminent strikes meant that there would be little hope of any operational surprise. The blow would be fully expected. This in turn both raised the risk to our aircraft and reduced the likelihood of significantly damaging the early sets of targets. This was precisely the kind of political-military tradeoff that chafed the air planners. But unless the risk to the aircrews was simply unacceptable, and we couldn't conclude that it was, there was no countering the over-arching political purpose of the strikes. We would telegraph our punch. We would simply have to accept its reduced military impact and make up for it later, if necessary.

There was another tricky feature of the air strikes: the targets. We knew that at all costs we needed to protect the secrecy of the specific targets we would be striking. This was critical to the safety of our air-crews, we believed, as well as to the effectiveness of the attacks them-selves. We had to keep the enemy guessing. Yet, we knew that there would be great curiosity at the political levels about the targets to be struck, and that they would insist in some way on asserting their polit-ical control by demanding to approve the targets or at least to review them. This wasn't unreasonable, because the targets would have to stand the legal test of the Geneva Convention and international law. In addition, striking targets would represent high national political and strategic statements for which public leaders would have to assume responsibility. It would have been naïve to believe that the top political authorities would simply turn every decision over to the military.

But for the military, the art was to gain political approval of the tar-gets as painlessly as possible. We wanted to be as certain as possible that military advice on target selection would be accepted and that political approvals would come quickly and well in advance of the strikes themselves. We wanted the greatest authority to pick the targets ourselves. Furthermore, we would want to restrict the circle of those political authorities in the know to the smallest numbers possible, since the larger the number of people looking at the targets, the greater the risk that the targets could be compromised to the Yugoslav military.

Over the previous months I had arrived at what I thought would be the right compromise. The operations plan would contain target sets—that is, the types of targets that we would attack—without disclosing the particular locations or numbers of targets in the set. Javier Solana seemed comfortable with this approach, and the ambassadors had also generally accepted it without discussion during the planning stages the previous summer.

I was deeply concerned about leaks, and with good reason. Back in October, one of the French officers working at NATO headquarters had given the key portions of the operations plan to the Serbs. The French Chief of Defense, General Jean-Pierre Kelche, and I had discussed the compromise then. It was not so specific as to disclose individual targets, and after analysis we decided not to throw out the plan. The officer was removed and corrective measures taken. Still, I knew that the Serbs had the concept of the phases of the air campaign as well as the types of targets in each phase. It was because of the possibility of future leaks that my staff and I had always insisted in retaining the tightest possible control of the specific targets.

At any event, the Serbs probably would have some difficulty in understanding the details of what we were about to do, because it wasn't as simple as a single operations plan. In the first place, we were going to execute two operations plans simultaneously, the first of which was the Phased Air Operation and the second of which was the Limited Air Operation. Both plans had been through the NATO approval process. While the Phased Air Operation called for a first phase limited to the enemy's air defense system and any deployed forces in Kosovo, it also provided authority to strike the air defense system throughout Yugoslavia. There were no off-limits areas. The Limited Air Operation, on the other hand, gave us the authority to strike headquarters, forces, and facilities in and around Kosovo that were connected to the forces that had perpetrated the ethnic cleansing or some other incident.

When I had briefed the North Atlantic Council on these plans during the late summer of 1998, I had been vague about the numbers of targets that might be struck. I estimated there might be a hundred or more targets associated with the first phase of the Phased Air Operation in order to seriously damage Milosevic's integrated air defense system. And the Limited Air Operation, just to effect a single strike of significance against his forces in and around Kosovo, might entail twenty or more targets. Thus I was reasonably assured that we had sufficient opportunity to plan a fairly robust and complex set of strikes from the outset.

The situation was different now. The Serb forces had been built up to more than 30,000, and they were no longer in their cantonment areas. Instead they were deploying to field bivouac and dispersal sites. And they were already engaged in the very attacks against the population that we had feared. The question was, could we do more with our targeting to achieve an impact or deterrence against these forces? Alternatively, what would we do if the forces really did attack primarily against the civil population?

But even as we examined and evaluated various target sets, I faced a bigger strategic challenge from within NATO. This was the idea of a bombing pause.

The logic behind a bombing pause was that it would serve as an inducement on the other side to begin the negotiations to forestall the resumption of wholesale bombardment. In the military we had always been skeptical of the notion, a skepticism reinforced by its ineffectiveness against North Vietnam in the 1960s.

From the military perspective, bombing pauses give the enemy the chance to recover from the effects of the strikes. Infrastructure like bridges and roads can be rebuilt, ammunition dumps concealed, and, perhaps most importantly, the air defense system can be rested and repaired. There were usually problems getting the air strikes restarted, because governments would traditionally stipulate a purpose behind the pause, such as permitting negotiations to begin, which, if not met, would seem to argue equally well for further postponement. Indeed, there would always be those who would seize on a bombing pause as an implicit admission that the policy of bombing was failing. Hence pauses seemed to undercut resolve.

Still, the NATO limited strikes that worked so well in Bosnia in August 1995 had incorporated a bombing pause, and as a result, bombing pauses were now a fixture of political thinking in NATO.

It was clear from Secretary General Solana, the tenor of the Council meetings, and the informal discussions on the margins that several NATO nations would expect a bombing pause almost immediately to encourage the Serbs to come back to the table at Rambouillet. In fact, they wanted the initial strikes expressly limited so that we didn't force the Serbs into a full military campaign in response. There was a spirit of hope at the political levels that Milosevic might recognize that NATO was actually going to follow through with its threat and then quickly concede in order to cut his losses.

As a military commander what I had to do was insist on my own "red lines." I had made clear throughout the planning process that I would not commit the airmen unless we had the full authority to go after the Serbs' integrated air defense system in a robust way, regardless of where the targets were located. We weren't going to be restricted to just "pecking" at it, nor were we going to permit Milosevic to protect his air defense by establishing a sanctuary in some part of Serbia.

On this basis I had determined that we should go after a significant number of targets on the first night, and, based on what we had already planned, we created a fifty-one-target strike plan directed at Serb air defenses, airfields, and communications. This would constitute a serious attack, with some margin left over, and one which I felt would move us smoothly into the next stages of the operation if necessary.

I convinced the Defense Chiefs, including General Jean-Pierre Kelche of France, that without at least this number of targets planned there would be a possibility that bad weather or other factors could undercut the initial strikes so much that they would be perceived as just pinpricks. We also agreed that we would need a minimum of two nights, perhaps more, before considering a pause. I knew that if I carried France, the other nations would go along. If we could get through the first night's strike and move smoothly into the second night, then we could continue to shape the campaign according to military logic until its objectives were met. Though I knew that the issue of a bombing pause wasn't going to go away, I could now turn my attention to getting the targets right and to seeing how quickly we could have an impact on the forces on the ground.

But in a conversation over the weekend, General Hugh Shelton placed another requirement on us. "Wes, how soon are you going to get me your Phase II targets?" he asked, referring to the hundred or more targets that we would want to strike in southern Serbia. "I need to get them across the river for approval."

Following the pattern established in the Desert Fox strikes against Saddam Hussein in December 1998, the White House intended to approve all targets. This was not good news—it meant a problem for us in moving from target to target, and it also meant that we would be placing stress on NATO, eighteen of whose members would be denied access to the targets in advance while one country, the United States, would have all the information. The process would put me in a difficult position.

We worked late that Saturday night reviewing all the targets for submission to Washington. But the problem didn't end there. The Joint Staff itself was determining a format for the targets that would address the political concerns at the White House.

"Wes, you'll have to get the estimates for the collateral damages and unintended civilian casualties," Shelton told me. There was always the risk of weapons malfunctions or pilot error, though we would do our best to minimize these. But in addition there were blast and fragmentation effects from bombs which could reach some distance beyond a target. We had mathematical tables to calculate these danger zones but of course there would be no way of knowing how many people might be in the buildings or in the vicinity, and without this knowledge estimates were unreliable.

This was the kind of political calculus that always made me nervous. "Well, how would we know that?" I asked. "You know how unreliable that kind of estimate is."

"Well, you have to use the formula for that."

"And where is the formula?" I asked.

"I don't know what it is exactly, or where it came from, but I think it came from your headquarters," he said.

Sure enough, my own intelligence analysts, working quietly with the Joint Staff target team in the Pentagon, had created a formula for estimating the numbers of people in buildings. But they had given the formula to the Joint Staff without telling the rest of my staff. This was a real foretaste of the kinds of issues raised by open-architecture, Internet-based communications. We scrambled to reassess all of our targets in accordance with the new formula.

We still weren't certain that we were headed for war. I knew that this was the period of maximum leverage for an agreement, and that Washington would be planning one last, full-court press to bring Milosevic around.

Not surprisingly, on March 22, Dick Holbrooke and his team came through Brussels to brief us on how Washington saw the issue, to give us their general approach, and to seek any additional details from us on our plans that could be used to persuade Milosevic about the gravity of his predicament. Then Holbrooke was off to Belgrade.

By the end of the day, Brigadier General George Casey, our Joint

Staff point of contact for the Holbrooke mission, called in to report that Milosevic wasn't budging and that he was predicting the elimination of the KLA within five days.

The report didn't sound too promising, but I had been on enough missions with Holbrooke to know that if there was any way to secure an agreement that was within the bounds of his instructions, he would find it.

I left the office to go home and, along with others in Washington, make contact with various members of Congress who were seeking information about the prospective military action. Senator Max Cleland of Georgia was concerned but ultimately supportive. Congressman Steve Buyer of Indiana told me that he really disagreed with our involvement in the Balkans because of the impact on our Armed Forces, but he said, "I'll never vote against a U.S. commander in the field." It was a pledge of support that I was to reflect on often during the coming weeks.

By the morning of March 23, the stress level at SHAPE had risen appreciably. This was to be the first run on our "battle rhythm," with briefings and videoconference meetings at set times throughout the day. And it was to be the last day of hope for the Holbrooke mission in Belgrade.

The NATO video teleconference kicked off at 9:00 A.M., on schedule. Serb ethnic cleansing activities were in evidence, as reported by a few of the international civilians who remained behind after the withdrawal of the OSCE mission. The forces on the ground in Macedonia were still in varying states of preparation for possible hostilities. And we recognized we were going to have a potential problem with the Yugoslav Navy. If Milosevic were to use his naval force to mine the Adriatic, launch missiles, or otherwise go after NATO or neutral vessels, there were no special NATO authorizations or instructions for addressing this problem.

After the NATO meeting ended, I had a long conversation with Hugh Shelton on targeting and on the Holbrooke mission, and then I briefed the American commanders at the U.S. VTC at 11:00. We knew that the targets were on their way to President Clinton for approval, so this was just a chance to exchange views once again with the U.S. command team.

In midafternoon, Lieutenant General Ed Anderson, the J-5, who was in Belgrade with Holbrooke, called with a further update. Milosevic was still dodging compliance with the earlier commitments to NATO and refusing to agree to the Rambouillet proposals. He claimed to be having trouble with his military responding to orders, asserting that he had sent out directives for them to comply, but also justifying their actions as just "proportional response" to the Albanian terrorists. In Anderson's view, the discussions were going nowhere; it was "a wild goose chase." Anderson explained that the critical time would be the vote of the Serb national assembly late in the afternoon and that Holbrooke would probably remain until then. I then went over the latest intelligence reports with Anderson, explaining that we saw indications of Serb forces repositioning.

By 5:00, Anderson was back on the phone. "There's been no breakthrough here," he reported. "We'll be leaving and heading to Brussels sometime shortly after 1800." That really did sound like the end. Milosevic was going to continue to play rough.

After a few more calls, I drove to NATO headquarters in Brussels to be there for Holbrooke's report to Secretary General Solana. It was somber and without hope. Anderson and I then returned to Mons. During the few minutes we had that evening, he filled me in on the atmospherics in Belgrade, and in Washington. He was especially strong on the idea of striking the ground forces.

"You know, Wes, the Chairman really wants to get at the ground forces."

"So do I, so do I."

"Well, I talked to him about the Apache helicopters and he was very high on the idea. He is very serious about wanting to get these into the fight, if you think they'll be useful."

Shelton had already asked me to evaluate whether I could use the Apaches, and I had replied that I could. With assistance from a Corps-level deep-battle targeting team, the Apaches could strike fifty miles into Kosovo against pinpointed enemy forces, whether they were in large groups or hiding individually among houses and trees. Flying in at night, using the folds in the earth for cover, they could hover long enough to verify their targets and then engage from more than four miles. They would be protected by attack aircraft flying high above and would also have long-range artillery and rockets in support. This was the very mission we had practiced with the Apaches in exercise after exercise for over a decade in the U.S. Army.

"Well, you know I've asked for them already, and haven't heard anything, but I'll continue to push. I appreciate your support in this." His personal support was particularly encouraging news, as Anderson was an artilleryman who was very familiar with the Army's ability to strike deeply and had considerable influence in the Pentagon. I continued to worry about the Serb reaction against the populace in Kosovo when the campaign began and was seeking whatever means might be available to strengthen our striking capabilities.

I had already turned in that night when Secretary General Solana called me from Brussels to tell me the decision: "Wes, you have the execute order for Phase I of the air campaign. I am giving you the execute order. You will have it in writing tomorrow morning, but this is the order, do you understand?"

I understood, but we both knew that the order could be revoked and the attacks called off as late as three hours prior to the scheduled time on target on Wednesday evening, March 24. After assuring Solana that we were ready, I called Admiral Jim Ellis in Naples and passed the execution order to him. I also called Admiral Steve Abbott, my deputy in Stuttgart, EUCOM headquarters. The staff assistant with me notified my executive officer, Pete Chiarelli.

When I arrived in the office on Wednesday morning, the execute order was there, dated March 23. At the NATO video teleconference at 9:00, I made the formal announcement to the commanders and staffs. "We are now in the execution mode," I said. "It's the first time NATO's ever done something of this magnitude. And we have ground forces at risk in two neighboring countries, and we have an indefinite duration for this operation." I had to be sure that my key leaders saw the full range of issues from my perspective.

"I received the execution directive from the Secretary General last night before midnight, so unless there's a sudden change of heart by President Milosevic prior to late this afternoon, this operation is going to proceed," I continued. "It's our estimation that there will not be a sudden change of heart by President Milosevic. He has dug himself into the hole, he's backed in, and his claws are hanging out right now.

So, we're going to proceed with this operation as planned and we're going to sharpen it and refine it with each successive day." In other words, don't plan on a short campaign.

But we had to move the campaign along some general paths, in addition to minding the legal constraints in the order. I termed these "measures of merit." Though the term cannot be found in any of the dictionaries of military doctrine, it seemed to fit here. I dropped them onto the command.

"As we start working through this, there are three measures of merit for the operation overall from the military standpoint. The first measure of merit is not to lose aircraft, minimize the loss of aircraft." This addressed Mike Short's biggest concern—to prevent the loss of aircrews. It drove our decisions on tactics, targets, and which airplanes could participate. But I was motivated by a larger political-military rationale: If we wanted to keep this campaign going indefinitely, we had to protect our air fleet. Nothing would hurt us more with public opinion than headlines that screamed, "NATO LOSES TEN AIRPLANES IN TWO DAYS." Take losses like that, divide it into the total number of aircraft committed, and the time limits on the campaign would be clear. Milosevic could wait us out.

"The second measure of merit is to impact the Yugoslavian military and police activities on the ground as rapidly and effectively as possible." We had to attack and disrupt—destroy if possible—the actual elements doing the ethnic cleansing. We knew we could strike the fixed targets; we had the initial sets of targets planned and approved, we would use improvements to the processes we had developed in the Gulf War in 1991. This was right down the center of Air Force conventional thinking, and we were very good at this. But the moral and legal imperative was to go after the Serb ground forces that were committing or aiding the ethnic cleansing and directly causing the humanitarian issues. Going after these ground forces was going to be very tough, without our own troops committed to the fight. It was not a conventional role for the air forces, and we would have to learn how to do it.

"The third measure of merit is to protect our ground forces—and in the case of SFOR, the elements of the international community—from retaliation or other attacks by the Federal Republic of Yugoslavia or their associated elements." Both General Montgomery Meigs, who had taken over command in Bosnia from Ric Shinseki, and Mike Jackson in Macedonia had force-protection worries. Altogether we had more than 30,000 troops on the ground in these two commands, and they were all within reach of the Serbs if the Serbs wanted to take the risk to go after them. We couldn't give Milosevic an easy opportunity.

"At the political level the measure of merit is to retain Alliance solidarity and the full support of our regional partners." Handling the various national concerns at NATO and in Macedonia was going to be difficult. But without political backing the campaign was over. Each of us who had been through Vietnam had learned this lesson very well.

We continued through the rest of the agenda in the VTC, including the diplomatic state of play in NATO, the intelligence update, and the concerns of the commanders. There was worry about Serb long-range rockets, problems in controlling the locations and dispositions of allied forces in Macedonia (which had not yet been formally transferred to NATO command), a discussion of Serb options against the NATO forces in Bosnia, and the possible reaction in Bosnia of the Russian brigade that was part of SFOR. There was concern about a possible maritime threat from the Serbs in the Adriatic, and anxiety that due to legal constraints in Washington imposed by Congress, the U.S. Marines Expeditionary Unit was going to be delayed. I wrapped up the meeting by emphasizing the importance of strategic coordination, working the details, and keeping a grip on all the pieces.

We had, in a few moments, previewed the campaign, the themes and issues we would work again and again in the coming weeks. The air campaign was to be relentless and intensifying, the constant drumbeat of NATO. But if the air strikes were the underlying rhythm, then the melody would have several variations, and it was going to be pure hard rock.

I returned to the office to place a call to General Ojdanic in Belgrade. I wanted to use a little leverage on him before the air campaign began.

"General, let me give you a very clear warning," I said after the preliminary greeting. "Any attack on NATO forces in neighboring countries will be met with very strong consequences. And leave your naval vessels in port or they will be attacked and destroyed."

"I understand your warnings," he replied, in a serious and respectful tone. "We know who are our enemies that cause problems. Forces in neighboring countries must act properly. But I don't understand why our maritime forces must stay in port."

I was firm in my response: "Your maritime forces are armed, and therefore they will be assumed to pose a threat if they move from their port." I followed up with more general admonitions to cease the military action in Kosovo and to accept the demands of the international community. Ojdanic said little, but it seemed that the warnings had at least given him pause.

It was time to go to Brussels to meet the North Atlantic Council. I knew that this would be a tense and difficult time for the Council, and that there would be many second thoughts and much guidance given. Of course, the ambassadors were speaking for their governments, not just personally, but I also believed that many of them were actually driving their governments' policies in NATO. This would be important.

When I arrived at NATO headquarters, I headed for the Secretary General's office to learn what he wanted from the meeting. Solana was in good form, relaxed, poised, thoughtful yet determined. We went over the target categories and timing to be briefed to the Council, then headed down to the meeting room. The ambassadors from Czech Republic, Hungary, and Poland were now seated alphabetically at the large circular table, befitting their new membership in the alliance. Each of the nineteen nations was also represented by its three-star military representative and by numerous assistants. A packed house, adrenaline flowing.

Klaus Naumann and I began our briefings. He covered the overall situation in Kosovo, while I outlined the situation with respect to the Serb air defenses, the status of NATO forces in Macedonia, and general plans for the air campaign. I stressed in particular that there could be no sanctuary for the Serbs when it came to attacking their air defenses. I tried to portray a measured and tough campaign, but I didn't want the targeting agreement to come unglued.

The questions and concerns came back immediately. How many casualties might we inflict on the Serbs? What if Milosevic wanted to comply, how could he contact us? Though I had support as we went around the table, it was clear that some nations were still hoping that merely a demonstrative strike would be sufficient to persuade Milosevic to change his mind. While the ambassadors were careful not to get too far down into the military details, the clear impression they conveyed was that this was not to be a war on Yugoslavia. Meanwhile I had to get them to think ahead, to what we would be doing on the third and fourth days, and to what the risks might be for our troops on the ground in Macedonia.

I returned to my headquarters as soon as possible after the meeting, to find that I had received calls from Joe Ralston and from Hugh Shelton's executive officer, each with separate questions. Shelton's question was urgent: What was the name of the operation?

We huddled around the desk—General Dieter Stockmann; Major General John Dallagher, the operations chief; Brigadier General Pete Chiarelli, my executive officer; and I—and we spoke to Admiral Jim Ellis at his Naples headquarters. The name? "Eagle"? "Allied Eagle"? "Joint Eagle"? "Determined Eagle"? "Determined Force"? "Eagle" seemed too cute, and "Determined" had already been used. "Allied Force" seemed the simplest and most descriptive. I had Pete Chiarelli pass it back to Washington.

Then I returned the call from Joe Ralston on the red-switch phone that was my direct line to the Pentagon. It was a little after 7:00 A.M. Washington time. "Wes," he said, "Sandy Berger is already asking, 'How soon are we going to attack tanks?' I'm saying to him, when we take the Integrated Air Defense down and the weather clears, then we'll go after the tanks. Is that right?"

"That's exactly right," I said. But I also understood the message from the political levels: Get after the forces that were attacking the civilians. It was the same understanding I had already reached with Solana and the Council in Brussels. We would go after those forces as soon as possible and as directly as possible.

There was another quick teleconference with EUCOM for possible last-minute changes, and then more phone calls back and forth with the Pentagon on how and when to do the Battle Damage Assessments and public releases. The Pentagon was supportive on controlling the release of information and on running the release on a European rather than a U.S. time zone basis. We agreed to release minimal information initially until we could assess our operational security needs. It was agreed that NATO would be responsible for the key press conferences and information releases that would define public support for the war.

Simultaneously we were wrestling with the issue of who would be the press spokesman. Brussels was insisting that it be a European general officer, but we had no generals on our public affairs staff. So we selected a British one-star, Air Commodore David Wilby, who was actually assigned to do nuclear planning, and we had to pull him off his planned ski vacation in the Alps and read him into the operation. By the time I confirmed the selection, General Stockmann already had him moving back to our headquarters at SHAPE so that he could be with me as we began our operations.

Joe Ralston called back to inquire about tanker support for the air assets protecting Hungary, which was the only NATO member that bordered Yugoslavia. Was it adequate? He was trying to help, taking issues he was picking up from the Joint Staff or Air Staff back in Washington, or perhaps concerns from the political level in Washington, double-checking the operational planning and backstopping our detailed military work. His call reinforced my appreciation of the incredible juxtaposition of strategic concerns and tactical details converging at my headquarters, but it was also a reminder of Washington's thirst for details.

Sitting in the office that day, between the phone calls and the teleconferences, Rupert Smith, Dieter Stockmann, and I discussed the strategy we would have to follow. The air strikes, of course, were the top priority. We had to move quickly to escalate, making the strikes stronger and more effective. The key to gaining more freedom of action was to destroy the Serbs' integrated air defense network. We would have to create innovative new processes to increase our capabilities against the Serb ground forces. The Apaches were to be part of this and perhaps other measures, too.

Another continuing line of effort would be protecting our forces and maintaining enforcement of the Dayton Agreement in Bosnia. Casualties would undercut our credibility and reduce political support for the campaign. We had to take actions to safeguard the NATO forces in Bosnia and in Macedonia, as well as our naval vessels in the Adriatic.

A third strategic effort had to be maintaining the support of the key front-line states, Macedonia and Albania. If we lost Macedonia, especially, there would be no chance to escalate to further operations, including the Apaches, and having to evacuate the thousands of NATO troops there would be traumatic. If these countries were so important to us, then they would certainly be targeted by the Serbs.

Next there was the matter of maintaining Allied cohesion. We knew that we had to conduct the military operations in a way that held the Alliance together, despite the differing national perspectives that would be brought to bear. This would mean reaching out to the Chiefs of Defense, and to the ambassadors, as well as to public opinion on both sides of the Atlantic.

That led to the problem of providing information to the public. The media and press were going to be vitally important. While the North Atlantic Council in Brussels was going to be in charge, all of the information, we assumed, would come through us. How were we going to generate sufficient information, and clear it through various national systems to control classified and sensitive information, and then be able to release it in time? We knew that this was potentially a problem, but we hoped to buy a few days by minimizing the initial public releases while we refined the system. And we had to think about how the air operation could be escalated, and what would happen if air power alone were not enough to compel the Serbs to stop their actions in Kosovo.

The next day, continuing the discussions, we added two more key elements to what would become the strategic road map for the campaign. We needed to isolate the theater of operations, so the Serbs couldn't be sustained and rearmed. This principle was a basic requirement at the higher levels of strategy, but, because it entailed a broad array of diplomatic and legal measures, as well as military efforts, it was never really considered in any of the existing NATO operations plans. I could only reflect back on my study of the Vietnam experience, and the tragic consequences for our air and ground forces of allowing unimpeded Soviet and Chinese reinforcements of North Vietnam for most of the war there. We would not be successful here if we allowed a large military assistance pipeline to be created to funnel high technology weaponry, advisers, and other sustaining strength into Serbia at the very time we were trying to compel Milosevic to cease his actions in Kosovo. Countries like Macedonia, Bulgaria, and Romania were going to be hugely important in this effort. While a lot of the work would be done above our level, we had to recommend it to our political leaders, and we had to do our part, too.

We also recognized that we would be drawn into the mission of providing humanitarian assistance to the Kosovars themselves. Our involvement would be morally and legally necessitated by the need to be humane, in response to the emerging outlines of the Serb strategy. And we were likely to be ordered to do this, in any case, by NATO political authorities in Brussels. At a minimum it would distract the chain of command from its primary focus on the air campaign. It might also greatly increase the risks to our forces.

Together these were the lines of effort that guided us, day by day, and with very little modification, through the entire campaign.

But for the time being we had to think about the immediate problem at hand. We were approaching the final moments when the strikes could be called off. In fact, Washington did call at 5:31 P.M. It was Hugh Shelton, passing on the final execution order from the U.S. National Command authorities.

"Wes," he said, "it's a go."

PART III

THE AIR CAMPAIGN

EIGHT

BATTLE RHYTHM

COULD PICTURE IT so clearly in my mind's eye. The B-52s up there all alone, the missiles dropping out of the bomb bay, the tiny wings unfolding, then the small jet engines igniting, and the missiles diving down as they winged their ways to the targets.

The Tomahawks, the Navy's Tactical Land Attack Missiles, came just a few moments later. I could picture these, too. The greenish-blue of the Adriatic just a few minutes before nightfall. The bursts of flame as the booster charges eject the missiles from the launch tube of the frigates and cruisers. The spouts of seawater as the submarine-based missiles catapult out of the ocean, fins unfolding and boosters igniting.

It was a synchronized attack. We were going to blind the Yugoslav military by taking out their radars and cripple them by destroying their anti-air missile systems. Then we were going to sweep in with the manned aircraft. We would lead with the least vulnerable birds, the stealth aircraft that couldn't be easily detected by radar, and we'd have some regular fighters and fighter-bombers along, too. I could imagine what the airmen felt like on this night, helmets tight, masks on, a head full of code words, target descriptions, and mental reminders.

But I couldn't be there in those cockpits. I could only imagine.

We had to respect Serb military capabilities. I knew there was a possibility that Milosevic might have been receiving information from Russian military sources, or even from other nations. The Yugoslav military had also purchased some relatively high-quality Westinghouse and Marconi radars to supplement the old Soviet-bloc network that Tito and his generals had built. Many of their sector control posts were located underground, tunneled into the sides of mountains, and there was even a system of underground cables. We also wondered if they could monitor our air activities by somehow using the European commercial air traffic control system.

We wanted to take out targets in a particular order, starting with the radars closest to the coast, which posed the greatest threat to our aircraft, and then going after the air defense missile launchers and radar control posts. We were under no illusions about the difficulty of taking down the Serb's early-warning and control systems. But we believed that by striking them first and heavily we could confuse and degrade them enough to operate successfully within his airspace with manned aircraft.

Shortly after 7:00 P.M. my staff and I at the chateau were in place, tuned to the television, and monitoring the computer. I got the call from Admiral Jim Ellis, the commander in chief of Allied Forces Southern Europe, at his headquarters in Naples: "Missiles are launched!"

I quickly placed a round of phone calls to my superiors. First, to Javier Solana in Brussels, who would inform the NATO ambassadors and governments that the operation was under way. Next was a call to Hugh Shelton in Washington, keeping him well informed to ensure that we had full U.S. backing in the hours ahead. Finally, I called Klaus Naumann at NATO headquarters, who kept the NATO ambassadors and the Military Committee generals up to date. They and the nations they represented usually had their own ideas, and I knew I would need Naumann's support to sustain teamwork and cohesion in the days ahead.

I had just over an hour until the missiles would begin to impact.

At our nighttime operations center, there was no way to see the actual radar screens or monitor the pilots' radio traffic, but that wasn't necessary at my level of command. Those activities properly belonged to the air commander, Mike Short, and his team in Vicenza, Italy. They needed the real-time communications and the ability to interface directly with the airborne air control aircraft in order to exercise their command functions. Of course, I had the special secure phones for direct communications to U.S. commanders anywhere.

My real window on the operation was going to be provided by the senior U.S. airman in Europe, John Jumper. Although he wasn't in the NATO chain of command for this operation, as the senior American airman he was my adviser and had all the technology and communications to keep a real-time read on the operations. As Mike Short's commander in the American chain of command, he also had a certain amount of influence in an advisory capacity. And, of course, he could control the American support provided to the NATO effort.

We settled in to wait. I had expected it to be a long night, but the news broke fairly quickly. Tom Brokaw appeared in a special report that we received by satellite, reporting that the "American-led air strikes" had begun. For us, Brokaw's choice of words indicated that we had gotten off on the wrong foot with the public. Allied participation had been a sensitive issue throughout the planning phase of the operation, with the Pentagon pressing to ensure that as many Allied aircraft as possible were involved in the operation in order to deflect the inevitable criticisms that would come from Capitol Hill about burden sharing. I directed our public affairs staff officer to call NBC about correcting the report—these were NATO air strikes, not American-led air strikes. We cited the number of Allied aircraft involved, about 40 percent of the total. NBC promptly changed the way it was characterizing the strikes.

By 10:00 P.M. the first aircraft had flown through Yugoslav airspace. On the secure E-mail came a report that one of our aircraft might have downed an enemy fighter—though this was unconfirmed. I didn't want to distract Jim Ellis or Mike Short, who were in the middle of monitoring the operation, so I picked up the red switch and pushed the button to reach General John Jumper at his headquarters in Germany.

Jumper reported that he was monitoring the communications, and that we had shot down one, and perhaps two, enemy aircraft. A few minutes later he called back to confirm that at least one of the aircraft was a MIG-29, a top Yugoslav fighter, and that one of the shoot-downs had been accomplished by a Dutch F-16.

I called Javier Solana to report the news—the Serbs had risen to challenge us and we had defeated the challenge. I expected Solana to share my pride in the reaction of the aircrews to the Serb threat, but Solana surprised me. "This is not good. This is not good," he said.

As we discussed the incident it became clear that the Secretary General reasoned that if Milosevic and the Serbs were going to fight back, then the fight might go on for some time, and that the losses of aircraft might draw the Serbs deeper into the conflict. True enough, on both counts, but after talking with General Ojdanic earlier in the day and hearing the reports on Ambassador Holbrooke's final meeting with Milosevic, I hadn't expected anything else. I was just happy that we had taken down their aircraft, and not vice versa. The harder the Serbs fought, I thought, the sooner it will be over. Solana acknowledged my views but saw too clearly what lay ahead.

I also called the Dutch Chief of Defense, Admiral Luuk Kroon, to congratulate him on the performance of his aircraft. He had already heard the news, a good indication of how strong the national reporting channels would be during this campaign, and he was a little concerned about too much publicity for Dutch efforts. "Please don't announce that it was one of our aircraft that was involved," he said. He would want time to make all the appropriate notifications within the Netherlands before this came out publicly. It was an indication of the sensitivity of the operation in many nations.

Soon after midnight, we were done. It had been a good night's work. Three MIG-29's downed, including one by a Dutch F-16, which underscored the Allies' involvement. All our command and control systems were working well and we struck over 80 percent of the planned targets. We had gone from one end of Yugoslavia to the other, hitting airfields, an aircraft repair facility, electronic intelligence sites, and army headquarters.

We had suffered no aircraft losses, while definitely releasing enough weapons to make an impact. The Serb air defense missiles had not really engaged us, perhaps because they were too busy trying to fly their own aircraft, we thought. We had proved that we could execute these strikes and do it well.

Morning came quickly after the first night of strikes. I made as many calls as I could to NATO colleagues, including General Jean-Pierre Kelche, the French military chief, and General Harmut Bagger, the German Chief of Defense, as well as to Solana and Nau-mann. At the 9:00 A.M. NATO video teleconference, there were a number of serious issues to be dealt with. Jim Ellis was concerned that the Serbs were moving their air defenses and not activating the systems in ways that would facilitate our attack and destruction of the network. We debated whether they were so smart that they were doing this deliberately, or whether it was a problem for them to coordinate their air defense ground systems with the MIGs that had been trying to attack us during the night. It was too early to be able to know for certain, but the Combined Air Operations Center assured us that the attacks on the system would continue.

Next was Mike Jackson, reporting from Macedonia. He explained that he had redeployed his forces during the evening to establish a screen line out front of his main facilities to give him early warning of any trouble. He was concerned that he still had not received operational control of all the forces on the ground in the area. The U.N. Preventive Force, some 700 soldiers from the Scandinavian countries, was under its own U.N. commander, and the units were generally intermixed among the NATO units. Jackson reported that they were "cooperating and coordinating." It could have been worse, of course, had they been uncooperative, but this was still a major issue, because it meant that passing of orders and coordination of actions were essentially done on a cooperative basis, with various national contingents checking back with their capitals before complying. If Yugoslav forces attacked across the border, our response was likely to be fragmented, and that would mean increased risk for our troops. Jackson also reported that the airport in Skopje was closed that morning because the air traffic controllers had not reported for duty.

From Sarajevo, General Montgomery Meigs reported that he was maintaining order throughout Bosnia-Herzegovina, despite the stoning of a vehicle and some ugly words. I had also learned, earlier that morning, that the Russians were making noises about pulling their troops out of Bosnia. I wasn't too concerned by this. We could make up for the missing two battalions, and it would preclude the possibilities of any overt collusion by the Russians with the Serbs. A bad thing diplomatically perhaps, but no problem from the military side. I had great confidence in Meigs. He had already been in command in Bosnia for six months, a second tour following his command of the U.S. division in the northern sector in the first six months of 1997.

Back in my office after the teleconference was over, I was joined by Rupert Smith and Dieter Stockmann to confer about the various elements of the strategic effort that we would have to lead. There was the matter of the air strikes themselves. If the initial strikes didn't break Milosevic's ethnic cleansing campaign, we would have to sustain and intensify the strikes indefinitely. This was the first priority among our strategic efforts: striking more targets and homing in on his command and control, as well as the forces on the ground.

Of course we would need more targets than the initial one hundred or so currently ready to go, but I was confident that we had the process under way to generate the additional targets that were required. Jim Ellis and John Jumper had shown me a list of 175 targets some two weeks earlier, and I knew that this strategic effort was progressing.

More urgent was the matter of attacking the Serb military and police forces, especially those conducting the attacks on the Albanian population in Kosovo. We knew that this was going to be challenging for the Air Force. Much would depend on the weather, the activities patterns on the ground, the degree of resistance, and the continued refinement of our techniques for attacking ground targets. As Smith sensibly suggested, it wasn't necessarily a matter of destroying these forces; simply scattering them and driving them into hiding would help to disrupt Milosevic's plans.

I had also formally requested the deployment of a task force of Apache helicopters, along with command and control and fire support, to help us go after the ground forces. We had a number of Apache crews and controllers based in Germany, and we estimated that once we were given the go-ahead it might take a week or ten days to get them into the theater of operations.

But we knew we were sitting on two problems with the deployment. First, we couldn't do the real on-the-ground planning effectively, because the Army lawyers were interpreting new federal law to mean that until Congress was notified of the impending deployment, we were not permitted to spend any funds preparing for it. We tried to work around this problem using U.S. personnel already present in Skopje, but these people lacked the necessary qualifications to do the reconnaissance. This had the units in Germany highly frustrated. There were also some issues with the proposed location. Skopje airfield was actually in range of some of the Serbs' long-range rockets. Placing the helicopters there could invite Serb artillery attack.

Second, we needed to receive permission from the government of Macedonia to operate from their country. As I knew from my meeting with President Gligorov the week before, the Macedonians were wary. Macedonia might seek even further security guarantees. I knew that it would probably require me to make another trip in to see him, and since I couldn't spare the time away from headquarters, I determined to let the question remain open for now.

The second strategic effort was to manage the continuing enforcement of the Dayton Agreement in Bosnia, including protecting our troops on the ground. We didn't need an expansion of trouble there, and any violence would be in Milosevic's interest. We knew we had the upper hand militarily with our 30,000 troops on the ground, and Monty Meigs would have to maintain the level of dialogue and react quickly and appropriately to prevent any incidents from escalating. He would also have to reassure the civilians who represented the international agencies and the various nations' diplomatic missions.

We had invested over three years of effort in Bosnia with substantial NATO forces following the Dayton Agreement, and we didn't want this effort to be lost. I intended to help by trying to insulate Bosnia and the forces there from any involvement in the operations in Serbia. We also had our naval forces in the Adriatic and our ground forces in Macedonia to consider.

The third strategic effort would be to sustain our base of operations in Macedonia and Albania. With its Albanian and Serb minorities, Macedonia was vulnerable to destabilization as a result of the fighting or deliberate Serb activities. If the Macedonian government fell apart or we were asked to leave, there would be no way to stage the ground forces for the next phase of the operation. Also, the fall of the government in Macedonia would represent a huge setback for the West and for democracy in the region. Macedonia had done well accommodating 2,000 NATO troops as part of the Extraction Force, but there were thousands more on the way; this would inevitably cause friction and raise tensions among the local people. The NATO troops in Macedonia were within range of Serb rocket artillery, too, and a Serb ground thrust across the border would be difficult to prevent.

The fourth strategic effort would be to take care of refugees. We believed from previous experience that Milosevic would try to prevent their leaving the territory of Yugoslavia so he could claim that the entire Kosovo issue was purely an "internal" matter. Still, any persons who managed to escape Yugoslavia would be the responsibility of the U.N. High Commissioner for Refugees, Sadako Ogata, and her team. The UNHCR had estimated that a crisis would generate no more than 200,000 refugees, and Rupert Smith warned that if the UNHCR could not handle a job of this size, it would fall on us.

Another task facing us was to isolate the operational area and thereby prevent Milosevic from receiving support and assistance from other nations. An air campaign, I reasoned from the lessons of Vietnam, was a race of "destruction" against "reconstruction." We had to destroy and disable our targets faster than Milsoevic could repair them or work around them. This meant that we would be undercutting our prospects for success if we allowed military gear or related equipment and support to flow in to replace what we were disabling. And I remembered well the reports of the astonishing buildup of Vietnamese air defenses with the help of Russian and Chinese support during the early Rolling Thunder campaign. That support seemed to completely offset the effectiveness of our strike campaign there.

Finally, we returned to the subject of strategic information. In democracies, the public has a right to know as much about the ongoing actions as can be safely provided without endangering the operation or the forces themselves. We would have to release information, but we knew we'd have to navigate carefully. It was better to start with a restrictive information release policy and then gradually open up than to give too much initially and try to clamp down later.

We were also concerned with how information might be interpreted. We knew we had to work with as many reporters as possible to get our story out and to build the relationships for openness and accuracy that would be required to defeat the Serb "big lie" when it was trotted out. One thing I had learned from Dick Holbrooke was to communicate with reporters after the story was out, to give them feedback and correct any mistakes or misimpressions. Of course we had to convey information as well to the decisionmakers in the various capitals and at NATO headquarters.

As Smith, Stockmann, and I reviewed the strategic concerns we had sketched out the previous day, I sensed that we had a good common grip on the problems. This was the most important of the understandings we reached—a strategic vision that kept the three of us together in our work. I was counting on Stockmann to help carry the Germans, as well as working the staffs at SHAPE and NATO Headquarters, and Smith to bring the Brits along, as well as shore up the frontline states and serve as my back-up and trouble-shooter. I would have to work the Americans, the French, and the others as well as directing the military efforts. This division of labor was one of the keys to our leadership effort.

At 11:00 A.M., it was time for the EUCOM video teleconference. This is going to be a long campaign, I explained. We're doing just fine, but there's so much more to do. There were issues about striking targets in Montenegro, Serbia's smaller neighboring republic within Yugoslavia, and the likely impact of such strikes on the regime of the Western-leaning President, Milo Djukanovic. We also had problems because some of the targets for the second night's strikes hadn't yet received political clearance from Washington or from Solana. I told the planners to keep them on the list for now, but what was most important was to focus on those targets with low risk of collateral damage.

What was becoming increasingly clear to me, as I spoke, was just how difficult the process of target approval was going to become. Once we moved past the obvious air defense target set, every target—headquarters buildings, communications towers, ammunition storage sites, and military maintenance facilities—was, in one way or another, likely to become controversial. In the U.S. channel, we would need a complete analysis of each individual target—location, military impact, possible personnel casualties, possible collateral damages, risks if the weapon missed the target, and so forth. This analysis then had to be repeated for different types of weapons, in search of the specific type of weapon and warhead size that would destroy the target and have the least adverse impact elsewhere. And this had to be done to my satisfaction, then sent to Washington where it underwent additional levels of legal and military review and finally ended up on President Clinton's desk for his approval.

"You mean he's going to personally approve every target?" I had asked Hugh Shelton earlier in the week. I knew then that we were going to be working very hard on targeting, but now, as the details of the various targets unfolded in the VTC—"They're still working this one in the Joint Staff; that one is supposed to be taken across the River today, but the appointment has been delayed; this one they've asked us to reconsider"—the gravity of the situation became increasingly clear. I saw right away that this was going to be a time-consuming and intricate process in which we couldn't make a mistake. We had to establish a routine and work it consistently every single day.

For NATO, on the other hand, I was able at this point simply to describe the types of targets and give representative examples to some of the Chiefs of Defense. Of course, I kept Naumann and Solana informed, too.

We had to start going after the Serb ground forces. But without our own ground forces deployed, we were going to have difficulty taking the strategic targeting effort and turning it to support tactical warfare.

After the VTC concluded I had just enough time to return to the office and draft remarks for the afternoon press conference with Solana. I had done a number of press appearances with the Secretary General over the past year and a half, but this time we had agreed to go over our remarks with each other in advance.

After the usual helicopter ride to Brussels, I joined the Secretary General's press preparation meeting, and then he and I adjourned for a one-on-one session in his office. I read him my notes, including my key point, which was that we were going to attack, degrade, disrupt, and, ultimately, destroy Milosevic's forces, facilities, and support unless he complied with the demands of the international community. In this way we would clearly link the military actions to their intended consequence, convey our resolve and seriousness of purpose, and move past the idea that Milosevic could wait us out. Once we began to use force, we had to succeed.

Solana listened and nodded his assent. Then he gave me his quick read of the political situation. There was good support of the actions thus far, but many of the nations remained interested in a bombing pause—which I once again counseled against.

Then he asked how soon I thought we would be asking to move to

Phase II of the campaign, attacking targets in southern Serbia that were supporting the Serb campaign in Kosovo. I explained that while we still had a few Phase I targets, associated with Milosevic's air defenses, there was no need to destroy everything in the Integrated Air Defense System before we went to Phase II. We should move as soon as possible, I said.

Moving to Phase II, he said, would be difficult; first NATO would have to see the results of Phase I. So, I reflected, I was going to have problems with expanding the target list on the NATO side, too.

Solana and I were silent and thoughtful as we walked together down to the press room. We knew that the public information effort was going to be critical for our success and that this was an important moment, perhaps even a defining moment, for the campaign. There were at this time no airplanes in the air—this press briefing would be the whole campaign at this moment. The two of us were, in a real sense, on the front line.

We had to both explain what we were doing and convince the public in many countries that we were doing the right thing. And I knew that Milosevic and his men would be watching from Belgrade, assessing our seriousness, looking for any openings or hint of doubt.

The press room was packed. We stepped up onto the stage at the front and Jamie Shea, the NATO spokesman, introduced Solana. He spoke first, reading from his text and looking out at the field of several hundred reporters and a score of TV crews and cameras. I thought he sounded confident and determined, exactly the right message to convey.

I then stepped forward and delivered my statement, citing Solana's remarks and the statements of the various heads of government. I then got to my main point. "The military mission," I said, "is to attack Yugoslav military and security forces and associated facilities with sufficient effect to degrade its capacity to continue repression of the civilian population and to deter further military actions against its own people. We are going to systematically attack, disrupt, degrade, devastate, and ultimately destroy these forces and their facilities and support, unless President Milosevic complies with the demands of the international community. In that respect the operation is going to be as long and difficult as President Milosevic requires it to be." I went on to echo Solana's words that this wasn't an attack against the Serb people and then described the operation the first night in general terms. I also made the point that we weren't going to permit the emergence of a sanctuary area in the Belgrade region. This was not only imperative strategically, it was also something I owed to our airmen. This wasn't going to be like Vietnam, where Hanoi had become a sanctuary and our Air Force couldn't strike the bases and headquarters directing the air defenses against us.

The questions from the press were astute. They brought out most of the key points and issues that were to surface in later days. How long would the attacks go on, for weeks? When would the bombing affect Serb forces on the ground? What if the Serbs were holding back on their air defenses in order to save them? What would happen to U.S.-Russian relations? Were we planning to hit targets in downtown Belgrade? Wasn't the ultimate aim to depose the Milosevic government? What about the harm to civilians?

The serious atmosphere of the press conference was impressive. There was no trace of the cynicism, sarcasm, or bitterness that we in the military remembered from Vietnam. There was a sense of underlying moral purpose and unity here (except for the one Serb journalist present) that was reflected in almost every question. The reporters just wanted the facts, and to understand what this was really about. I didn't expect any favors from the reporters, but they were doing their job in a straightforward way and that was what I had hoped for.

Solana was quiet as we moved back toward his office. "What do you think?" I asked, hoping to compare notes and draw him out a little.

"The word 'destroy,' " he said. "I am worried; that is all the press will focus on tomorrow."

I sensed it, too. It was a strong statement of purpose, and I knew from personal experience that this was the kind of straight threat that would carry weight with Milosevic and his cronies in Belgrade. If we could persuade them at the outset that they couldn't and wouldn't succeed against NATO, then we might undercut their willingness to continue their repression in Kosovo.

But I also recognized that my language might sound too bellicose for some in Europe. I had made explicit what all the military had been saying for almost a year: once we started, we had to stay with this until we succeeded. After the press conference it would be more difficult to find some excuse to call off the air strikes after a few days, though that wasn't my intent. I knew that Solana wanted to see this operation through to the end. And I saw no sign of any softening in Washington, either. In fact, as I thought about it, when the United States launched the initial air strikes against North Vietnam in the mid-1960s, Washington had never expressed a clear linkage to an objective and the intent to see it through. To be true to its mission, NATO had no alternative but to follow through until Milosevic complied. In any event, it had been said. We would have to await the next day's results.

Back at my headquarters in Mons, Dick Holbrooke was calling from Budapest to see if I thought a bombing pause would be a good idea. I explained that I did not. I reminded him how much difficulty we had in getting the bombing campaign started in 1995. I also explained that there was no need for a pause for diplomatic purposes, that Milosevic and his generals knew exactly how to contact us if they wanted us to stop the bombing.

"But if we had to take a pause, how soon could we take it?" he persisted.

"Not for at least five to seven days," I said. I had to keep this campaign going long enough to hurt Milosevic, if we were to have any chance of his accepting our conditions. Even then, I could imagine, just think about the labor we'd have to go through trying to craft the conditions for a pause that would allow it to start again if he didn't comply. I had to keep booting the pause downfield.

Later that afternoon, as I conferred with Rupert Smith and Dieter Stockmann, we were interrupted by a call from the State Department. The U.S. embassy in Macedonia was under attack by a mob of people protesting the air strikes. They had burst through the front door and had tried to attack the staff. Ambassador Hill had locked himself in the basement vault. There were fears that the embassy was going to be burned. The Macedonian police had been contacted but were not responsive. The embassy staff couldn't see what was going on.

I called Mike Jackson in Skopje to get him involved. I also called the small American contingent there under the command of Brigadier General John Craddock. I directed Jackson to use the American capability to get a reaction force in to help the ambassador, and then called Craddock to ensure there would be no question that he would take instructions from Jackson, though technically the American contingent was not part of the force that Jackson was commanding. Jackson informed me that he would dispatch Craddock's men immediately, and he advised me that the German embassy was also under assault.

After an hour or so, the situation came under control. The American ambassador freed himself from the vault, the embassy was damaged in the attack but not burned, U.S. troops had arrived on scene, and the Macedonian police had promised to take charge. Chris Hill came on the phone to explain that the pro-Serb crowd had been bused down to the capital from a northern town that had a largely Serb population.

This last fact confirmed my view that this was a planned attack, designed to spark resistance to NATO in Macedonia and contribute to destabilizing a friendly, democratic government. It was part of the way Milosevic would fight back against NATO and his neighbors. These were the games we had to expect from Milosevic or the Serb government.

From the press it seemed that President Clinton had ruled out the ground option, declaring that he "had no intent" to deploy American ground forces against the Serb army. I hadn't been warned, but the announcement was not surprising. No nation wanted to think about invading Kosovo—at least not at this early stage in the air campaign. I interpreted the President's statement as a preemptive political move designed to head off a potentially divisive and, at this point, unnecessary debate. Milosevic, of course, would have been impressed if he believed that we were so serious that an invasion was being prepared, but a series of painful national debates about the ground option at this point would, in the near term, have added no coercive pressure to the NATO air campaign. Anyway, I never took the statement to mean more than that the President had no current intent to use ground forces; if necessary, he could change his intent. As I was to discover, though, the statement did become an impediment within the U.S. channel to commencing ground force planning.

That second night we had a well-planned, integrated strike. Once again we had over fifty targets, ranging from the major airfield complex at Batanjica, just a few miles from downtown Belgrade, to the headquarters in southern Serbia of the Serb police and military forces, who were participating in the action against the Kosovar Albanians. Radar sites, air defense sector headquarters, electronic warfare and radio intercept sites, missiles storage facilities, airfields, microwave relays, regional army and police headquarters—these were substantial and serious targets. Their loss ought to give a real kick to the Serbs, I thought.

We had good flying weather, and it all went off like clockwork, except for one plane with engine trouble. We monitored the reports from my study. It was calm and business-like in the command networks, a little too calm.

No Serb aircraft rose to meet us. The air defense fires coming up were scattered and only one surface-to-air missile launch was reported. There were no immediate indicators that we had delivered a war-winning knockout blow, and we hadn't.

By the next day, the battle rhythm seemed routine. Morning meeting, NATO VTC, EUCOM VTC, press and media, follow-up. We worked off the strategy we had developed. Make the decisions as necessary on the targeting and ramp up the campaign. Protect our troops. Keep Macedonia stable and on our side. Isolate the theater. Prepare for humanitarian assistance. Provide strategic information and win the public affairs fight. Sustain Allied consensus.

The field commanders reported concerns in Macedonia and Bosnia. The Macedonian government had been shaken by the previous afternoon's riots; the government was supportive of us, but felt it was vulnerable to Serb pressures and was being somewhat taken for granted by NATO. In Bosnia, Serb crowds in Banja Luka, the capital of Republika Srpska, had ransacked the American, British, and German consulates, and a U.S. helicopter on patrol had been hit by small arms.

All morning, as I went in and out of meetings and video teleconferences, the press play was ramping up. We were besieged by requests for interviews at SHAPE, including some personality pieces. That the public affairs work could be an all-consuming effort was obvious. I couldn't afford it. Colonel Stephanie Hoehne, my public affairs officer, was in and out of the office trying to sort through the requests.

"Sir, you don't have to do any of this," she said. "But if you want to get out your message and anchor it in the public, you're going to have to speak out now and make your points known. You've got to stay in the fight."

She was right, of course, because this was a NATO campaign, and there wasn't any other headquarters that could see the operation from this perspective. I had to protect the credibility of the campaign and the men and women flying. We picked the *Today* show and an interview with Christiane Amanpour of CNN, with whom I had a wide-ranging discussion about the purposes and methods of the campaign. I explained that attacking the ground forces was part of our strategy but added that it was "always understood that there was no way we were going to be able to stop Serb paramilitary forces who were going in and murdering civilians in villages." This was rapidly becoming one of the key issues.

Meanwhile, Solana was trying to assuage public concerns by estimating that the length of the campaign would be "days, not months." And, in answering the questions about our ability to stop the forces of ethnic cleansing on the ground, Jamie Shea was still alert to the concerns of the diplomats that we might extend the conflict if we killed too many Yugoslav troops: "We are not going to systematically target troops but we are going to systematically target the heavy artillery and tanks and the equipment without which the troops would not be able to carry out their brutal repression." Several governments still hoped that the mere expression of force would sway Milosevic, while significant losses might harden Serb resolve.

Many in the press were focused on one question: What were NATO's objectives in the campaign? A halt to the Serb repression? A Serb return to Rambouillet? The destruction of the Serbian military? There was speculation that the ambiguity in goals was intentional, to enable NATO to meet its obligations to help protect the Kosovars without having to achieve Serb participation in a peace settlement or do too much militarily.

I had no doubts about what we had to do on the military side, but a number of us had begun to ask in private about the political goals of the campaign. If Milosevic continued to defy the attacks and continued the campaign of repression in Kosovo, wouldn't it become impossible to return to the negotiations at Rambouillet? Rambouillet would have let the Serbs keep several thousand police and military in Kosovo. Would any Albanians be likely to accept that now? If not, did this mean that the somewhat limited military actions they had anticipated would have to be sustained and intensified? The answers were also important in considering the follow-on peace support operation.

Concurrently, there were mixed signals from above. There was word that Greece didn't support continued combat operations and conflicting press reports on the Italians' desires for a bombing pause. The Ukrainian foreign minister was visiting Belgrade, seeking a solution to the crisis. Russia introduced a U.N. Security Council Resolution (later defeated), calling the NATO action a "flagrant violation of the U.N. Charter." There were also rumblings of Russian and Belorussian aircraft movements and repositioning of forces.

The phone calls and issues never slowed down. We had to plan and adapt as we executed.

From Rome: Could we not actually commit the Italians to bombing runs until their parliament approves?

From Greece: An assassination threat against a U.S. officer; and the Greek deputy foreign minister has called for an immediate halt to the bombing.

From Admiral Jim Ellis: Can we attack a parked MIG with a hasty launch of a Tomahawk missile? Yes, you have standing approval for such fleeting targets so long as no collateral damage is anticipated. And good luck.

From Brussels: The Secretary General wants an update on the operation.

From General Shelton: The President has authorized us to take our place in the staff of the headquarters in Macedonia, but, Wes, how badly do you need the Apaches? I came on strong. We need them.

Back to Stuttgart to my deputy there, Admiral Steve Abbott: We need a cross-servicing agreement with Macedonia so we can give their police some fuel.

From Washington: Ambassador Gelbard wants to know why the British troops failed to protect the consulates in Banja Luka.

In the middle of this we were informed that our airmen had just shot down two MIGs that were leading an air attack from Serbia into Bosnia. This was a second "strategic shot" at us, following on the mob attack on the embassies in Macedonia. (It was later determined that after the two MIG-29 aircraft were shot down about twelve miles from the U.S. headquarters at Tuzla by a U.S. F-15C using the new beyond-visual-range missiles, our soldiers near Brcko watched several Serb ground attack aircraft flee back to their bases in Serbia.) We didn't even pause. Monty Meigs would take care of it, along with protection of the NATO governments' consulates in Banja Luka. However, the next day there were disconcerting rumbles among my subordinate commands about whether the Air Force would allow American aircraft to continue to fly overhead in Bosnia if our ground forces issued their Stinger missiles to the troops. Subsequently, no missiles were issued, and the Serbs never reattacked. But this was an old Army–Air Force squabble I was disappointed to see reappear here.

At our level we were working the big issues, trying to get ahead of current operations to strengthen future operations. We continued to discuss how best to position and employ the Apaches with the Army planning staff in Heidelberg. We determined that, because of the reports of atrocities, we should seek authority to strike the Phase III targets, those headquarters and support facilities located around and within Belgrade, as soon as possible. I made a call to Jim Ellis to confirm that we were continuing Air Force planning to put heavy bombers against Serbs' ground force assembly areas in Kosovo.

That evening, Klaus Naumann and I met with Solana to discuss the operation and the way ahead. We went through the campaign objectives, the character of our adversary, the numbers of aircraft, targets, weather conditions, and Serb actions on the ground. "Will it be over by Easter?" Solana asked. Easter was April 4, nine days away. I couldn't promise such a quick solution.

The immediate issue was the prospect of a bombing pause. Please don't let it happen, I pleaded. Solana listened, and then he explained, "The Pope is going to give a speech on Wednesday, before Easter, and he will call for the strikes to cease." The Secretary General was very concerned.

I asked how the Pope could do this if the Serb campaign was still under way. Couldn't someone explain it to the Vatican? I asked.

"You do not understand the impact he will have," Solana said. "When the Pope speaks, people and governments listen. They will find it very difficult. Try to think like a Southern European Catholic."

"I am a Catholic," I protested, half jokingly. He knew it very well, as we had often talked about our religious views.

"Then perhaps you are not a good Catholic," he rejoined, smiling a bit at the crazy position we were in, fighting a campaign for moral and humanitarian purposes and having to defend our freedom of action against Christian virtues. I tried to joke that he, a physics professor and a socialist, had some nerve accusing me of not being a good Catholic.

As I left to go back to Mons, I reflected on what we had covered. It had been a good discussion, and despite the pressure and fatigue we could still joke with each other. We had succeeded in keeping the strikes going past the first two nights, but we were not yet close to accomplishing the Phase I objective of destroying the enemy's integrated air defense system. We were striking at the facilities of the Serb ground forces that were doing the ethnic cleansing, but we hadn't yet struck those forces. We were departing from the original concept of the phased air operation by moving beyond Phase I targets before the Serbs' integrated air defense system had been broken—the aim of that phase. We were also pressing for more resources and more options. Commanders had to do that; it was what we taught in every training exercise.

In fact, if this were an Army training exercise, I thought, this would be the point that we would stop for an after-action review, letting an outside team of observers help us conduct a candid self-appraisal, and then we would make the adjustments and move on. These outside teams always featured a retired three-star or four-star general, called the senior mentor, to help keep everything in perspective.

I thought that we could use a senior mentor right now, and that the perfect man for the job was General Ed Burba, a retired four-star who was working with the Army Battle Command Training Program as a senior mentor. I had known General Burba for twenty years and had worked for him in a couple of different assignments. He had superb military judgment. I reached him in Atlanta by phone as I traveled home.

"Sir, you know what we're engaged in over here?" I said.

"Oh, yes, we've been following it as best we can from here. Looks like you've got quite an operation going there," he said.

"Well, it's one of the most incredible things I've ever been involved in," I told him, and I sketched out some of the press play and publicly known issues. "I'd like to invite you over to take a look at what we're doing. I'm not sure what you'd actually be doing, but I'd just like to bounce some ideas off you, and it would be helpful if you could come right away."

He agreed to come as soon as possible. This would help.

Then I had to face the more immediate concerns: the ominous weather forecast. This was supposed to be our first bad-weather night. How would this affect us?

It turned out to be a bad night. Most of the air strikes were canceled. The weather in southern Serbia and over Kosovo prevented manned aircraft from flying with enough visibility to be safe if engaged by enemy missiles or to deliver weapons accurately. But we did have some weapons, Global Positioning System–guided bombs and missiles that are precise even in bad weather. These were all that was going to see us through these kinds of nights, I thought.

We also had the cruise missiles. Twelve launched tonight from the B-52s, plus the Tomahawks launched from the ships, and some other strikes around Belgrade. So despite the bad weather, we were able to keep the pressure on, hitting some key Serb police and military headquarters.

The next morning, day four, a new concern surfaced: the Russians had announced that they were going to deploy several warfighting vessels to the Mediterranean. They had notified the Turks of their intent to pass through the Dardanelles from the Black Sea to the Mediterranean in early April. It was an unmistakable signal.

It was also a threat to the air campaign. At the very least these ships could complicate our use of the Adriatic, where the Yugoslavs had not yet ventured from port after my warning to them. The Russian ships could provide early warning of our strikes to the Serbs, harass our naval movements, or even block the flight paths of some of our systems, all without engaging in any hostilities.

Jim Ellis was on top of the Russian naval issue, but there wasn't much that he could do. He had neither the forces nor the authority to take any action should the Russian battle group appear. It was my problem.

I wanted to be certain there was no misunderstanding of my intent as we set out to work this. We just could not allow this threat to materialize. "We're not going to let them come into the Adriatic, or through the Straits, if I can help it." I said. "We're going to get this stopped, or pull in the forces to block them."

Later that morning, in a phone conversation with Klaus Naumann, I passed on my concerns about the potential Russian naval presence.

"If they come through the Straits and into the Med, they will really be a problem," I said. I needed Klaus's help in building up diplomatic resolve against the possible naval movement, and we had to begin to think about requesting additional forces to deal with the Russians. "This is a major problem, not a war problem, but a major problem," I told him.

I was also worried about some Serb artillery that was positioned in southern Serbia but was aimed into Macedonia. It wasn't participating in the ethnic cleansing, but it was aiming south; some of our troops were within its range. If we could attack it and destroy it all at once, well and good. If we attacked and they responded, then we would have brought a shooting war to Macedonia. And if we used aircraft, wouldn't we then be diverting efforts unnecessarily from attacking those forces actually participating in the ethnic cleansing? I decided to keep the artillery under observation and stay focused on the Serb forces operating inside Kosovo for now.

I also worked the target approval problem through most of the afternoon, including extended phone discussions with Hugh Shelton. We needed to be striking targets in downtown Belgrade in order to make an impact, and I laid them out. He reiterated strong guidance from the Administration to do more to impact Serb atrocities on the ground.

In the middle of this, General Mario Arpino, the Italian Chief of Defense, called to warn that if we tried to move ahead too quickly on targeting, then Italy might face another governmental crisis. Italy, he said, might be able to withstand only another three to four days of bombing. Arpino had been Italy's Chief of Defense for only two months, but he conveyed great confidence and authority. I always listened to his insights and requests.

We had also been examining claims of unintended damages from our attacks. In this case, there was a rumor that one of previous strikes on the airfield and missile facilities around Belgrade had somehow led to the release of toxic chemicals. We faithfully ran down all the facts to verify the location of the pharmaceutical plants. We finally concluded that it had been burning rocket fuel from the Serb antiaircraft missiles and from the storage facility that we struck that was responsible for the eye irritation being reported by the media from Belgrade.

We were also dealing with the reports of a U.S. missile that had landed within Bulgaria. Not good.

As I headed home that evening, I was anticipating our first strikes against the assembly areas for Serbian troops. But I also recognized that we were, step by step, making the transition to an operation that was going to be broader and more intense than the original plan had anticipated.

Saturday night was a routine evening until John Jumper called on the secure phone shortly after 10:00. "Sir," he said, "we've got one of our 117s unaccounted for coming out of Yugoslav airspace."

It was the call I had been dreading. "John, what does this mean? Did we lose one, or what?"

"Sir, we don't know yet. He hasn't checked in. It could be commo problems, or he could be down. Right now, we're trying to get confirmation."

A few minutes later Jumper called back. "Sir, it wasn't coms. We don't have him. He's down somewhere in Serbia."

I called Hugh Shelton to let him know the bad news. "Well, sir, here it is, what we've been expecting."

Shelton took it straight, without any emotion. "Well," he said, "the SecDef and I have been saying that we would lose some aircraft. And that's what the models showed. I'll let him know."

Rescuing the pilot was out of our hands at SHAPE. A set of preplanned procedures kicked in, including linking up helicopters, fighters, and refueling aircraft, and they'd have to determine how to make a run into Serbia to snatch the pilot. We had about seven hours of darkness remaining before daybreak.

We received the periodic reports. The pilot has checked in; we know his location. He's OK and evading capture. The aircraft are delayed; they have to link up with the tankers and refuel.

The pilot is moving.

In the meantime the word had gone out to the press from Serb sources. In response to queries, we refused to confirm a missing plane; we were still checking. The longer we could protect the fact that a plane was down and a pilot potentially missing, the greater the chance that we could rescue him.

I couldn't reach Solana on the secure phone, so I couldn't even tell him what was going on.

We were engaged in three all-night duels, on the ground between the pilot and his pursuers, in the air between our combat search-and-rescue and Serb defenses, and in the media—the so-called information war—with the Serbs seeking to take credit for shooting down their first aircraft and our determination to deny it as long as possible in order to protect the pilot.

Around 12:30 we partially lost the third fight. The burning wreckage of the aircraft was being shown on international television broadcast, with ecstatic Serbs clamoring over the area. Now we could only say that we weren't sure whether the plane had been shot down or whether it had had some malfunction.

But we were still ahead in the two duels that counted. And by 5:30 A.M. we had won both; we had the pilot, safe and sound, and back in our airspace.

I called Solana to tell him the results. Despite the delays caused by the positioning of some of our aircraft, the need for air to air refueling, and intensive Serb efforts, our team succeeded in pulling out the pilot. "Good," he said. "This is spectacular. It is a moral victory."

It didn't feel like much of a victory. Bad weather had caused us to cancel two of the night's strike packages, and we lost other strikes in the north while we were working on the pilot's rescue. This also meant that we hadn't hit the planned assembly area targets.

For the next night, my concerns were to hit the troops on the ground and to ratchet up the pressure against Belgrade. Once again we had found some assembly areas to strike; it seemed that somehow we could get fresh photo imagery of the targets but couldn't get the aircraft in to strike them.

Flexibility. That's what this was all about. How do you reduce the planning time and attack more spontaneously without running unacceptable risks for your aircrews? We were doing well at making the targeting for the missiles more flexible. They were becoming more responsive than the manned aircraft, I reflected.

We were still suffering from a shortage of approved targets. When I announced that we had received the North Atlantic Council's approval to go to the Phase II targets, Jim Ellis noted that the only thing new in Phase II were eight bridges to be struck. Everything else had either been hit already or entailed too much risk of unintended damage. So I continued to push both Washington and the NATO leadership for approval to strike the Phase III targets around Belgrade, and I made sure that we would be ready to strike as soon as the approvals came in.

But the immediate priority remained the ground targets in Kosovo. We had to hit them and it wasn't going to be easy.

We also had to be innovative in going after the Serb air defenses, I thought. The Serbs were shifting them around from position to position, blinking the radars off and on, and avoiding our strikes. The Serb tactics weren't totally effective, but then, neither were our attacks. We needed a weapon with a rapid kill capability, like the Army Tactical Missile. With a range of over one hundred miles, a two-minute time of flight, and a big warhead, it would be perfect for smashing Milosevic's air defenses. We had used it like that a few times against the Iraqis in Operation Desert Storm.

The trouble was, we didn't have any missiles or launchers nearby. We had asked for them as part of the Apache deployment, but even after they arrived that would only give us range into Kosovo. We needed them in the north, where they could strike the area around Belgrade. I explained the situation to John Jumper, and he agreed to have the Air Force ask for them. I also asked Steve Abbott to work Navy channels to get permission to fire these missiles off ships, a "joint" services experiment we had done a few years before.

That afternoon I also ran the idea by Hugh Shelton, and got his support. But there was concern about our expenditure rates for some of the types of ammunition, which targets we were striking, and why.

I asked Shelton for Washington's help in supporting the government of Macedonia, urging that a high-level State Department official needed to come in and work with the Gligorov government on an assistance package. And I raised the "end state" issue. What was our objective, to deter ethnic cleansing? Surely, no one could think that Milosevic would now return to Rambouillet. And if he did, was this enough?

Shelton didn't want to get into political or policy issues; these were questions for Sandy Berger, the national security adviser, he said. But the answers were vital, and I had learned before that military advice was often required on such questions. I switched gears and gave him an update on the good work being done by John Jumper and his head-quarters in backing up the strikes, and we signed off.

Of course the end state was a political and policy question—I had been in enough meetings in the White House Situation Room to imagine the effort going into the addressing the problem in Washington—but it had profound military implications as well. If Milosevic signed the Rambouillet agreement and we put our forces in, we would be obligated to allow some of the Serb military and police forces to remain in Kosovo, greatly increasing the difficulties of enforcing any agreement. This raised the broader question of NATO credibility: with all the signs of ethnic cleansing and the attacks against civilians, were we really going to be able to let Milosevic return to the terms of Rambouillet? There was another troubling aspect to this question: If we asked for more from Milosevic, would the bombing be enough to achieve it?

Chris Hill called to update me on the situation in Macedonia, and to press his ideas on which targets would be most effective in coercing Milosevic to call off the campaign. I asked Hill to think about our end-state objectives. He had run the negotiations with Milosevic during the summer and autumn and also knew the Albanians well. Is Rambouillet dead? Can this formula ever work now? He seemed to share my concerns.

Then General Ferenc Vegh, the Hungarian Chief of Defense, called. I tried to imagine how he must feel; he and his wife had come for dinner just two weeks ago when we were celebrating Hungary's admission to the Alliance. Welcome to NATO; you're now at war! He and I discussed the situation, the ongoing operations and the risks to Hungary. I assured him that there would be no problems for Hungary.

I also spoke to the F-117 pilot we had rescued. It was difficult to be so far away from the men and women who were doing the job. He sounded good, all things considered, and had already talked to his family.

"Sir, I have just one request," he said.

"What's that?" I thought he might want a couple of days off or a quick flight home.

"Sir, please don't let anyone release my name. I love the United States Air Force, and I want to stay in it and continue to fly."

He didn't want any publicity. He certainly had my support.

After being awake for thirty-six straight hours, my battery was running down by late afternoon. It was time for a nap on the little bed in the dressing room behind my office. This was going to be an important evening—dinner with Solana and Naumann and our first chance to really reflect on our strategy. And to put the pressure on for the Phase III targets that we really needed. Fifteen minutes with eyes closed, flat out, and then I was ready to go.

Solana lived in the official residence of the Secretary General, a large town home in a gated community in one of the nicest areas of Brussels. There was the usual warm hospitality and fine food, but after the opening discussion about the rescue of the pilot, the issues were difficult and my answers unsatisfying. How are we doing against the air defense? Fine, but we haven't taken out their system yet. When will you take out their system? Can't say. When are you going to start attacking the ground forces? We're ready now, but the weather is preventing us from striking. What can you do to stop the humanitarian outrage on the ground? For now, nothing more than we're doing. You must do more. How much will the Phase II approval help us? Not much.

We were doing what we'd signed up to do in the plan, but it was too slow, and even if it had been faster, the air actions still wouldn't hit the paramilitary units that were causing most of the damage. Bad weather, the loss of Saturday night's strikes, and concern about Serb air defenses were impacting strikes against Serb gound forces. And political pressure was building for a bombing pause and for seeking some other means of addressing the humanitarian issues. I could see the pressures closing in on the Secretary General.

When the conversation moved into the diplomatic area, I raised the issue of the political objectives of the campaign. What really was our aim? I asked. Surely not just a return to Rambouillet?

It was clear that Solana had worked a good deal on this issue and was moving the answer beyond Rambouillet. This reassured me. Most everyone with whom I had spoken felt that it would be impossible for the Serb military and police to remain in Kosovo after what they had done.

It was time to seek approval for the Phase III targets. These were the more significant targets associated with Serb repression that were located in the central and northern part of Serbia, including in Belgrade.

"Javier, we need to strike at these police headquarters in Belgrade. They are directing the ethnic cleansing." I showed him the aerial photos of the targets, located in downtown Belgrade.

He was dubious. What was nearby? Hospitals, schools, embassies, but I can't show you exactly on this photo. Can you guarantee that you will hit only the target and not anything else? No.

Klaus Naumann was also concerned. This would be a big jump in the risks, and if there was collateral damage, we would have trouble keeping all the nations on board. It had been difficult enough to secure the approval of Phase II targets.

Naumann reminded me of the German strike on Belgrade during World War II: German bombers had hit hard at the center of the city, killing 17,000. Europe, and Germany, had not forgotten the shame; sensitivities were acute.

"Can you guarantee me that if you strike these targets Milosevic will surrender?" Solana asked. He was clearly seeking arguments to use with the ambassadors.

"No," I said, "But I can guarantee you that if we don't move ahead with strikes like this he won't surrender."

We wrestled the issues back and forth and ended with an agreement that we would do everything we could in the next two or three days to attack the ground forces and that he would work to get approval for a few key targets in Belgrade.

I rode home reflecting on the dinner, my head still buzzing, determined that we weren't going to fail. I knew what I had signed up for, but I didn't know how I was going to deliver the results he needed on the ground targets. I was confident that he would get the Belgrade targets approved for us, and he was confident that I would produce the results against the ground targets. I couldn't let him down.

The strategy we had embarked on was proving to be extraordinarily difficult, not only because we were not able to strike the ground forces as rapidly as desired, but also because the political discussions and diplomatic activities were sending mixed messages. This was the inherent contradiction in any strategy combining the use of force with continuing diplomacy: Would Milosevic really believe we were persistent and united enough to defeat him when so many nations were publicly questioning the strategy or seeking to negotiate with him?

It was late by the time I got back to the chateau. On this night the weather was relatively cooperative; the strikes went in and all aircraft returned safely.

Before I turned in for a few hours of rest, I reflected again on the problem of hitting the targets on the ground. We were working on the problem every day in the VTCs, John Jumper had been down to Aviano to work with Mike Short on some new techniques, and Ed Burba had arrived from the States to serve as my sounding board. And I was still pushing for the Apaches. They might really turn the tide, I hoped.

A commander always has to have a plan. I had several plans. For the first time in two days, I could sleep. But it was odd, I thought, that I had not been invited into discussions with Washington that went into the strategy and implications of what we were doing, as I had discussed with Solana and Naumann. In fact, beyond the several actions I was pressing with Shelton, I hadn't discussed overall strategy with Secretary Cohen or the President at all.

NINE

APACHES AND TARGETS

AFTER THE FIRST DAYS of the air campaign, we needed better means to measure our efforts. I asked my staff to develop a system, setting our objectives against Milosevic's probable objectives, and then rating each side. The results did not look good.

In Phase I we had wanted to destroy or neutralize Milosevic's air defense system. Our analysis showed that we were still short of our objectives in destroying his early warning system, taking out his surface-to-air missiles, disrupting his command and control, and taking down his radio relay and communications sites. Moreover, the Serbs still retained their surface-to-air missile capability, some airfield capability, and so on. Now we were moving to Phase II strikes against forces facilities and support, including lines of communications in southern Serbia, and to frustrate us here, all Milosevic had to do was disperse the Serb heavy weapons and headquarters, continue operations against the Kosovars, and avoid a NATO ground intervention. We had lost the element of surprise, so the results were disappointing in purely military terms.

I conveyed this assessment in draft form at the U.S. video teleconference, just to help us put our efforts in perspective. Afterward I got a call from an angry John Jumper, who was outraged at the methodology. It was constructed, he said, in a way that demeaned the results of the airmen, because the objectives were set too high, and there was inadequate recognition of what we were accomplishing by continuing to strike.

He was right in sensing something wrong. While the methodology looked logical, it was too mechanical. We weren't, ultimately, in a battle of attrition, but rather we were using military power to force Milosevic to comply with the directions given by the international community. While accomplishing all the military objectives quickly and decisively would be ideal, we could still succeed by persevering and steadily intensifying the strikes. What we could not do was measure ourselves against a mechanical standard that was going to cause us to lose heart.

Of course, the press and media also saw that the air strikes were not achieving decisive impact. Sunday newspapers and talk shows were full of questions about the strategy and competence of the campaign, with many commentators believing that the NATO strikes had caused the ethnic cleansing and others calling for the use of ground troops.

I was doing all I could to offset the criticism and to maintain support for what we were doing. In the first six days of the air campaign, I had appeared before the media and press several times each day. I tried to play down any expectations for a rapid military success and put the burden of ending the fighting on Milosevic.

It was also necessary to maintain Congressional support. On Monday afternoon, March 29, the first congressional delegation arrived for a briefing and discussion at our headquarters. House Speaker Dennis Hastert and twelve other Members, who had been traveling through Europe during Easter recess, diverted to visit SHAPE. They listened attentively to an introductory briefing and then cut to the heart of the issues with their questions: What is the endgame? Do we have to get rid of Milosevic? Do we need Phase III targets? Wasn't the decision-making that got us into this bad? Is this an American war or a NATO war?

They listened carefully to the answers that U.S. Ambassador Sandy Vershbow and I gave—that U.S. leadership was required, that we had to be patient and combine force with diplomacy, and that it was premature to focus on other strategies. At the end, the Speaker closed by saying that we ought to stay with the operation and see it through. This was some very encouraging news.

But on the way out a friendly congressman pulled me aside. "They're settin' you up," he said.

"Excuse me, what do you mean? Who's setting me up?" I was surprised.

"You know who," he said. "First they went after Albright, now they've got their sights set on you."

"Well, uh, thanks," I mumbled. I didn't know who he was talking about. Nor did I want to go down that line of thought.

Meanwhile, according to our reports, the diplomacy continued at a frantic pace. Yevgeniy Primakov, the Russian prime minister, was going to Belgrade to see Milosevic; the United States was working to reassure the front-line states like Macedonia; and the diplomats at NATO were growing increasingly concerned about the human suffering in Kosovo. Moreover, there was still discussion in European circles about the possibility of a bombing pause.

Rupert Smith, Dieter Stockmann, and I met that afternoon for our usual end-of-the-day meeting. "We have to help people understand what could happen if we were to call a bombing pause," I told them. "When you pause, people believe you've lost faith in what you're doing. When you want to restart, those that didn't believe in the bombing in the first place are still opposed, and accuse you of a second failure, not taking advantage of the bombing pause to achieve peace, while those who would have supported you are now confused that you seem uncertain about whether to renew the strikes. And from the military side, the pause lets the enemy recover, reset his defenses, and continue the ethnic cleansing unimpeded." I asked Stockmann to have the staff prepare a paper for NATO headquarters on the ten best reasons not to have a pause. Stockmann took care of it. I never heard anything else about a bombing pause from within military channels.

The troublesome issues weren't just from European sources. In a drumbeat of phone calls over several hours, Washington had turned critical. Officials there were concerned about the information flow, about the use of key munitions, and about why we were attacking targets repeatedly. According to my staff in Stuttgart, the Joint Staff voiced many reasons against Phase III targets and deploying the Apaches as we requested. In a special meeting of the Joint Chiefs, the Army reportedly opposed the deployment of the Apaches.

All the questions reflected deeper concerns at work. As one senior officer in a position to know told me that evening, "I don't know where this is going, to tell you the truth, Wes. They're looking for a way out back here."

Through the night the phone calls continued with Washington, the Allied capitals, and Brussels. Broad themes began to emerge. Some countries wanted to add new targets and strike harder at the Serb ground forces. Other countries wanted to find reasons to announce a bombing pause for Easter. No consensus had emerged on the ultimate objective of NATO's efforts, or the extent of our resolve to prevail..

The processes of approving the targets, striking the targets, reading the results, and restriking were confusing. The original plans had presumed that the SACEUR would have the authority to strike targets within overall categories specified by NATO political leaders, but Washington had introduced a target-by-target approval requirement. The other Allies began to be increasingly demanding, too. It was British law that targets struck by any aircraft based in the United Kingdom had to be approved by their lawyers, the French demanded greater insight into the targeting and strikes, and of course there had to be continuing consultation with NATO headquarters and with other countries, too.

One key variable in the approval process was the possibility of unintended damages, or, as we called it, collateral damage, and differences between our interpretations and those in Washington were continuing to hinder the approval of certain targets. We did our best to reduce the risks to innocent civilians, but every change meant a new target document and a new run through the approval process.

Most targets, moreover, required more than one bomb, and in the case of ammunition depots and airfields, several dozen strikes were required. Sometimes planned targets would not actually be attacked if a radar or antiaircraft system was found to have been moved. These details were difficult to track at the higher political levels and triggered a steady stream of questions.

The change of command ceremony at Supreme Headquarters, Allied Powers Europe (SHAPE), near Mons, Belgium, on July 11, 1997. The flag of the command has been passed from General George Joulwan, the outgoing Supreme Allied Commander, Europe, or SACEUR (rear, center), to NATO Secretary General Javier Solana, who is passing it to me.

General John Shalikashvili, who served as Chairman of the Joint Chiefs of Staff from 1993 to 1997.

Ambassador Robert Gel-
bard (left) and General
Eric Shinseki join me at
the memorial service on
Bosnia's Mount Igman
on August 18, 1997,
honoring the three Amer-
ican diplomats who had
been killed in a tragic
accident there at the
start of the Dayton
peace process two years
earlier.

The morning update in my office during the first Kosovo crisis, in early
October 1998. From left, Colonel Doug MacGregor and Minister-Counsellor
Michael Durkee of the United States; General Sir Jeremy MacKenzie of
Great Britain, the Deputy SACEUR; myself; General Dieter Stockmann of
Germany, the SHAPE Chief of Staff; Major General Geraard Bastiaans of
The Netherlands; and Major General John Dallagher of the United States.

In Belli Dvor, the Yugoslav Presidential Palace, preparing to sign the NATO Air Verification Agreement in October 1998. From left, General Klaus Naumann, the Chairman of the NATO Military Committee; myself; Secretary General Solana; and Yugoslav President Slobodan Milosevic.

Some final words from Ambassador Richard Holbrooke on March 22, 1999, as he prepares to depart NATO Headquarters en route to Belgrade for the final efforts to persuade Milosevic to return to the negotiations at Rambouillet and avoid NATO air strikes.

Secretary of Defense William S. Cohen (left) and General Henry H. (Hugh) Shelton, the Chairman of the Joint Chiefs of Staff, at a Pentagon briefing in 1998.

General Joseph W. Ralston, the Vice Chairman of the Joint Chiefs of Staff, at a briefing during the war.

TOP The afternoon wrap-up sessions with Deputy SACEUR Rupert Smith and Chief of Staff Dieter Stockmann were key to maintaining strategic direction and Allied cohesion in the campaign. MIDDLE The first morning deskside update, with my executive officer, Brigadier General Pete Chiarelli, at 8:00 A.M. on March 25, 1999. The desk is the one that was used by General of the Army Dwight D. Eisenhower when he signed the activation orders for SHAPE in April 1951.

Virtually chained to the Headquarters by an unending stream of issues, problems and concerns in the early days of the war, I am seen here handling the "red switch" connection to the U.S. chain of command, while my aide-de-camp, Major Jay Silveria of the U.S. Air Force, readies another call on the "secure" connection to the Allies.

Strategic information was a key aspect of the campaign, especially at the NATO Summit in April 1999, where Secretary General Solana and I briefed the press on the progress to date.

President Bill Clinton, shown here with Secretary General Solana and me on May 5, 1999, was one of several NATO heads of government to visit NATO Headquarters in Brussels to receive an update on military efforts and to reinforce Allied efforts in the campaign.

LEFT General John Jumper, the Commander of U.S. Air Forces in Europe, was not in the NATO chain of command for the operation but, as the senior U.S. airman in Europe, played a critical role in supporting the planning and direction of the campaign. **RIGHT** Waiting with me for the arrival of an important visitor are two of my subordinate commanders: Admiral Jim Ellis (center), Commander of NATO Allied Forces Southern Europe and of U.S. Naval Forces, Europe; and Lieutenant General Mike Short of the U.S. Air Force (right), who commanded the air effort under Admiral Ellis in both NATO and U.S. channels.

LEFT Though recently retired, General Ed Burba played a critical role in planning, coaching and suggesting innovations during the campaign. Here he is at Rinas Airfield, Albania, with Lieutenant General Jay Hendrix, Commander of the U.S. Army V Corps and Task Force Hawk. **RIGHT** General Montgomery Meigs was the Commander of the Stabilization Force (SFOR) in Bosnia-Herzegovina, where he was in charge of monitoring and ensuring compliance with the Dayton Peace Accords, and also commanded U.S. Army Europe.

Working to transform the Kosovo Liberation Army after the operation succeeded. Here Lieutenant General Sir Michael Jackson, the commander of the Kosovo Force (KFOR), and I meet with Brigadier General Agim Ceku, the KLA commander.

After the war's end, on June 24, 1999, Secretary General Solana and I arrived in Pristina, the capital of Kosovo, to be greeted by a spontaneous welcome and large crowds.

Often assessing the damage to a target in real time was impossible. Even if the bomb hit, it sometimes took several hours or even days to confirm that a target was functionally destroyed. It was therefore difficult to convey to Allied political leaders a clear sense of the battle damage results. Britain's Charles Guthrie called to ask why we weren't striking more significant targets. Did we need more aircraft? Should we be flying lower? Taking more risks? How can we be more effective?

We listened carefully to each Chief of Defense. We needed their insights and good ideas, as well as their support. I was asking the same questions. It was clear that we could use more aircraft. The airmen assured me that we were flying at the right altitudes to optimize their weapons without slipping down into the range of most of the antiaircraft weapons. And the political impact of aircraft losses would still outweigh any potential benefits of a few Serb vehicles hit.

Washington asked why we sought approval for certain targets in Phase II, since they had been in Washington's view reserved, to be used if the Serbs struck our forces. These included targets such as petroleum storage and electric power facilities. Other targets we had sent forward, meanwhile, hadn't received approval because of collateral damage concerns. Everything possible was being undertaken to ensure that the strikes met strict legal standards and minimized risks of harm to innocent civilians.

By Tuesday morning, I had learned that the Joint Staff in Washington had apparently disapproved our requests to go after some of the bridge targets that should have been approved as part of the NATO Phase II package. There were other targets disapproved as well, including some petroleum storage locations in Kosovo. My staff and I believed that the Joint Staff estimates of collateral damage simply had not been updated, making the bridge targets look much more risky to innocent civilians than we believed to be the case. We would lose at least another day, and more hours of our time, sorting it out.

We were pressing hard to get the additional targets approved, naturally, because these approvals were critical to ratcheting up the pressure on Belgrade. But the bridge targets were especially sensitive. Our intelligence analysts were predicting that the Kosovo Liberation Army might survive only another two to three days, and we were also hearing of additional Serb forces moving south to Kosovo. Destroying the bridges might impede their movement and be the most rapid means at hand to prevent Milosevic from accomplishing his purposes in Kosovo.

The weather continued unfavorable for air strikes, and although we had flown some two-thirds of the sorties planned over the previous twenty-four hours, many of the aircraft hadn't dropped their bombs because of poor weather in the target areas.

An additional complication was Russian Prime Minister Primakov's visit to Belgrade. Of course we wanted to ensure that his visit was safe, but this meant further restrictions on strikes in the Belgrade area. This impeded our efforts to degrade key assets around Belgrade and keep Milosevic's military and civilian leadership under pressure.

Russia's role was worrisome. At the political levels, Russia was playing hard by breaking off contacts, and this worried the civilian leaders. There were also military concerns. The Russians had turned increasingly negative over the months of the crisis. In February they had pulled out the Russian deputy from my headquarters and brought him home more or less in disgrace for being "pro-NATO." There were also various rumors of their intent to help the Serbs. We were still expecting their ships to pass through the Dardanelles and enter the Mediterranean, and in Bosnia the Russians had announced that they would no longer take orders from the U.S. commander on the ground. U.S.-Russian military contacts were being canceled and the Russian group at SHAPE was preparing to depart. I directed Jim Ellis to be prepared to implement a naval exclusion zone to keep the Russian naval vessels from interfering with us. And I told Monty Meigs in Bosnia to be prepared to handle the Russians if necessary.

There were other complications as well, such as the ongoing active air campaign against Saddam Hussein in Iraq. Starting in late December 1998, Hussein had begun to try to resist the enforcement of the U.S. no-fly zone in northern Iraq, and in response to his antiaircraft fire against our planes, we had been attacking the Iraqi air defense system.

At the start of Operation Allied Force, I had pulled some of EUCOM's early warning and electronic warfare aircraft out of the mission in northern Iraq to meet key shortfalls in our current operation against Yugoslavia. Now the Joint Staff was asking when we could return these aircraft. Clearly they didn't understand that this was a war, that NATO's future was at stake, and that these assets were absolutely vital to escalating the pressure against Belgrade. Enforcement of the no-fly zone over northern Iraq was a lower priority for my command. The U.S. Central Command, under General Anthony Zinni had the bulk of enforcement responsibilities. I was asking for the *Theodore Roosevelt* battle group to be placed in support of the NATO operation, for the Apaches, for the Army Tactical Missile System, and for more aircraft, and they were asking us to consider giving up aircraft to what appeared to be a secondary mission? They should be sending aircraft to NATO, I thought, not taking them away.

When Hugh Shelton called to discuss the Apaches, I continued to press for their deployment. They had completed their training in Germany, and the deep attack team had been validated by the Army as one of the most proficient ever. This is what we'd been training them for for years. "But, Wes," Shelton said, "you should know that I'm having a hard time back here with the Chiefs. The Army Chief just doesn't want to send them in."

Though Shelton's words merely confirmed the information coming through other channels, it was chilling to hear it from him. It was also inexplicable. I had been through the planning of the package and the operational concept. I had no illusions about the ease of the mission, but then, we weren't doing so well with airpower at that point either.

I pressed the case for the Apaches. "Sir, they can get there and do what nothing else can. And we are in this fight. It is war, as far as we're concerned, and we've got to have the means to win it. Surely we're not going to deny a wartime commander in chief the assets we need to win?"

I remembered from my time as J-5 how careful General Shalikashvili had been to meet the requirements of the commanders in chief in the field. The cardinal rule was: always support the CINC. Always. Surely the Joint Chiefs would ultimately support me on the Apaches. Shelton didn't sound confident.

Meanwhile my requests for additional targets were still ricocheting around NATO headquarters. Klaus Naumann called to request more detailed descriptions of the so-called "high value" targets around Belgrade. He promised to work to build consensus for escalating the strikes, but urged again that we do as much as possible against the Serb forces on the ground.

Meanwhile, the Serb operations on the ground inside Kosovo were grinding forward. We continued to receive reports of Serb brutalities and ethnic cleansing against the civilian population. Estimates put the refugee count at 100,000 already, largely in Albania, with another 100,000 persons en route out.

On the morning of March 31 my mind was on the strategic problem facing the campaign: how to generate enough pressure on Milosevic to make him quit his deadly mission in Kosovo. I was especially buoyed by two phone calls: one from Hugh Shelton, confirming that the State Department would oppose any bombing pause; and the other from Sandy Vershbow, conveying efforts by the NATO ambassadors to reach an arrangement to approve strikes against the more high-value targets.

But what was really gnawing at me was the Apache problem. I couldn't get over the Army Chief's deciding against deploying the Apaches without even consultation, without any reconnaissance having been done in theater, and without understanding how urgently NATO needed them. Even so, I directed Monty Meigs and his team to continue the planning for the Apaches. We had now switched the basing from Macedonia to Albania due to the sensitivities of the Macedonian government and the proximity of Serb artillery. This meant a much tougher transportation problem. But I didn't want to have to re-fight the battle of getting Macedonian approval—I didn't have time to travel there and work it personally, nor did I want to put the helicopters within range of the Serbs' long-range rockets.

Then Solana called to formalize the additional targets, and to underscore my responsibilities. But I had heard that Greece, Italy, and a few other NATO governments were concerned about the escalation in the campaign and had gone along reluctantly at the political level. So I knew not to take the additional targets for granted.

Sure enough, Klaus Naumann called a few minutes later, and when I told him that we wanted to go after the Danube River bridges, he said, "That's quite unacceptable."

But, as I explained to Naumann, we needed to escalate, and if he didn't push for NATO approval, then the Americans might also turn us down, as they had before, because NATO hadn't asked for the target.

I was pushing everyone hard to escalate the intensity of the campaign, out front of Washington and NATO, seeking resources and backing to achieve what we called "escalation dominance." This was what commanders are taught to do. In my next phone call, to Hugh Shelton, I brought him up to date on the issues and then, sensing a certain weariness in his voice, I asked, "Sir, I need some guidance: how hard should I continue to push?"

I expected some measure of support. Instead, he replied, "Wes, I don't know."

I needed to keep Shelton with me in this. I knew that he, as a former commander himself, appreciated what it felt like to be on the hook for the operation without the resources and authorities to complete the mission. Regardless, I just couldn't let up. Pushing to escalate and intensify was the strategy. There was no real alternative.

In the middle of the struggle over target approval, we had another incident in the continuing Serb campaign against our presence in Macedonia: three American soldiers were fired on and disappeared. It was the first loss among ground forces. A quick reaction force was dispatched immediately, as well as a British search helicopter, but the missing team was nowhere to be found.

Later that evening, we learned our soldiers were in Serb captivity, under interrogation, with their actual condition unknown. I explained to Secretary Cohen that it was almost certain the men had been kidnapped. After talking to the chain of command, I was fairly confident they hadn't strayed over the border. This was the kind of thing the Serbs were very good at, and from discussions on the margins at Dayton, I knew they doubted our resolve to withstand any casualties. This was their way of fighting back.

The kidnapping of our soldiers reinforced for me the need to work strategically against the Serbs. One resource we most needed was the Apache task force to help us intensify strikes against Serb ground forces. When Secretary Cohen first spoke to me, several days into the war, I asked for his support, but he didn't know I had asked for the Apaches. ("The first I've heard of it," he had said.) Subsequently, he arranged a video teleconference together with Shelton and the Service Chiefs on the evening of April 1, focused on the Apache issue. After my conversations with Hugh Shelton, I was under no illusions about the

steepness of the hill in securing Pentagon approval, but I was determined to engage the Secretary on this issue. In fact, if the Apaches had
been approved when I first asked for them, I thought, they would be
arriving about now.

At 8:00 P.M. on April 1, Lieutenant General Jay Hendrix and Major
General Dave McKiernan arrived to join me for the briefing of the
Apache mission to the Secretary of Defense, the Chairman of the Joint
Chiefs, and all the Service Chiefs, which was scheduled to begin at
11:30 P.M. I was glad to have a few hours to look over the details we
would present and to collect my thoughts, because as soon as I saw the
draft brief, I could see the influence of the reluctant Army mind-set in
Washington at work. In the section on risk, the briefing simply listed,
in a column that went for two or three pages, all the weapons that were
capable of perforating the skin of an Apache helicopter. This wasn't
risk, I thought; this was just a way of saying, "Don't do the mission."

"Jay, do you guys want to do this or not?" I asked. "If you don't, just
say so; don't submarine it in the briefing. What is it, I want to know." I
was disturbed.

"Sir, we can do this mission," Hendrix replied strongly. "We just
were showing some of the dangers involved, and, anyway, these slides
can be changed."

"Then fix this so that we address the risks the right way. We have to
manage those risks, find ways to mitigate them—not just throw up
some inflammatory lists and pass the problem upstairs. I can guarantee
you that if we don't want to do this mission, then no one else in Washington will."

I knew I was asking a lot. In the corporate mentality of the Army,
we had learned seldom to volunteer to do missions. It was part of the
Vietnam hangover. The standard reply was, "We'll do it if you direct
us, sir, but here are the risks," and we always managed to convey that if
you direct us to do this, then you'll be responsible for the losses. But
weren't we responsible for a sensible plan mitigating risks?

Hendrix and McKiernan redrafted a few slides in short order. Hendrix was prepared to take the responsibility for the mission, and so was I.

As we went into the VTC room, the atmosphere was heavy. I took
my place at the center of the semicircular table, and put Hendrix on
my right and McKiernan on my left. I was uneasy about having to press

so hard for support. The system came on and I looked into the screen at the wall of grim faces, with the Secretary in the center. The view was anything but comforting. They were six or eight around the table, and a few others in the background. This was feeling like a trial, with a tough-minded jury, and I was going to have to defend the plan at almost midnight and by VTC.

I began with a brief recap of how I saw the situation. Hugh Shelton and I had been in continuing communication. I had already discussed the concept with Shelton, and knew that he supported us. But it had been difficult to break free to update the Service Chiefs. For everyone else's benefit, I sketched out the Apache concept myself, describing how the helicopters would be used to cross the border into Kosovo and attack the Serb ground forces. I wanted to make it clear that I was behind the request, not just escorting Jay Hendrix into the courtroom. I then asked Hendrix to cover the plans in detail.

His briefing was straight doctrine, exactly what we'd been developing for years in the Army: penetrate behind enemy lines and attack enemy forces. We would go in with lots of Air Force and Army support; fighter aircraft and artillery would suppress the enemy; electronic warfare would blind the radars. We would rely on unmanned aerial vehicles to find the targets, and we'd go at night. The target areas were well within the ranges of the Apaches. And we had an extraordinary amount of Air Force and national level support available.

It was true that there were no U.S. forward ground units, a departure from how we had trained, but there was a defined border, and we knew where to begin suppressing potential air defenses. It was also true that we couldn't yet guarantee what the targets would be—but if we waited to deploy until the targets were identified and approved by the Pentagon, we would always be too late. In fact, in every exercise we ran, the biggest challenge was always finding the targets, and you could never guarantee them in advance. I was confident in the soundness of what we were presenting.

The first question was about how many losses we might suffer. That wasn't a neutral question. If your first focus is losses, then you're not thinking about winning, I figured. Everyone in the teleconference knew that predicting losses was just guesswork. I retraced why we needed the Apaches, concluding they would buttress the air campaign and reduce the likelihood we'd have to deploy ground forces. Hendrix estimated that the losses might run from none up to 5 percent, but stressed there was no way of accurately estimating them.

After this discussion, the Chiefs began to raise other issues. Surprisingly, the Army Chief was absent. Instead, General Ric Shinseki, now the Army Vice Chief after having commanded in Bosnia, and the insider choice to be selected to be the new Army Chief in June, was representing the Army. He read off the official Army position. There were policy concerns and operational concerns. What about the prohibition on ground troops? Why Albania and not Macedonia? Didn't that raise force protection problems? Wouldn't using the Apaches broaden the conflict? Did we have enough support? Where was the detailed analysis of the Serb air defense threat and the ground forces we were targeting? Why not more helicopters?

When a service doesn't support the use of its own assets in combat, assets developed over two decades and at a cost of billions of dollars, there's no end to the detail of the questions that can be asked. I had been forewarned, but to listen to the Army's questions was still painful. The policy questions were up to Washington, though since Hugh Shelton had offered the Apaches, I believed that he should address those concerns. As for how many were needed, and how to use them, this was ultimately about professional competence and command judgment. This was the very kind of situation that the 1986 Goldwater-Nichols legislation intended to address by enhancing the authority of the theater commander in relation to the Service Chiefs. I refuted each reservation and insinuation and restated a forceful case for the Apaches.

Then it was the turn of the Air Force and the Marines. There were questions, and our answers, but no indication of support. The issues went from mundane detail to the very legitimacy of the campaign and our strategy, though the strategy had never actually been laid out and agreed to by Washington. It was clear that the Services' objections were affecting Secretary Cohen. I repeated a strong request for the Apaches. And then the VTC was over.

I went home and tried to sleep. It was for me the most difficult moment of the war thus far. In one sense this was simply the latest effort in a week of pushing hard to escalate the campaign in order to bring the operation to closure. But it was also the culmination of almost two years of trying to ensure NATO success in the region, despite a reluctant Pentagon.

The next day Hugh Shelton told me that the Apaches were likely to be approved for deployment, despite the objections of most of the Chiefs, though he cautioned that this was tentative. I was also encouraged by the news from Brussels that there would be no Easter bombing pause. Shinseki called to say that he personally supported the deployment decision.

In Washington the dynamic appeared to be shifting. Having struggled in the early part of the week with whether to approve intensified strikes, and having ruled out any intent to use ground forces, the Administration was now anxiously pushing for heavier strikes. Can you use more pilots? Why are you hitting the same targets again? And there was no sympathy for bad weather. It was clear that the strategic bombing advocates were gaining the upper hand in the interagency discussions.

I was certainly willing to take more resources and go after more targets. We already had studies under way to determine how many additional aircraft we would need. But we also knew that a much broader effort was needed.

That Friday afternoon, I pulled my four-stars together for a private, commanders-only VTC. The issues were fundamental. Were we meeting our military objectives? How were these linked to the political objectives? What were the political objectives? What is the end-state? When could we reach it?

Monty Meigs was concerned about the pace of events, and our ability to respond. As he saw it, Milosevic was doing everything he could to destabilize Bosnia, too. Meigs was right; NATO needed to decide and act quickly. Allied Force wasn't unfolding like the Gulf War or the military textbooks taught us.

There was a deep concern about our overall strategic position. John Jumper was especially articulate. "We watched the buildup and invasion," he said, referring to Milosevic's actions. "He acted under the strategic deception of peace talks. Now we're hitting things and he's killing people. What we're doing looks like retribution, and I don't feel the support at the political level."

Each of the commanders was plugged into Washington, talking with his subordinates, and watching the media and press. In modern war, high-level issues seep deep into military organizations. You can't fence off a command.

So, will this bombing campaign be effective in breaking Milosevic's will? I asked. That's what it was really about. The commanders' assessment was grim: No, not for a very long time. No one could accuse us of overconfidence, I thought, but their candid views were a necessary prelude.

We next covered about our own processes within the command, and what we needed to improve. Then we signed off. I thought it was a critically important session, to help them see the big picture and strengthen our efforts. Four-star generals and admirals have a lot of experience; they don't do as well when they're "just working their lane." Neither does a command. You have to create a sense of shared responsibility and teamwork at the top. In this case, they had reinforced my conviction that we had to have a ground option to fall back on, and that the air campaign would take a long time.

A new factor was at work as well: the mass expulsions of Kosovar Albanians. The Serbs had begun organizing trainloads of Albanians from Pristina, the capital of Kosovo, rounded up at gunpoint off the streets or from their homes, some robbed and raped in the process, and shipping them south to be dumped at the border with Macedonia. Mike Jackson was estimating up to 40,000 refugees on the northern side of the main road from Pristina. Jackson reported that the government ministries in Macedonia were not coordinating well and that the UNHCR didn't have a grip on it, either. It was, he concluded, "without a doubt a serious situation."

Our figures were already showing some 540,000 internally displaced or refugees, including over 100,000 in Albania and almost 50,000 already in Macedonia.

At 3:00 A.M. on Saturday, April 3, I received a call from Mike Jackson. "President Gligorov has called me in to complain about NATO's lack of assistance with the Albanian refugees from Kosovo," he reported. "They are entering by the tens of thousands. The Macedonian government is in danger of collapse. He has ordered me to vacate all the facilities occupied by our force so that refugees can be settled there. And he has asked that you call him at 9:00 A.M. What should I do about leaving the facilities? If I pull out, we'll really be in a mess."

Milosevic had no doubt been behind the burnings of the embassies in Skopje last week. He had probably kidnapped our three soldiers. Now he was using refugees to destabilize the country. What all the pressure from Serbia hadn't been able to do, tens of thousands of Albanian refugees could: they could split the government apart, and the country with it. Macedonia was Yugoslavia's deep battle. If Milosevic could knock it out of the war, NATO would be driven away from his southern border, lose its base areas, and forfeit any realistic ground option.

The phone call with President Gligorov was going to be critical, I knew. We had a relationship. He trusted me. We connected a little after noon. "Mr. President," I said, "please be sure that NATO is going to help you. In fact we're not only going to help you, we are going to make you successful. Our goal is to create conditions so that the refugees can return to their homes. They will not remain in Macedonia." When he forced the issue, I told him that we would evacuate our facilities at Camp Able Sentry, near the airport outside Skopje. It was a stall for time, as well as an effort to avoid the issue being raised at higher levels.

Gligorov was listening on the phone, but I wasn't getting much feedback. I pressed harder. "Mr. President, we will do everything possible to support your country, you, and your vision for a democratic Macedonia. You must tell your people that it is Milosevic, not NATO, that is causing these difficulties."

I could tell I was succeeding when he replied, "Exactly."

I also knew that Mike Jackson was strongly opposed to giving up facilities. He was right, from a military point of view. Our facilities would make little difference in accommodating the refugees—we just weren't occupying that much space. And at the very time the ARRC and its elements were most needed, they would have been involved in relocating and taking care of themselves. But politically the promise was necessary to shore up the Macedonian government. We would have to sort out the space for refugees as we went along.

Meanwhile the struggle to intensify the air campaign continued. We'd clearly achieved a break in the logjam of the target approval process within Washington. We had over a hundred targets now ready to be struck—radio relay sites, barracks, ammunition bunkers, minor bridges, and petroleum storage. Washington was preparing to authorize me to approve on my own any targets that were projected to generate only small numbers of accidental casualties.

The problem was that these targets were unlikely to be decisive. Unless we could truly destroy all of Milosevic's stored ammunition and fuel, take out all his communications, block all of his roads, and so on, we were degrading and disrupting him, but not decisively. I knew that eventually we would run out of easy-to-strike targets, or that Milosevic would receive improved air defense equipment, or that the NATO governments' patience with the air campaign would run out.

I had begun reiterating the limitations of the campaign, setting the stage for the move to a ground option, if necessary, and keeping the pressure on for more target approvals. I reminded Joe Ralston that we weren't having the desired effect with the air campaign. I also talked to Hugh Shelton about the need to begin to consider preparing a ground invasion. I had heard that the ground option had been taken up at the White House, despite the President's statement the week before that he had "no intent" to put ground forces into Kosovo in advance of an agreement. No one "wanted" to use ground troops. It would be far preferable if we could do the job with airpower, but having the ground option ready to go would apply great pressure against Milosevic.

Most of the Americans had begun to believe that the quickest way to win the air campaign was to break Milosevic's will through strategic strikes at the elements he used to direct and support the repression in Kosovo and to maintain himself in power. These were the politically sensitive targets: top headquarters, communications and the television stations (part of his command and control network), the presidential residences and retreats (with their bunkers and communications), the electric power system, and other key targets in Belgrade. Here we were still ensnarled in political approvals.

The French in particular wouldn't budge on the sensitive targets. It was too soon, they said. My French liaison officer explained the French doctrine, and what he believed to be the view of their president, Jacques Chirac: the best way to pressure Milosevic was to ensure that he had more to lose in the future than he had already lost. In other words, they seemed to be saying, if he feels like he's already lost everything, he'll have no incentive to stop. It was plausible, I thought, but we were a long way from that point. And if we didn't increase the pressure on him, our own people would grow discouraged.

On this issue we were exposing what I came to understand as a fundamental difference within the Alliance on the nature of the campaign. The United States was increasingly committed to the idea of strategic strikes, going after the heart of Milosevic's power. The Europeans, or at least the French and a few others, were more interested in limiting the strikes to Kosovo, trying to hit the ground forces, and avoiding actions that might antagonize or damage Serbia further.

Obviously we had to work on both sets of actions. If we couldn't quickly break Milosevic's will with strategic strikes, then we had to take away his capabilities to fight in Kosovo. Losses to his forces there might also affect his willingness to continue. I had to keep pushing to intensify the strikes on both strategic and tactical sets of targets.

The weather also continued to bedevil us. On Friday night, we aborted almost all of our strikes, and the forecast was bleak for the next few days. The aircraft weren't that flexible. If we planned for a set of strikes in the south and the weather was bad there, but good in the north, then we simply forfeited the use of those aircraft for that period. We were also trying to operate on a seventy-two-hour cycle, so if certain strikes were canceled on a Friday, they couldn't be restruck until Monday or Tuesday. The whole operation came to seem like some kind of unpredictable roulette game. If we bet on the weather, planned the target, and the weather was poor, we lost the strikes and wasted the aircraft that night. If we planned the same targets for the following night, anticipating the possibility of poor weather on the first effort, but were able to complete the strikes as originally planned, then we probably lost the use of the aircraft on the following night. The most flexible assets were the missiles—they could be re-targeted in a few hours—but they were best suited for the high-value, politically sensitive targets that I couldn't get approved.

It was little wonder that the political leaders and some of the press were complaining that the strikes weren't intense enough. We used the best planning system that we had in the Air Force, but it didn't do well with bad weather. I began to think that we had learned the wrong lessons from the forty-four-day air campaign in the Gulf War, which didn't have to face such weather-related problems in the desert.

However, the Air Force was getting rough treatment from some of the desk jockeys and so-called experts back in Washington, which was a bad rap. The truth was that this was a theater with significant distances, no matter how small it might look on a map. Each mission for one of the single seat F-16's, for example, was the equivalent of taking off in Washington and flying almost to Chicago before facing Serb defenses. Then flying through hostile airspace, and returning to Washington. Usually two air-to-air refuelings were required, and flying times of five, six, seven, or more hours were routine. On a sustained basis, it wasn't possible to crank out two missions per aircraft per day.

We also maintained a healthy respect for the Serb Air Force. Of course, if we could catch the planes airborne, they were no match for us, but this meant that we had to maintain air-to-air interceptors airborne around the borders of Yugoslavia twenty-four hours a day, along with the big AWACS aircraft, the Boeing 707s with the radar dish on top. The Serbs had already tried once to strike our troops in Bosnia. We didn't want any other similar efforts to stand a chance.

One problem we had avoided was unintended civilian casualties. We had been careful in picking the targets, the cruise missile planning had been exquisite, and the pilots had been careful and, perhaps, lucky. But I remembered the impact from the Gulf War when the Air Force targeted a command bunker, and inside it several hundred Iraqi civilians were killed. I also remembered the problems during Somalia and other operations when we were shooting or operating in close proximity to civilians. We knew we had to take extraordinary measures to ensure that we reduced to a minimum the chances of accidental injury to civilians.

The system we had put in place had worked well. Basically, we knew the accuracy and the radius of damage of each of our bombs and missiles. Using precision photography and sophisticated modeling of the explosion, we were able to accurately project damage to structures, window breakage, and even eardrum rupture. We then adjusted weapons, delivery angles, and, in many cases, simply didn't strike targets that would have risked significant civilian injuries. It was these calculations, among others, that the President was using in determining whether to approve our targets.

But now, after ten days of the campaign and over one hundred targets attacked, the choices were getting more difficult. Many of the most lucrative, isolated targets had been struck. The remaining targets were often in more populated areas, some with houses or apartments nearby. If we were going to ratchet up the campaign, we were going to have to accept the risks of increasing numbers of unintended civilian casualties. It worried me, but I worried more about the prospect of the air campaign losing momentum and having to be completed with a ground invasion of Kosovo. That would be far more destructive.

On the morning of Easter Sunday, April 4, I reviewed the situation with my commanders. Collectively, we sensed that events were moving in our favor, despite the continuing poor weather. Mike Jackson reported that we were achieving cooperation with the U.N. in dealing with the refugees and that the Macedonian government had settled down, even though we had decided in the end not to give up our barracks after all.

In Bosnia, SFOR had severed the Serb rail link into Montenegro, using explosives to sever a section of the line that cut through a corner of Bosnia. In the upside-down logic of the Balkans, the hard-line Bosnian Serbs chose to interpret this action as SFOR's way of trying to provoke a confrontation so that SFOR would have an excuse to destroy the Bosnian Serb military. After Monty Meigs had described this rather surprising interpretation, he said, this is a way of saying to the Serbs to stay home and in your barracks. "That's called deterrence," I said.

The EUCOM commanders were equally upbeat. The weather was about to break for a few days. I was keen to take advantage of this period to put maximum pressure on Milosevic, and we were still pumping out targets for the President to approve. Our flexibility in using the missiles was improving, making us more responsive in following up on current intelligence. The aircraft carrier USS *Theodore Roosevelt* was returning to the area, and it appeared we would be able to fold it into the campaign. Deputy Secretary of State Strobe Talbott had arrived in the region to assess and reassure the regional governments. It was the diplomatic assistance we had been seeking for several days.

It was Easter, and we were still bombing. NATO resolve had survived, despite the concerns of the Pope and several nations. The political end-state was being defined, and the NATO nations were toughening their expectations. Now, it was likely that the Serbs would have to pull all their military and police out of Kosovo, allow the refugees to return home, and accept an international military presence on the ground.

President Clinton called from Camp David as well, just to wish us Happy Easter, and encourage us to stay with it.

Above all, we had a sense from the press and public reaction that Milosevic had made a serious strategic blunder by pushing the Kosovar Albanians out of Pristina. It was a galvanizing moment for public opinion, and the sight of such human misery was certain to bring additional support to NATO.

In reviewing the press coverage that morning, I noticed a revealing article in *The Washington Times*, which described a tug of war between the European Command and the Central Command over the aircraft carrier *Theodore Roosevelt*. It was probably a leak by the Navy, to justify the importance of its carriers, but perhaps it illustrated what was really going on within the Joint Staff, unknown to me at the time. If so, it was a replay of other struggles, from other wars, as one theater commander competed against another for key assets like landing craft, the latest fighters, or long-range bombers. However, the difference was that there was the only one commander at war.

Hugh Shelton called in the early afternoon to discuss his concerns with the Allies. He spoke of the frustrations of clearing targets with the other NATO governments. Someone in Washington was pressing to hit the electric power targets not later than tomorrow, Allies or not. "Please don't break with NATO over this," I urged. "If we blow up a couple of transformers, without NATO approval, some of the Allies may walk away from this thing. Just keep the pressure on, and stay steady." He and I both knew that we had to keep NATO as a whole engaged, but we were both impatient. We knew there was, somewhere, a political limit as to how long we could extend the campaign.

Shelton put another issue on the table as well: formal planning for an effort to prevent or strike back if Milosevic went after Montenegro. Over the last week, concerns for Yugoslavia's other republic had grown increasingly prominent. We had hit targets in Montenegro at the start of the campaign—we had had no choice, since the air defenses there were a vital part of the Serbs' integrated air defense network. But almost immediately various countries had begun to object. Now we weren't getting any targets cleared in Montenegro. Instead, we were treating Montenegro almost as an Allied country. We had already struck at bridges designed to make it more difficult for Milosevic to move his forces into Montenegro. And we had sent SFOR to disrupt the sole rail line from Serbia into Montenegro. More detailed and systematic planning was needed, but we had to recognize that, however much the politicians might believe that Montenegro was friendly, there were Serb forces there actively opposing us, including radars, antiaircraft missiles, the command and control for several thousand Serb troops.

As the new week began, the fissures between the American and European views were becoming more pronounced. The NATO ambassadors wanted to know why we weren't doing better against the ground forces and wanted to know why the Apaches weren't arriving sooner, since the Pentagon announcement about the Apaches a few days earlier had really raised expectations.

On the ground in Kosovo the situation was worsening. The number of refugees and internally displaced was over 350,000, and the Serb military were continuing their attacks against the KLA. Tension was building inside Montenegro, too, as President Djukanovic tried to maintain his power in the face of Milosevic's pressures.

For my part, I was pushing for success against the ground forces, an effort that I considered the top priority of the campaign. It was a political, legal, and moral necessity. The world was watching as the Serb military was creating the refugees. European political leaders were having to defend the bombing to their domestic publics without seeing any effects on the Serb ethnic cleansing machine. The U.N. Security Council Resolution being cited as our legal authority was addressed to the humanitarian situation. It seemed to me that we simply ought to do as much as we could do to relieve the direct pressure the Serbs were putting on the Kosovars. How could we morally justify not striking at the Serbs on the ground, if we had the ability to do so?

Attacking the Serbs' military machine and police in Kosovo also made excellent military sense. We wanted to go after Milosevic's "centers of gravity," the sources of his power and strength. But in the end, it was the support of these organizations that was critical to Milosevic's grip on power in Serbia.

I had seen first-hand Milosevic's keen interest in and knowledge of military matters. He had been in the Army reserves for years, and became a well-trained and educated reserve officer. I knew that he had been trying to insert his men into the top leadership positions in the Armed Forces and that he already dominated the police. And I knew that when he couldn't work through certain leaders, he worked around them, skipping echelons in the chain of command to drop down and give specific orders when necessary. He couldn't stand to have these forces seriously hurt.

The way I looked at it, the point of the campaign was either to break Milosevic's will (or the will of his supporters) or, ultimately, deny him the capability to continue the ethnic cleansing in Kosovo. On the strategic level, we continued to push for approval to attack the strategic communications targets, including TV stations, key bridges, and electric power stations—high-profile elements of Milosevic's system for command, control, and sustainment of the Armed Forces in Yugoslavia. That was one center of gravity. But the Serb ground forces were another center of gravity, and they were the priority.

TEN

THE STRATEGIC BATTLEFIELD

AS THE STRESS and frantic pace of the first ten days gave way to the more steady and intense work of the campaign, some of my American commanders subscribed to a more doctrinaire view of the conflict. In this view Milosevic was an uncaring leader, a man who would be unaffected by losses among his military and police. This was the classic view of the American airpower adherents, combined with a perception of the parallels between Saddam Hussein and Milosevic–only the bombing of strategic targets was going to be effective. Forget about attacking the Serb forces in Kosovo.

This view was conveniently buttressed by the obvious difficulty the Air Force was having in attacking the Serb ground forces. As Mike Short said to me, "Boss, you show me the targets, and we'll strike 'em." But we were going to rely on the Air Force to find the targets. In practice this meant seeking additional means of information, a new way of processing intelligence, more flexible mission planning, potentially higher risks from Serb antiaircraft fire during the attacks, and higher risks of costly mistaken attacks on civilians or friendly elements on the ground.

This was also the classic struggle between Army leaders, who want the Air Force to make a difference in the fight on the ground, and some adherents of airpower, who saw airpower as strategically decisive, without recourse to the dirty business of ground combat. It was a struggle impelled by the losses in the trench warfare of World War I. Everyone sought another, better way of fighting than that.

In a way we were reliving the old tensions of the post-World War I era, and of World War II, when the advocates of strategic bombing fought against the ground force commanders for the resources and independence to go after German strategic industry and Japanese cities in an effort to preclude long and costly ground campaigns. Also, we were reliving especially the lessons of the Gulf War, when a long air campaign had preceded a short ground operation and, in the process, persuaded the analysts of the virtues of "precision strike" with laser guided bombs and missiles against key Iraqi targets.

The disagreement about what to strike, and in what priority, crossed another old battleground as well: the dichotomy between political aims and military means. It is in the nature of senior military officers to grouse about the political aims and restrictions of an operation, since these aims and restrictions define the military tasks and responses. Correspondingly, diplomats and politicians often chafe at the military's performance.

What made this situation deeply personal was that I operated in both worlds. As SACEUR I had more than purely military responsibilities–I was a close adviser to Secretary General Solana on the overall policy and strategy of NATO's effort in the Balkans, had frequent discussions with NATO ambassadors and ministers, and of course conferred regularly with General Klaus Naumann. In these conversations I offered advice on the political and military situation inside Serbia, as well as on NATO's military capabilities and requirements. I had to say whether particular strategies could work, considering both the political world above me and the military structures and capabilities. Obviously I couldn't control decisions at the political level, but my comments could affect them. It was the nature of the job to engage both levels within NATO, though I was never certain that the Pentagon understood this.

I was also charged with implementing the political decisions. As the top military commander, I would be held responsible for the military success or failure in the NATO operation.

Thus I was deeply involved in the process that gave me the orders that I then had to execute. I understood precisely why it was necessary to go after the Serb military and police forces. But some of my American subordinates just didn't agree. It was a strictly "professional" disagreement. There was an impact on the command as we moved deeper into the campaign. Compared to the whole-hearted Air Force work against the strategic targets, there was an inertia in adjusting and innovating to attack the Serb military machine in Kosovo, an inertia manifest in several ways. Problems with weather, with massing aircraft, or with the threat from Serb antiaircraft systems always seemed more troublesome when the object was to attack the ground forces than when it was to attack the strategic targets.

I found myself doing a lot of explaining about what was happening at the political level, as though my subordinate commanders would agree with me if they understood what I understood. I recognized that I was being extraordinarily candid, far more so than would have been expected. I hoped it helped.

Because we were having to devise new methods, I was interested in every detail of the fight against the Serb military and police forces in Kosovo. Our lack of early successes gnawed at me, especially before each video teleconference, when I would ratchet up my determination to make an impact and take the command where it needed to go.

I found myself reiterating our priorities again and again. "You must impact the Serb forces on the ground." "Do you understand that attacking the Serb forces on the ground is my top priority?" "We're going to win or lose this campaign based on how well we go after the ground targets." I also worked indirectly, through those in my command who clearly did understand, and wanted to press home the attack.

Many times I found myself working further down into details than I would have preferred, in an effort to generate the attack effectiveness against the ground forces that I knew we needed. "Can't we keep the aircraft on station longer, by letting them refuel again, while we wait for the weather to clear?" "Can't you get more aircraft into the airspace by splitting it three ways instead of two, and stacking the aircraft overhead?" "Isn't there some way we could entrap that SA-6, make him turn on his radar and take him down?" "Why can't we use the AC-130 gunships from a greater range?"

The Apaches turned out to be unexpectedly contentious within the command. "Too risky to use—the gain wouldn't be worth it." It was said forcefully, though not to me, by some of those who had never worked with Apaches, didn't know the doctrine, or didn't appreciate how to mitigate the risks. And it was said even after the approval of the deployment. It was partly, at least, a problem of crossover skills and knowledge between services. It was similar to my debating submarine tactics with a submariner, or telling a fighter pilot what kind of maneuvers to use to defeat a certain type of antiaircraft missile. I listened, but I had confidence in the outstanding Apache team we had assembled. The V Corps deep battle team, which would develop targets and direct the Apache strikes, had just been validated on its annual exercise as probably the finest in the Army. And we were joined by Brigadier General Richard Cody, who had led the first Apache missions against Iraq and was reputed to be one of the most competent trainers and leaders in the Army. With Cody there, and senior leadership from Jay Hendrix, I was confident that we weren't going to attempt anything beyond the capabilities of the aviators and our equipment.

Moreover, like any good submariner or fighter pilot I had confidence in my own judgment. I had worked extensively with Apaches, had helped develop the doctrine for their use at Fort Irwin at the National Training Center and with the Battle Command Training Program at Fort Leavenworth, evaluated their lessons from the Gulf War, and had commanded and trained them in my division at Fort Hood.

I knew that the questions about the extraordinary efforts I was making to go after the ground forces were being reported to the Pentagon. I could hear some of the issues that I answered with my own commanders raised again by members of the Joint Chiefs in the occasional calls we had. And I could sense, in the way the United States so strongly supported the strategic bombing and more weakly supported the campaign against the Serb ground forces in Kosovo, the ongoing under-current, back into the Pentagon from within my command. I could also sense it from some of the press comments that were written about alleged "micromanagement."

In fact, it was a two-way dialogue, as some of the political uncertainty and military reluctance in Washington and in the press was impacting my command. Some could sense that the support from their own services in Washington wasn't there. Some disregarded that, and soldiered on. Others were buffeted, dubious, and sometimes resistant, as they sensed the doubt, hesitancy, and differing perspectives in Washington. Longstanding loyalties and personal relationships were at stake, as always, as well as the accomplishment of the immediate mission at hand. But the issues always came out as professional, not personal.

One member of my team told me, "Sir, I'm concerned with the political implications that have to be worked from the top down." It wasn't really his concern directly, though I appreciated his sensitivity to it. But what I really needed were his military recommendations from the bottom up. Everything was crossing my desk.

For each of us, it was a difficult position. My American commanders all held responsibilities in their own services for command of their assets in the region. The Air Force commander reported to the Air Force Chief of Staff; the Navy commander to the Chief of Naval Operations, and so on. But the operations of the force were my overall responsibility.

Technically, all the operational recommendations were my responsibility, and protocol required all such communications to route through my headquarters. So far as I know, they did. But in practice, I suspected that when the service chiefs or their deputies asked their men, "How's it going?" they were obviously discussing the operations, too. I heard that this had happened within the Army channels during the Gulf War. There was probably a similar dialogue with the Joint Staff. And when the Joint Chiefs meet, they don't just work to meet every CINC's requirements, the way the books portrayed it to work; but they evaluate the requests as well, perhaps judging them against whatever dissonant voices emerged within the commands: In this day with the communications technologies and virtual organizations, you can't seal off commands. Nor, when issues are still open and under discussion, will everyone always have the same opinions.

Handling the Chiefs was actually Hugh Shelton's responsibility. I knew there were difficulties there, but it was his job to support the commander in chief in the field. My responsibility was to grow the command to meet its requirements during the operation, through coaching, training, and oversight. However, operating without a clear, agreed strategy or a strong, unified Washington made leadership feel like physical conditioning using some kind of "resistance training." It was like running in the loose sand on the beach. Ultimately, as the commander, I would bear the responsibilities for the outcome and for the command judgment on issues like targets, air reinforcements, and the Apaches, unless they were assumed by higher authority.

Despite their reservations on strategic targets, the NATO Allies were remarkably supportive of the air campaign. At the urging of Charles Guthrie, we gathered some of the NATO Chiefs of Defense together at my headquarters on April 6 to review the campaign to date. Both the Europeans and Shelton endorsed our actions and strategy, including putting the priority on attacking Serb ground forces, and supported my call for additional resources for the campaign. The key problem for them, they said, was to receive more information, faster, each day, so that they could keep their ministers informed. "We have to win the battle in the press," they said.

Congressional delegations began to arrive, too. Secretary Cohen and a few key senators came to Mons on April 7. I laid out the results to date, explained my priorities, described the additional targets that needed to be struck, and the need for additional aircraft. "What about ground forces?" one senator asked.

"We may need them at some point, but let's give this air campaign time to work," I answered, and explained that even if we had had ground forces standing by at the borders, we would not necessarily have pushed them in without giving the air forces time to work over our opponents.

"Then when would you want the ground forces?" he asked.

I didn't yet have a timetable worked out, but it was clear that we would need them before winter. "Senator, we will have to work backwards from any ground force objectives, considering how long it will take to ready and stage the forces, and so on. But we're probably several weeks away from having to make that call now." This was the question that put the problem in focus. We were going to have to move ahead in facing the ground force issue, because snow could begin falling in the mountains in October, only about six months away. We wouldn't want to fight a winter war.

The delegation was supportive, and after hearing the briefing, the Secretary told the press, "Whatever General Clark feels he needs to carry out this operation successfully, he will receive." It was a welcome public vote of confidence.

In the meantime I kept the pressure upward, seeking to get approval for the strategic target sets. There were three areas of contention: the TV system, the bridges, and the electric power. It was difficult to get political approval for striking the television stations, because strikes on television facilities seemed undemocratic and perhaps illegal. The bridges raised the specter of collateral damages. Serb civilians were still using them, and there was concern that these bridges weren't militarily relevant. The electric power was connected regionally—into Macedonia, Romania, and Kosovo itself, and there were humanitarian considerations. All these issues had to be addressed, but, as I discovered, there would almost always be reasons why any specific target should not be attacked. If we didn't continue to seek approvals, the air campaign would simply wither away irresolutely.

For each set of targets there were supporters and doubters. Positions shifted from day to day, and there was no clear authority for resolving the issues. I found myself sometimes applying pressure in any direction where I encountered resistance.

At one point I had secured French permission to attack the Serb television transmitter, as well as American approval, only to have NATO balk when some of the ambassadors questioned whether the target was truly military. Air Commodore David Wilby, my representative at the NATO press conferences, and I tried to craft a public explanation of the military value of the transmitters, which didn't succeed. And, of course, there were international newsmen in the stations of the Serb government television. Stronger resistance to attacking the television facilities emerged. This turned out to be a heavy blow to NATO's confidence in our support for its public information efforts, especially since we had mistakenly released information earlier in the campaign that several prominent Kosovar Albanians had been murdered.

Shortly after the press conference, Solana called. "This is unacceptable," he said. "There have been too many mistakes in public affairs. You must find a new spokesman."

I wanted to explain that if there were problems, I was responsible.

But he wouldn't budge. It was the most intense and determined that I had seen him, an indication of just how critical the public information operation was. But it was a hard blow, for I thought highly of Wilby, who had become a genuinely close member of my team.

The next day Jamie Shea announced that we would not be targeting the Serb television transmitters directly.

Intertwined with the targeting efforts was the requirement for additional forces. Our total number of aircraft had been constrained by the initial context and objectives of the operation. The operation hadn't been seen in its planning stages as the all-out attack on Serbia it was evolving into.

When I discussed the issue with Hugh Shelton, he was supportive. "Sure, we can get you additional assets," he said, "but just ask for them all at once. Don't incrementalize it." He was trying to dodge the charges from some in the press and in Congress that we were guilty of "incrementalism," that is, not using decisive force.

But how could we know all that we might need weeks and months hence? This was an operation designed essentially to break Milosevic's will. It might have to transform into a more conventional full-scale ground attack into Kosovo. So it was necessary to ask for a wholesale reinforcement of the theater.

My decision was jarring to some of my team. As one of my commanders told me, "We have a process challenge, not a resource challenge. We should not substitute force flow for strategy. We do not need additional resources."

Technically the commanders were right, for the moment. I knew they were haunted by the fear that they would be launching aircraft that had no targets to attack, and that they would be judged to have overreacted. But we needed to move simultaneously to fix the targeting problem and to bring in additional aircraft. There was also political leverage to be gained by announcing significant reinforcements. I was determined to show that we weren't going to allow the campaign to wither away.

We were already hard at work on the targeting issue. I wanted to expand our target base to some 2,000 targets. It was a large round number, large enough to get us past the daily struggle over the number of targets approved for that day. And I was pushing the targeteers to think broadly, to formulate plans to target the forces dispersed along the border with Hungary, the equipment in the garrisons at Novi Sad, the bridges and networks Milosevic was using to transfer fuel around the country.

Turning the information we had about Serbia into actual targets was a painstaking process. We first had to collect current photographic imagery, assess the actual construction and vulnerabilities of the targets, and develop the appropriate attack tactics. An important step in the process was to estimate the risks of accidental casualties if we struck and to repeatedly reconfigure our attack tactics, substituting the type and size of the weapons, to minimize this. The information architecture we had established, and especially the ability to pass detailed photographic images containing millions of bits of information, was enabling us to fight a new way. We were creating a virtual intelligence organization.

This was the essence of what all the theorists had been describing as the future of warfare. My intelligence officer, Brigadier General Neal Robinson, had created a vast, horizontally integrated team of experts. They were nominally working for many other commanders, but he was the actual coordinator. The work was being done collaboratively, in real time, in a multi-stepped process. Without the information technology, we would have had to pull together hundreds of people in one place. Instead we had a virtual organization.

But we were fighting a competent adversary. At the military level in Kosovo, the Serb military and police forces had step-by-step attacked the large base areas that the KLA had established in the forested mountains. Each day, the organized KLA resistance diminished. And this, in turn, meant that the Serb forces could reposition, disperse, and hide from our aircraft. After two weeks most of their large-scale operations were over. "Sir, those big base areas we were targeting just aren't there anymore," the staff reported. And, "there's just very little movement down there. When they see us coming, they hide."

"Just get twenty-four-hour-a-day dominance in the skies over Kosovo," I directed.

The constant attention and a spell of good weather over Kosovo were finally starting to produce some results against the Serb forces. Several trucks and vehicles carrying ammunition and fuel were attacked and destroyed.

In the meantime, the Serbs were playing a cagey political game. On April 6 Milosevic declared a unilateral cease-fire, saying that Serb operations had been completed. Unfortunately for Milosevic, the expulsion of the Albanians had gone too far in incriminating Serb conduct for a unilateral cease-fire declaration to have any political impact in the West. It was seen as the insincere gesture that it was.

I knew that an air campaign was a race of our destruction against Milosevic's improvisation, repair, work-arounds, and reconstruction. In Vietnam it had taken us too long to recognize that we were in a competitive game—we had to tear up the enemy's capabilities faster than he could rebuild them, and we didn't or couldn't do that. In Yugoslavia, we seemed to be winning, but we had to keep the pressure on and intensify it. And we still hadn't struck the important TV network, the presidential residences and bunkers, or the electric power.

Though I had had no real strategy discussion with Washington, we were working the strategy through NATO. In a meeting April 9 with Javier Solana and Klaus Naumann, I argued that we had to give the air campaign time to work, but that, frankly, it had not been designed, resourced, or conducted as necessary to rapidly degrade the Serb forces deployed to Kosovo. I warned that we would need several hundred more aircraft and several more weeks for the air campaign to have a chance of working. Even then, there was no guarantee. But, I said, an expanded air effort would be a necessary precursor to a ground campaign, and we would want to launch a ground campaign in July—which meant we had to make a decision to begin preparations in late April.

Solana fully supported quiet work on looking at options, military as well as diplomatic. But the work must be done discreetly, he said. Naumann reinforced my views, also adding that the air campaign was achieving results.

As we discussed the details of the various alternatives, we each recognized that the nations of NATO had not really accepted that we were at war. Going back to my Vietnam experience, I contended that war has a logic and dynamic all its own and that a strategy of half-hearted incrementalism was likely to fail. We needed to decide now on a political strategy, either cut losses and accept a deal with Milosevic or take all measures necessary, including an embargo on all trade and a major build-up of ground forces, to convince Milosevic and his followers they must pull back. But if we continued on the present course of incremental escalation, I warned, we were headed toward a protracted and potentially inconclusive conflict. There was a growing perception that NATO wasn't committed to winning, a perception that was already undermining our efforts.

Solana and Naumann listened, nodding, and adding issues for consideration. We each left with an appreciation that important decisions would have to be made before or during the NATO summit to mark the Alliance's fiftieth anniversary, which was scheduled to be held in Washington on April 23. I departed determined to accelerate the pace of our work on the ground options. I had less than two weeks until the summit.

I had another chance to make my case against incrementalism to Secretary of State Madeleine Albright in a one-on-one breakfast meeting on Monday, April 12. It had been a little over four weeks since our last meeting, before the war had begun.

"Well, Wes, it's up to you," she said as she sat down. "I've done my best, and they've called it my war, and they've turned on me. Now they'll turn on you." I didn't want to ask who "they" were; it was too painful.

"So, we did diplomacy backed by force, and now we're into force backed by diplomacy," she explained as she recounted the herculean efforts she was making to keep NATO foreign ministers committed to the effort. She agreed that we could not allow this conflict to become another Vietnam, and she supported my efforts to intensify the action against the Serbs.

"But Madeleine, can I just go back to something you said earlier? You know, thinking about Vietnam, and what we're doing today, do we really want to give up on the diplomacy right now? Even if we bomb him much harder, someone's still going to have to go in and close the deal. Isn't our leverage for diplomacy now even greater than it was when we were just threatening to use force?"

"Yes," she said, "but who's going to carry the messages in? Certainly not the Americans, and not our Allies."

"What about the Russians?" I speculated. Who better than the Serbs' best friends to tell them to surrender?

"Well, they won't even speak to us about it now," she responded. But she took it as a serious suggestion.

As she spoke to me I saw that we had been mislabeling much of what we had said: before the air strikes, we were using "diplomacy backed by threat." Now, as I saw it, as we were actually dropping bombs, we should be into "diplomacy backed by force." Only when we invaded, using ground troops to wrest Kosovo away from Serb control, could we say we were really using "force backed by diplomacy."

I used this formulation as I explained the current situation to the Service Chiefs and Secretary Cohen on April 13 in the first of what were to become twice-weekly VTCs with Washington. Although I had continuously worked to keep Shelton informed of my thinking, this was the first comprehensive discussion on strategy in U.S. channels, and my first opportunity, aside from the congressional visit, to lay out the big picture for the Secretary of Defense. This fight is coercive diplomacy, I explained, and took them through the stages and labels I had worked out during the meeting with Secretary Albright. I explained the requirements for intensifying the air efforts. I laid out what I saw was the need to go ahead with preparations for ground options, following discussion at the NATO summit, with preparations to begin thereafter. As the Chiefs raised their issues and questions, it was clear that the gravity of the situation had finally sunk in—this was a serious discussion. They followed my logic through the intensification of the air campaign, though some voiced concerns about potential Alliance support for a ground option. Still, I was encouraged that we were at least talking strategically.

We also had to deal with the challenge of minimizing civilian casualties, underscored by two recent incidents. The first was an attack on a railroad bridge near Leskovac on April 12. The pilot's mission was to take out the bridge, but a train happened to be approaching as the missile hit but failed to destroy the span. The pilot, thinking that the first missile had hit and halted the train, fired a second missile at the other end of the bridge, not realizing that the train had continued forward, into the missile's path. It was a tragic incident, with some ten people killed and many injured, according to Serb reports.

The second incident occurred two days later, as the weather began to clear over Kosovo, and our forward air controllers reported convoys of military and civilian vehicles interspersed. They also reported receiving ground fire. One of the forward air controllers watched a column snake toward Djakovica, stopping along the way to burn Albanian houses. Using his own weapons, he struck at one of the vehicles. Nearly simultaneously another forward air controller, several miles southeast, watched another column of 100 vehicles moving. He saw ground fire coming at him from what he believed to be the vicinity of the convoy. He also struck back, until the weather closed in.

Almost immediately there were Serb reports of civilian casualties, and by that evening pictures of a horribly mangled tractor were on CNN. We couldn't get further substantiation on the Serbs' actions. After a series of late-night discussions I called Solana early the morning of the fifteenth. "I think we did it," I said. "It seems to be a clear case of misidentifying the target, and I recommend we announce it at the news conference." This kind of bad news doesn't get better with age. Several days later, after some of my commanders and I had spent many hours sorting the information, we learned that two convoys, one north of Djakovica, one south, had been struck at nearly the same time. Several bombs from different aircraft had hit. There had apparently been military and civilian vehicles intermixed in at least one of the convoys. We couldn't confirm the casualty figures, but we did note that the scene of the second convoy wasn't presented to the media by the Serbs until the next day, and some elements appeared to have been rearranged. What was the truth? We may never know.

Around this same time, as we were bringing the Apache force to Albania, we were growing increasingly concerned about the nearby Serb air base at Podgorica, in Montenegro. For days we had been asking for authority to strike these forces, but we had been stopped at every turn by concerns, especially from the French, that we would undermine the tenuous grip on power maintained by Montenegro's Western-inclined president, Milo Djukanovic.

As a next best measure we had already established a combat air patrol over the Adriatic that might be able to intercept a large force if it were to stage and attack the growing international force at the airfield in Tirana, the capital of Albania.

I was pressing NATO and Washington hard. This was a matter of protecting our American and NATO forces.

The Germans mentioned something about a three-way phone call among the French minister of defense, the German minister of defense and Secretary Cohen, in which the French had agreed that Montenegrin targets could be struck if there was a risk to our forces. Meanwhile, French sources knew nothing of such a conversation.

On the afternoon of Thursday, April 15, Joe Ralston called in response to my requests for help from Washington: "Launch the aircraft against the airfield," he said. "Sandy Berger is making one final check; we'll call you back if necessary." When we got the word that the White House had approved the strikes, we went forward, with good results—the hangars torn up, radars destroyed, and the tunnel to the underground fuel storage destroyed.

The French were not happy with the strikes, and told me so. They wanted only "reactive" strikes, not "preventive" ones. But French troops weren't at risk there, either. And in the way that NATO operates, I had to accord the greater weight in decisionmaking to the countries most strongly affected. The North Atlantic Council in Brussels later endorsed the strike. It was a measure of the strength of the Alliance that the strong daily cooperation with France continued unaffected. And Djukanovic's government did not fall.

By the weekend the weather was uncertain again in Kosovo, but I was pleased to be traveling into the region for my first visit since the start of the campaign. Except for my occasional trips to Brussels, I had been chained to the VTC and the Red Switch secure telephone network since the start of the campaign. I was eager to see the airmen, check in with local leaders, and look at the situation on the ground in Tirana as our force was arriving there. I left Rupert Smith and Steve Abbott to handle the teleconferences and work with higher headquarters.

The visit to the field on April 17 was everything I hoped for: a chance to reassure the Macedonian and Albanian governments, a talk with the airmen, a look at Task Force Hawk and the Allied Command Europe Mobile Force (Land) as they were setting up in Tirana, and a chance to speak face-to-face with Mike Jackson, Jay Hendrix, and Mike Short.

Inside the big, dark presidency in Skopje, Macedonian President Kiro Gligorov gave us a cordial greeting in the reception room and then ushered us into his office. Gligorov was, as usual, composed, insightful, and supportive. Whereas a few weeks earlier he "would not allow the soil of Macedonia to be used for attacks on Serbia," he was now saying that he "would not permit the soil of Macedonia to be used for aggression against Serbia without parliamentary approval and public debate." He was sensitive to the need for a possible land campaign, though I explained that no decision had been made to conduct such an effort. His position was a step forward in my view, since he certainly wasn't intending to sponsor a vote he would lose.

In Albania, the reception was overwhelmingly positive. The young prime minister, Pandeli Majko, fluent in English, approved every request. May we use an additional airfield? Of course, use all airfields. May we repair the highway to Kukes? Please do so. And the road to Skopje? You may have all roads and all government facilities—take anything you need.

The defense minister, Luan Hajdaraga, escorted me throughout my visit, explaining how he had deployed his small Army, and was perpetually cheerful. The presence of the thousands of American soldiers was proof positive that NATO was committed and would win. Albania, in his view, was now saved. He was eager to see the Apaches lift off, and hear the sound of our rockets firing into Kosovo and Serbia.

Rinas Airfield, near Tirana, was bustling with activity of all kinds, both humanitarian and military. The parking aprons were full. But as I toured the facilities, there were clearly "two classes of citizens." On one side was the Air Force, with nifty, clean accommodations and a first-class field medical center. They were the first part of the American contribution to humanitarian assistance, part of our Joint Task Force Shining Hope, under the command of Air Force Major General Bill Hinton. On the other side of the runway, over a taxiway blocked by a French refueling operation, several hundred muddy, wet American soldiers were scrambling to set up close-in defenses and find enough dry ground to park their vehicles and pitch tents. It was a scene from any war—desperate, hustling, dirty soldiers, fully armed and equipped, nervous with uncertainty. In the distance I saw two female soldiers struggling to escape from the knee-deep mud that had immobilized their Hummer and its trailer. They were in full field gear, straining to move as the mud sucked at their overboots.

Walking toward us was a group of senior NCOs, looking uncertain, dropping their gazes, and trying not to see the highly visible party of senior officers moving toward them. Was it poor morale, I wondered, or were they just worried about the problem of whether to salute in the field? It was an old, familiar scene as I stopped the first of the senior NCOs.

It wasn't morale. "Sir, they told us not to salute here—it might be too dangerous," he said, referring to the idea that snipers might see the salutes and then target the officers. It was clear that he was committed to following the force protection orders he'd been given despite the obviously relaxed Air Force posture across the runway. I reassured him and encouraged him to take care of the two soldiers and their mired vehicle a few hundred meters down the runway.

I soon linked up with Jay Hendrix, who had flown in early in the deployment. He explained his plans for the layout of the field, pointed out the problem of the French refueling point (which blocked access from one side of the airport to the other), and discussed the force flow, training plans, and force protection issues.

There were delays with the deployment of the Apaches. The weather was difficult en route, and the Apaches themselves, flying from their bases in Germany and denied overflight of Austria, were making a long trek across France and through Italy to get to Albania. Finally, the size of the Task Force had grown to over 5,000 soldiers, as the Army leaders, with some encouragement from the Pentagon planners, had become ever more concerned about the proximity of Serb forces and the difficulty of defending the airfield against terrorists reported in the area. I wasn't unhappy to bring in more forces, but the truth was that we were far less exposed here in Albania than we would have been at the airfield near Skopje, within range of Serb rockets. Still, what had looked like an eight-to-ten-day deployment of 1,800 troops to Macedonia, as I had originally envisaged and requested, was now bringing three times as many soldiers to Albania, into the middle of a more complex security environment at an overcrowded airport struggling to meet humanitarian requirements. That it was going to take only three times as long as originally estimated struck me as remarkable. I still hoped Hendrix would be able to make the first Apaches ready for a mission before the NATO summit on April 24. But the chances were diminishing with each day of weather delay.

By Saturday night I was back at the chateau, well aware that we were less than a week away from the NATO fiftieth anniversary summit in Washington. This would be the key meeting that would review the results and set the course for the rest of the campaign, I reckoned. The air campaign was basically "on track" as I saw it, despite continuing difficulties with the weather. We now had a working system to strike Serb forces on the ground, the unmanned aerial vehicles were being integrated into the targeting process, and the flow of intelligence had improved greatly. We just needed good weather to apply our capabilities.

On the strategic axis, going against facilities in Serbia, we were definitely having an impact on ammunition and petroleum storage, roads and bridges, and the radio relay system.

There was still much to be done. Despite another week's pushing, we still hadn't received the go-ahead to strike the Serb TV. Nor were we permitted to go after the electric power. And the general flow of targets for approval in Washington was still slow at times. But I was particularly concerned now to deepen the isolation of Serbia. One method was to cut off all petroleum imports, while we were continuing to seek out and destroy oil storage as well as remaining portions of the refineries. The other method was to obtain clearance for NATO overflights of Bulgaria and Romania, thereby encircling the Serbs.

The petroleum problem was primarily legal. Laws of warfare were, strictly speaking, not fully applicable, since the NATO nations had not formally declared war. This meant that some countries were unable to take legal measures to stop the flow of oil into Serbia. France, in particular, wanted careful consideration of these legal concerns. Nor was France amenable to targeting the petroleum storage facilities in Montenegro, even though it was inevitable that Montenegrin facilities were being used to supply Serbia.

However, we were making real progress in achieving the aerial encirclement of Serbia. I wanted to send the message to Milosevic that he had no hope of a friendly neighbor as a conduit for resupply. We had been working on the issue informally for several days, and now high-level phone calls were taking place to "lock in" our understandings. We anticipated parliamentary and constitutional delays, but that was really the point of the request—to engage the political system and the public in Bulgaria and Romania. While our airmen were happy to have the use of the additional airspace, this would be much more important in later phases, as additional aircraft arrived, than it was now.

By Monday, April 19, refugees and displaced persons were totaling almost 900,000, with over 350,000 in Albania and 130,000 in Macedonia. And we had reports of over 250,000 persons displaced inside Kosovo, many of them hiding in the mountains without food and shelter, and driven back and forth by Serb operations. We had to move quickly to make operational in Albania the small NATO headquarters of Allied Command Europe Mobile Force (Land), or AMFL, as we called it, under the command of British Major General John Reith. And, thinking ahead to stabilize Macedonia and prepare for a possible land campaign, we had to orchestrate the flow of the Albanian refugees from Macedonia into Albania, out of the areas where they could be vulnerable to Serb artillery fire.

But my principal concern was to get ahead of the press of daily events by developing the idea of the ground option, an invasion of Kosovo itself. As I sat around in the evenings with my old friend and mentor, Ed Burba, and reflected on our progress in our meetings each afternoon with Dieter Stockmann and Rupert Smith, the ground option was constantly on our minds. There were limits as to what the air campaign could realistically achieve. Airpower could threaten, punish, destroy facilities, and attack forces on the ground. But without a ground force, there was no assurance that we could actually force Milosevic out of Kosovo. Break his will and the forces would leave, but whether we could do it from the air was simply unknowable.

A ground attack would represent a major new commitment, and major increases in costs and risks. But with our advantages in firepower, with the potential support of the Albanian population, and with favorable weather during the summer and early autumn, there was every reason to expect we could achieve a complete success in forcing the Serb forces to evacuate the province. More immediately, in my view, the decision to prepare for ground operations and the visible preparations would significantly raise the pressure on Milosevic. The Serb forces were one of his centers of gravity; the ground threat would strike at his own survival.

Finally, I had always believed that a military commander has to have a follow-on or back-up plan always. It would be irresponsible to grind ahead with an air campaign without planning a transition into ground operations.

I had laid out the case for this to Hugh Shelton a week earlier, and he had seemed to agree. In fact, the Army had already sent over a small planning team. The British and Canadian ministers of defense had already talked to me about the possibility of moving ahead to plan for the commitment of ground forces. And the press was full of speculation. Based on the timelines I had discussed with Shelton, I expected that this would be an important behind-the-scenes topic at the NATO summit. I wasn't interested in any formal announcements. I was just concerned about the need to get on with the preparations so that whatever we did could be completed before the autumn snows made passage across the mountains difficult.

On the afternoon of April 19, I spoke with Shelton again. I reminded him of the timelines, that troops would need to be deploying by June 15 in my estimation, and informed him that the topic was likely to come up in my meeting the next day with the Tony Blair, the British prime minister, who had scheduled a visit to SHAPE.

The conversation turned difficult as I talked about the need to work the ground troops issue at the summit and how I might help. "You're not coming to the summit, are you?" he asked in an alarmed tone. But this was customary and already scheduled. The entire Military Committee, of which I was a nonvoting member, was to attend. It had been in the plans for months. And I would give the key briefing on the operation to the heads of state. That was my responsibility.

"Of course," I said. "The SACEUR always comes to the summit, and besides, if we're working the ground option behind the scenes, and there's some selling to do—"

"If that option is going to be sold, it will be sold by the President, not by you," he said sternly. "Why are you coming to the summit?"

"I understand that this is the President's role," I said, "but in the past, the SACEUR has always presented the operation brief." This was so basic to the responsibilities of the commander, and to the relationships with the European military and political leaders and their governments that his resistance was surprising. We had finally come head-to-head about the responsibilities of my command.

In his view, perhaps, I was just a subordinate who should take military orders and leave the policy to the civilians. But in NATO it could never work that way. At the senior levels military action and policy making were totally intertwined, and I had to participate in both worlds. The summit was going to be the key location on the strategic battlefield, both for the policies and for the military plans. It was the decisive point. I could easily command for a day or two from Washington and from my aircraft, with its sophisticated communications equipment. But if the SACEUR wasn't present at the decisive point, it would be taken as an indication of problems within the command or worse, problems with the strategy and results of the operation. Further, the Europeans were aware of Washington's ambivalence about Operation Allied Force, and they were becoming increasingly aware of problems within the U.S. command channel. My presence at the summit could help correct that. And whatever needed to be done at the summit, I believed that I could help.

Shelton dropped the topic. The phone call ended with a further discussion of target sets and clearance procedures. But I took his comments as either a real lack of understanding of the role of the Supreme Allied Commander or some other underlying issue. Either way it was trouble.

A few minutes later Javier Solana called. He came straight to the point. "Sandy Berger has just called to tell me that Secretary Cohen is uncomfortable about your attending the summit. Do you have any idea why?" he asked.

I told him about my conversation with Shelton about ground forces and the summit.

Solana was thoughtful. "I see. Well, I have told Sandy that I must hear about this directly from Cohen," he said.

Solana was somewhat aware of the occasional challenges I had had in dealing with the Pentagon over the past year and a half, but I knew there were real limits as to how much help he could provide. He was also aware of my concerns about the need to start thinking seriously about ground forces.

I called in a few key advisers and asked them what they thought. They were unanimous in their recommendations. This was simply a critical issue. It wasn't personal, they said, but had to do with the position of Supreme Allied Commander as Eisenhower had established it and as eleven previous SACEURs had operated. For the first time, NATO was at war, and the position was functioning as designed. Sir, they told me, you have to go.

An hour or so later, Solana called back. "I have heard from Secretary Cohen," he said. "He does not want you to come to the summit. He feels you are too busy here to be spared. I have told him that you are the Supreme Commander, that I would relay his views, and that I will support whatever you decide. What is your intent?"

"I feel I need to go. I have to report on the operation to the leaders, regardless of whatever else is discussed," I said. Solana knew the significance of my attendance.

"Then I will support your decision, and I will inform Secretary Cohen," he said.

Because I was coming in my NATO capacity, Washington apparently didn't feel it could simply order me not to attend. Had they done so, I would have had no choice but to remain in Belgium. But as it played out, I was given the choice and took it. As I reflected on it, this was the continuation of almost two years of tension with the Secretary, the Chairman, or both stemming from the inherent requirements of the SACEUR position. Previous SACEURs had faced similar issues due to the unusual nature of the job. But I had never been able to convey to Shelton and Cohen what the job entailed in a way that they appreciated. Restraining my contacts with others in Washington, the media, and the Congress was one thing. Seeking to restrain my contacts within NATO itself was quite another matter. I was loyal to Cohen and Shelton. But at this point, caught up in the middle of an operation whose outcome was still in doubt, I had been given a choice. I was at the very fulcrum of the policies, the strategy, and the operations. If for no other reason, I had to go back to see people in Washington and at the summit face-to-face to hear and understand what people there wanted, and to explain my assessment and recommendations in a very fluid, evolving situation to NATO decisionmakers, including the Secretary himself.

In the meantime, work continued. Hugh Shelton called back to tell me that the Chiefs had agreed that planning should start for a ground operation, and that it should be NATO planning. Improving weather enabled us to intensify our strikes into Kosovo. We were still working with the French to try to get their approval to strike the electricity system, and we finally achieved French approval to strike the official Serb television transmitter in Belgrade, weather permitting.

We were trying to convey a degree of warning so that as many people as possible would leave the transmitter. The previous day we had planted a question at the Pentagon news briefing, hinting at a possible strike at the television facility; in response the Serbs had ordered all international journalists to report to the Serb television building. This was worrisome. The French then withdrew their approval to strike and authorized us to strike at Socialist Party headquarters and its TV station instead.

That Tuesday morning Prime Minister Blair arrived at SHAPE during the NATO VTC, spoke in inspirational terms to the commanders and staffs throughout the Alliance, and then moved to my office for a private meeting. As we sat down, he came right to the point. "Are we going to win?" he wanted to know.

"Yes, Prime Minister, we are going to win," I assured him. Twice. He looked at me searchingly. This was about will.

Then he leaned forward on the couch. "Good. European governments have a lot riding on this, you know." In other words, the outcome of this campaign was a lot more significant to the Europeans than to Washington.

He continued, "Now, are we going to win without ground troops?"

"I'll do everything possible to make it happen, but I can't guarantee it with air power alone," I said, and discussed the air campaign in more detail.

Then the Prime Minister wanted to know if we would be able to put together a proper plan to bring in ground troops and successfully take Kosovo. At that point I couldn't give him a full assessment, but said that if it came to ground troops, his support would be critical. I knew the British were leaning hard to push ahead for planning the ground option even though all of us hoped for victory short of that. I reviewed where we stood on the process of preparing and deploying ground troops. The timelines were very short.

From my perspective it was an excellent meeting, with the British Prime Minister seriously committed to winning and determined to do all he could to bring it about. He left assuring me of his support in moving the overall campaign forward.

By late evening the French had reversed course, approving strikes at a few of the high-value targets I had requested, including the television transmitter. The missiles struck right on target. The strike would dominate the news the next day; it showed NATO's resolve once more.

At the morning VTC on Wednesday, April 21, my commanders and

I discussed how to reinforce the air campaign with the several hundred additional aircraft that I had requested two weeks earlier. After intensive work, the package of requirements was about to go to Washington for approval. I saw the package as critical, not only to intensify the air campaign, but also to be positioned with aircraft sufficient to support a ground intervention in mid to late summer. If we were to decide for a ground option, I thought, at least we would have the necessary air power already in place. My commanders, on the other hand, were looking at the problem from a different level. They were trying to prevent a sudden influx of aircraft that might too rapidly consume the available supply of targets. They said they wanted an "orderly flow."

Jim Ellis in Naples and Mike Short in Vicenza knew exactly what was bothering Washington. Continuing questions were coming out of the Services, the Joint Staff, and from high-level civilians about the efficiency of the campaign. Why are you restriking the same targets? Why are you using the scarce all-weather precision munitions against airfield runways? Why can't you fly the aircraft more? These were good questions, all of which I had been dealing with, but they also reflected the central Pentagon problem of trying to manage a limited war that wasn't the top Pentagon planning priority and hadn't received full national commitment and support.

There were answers to each question. As far as the restrikes were concerned, each target had usually had several different aiming points—different buildings within the compound or different ammunition storage bunkers, for example. With precision weapons, you have to take out discrete targets; it's not "carpet bombing." When we restruck a target we usually were striking a new aim point.

The targeting issue had become the favorite "whipping boy" within the Pentagon. There simply weren't enough in queue or being generated to satisfy the air planners. I certainly wanted to generate more targets, but my more pressing concern was political approval to go after the sensitive targets aimed at the command and control at the source of the problem, Milosevic and his cronies—and we had many of these already—and then having enough aircraft and eyes overhead to dominate the skies twenty-four hours a day. I believed that the very presence of the additional aircraft in theater would lead to new approaches to targeting, to make use of these assets at our disposal.

But the disjuncture in perspective between SHAPE and Washington was enormous. I was trying to achieve sufficient strategic leverage against Milosevic to break his will. For me the short-term efficiency was important, but ultimate effectiveness and success were critical. Time would eventually run out on public patience with the air campaign, and all the good management of resources wouldn't help us in that case. We needed to escalate the air campaign's intensity as rapidly as possible, to avoid confronting the painful decisions about ground options. I continued to press my perspective on Washington as well as explaining it to my commanders in phone calls, VTCs, and in person.

Wednesday evening, before departing for the summit, Javier Solana and Klaus Naumann and I met in Solana's office. For me, it was a critical opportunity to lay out once again my concerns about the strategic direction of the campaign. I pulled out a letter that we'd been working for several days in my headquarters and outlined it to Solana and Naumann. It assessed the campaign from a purely military perspective, addressing the difficulties of getting at the Serb forces on the ground in Kosovo, and recognizing that by July the air campaign would have peaked even with the additional aircraft, leading to mounting political pressures to halt the bombing. Everything possible would be done to win from the air, but there had to be a follow-on option. Working backward from the first snowfalls in the mountains of Albania and allowing time for "slippage" in planning and deployment, my letter called for national decisions to begin preparation of the ground forces on May 1.

We all recognized that Milosevic might fold earlier, through a loss of will or other pressures, but we had to consider our alternatives if he did not. The atmosphere was grave as we discussed our situation. Solana said he would do what he could. He would be meeting with President Clinton and Prime Minister Blair the next afternoon. But none of us knew where the summit might take us.

That night we struck at President Milosevic's command bunker, located beneath his house at 15 Uzicka Street in Belgrade. The strike was on target.

Then it was the day of departure for the States. I planned to be on the ground for twenty-four hours, including a breakfast with the Secretary and Chairman, a briefing to the heads of states, a meeting with the ministers and Chiefs of Defense. No social stuff. Then, depart Friday afternoon, April 23, for the seven-hour flight back to Belgium.

On board my DC-9, I reflected on how far we had come in four weeks. Some nations had wanted only a demonstrative strike, but we had succeeded in mounting a full-fledged air effort now involving almost 600 aircraft. There had been no bombing pause. We'd struck hard at the Serb's military installations, petroleum, military sustainment, transportation, and communications. With the strikes on the television facility and the command bunker we were hitting the heart of Milosevic's command and control. We'd lost only one aircraft and no pilots. Our forces in Bosnia, Albania, and Macedonia were safe thus far. We'd had only two serious incidents resulting in civilian casualties. The governments of Macedonia and Albania remained stable, despite the pressures of accommodating the refugees and NATO. The assistance to refugees had been successful. The Russians had not intervened, and Bulgaria and Romania were rapidly being drawn in to complete Milosevic's isolation. The press had been tough but for the most part fair. NATO consensus had held, despite the pressures.

On the debit side, we hadn't stopped the ethnic cleansing, and the latest figures showed over 800,000 Kosovars internally displaced, hiding in the mountains and forests. Despite continued discussions, we had found no practicable, safe way for our aircraft to provide them humanitarian relief. The Serb forces in Kosovo were under attack, forced into hiding and dispersal much of the time, but not significantly damaged, thanks in part to some really difficult weather. The Apaches hadn't flown their first mission. Petroleum was still being delivered into Yugoslavia legally, even by ships from NATO nations, despite weeks of NATO planning and studies. And the Yugoslav football team was still playing matches throughout Europe.

I also knew that my command was not receiving the support it should. It was important, within the Pentagon, to prevent a misunderstanding about the SACEUR's responsibilities from undermining the campaign. I hoped for a good breakfast meeting with Shelton and Cohen the next morning. It would be my first chance to sit down face-to-face privately with the two of them since before the campaign began.

I added it all up. On balance we were winning and Milosevic was losing. And I believed he knew it.

ELEVEN

THE GROUND OPTION

FRIDAY, APRIL 23, was the big day—NATO's fiftieth anniversary summit in Washington. As I began work early that morning, I learned about the stormy discussion on ground troops between the President Clinton and Prime Minister Blair, the result of which was that there would be no discussions of the ground option at the summit. However, Javier Solana had issued a press statement authorizing NATO to do an "assessment" of its ground intervention plans. It wasn't what I had hoped for, but then it wasn't yet May 1, my deadline, either. And "assessment" was one of those words that could mean anything from a one-sentence appraisal to a complete new plan.

Secretary Cohen gave me final guidance at breakfast at 6:30 A.M. in his office. I expected Hugh Shelton to join us but he didn't. As I reviewed the status of our efforts and gave a brief synopsis of the Allied Force briefing I would give to the heads of state in a few hours, I made sure that the Secretary understood my views on the ground operation. I was pressing for beginning preparations by May 1 because there were many nations that would need a long time to be ready; I wasn't pressing to commit to a ground operation, I said, because I didn't have a workable plan at this point, and I knew we could do still much more from the air. But how could we not have a follow-on option?

The Secretary expressed his conviction that we would eventually get a diplomatic settlement, though not without more intense air strikes. It might take another ten days or so, he felt, though he disclosed no basis for his optimism. He also clarified the U.S. position, at least as far as this summit was concerned: "Nothing about ground forces. We have to make this air campaign work, or we'll both be writing our resumes."

It was clear guidance. "Yes, sir," I said. "I'm not going to spoil the summit. I'm not going to be the skunk at the picnic." I knew how important NATO consensus was.

In any case, I still had the authority to do an assessment.

We drove to the summit site, and I found the temporary office they had set up for me, right next door to Klaus Naumann. We exchanged insights, and then I followed up on a rumor I had heard. "Klaus, what happened to your extension in position?" I knew he was scheduled to retire after completing his three-year term as chairman of the Military Committee in early May, but I also knew that he wanted to stay until Operation Allied Force was finished, and I certainly wanted him to stay.

"It has been decided that I will leave on May 6," he said. It was rumored that one country had threatened that if the change were not made on schedule, it might be viewed as such a lack of confidence that its government might fall. Naumann would be departing and retiring.

I was terribly sad for him. He had had a magnificent career, helping steer German policy during the German unification, serving as Germany's Chief of Defense during the absorption of the East German military, and then as NATO's highest military official, the Chairman of the Military Committee. Departing in the midst of war was a heavy blow to him, and to the Alliance. I had worked closely with his designated successor, Italian Admiral Guido Venturoni, who had been extraordinarily helpful in assisting NATO in the Balkans.

Still, it hit me hard personally. Klaus Naumann was like a brother, and we were losing him in the midst of a war.

The summit's key event, so far as I was concerned, was the opening working session, the heads of state meeting to review the ongoing operations in the Balkans. I arrived early, hoping for a word with some of the delegations before the meeting began, and, for some reason, the security guards let me and Mike Durkee, my political adviser, in before the NATO delegations arrived.

As we entered the reception area I saw the U.S. hosts lined up, waiting for the receiving line to begin. There was President Clinton, Secretary of State Albright, Secretary of Defense Cohen, and General Shelton. It was our team, in the few moments prior to the start of an historic event, standing in line and ready, trying to relax. It was the first time I'd seen the President since the dinner he had hosted for the Joint Chiefs and Commanders in late January. I moved toward the group, in a gesture of respect and acknowledgment, intending to give a brief hello. It was instinctive courtesy, that you don't walk into a room with your military superiors and not acknowledge them.

As I approached, two or three of the team glanced at me. The body language was uninviting.

I turned away and halted about twenty feet behind and off to the side of the group. I stood with Mike Durkee in the center of the room. There was no place to go.

Then the ushers allowed the first delegations to enter the foyer, and at once I was surrounded by an interested and respectful group of ministers, deputies, generals, and staff assistants from the various countries. Then the heads of state stopped after they came through the President's formal receiving line, making me almost the center of a second receiving line. It was an indication of the relationships that existed, as well as a gesture of respect for the position of SACEUR. This was an opportunity to meet face-to-face and press my needs for target approvals and overall intensification of the air campaign. After an especially cordial and supportive chat with President Jacques Chirac of France, I asked General Jean-Pierre Kelche, the French Chief of Defense, half-joking, "So, do I get approval for the electricity system targets, or not?" Kelche just smiled.

As I moved to my place at the big circular table, I was very hopeful. There was an unmistakable determination in the air, a collective resolve to see this through, and a sense of teamwork that was stronger than before.

In my briefing I sketched out the various parallel efforts, including the air campaign, humanitarian assistance, isolating Serbia, and stabilizing Bosnia. In the air campaign I talked of our attacks on two "axes"—a strategic attack directed at Serb military and security targets, as well as Milosevic's instruments of control in Serbia, and a tactical attack, directed against the forces of ethnic cleansing in Kosovo. The Americans, and especially the American military, believed that the strategic air attack was the key. Most of the Europeans were at best ambivalent about the strategic attacks; they wanted me to attack the Serb forces. I said we had to do both.

I talked about our results to date and what we needed in the near future—more targets, more aircraft, and a more intense campaign on both the strategic and tactical targets. I also explained that it made little sense to bomb Milosevic's petroleum storage facilities and at the same time let him import oil. But my conclusion was upbeat. It was simply a fact that we were winning this campaign and that Milosevic was losing, and he knew it.

After the briefing, various heads of state spoke, all in favor of the operations and generally supporting intensifying our campaign. President Clinton reinforced my request for action to halt the shipments of petroleum to Yugoslavia. By the time of the defense ministers' meeting that afternoon, I had received authorization to create a "visit and search" system to inspect and divert oil shipments intended for Yugoslavia.

NATO also agreed formally on its objectives for the campaign, at last: stopping the violence in Kosovo; withdrawing Serb military, police, and paramilitary from the province; stationing an international military presence there; allowing all Kosovar Albanians safe return home; and working toward a political settlement based on the talks outside Paris.

Flying home, I realized there was no way of knowing whether Secretary Cohen's prediction about the early diplomatic settlement would work out, but the best way to achieve it was to continue to push to intensify the campaign, bring in more aircraft, and continue to work isolating the theater. We also had to move rapidly on the ground plan assessment if we were going to meet the timelines for an invasion before the autumn ended.

Alistair Campbell, Prime Minister Blair's public affairs expert, and others were working to strengthen the NATO strategic information effort. He was helping us work the public affairs aspect of operations in advance, so that journalists' lines of questioning could be anticipated and properly addressed. If we were targeting the Serb media, for example, shouldn't the NATO briefers have key background information and analyses on the Serb media in advance? Couldn't they even, if they were aware of the targets early enough, help us avoid the pitfalls of public outcry in a war that was almost as much about public opinion as it was about the destruction of targets in Serbia?

Campbell was also advising me on how I could be most helpful. Give only the very top-level analyses, he said, and don't make yourself too available. After all, you're the Supreme Commander. In keeping with this approach the public affairs office at NATO Headquarters asked me to give a post-summit news conference on Tuesday, April 27.

It was another in a series of public briefings, and I was prepared with briefing slides and photography. I explained that we were actually operating on four reinforcing efforts: implementing the Dayton Accords in Bosnia; providing humanitarian relief in Macedonia and Albania; prosecuting the air campaign in Yugoslavia; and trying to isolate Serbia.

I wanted to convey the overall complexity of the operation.

The air campaign, I explained, was proceeding on two simultaneous axes: strategic attack against the targets in Serbia, and tactical strikes against the forces and their supply routes in Kosovo.

I explained that we had doubled the total number of aircraft, and almost tripled the number of strike aircraft. The weather, I explained, had been awful, with more than 50 percent of the strike sorties cancelled in twenty days. Then I went through each of the target categories, including air defense, fuel, the road and bridge network, communications, and the ground forces in Serbia. Each set had examples of targets struck. And I was careful that our claims of the extent and effect of damages were conservative. I had always cautioned against "battle-damage bean-counting" and I certainly didn't want to contribute to it.

The press conference was going extremely well when, near the end, John Dugberg of the *Los Angeles Times* asked for more specificity about the effects of air attacks against the Serb forces on the ground in Kosovo. I restated the difficulty in gaining specific information without being on the ground, and warned that the actual counts of forces might not show Milosevic's losses because he was continuing to bring in reinforcements.

I didn't see much news in this remark. But to some reporters, this became the story of the day. Headline writers further distorted the comment. *The New York Times* proclaimed, "NATO Chief Admits Bombs Fail to Stem Serb Operations," while *The Washington Times* screamed, "Clark Reports Yugoslavia Pours Troops Into Kosovo."

To me this was a complete misunderstanding of my statement and of the facts. It was simply basic military doctrine to replace losses in the field, and it was not surprising that Milosevic was behaving in this way. So far as I knew, we had not ever claimed that we had sealed off Kosovo. Milosevic was certainly attempting to replace losses and maybe even to reinforce. In fact, the vigor of his efforts was itself good witness to the effects of the air attacks.

I didn't learn the Washington reaction until the next evening, when I was called away from our farewell dinner with Klaus and Barbara Naumann to take an urgent telephone call from General Hugh Shelton.

"Wes, at the White House meeting today there was a lot of discussion about your press conference," Shelton began. "The Secretary of Defense asked me to give you some verbatim guidance, so here it is: 'Get your f——g face off the TV. No more briefings, period. That's it.' I just wanted to give it to you like he said it. Do you have any questions?"

Unfortunately, the speaker phone was on, and several members of the staff probably heard the call.

As the discussion continued, it seemed that the President had read the complete articles and remarked that the stories didn't back up the headlines. He then read the transcript of my press conference and said there was nothing wrong with what I had said. Nevertheless, the Secretary's guidance stood, Shelton explained.

I knew that for military men, dealing with the media can be like drinking from a poisoned chalice. However heady the wine, at some point you may get a fatal dose. But we had recognized the importance of strategic information, and I was just following the master plan Alistair Campbell and the others had put in place. My answer, in context, was quite innocuous. Out of context the reporters may have interpreted my explanation as undercutting support for the air campaign and feeding

efforts to promote a ground attack. That was neither a fair interpretation nor my intent. We were doing everything we could inside the command and with the press to keep up the enthusiasm for the air effort.

The next day my public affairs officer, Colonel Stephanie Hoehne,
called to Assistant Secretary of Defense Ken Bacon's office for clarification. I was to be permitted to do interviews and media on the troop
visits, but no more briefings in Brussels. Within these restrictions,
though, I had to continue to work the European media, at least.

As a result of the summit, Washington had become even more
active on the targeting issue in bearing down on the French reluctance
to strike the electric power targets. By April 28 there were again rumblings that Washington was preparing to order me to strike the electrical grid regardless of the opinions of other nations. I hoped not.

On April 29 we received French approval for some strikes on the
electrical system, and we struck part of Serbia's power system on the
evening of May 1. According to press reporting, 70 percent of Serbia
was blacked out, though power was restored to Belgrade, at least, early
on the morning of May 3.

In the meantime we continued to work our way through the slowly
expanding approved fixed target list, pounding the bridges and ammunition and oil storage sites, and taking down the large television
retransmission and military communications site at Avala mountain
outside Belgrade. But we were also starting to encounter the kind of
incidents we had worked to avoid from the beginning. On April 27 a
laser-guided bomb had lost its course when clouds scattered the laser
beam. On May 1 we lost a Marine Harrier jet fighter over the Adriatic
due to mechanical problems. That same day we struck a bridge north of
Pristina, and, similar to the earlier incident with the train, in this case,
the bombs impacted just in front of a bus that was crossing the bridge.
Again, there were civilian casualties. Then, that night we lost our second aircraft in combat, an F-16 flying over central Serbia. It was a
reminder of the continuing threat posed by the Serbs' air defenses,
even though most of their missile technology was twenty to thirty years
old. But our search and rescue effort was up and operating smoothly,
and we had the pilot out in a little more than two hours and without
any losses, despite cannon and missile fire at the rescue helicopters.

On May 2, I spoke with Klaus Naumann about expanding the target list to include, with the lawyers' approval, more military-related targets associated with Milosevic himself—military-industrial electrical equipment manufacturing, and metallurgical processing facilities owned by Milosevic and his cronies. The next day I flew to Sofia to get the Bulgarian government's assessment of the situation. I had developed a great respect for the democratic leadership of Bulgaria over the past two years. They sought military, economic, and political reform, and looked to NATO for assistance, ideas, and eventual membership. The Bulgarians were proud of the support they were giving us, and optimistic about the results of the air campaign. The destruction of Milosevic's refineries would cripple his agriculture, they said, predicting that he would surrender before the end of June. They reported that the strike on his house was warmly received by the people in Belgrade, who claimed he had ordered the lowest-ranking employees at the TV studios to remain behind, so there would be victims when NATO attacked.

We also needed effective action against the Serb ground forces in Kosovo. Here the problem was the danger of civilian casualties and collateral damages, as well as the risks to the aircrews. The British and French governments were preventing their aircrews from striking ground forces if they were within 500 meters of a village. But the American pilots were also careful. The leadership in the Combined Air Operations Center in Vicenza, Italy, was engaged in real-time monitoring and approvals of the missions against the Serb forces in Kosovo.

We had tried to set up a system to use reports from the Kosovo Liberation Army to help us determine which villages were clear of Kosovars. The idea was that the KLA could tell us through intermediaries whether certain villages were unoccupied. We soon discovered that this method wasn't reliable. The KLA's information might be old, or the Serbs could have infiltrated their communications, or perhaps it wasn't really as accurate as we needed. I had suggested the system but quickly became disenchanted. We would have to rely primarily on unmanned aerial vehicles' real-time TV to help us avoid harming civilians, and we'd have to be very wary of striking villages.

What we learned later was that in fact the Kosovars were coming back into their homes at night, hiding for a day or two, eating, changing clothes, and then moving back into the forests. We were fortunate that we didn't rely on the KLA reporting.

We set up a system to enable our aircraft to descend well below 15,000 feet, if necessary, to identify targets on the ground, but the pilots reported that they were usually more effective using high-powered binoculars and orbiting well above antiaircraft machine gun altitudes. On the good-weather days we were able to strike effectively. On April 24 we hit trucks and an armor and support assembly area. On the 27th, ten vehicles were hit. On April 29 we had even better results: twelve trucks, two revetted tanks, and other military vehicles. But there wasn't enough good weather; instead we had day after day of low clouds and ceiling restricting our operations, especially in Kosovo.

It was an adaptive process, and the Serbs were learning, too. Earlier, they had abandoned their large assembly areas in favor of wooded dispersal sites. Now, they had stopped moving in convoys. Now, they were moving from the woods into the villages to hide.

For us, trying to precent unintended civilian casualties was a significant and frustrating problem. As John Jumper expressed it, we often saw a "picture of a farm house that has tracks going to the farm implement storage shed, and another with a hay stack with a tank clearly hidden underneath, or a treeline with artillery hidden in it. But when you go out from that and see that that's in the middle of a very populated area with lots of houses around it.... The translation from that high-resolution imagery into quality targetable data that you pass to the cockpit isn't as easy as it looks like it would be."

I re-emphasized that attacking these forces was my number one priority. I saw this effort as a necessary prelude to a possible ground campaign, and even a chance to avoid it altogether. I was especially proud of the innovations of the airmen and commanders, who hadn't had any opportunity to rehearse until the forces were deployed. The Desert Storm team had been assembled and was scrambling on the offensive plan and techniques for months before it attacked Iraq in 1991. We hadn't had that luxury. Our force came together at the last minute, the unmanned aerial vehicles hadn't arrived until after the operations began, the aircraft carrier came in two weeks late, and reinforcements were still arriving. Nor had our forces truly understood the nature of the battlefield and the intense political constraints to be imposed. We were fighting, planning, and adapting simultaneously, and each day of good weather brought good results. We seemed to have created a workable system; we just had to continue to strengthen it.

I was focusing attention now on the specific rules we were following in striking fielded forces. Congressional delegations would speak to pilots or air controllers, hear answers that were troubling, and bring them to me. I had to clarify the issues for the congressmen and, if necessary, fix the procedures in the command. It wasn't the best way to get "feedback" on my command, I recognized, but it was the system that was working now. Congress was asking questions like this: "If a MIG-29 or a tank is parked next to a house, you won't attack it?" I reminded the command (and Congress) that these were issues of military judgment, but that I would like them to attack the tank even if it was parked next to a house unless there were specific indications that civilians would be hurt. We weren't going to disregard risks to civilians but the alternative to taking risks with property damage was that we might ultimately have to put our troops in on the ground.

Strikes against Serb forces in Kosovo were further complicated by the continuing humanitarian convoys that were coming in from Greece, initiated by a nongovernmental organization attempting to alleviate suffering on the ground. These convoys were largely uncoordinated and out of communications, and they worried the airmen. The last thing we wanted was to hit a Greek truck by mistake. But we could neither block them nor control them. They were just another battlefield hazard.

Meanwhile, because the Air Force C-130 cargo planes wouldn't survive against Serb air defenses, John Jumper and I were working on a system to be able to drop food rations at high altitude from bombers. Some of the airmen didn't like this, but if we could use the system to keep the refugees in place and safe, strengthen resistance to the Serbs, and reduce the incentive for more Greek convoys I was willing to look at it. (It was eventually blocked by the Pentagon leadership, but at least it was given serious consideration.)

I also had to turn my attention to the Apaches, which were finally arriving at Rinas Airfield outside Tirana, under the command of Jay Hendrix and his Task Force Hawk. There were continuing deployment problems, just moving the 5,500-soldier force, totally by air. There were problems on the ground, in a cramped, muddy, and insecure airfield. There were problems with the command structure, including Hendrix's relationship to the humanitarian assistance operations run by NATO and by the U.S. Joint Task Force Shining Hope. And, most fundamentally, there were problems with the employment of the Apaches themselves. The crews needed training once they arrived, firm operating procedures, including complete rules of engagement, legal and political authority from NATO and the United States, and a lot of support from the Air Force to facilitate their mission. I would have to gain U.S. permission to commit the Apaches in combat. Unfortunately, I knew that their participation wasn't totally welcomed by my own command.

Over the summit weekend, some of my commanders had begun to state that the Apaches would detract from the ongoing air operations. They also were worried that there might not be sufficient targets to justify the risks and support requirements for Task Force Hawk, concerned about the diplomatic implications if the long-range Army rockets were used, and concerned that engaging Serb forces close to the border with Albania might cause the Serbs to strike us in Macedonia.

These were the voices of conventional air power. Though these commanders had no experience with the Apaches, all their concerns were reasonable and legitimate, I thought, and had to be addressed. But what I wanted was for my commanders to fix the problems at their levels and leave the politics and geostrategy more to me and higher authority. I also realized that ultimately, making the Apaches work would be my responsibility.

In war, the art is to focus as much combat power as possible at the decisive point. One of these decisive points was the destruction of the Serb ground forces, and the Apaches could help us here, I knew.

Hendrix and I went through the plan of operations and requirements. He had completed a considerable amount of planning already, but I sensed he was trying to plan and coordinate in a "resistant medium." So many questions raised about the Apaches, and the other pressures of ongoing operations were so intense, that every bit of progress was achieved only after considerable struggle. Planning and coordination that would have taken a few minutes in an exercise were consuming days. When I learned that General Reimer, the Army Chief of Staff, had been talking to my subordinates about whether they sought the use of the Apaches, I knew some doubts were seeping into the commanders responsible for execution.

Our plan called for us to fly across the border into Kosovo, using artillery, rocket fire, and Air Force assets to suppress any enemy air defenses that might threaten the Apaches as they flew past, and then attack Serb forces. In training we operated off both hard intelligence of the enemy's air defenses and off "templates," threat locations where an enemy might likely be. One of our first tasks was to practice the close timing of these suppressive fires. That involved "clearing" both the airspace, to avoid a midair collision between the artillery projectiles and an aircraft, and the ground, to avoid friendly or civilian casualties. So, we needed to establish in conjunction with the Combined Air Operations Center in Vicenza the actual procedures that we had talked about and used in our training exercises. We also needed the legal authorization to shoot the artillery and rockets, which would require approval of a specific set of legally binding "rules of engagement." And if no one else asked for it, we also had to determine how we would be able to avoid civilian casualties with the suppressive artillery and rocket fires.

Then there was the problem of knowing which targets to attack and how to attack them. We would have to know precisely where to look for armored vehicles and when it was permissible to shoot. We'd see tanks lurking under trees at the edge of a forest, or backed into a garage or a destroyed house. Artillery might be pulled up next to houses or mosques. We needed unmanned aerial vehicles with real time infrared TV always available for planning and coordinating the attacks. It would be able to watch as the enemy tried to conceal his equipment, alert the helicopters of movement behind them, or handle any of a dozen other tasks.

And we needed the use of an Airborne Command, Control, and Communications aircraft, a specially configured C-130 transport, to assure the uninterrupted line-of-sight communications to make the mission work. Then the staff needed to demonstrate that they could put all of the information and assets together to make a complete and effective mission.

I directed Ellis, Hendrix, and Short in my U.S. chain of command to pull all of this together, so that we could have a three-phased training plan: first, fly the Apaches to the border alone; second, assemble the complete package, fly to the border, and simulate the firing of the suppressive fires; third, assemble the complete package, fly to the border, and actually fire the suppressive fires, without bringing the Apaches across. Only then would we move to the real missions. I made it clear that they should conduct as many rehearsals as necessary, until the whole team was confident. All of my commanders supported this approach.

I envisaged Jay Hendrix with Task Force Hawk as a ground commander without forward troops. He had his full array of intelligence analysis and planning capabilities, and access to all the intelligence in theater. He could task special reconnaissance teams on the high mountains to look down into Kosovo or get information from the Albanian Army. With his rockets he would be able quickly to strike deep into Kosovo and beyond to hit enemy air defenses. And he would be the claimant for all the assets he needed to conduct what we called, in Army terms, "the deep fight."

In the absolute worst case, our inability to locate suitable targets, his force would become a highly effective reserve, able to reinforce the Albanian Army to halt any Serb invasion across into Albania.

Walt Slocombe told me in a telephone conversation that Secretary Cohen expected to see the Apaches in action soon. So did we.

Meanwhile the paperwork was flowing to authorize us to move forward. My concern was to get the Apaches into operation as soon as possible. To do that, I believed, it was better to keep them under U.S. operational control. This meant that the detailed rules and procedures for using the Apaches wouldn't have to be cleared by all the NATO governments but just by the United States—avoiding what was shaping up to be a possibly protracted debate—and that the flight planning would likewise occur in U.S. channels. Once we had the Apaches in operation successfully, I reasoned, we could then put them under NATO. I ordered the paperwork pulled back from NATO consideration.

This heightened unhappiness within the Alliance about the Apaches. They had taken far too long to deploy, given the public expectations, and there was some speculation that they might not be used at all. Now, I had removed the operational control, and the oversight, from NATO channels. Klaus Naumann remarked privately that all of these aspects of the Apache deployment were damaging the credibility of the Alliance, and he was right.

On the night of May 4, another rehearsal was done by Task Force Hawk. It was to have included live fire into Kosovo from our artillery and rockets, but I wasn't able to secure permission from Washington, so it was another dry run up toward the border. Then, at 1:40 A.M. local time on the 5th, an Apache crashed. This was the second aircraft loss in the mountains of northeast Albania, following one on April 26. But in this accident, both crewmen were killed. Two accidents, and now two fatalities, in two weeks of training.

The shock wave from this accident sent ripples, even though we diagnosed it almost immediately as an aircraft mechanical failure, not a pilot error. Task Force Hawk continued its preparations.

I was also deeply involved in the "assessment" of the ground option, coming out of the NATO summit in Washington. I knew that we would have to at least consider going through northeast Albania, as well as through Macedonia and possibly southern Serbia, in order to invade Kosovo. On my first trip into Albania after the summit, on April 25, I made a point of studying the terrain in northeast Albania carefully as we flew toward Kukes, on the border with Kosovo. General Ed Burba had already been in the area and was strongly in favor of using avenues of approach through northeast Albania. Here, unlike Macedonia, the mountains were on the friendly side of the border. Once there, the fight looked much easier.

The land rose quickly from the flat coastal plain into a series of steep hillsides punctuated by sharp valleys and draws. Only two roads led all the way to Kukes, and both had various weak bridges, narrow shoulders, and occasional cutbacks. From the air the pavement looked poor. Nevertheless, I could see buses, cars, and the occasional truck grinding up toward Kukes. Tough terrain, yes; impossible, no. But it would be very important to ensure that we kept the enemy out of this terrain, I thought. We didn't want to have to fight through it. And we would have to find some way to get the large, heavy vehicles like tanks forward. Perhaps the dirt airfield at Kukes would work. I was concerned, but also a little intrigued. This could be done, and it would spread the defender considerably.

Later, working with my subordinates on the ground war options, I acknowledged that we did not yet have a plan that I was comfortable with, and, as intended, that really opened up the discussion. Somehow I had to draw them out and then develop a greater common appreciation for the way ahead. Without this, I believed we would be ripped apart by the various factions in Washington. One school of thought was to go right to Belgrade. Geographically, Belgrade was Milosevic's center of gravity. It was the final objective they thought—why go for Kosovo alone, as an interim objective? The terrain was better, and fighting there avoided, they said, the possibility that the Serbs could fall back into the mountains of southern Serbia and conduct a counterinsurgency campaign.

Another group argued for the practical, and the need to do something this year, then, if necessary, move against a more strategic objective later. I added to the mix my report of Strobe Talbott's reaction when I had met with him on April 8 and mentioned the possibility of going into northern Serbia toward Belgrade: he went pale. It would be likely to bring down the government in Ukraine, he said, and would put Hungary under extraordinary pressures, maybe even leading to regional conflict. I knew that there would be strong political resistance to moving against Belgrade, but I had to work the arguments at the military level first.

We discussed the fact that, even before there was a decision to invade, the planning, preparation, and deployment of ground forces would also give us diplomatic leverage. In any case, if Milosevic surrendered to the air campaign, the presence of those ground forces would be critical to a speedy entry into Kosovo.

But the air campaign had perhaps a 70 percent chance of working, I said, and so we were going to make it more intense, take more risks with collateral damage, and push responsibility upwards while we worked the ground option. NATO was not going to lose. I told my staff to cut off the internal speculation on the ground campaign and help me prevent the press from seeing dissension here. "I need your support," I said.

It was an important session, both for gaining some of their views and for pushing some of mine. But I left knowing that not only did we have no real plan for ground forces, nor did we have an organizational structure. The two were closely interconnected.

By doctrine I knew that I would need to place someone in charge of the ground component. It could be Montgomery Meigs, the U.S. Army commander in Europe. He was a four-star, and this operation would justify a four-star, but he was committed in Bosnia. It could be Mike Jackson. He was a three-star but exceptionally able and already on the ground. But he was British, and if the Americans were by far the largest component of the force, then it might be necessary to have an American land commander. It could be Jay Hendrix, a three-star, but he was fully engaged with the Apaches.

Then there was the problem of the reporting channels. This was always one of the most controversial of the decisions made in modern warfare. Who would be the operational commander? For D-Day in 1944 the British General Bernard Montgomery had tried to persuade General Dwight Eisenhower to concentrate on being overall commander, allowing Montgomery to command all the troops on the ground. Eisenhower refused. In the Gulf War, General Norman Schwarzkopf actually had a U.S. Army Commander in Lieutenant General John Yeossock, who coordinated the operations and logistics of the two U.S. corps, but Schwarzkopf retained his control of the ground operations.

My situation was going to be even more complicated. I went over it again and again, trying to rationalize my instinct and experience with the intent of the NATO command structure. In the U.S. chain of command, I was in a position of the theater commander, responsible for operational control unless ceded to NATO. In the NATO chain I was even higher, a strategic commander responsible for multiple theaters—though there was war in only one theater—and my U.S. naval component commander, Admiral Jim Ellis, was, in the NATO chain, the operational commander.

I would have to consider this carefully; I wasn't prepared to resolve the organizational issues yet. This was too big. First, we had to move ahead with the assessment of the ground forces options. On this front, Dieter Stockmann was supervising the planning, with close coordination and counsel from Rupert Smith and Ed Burba. Under my direction, they were concentrating their efforts on the smaller option, the attack to free Kosovo.

It was a typical planning effort that required an analysis of the weather, terrain, and enemy as well as the development and assessment of various course of action for the so-called Option B(-), a designation we had given for the attack to seize and secure Kosovo. The idea was to work backwards from the battles we wanted to fight, and then analyze the required logistics, deployment, and force flow. There was no other way to do it.

We knew the terrain fairly well, and could readily identify three avenues of approach: one in the east, one in the center, one in the west. None was open or easy. In the east, there was a valley leading into southern Serbia, then a hard left turn through a narrow mountain pass to penetrate to Kosovo. In the center, there was a major defile with a river running through it north of Skopje, Macedonia. It was the main highway into Kosovo, with the rest of the border being blocked by mountains ranging up to 10,000 feet in elevation. However, the route was narrow and winding. There were several bridges and tunnels on this route, which was essentially a steep gorge of some fifteen miles in length. In the west was the toughest part of Albania, with poor roads, one dirt airstrip and constricted terrain. It had one key advantage: the high ground was mostly in Albania. So long as our side held the border, all we would have to do was move through the mountains; we wouldn't have to fight our way through them. Once attacking, we would have far easier maneuvers.

Of course, there was also the option of using parachute or heliborne forces to gain surprise and take key points.

The enemy situation was known in only general terms, but we anticipated that the 40,000 to 50,000 troops that Milosevic had currently deployed could be almost doubled in strength and backed with lots of artillery, tanks, and very intensive mortar fire. There were another 15,000 or so heavily armed police who could add to his defenses. And the Serbs were continuing to emplace minefields and prepare fortified positions.

Stockmann and Burba and their team quickly realized that the original estimate of 70,000 NATO troops was far too little, given the scale of actual and potential Serb reinforcements. We might actually need up to 100,000 combat troops, plus almost that many support and service support troops behind them. At this point I didn't want to force them to shrink their estimates—if I started doing that, to make the product more "saleable" at the political level, the planning would simply be unsound. Instead, we would have to look at the intelligence and weigh our assumptions more carefully as we proceeded.

The planners also studied the timelines. In their view, we were already too late to invade Kosovo before the snows hit the mountains if we stayed with the routine NATO planning process. If we were given authority to plan, and not just assess, we had to allow sixty days to plan and ninety days to deploy. On that timetable, we would be lucky to attack on November 1. So it was clear that we were going to have to commence preparations and deployments before we had a final approved plan.

I still wasn't comfortable with the courses of action developed for getting into Kosovo and defeating the Serb forces there. What were the appropriate objectives? How would we actually fight? How could we maximize our strengths and capitalize on our opponent's vulnerabilities? How could we achieve surprise? What would be the role of the KLA and the Albanians? How would we provide the logistics support?

I had to bring Washington along with me as we worked through this process; as always, Washington was the key to any effort within NATO, and especially in this campaign, where almost two-thirds of the aircraft and about half of the ground troops would likely be American. I knew that Secretary Cohen was determined to make the air campaign work, and make it work in conjunction with diplomacy. At the same time, congressional critics were questioning the President's decision to rely on air alone, though some of these same critics were opposed to the engagement in the Balkans on many grounds. There were others in Congress, however, who would have supported whatever was necessary to succeed.

The Pentagon leadership saw the political dimension at close range. Some believed that if the numbers required were to leak out publicly, the Administration would be accused of rigging the options to eliminate ground attack. Several retired generals were proclaiming that we could do a ground operation on the cheap, for less than half what our planners were seeking. Secretary Cohen seemed to believe that planning and preparation for a ground operation of this magnitude would generate a self-defeating debate by admitting that the air campaign wasn't viable and a ground option was too difficult and expensive. It was a true dilemma.

Hugh Shelton also raised an issue that had been troubling me: How could we incorporate into our estimates of enemy strength the results of the bombing that would continue until we launched the ground effort? Wouldn't this significantly reduce the size of the forces required?

As I worked through the issue, it was becoming clear that the assessment wasn't ready, nor would I have the Washington backing I needed to proceed to more detailed planning and preparations. We had to delay submitting the assessment to NATO headquarters. We needed more time.

I also continued to worry about the three soldiers from my command who had been kidnapped by the Serbs back on March 31. From the beginning, the operation appeared to me to be a Serb special forces gambit: when they failed to shoot down aircraft and capture pilots, they had gone to a back-up means of grabbing any Americans, just to attempt a humiliation. Some of my subordinates believed that the three soldiers had strayed into Serbia. I didn't. This was a straight kidnapping, and I wanted them back. We considered a variety of means to rescue them, but nothing looked promising. It was a waiting game.

In the week before the summit we received word that the KLA had captured a Serb soldier. Here was our opportunity, I thought. If the KLA transferred the prisoner to us, then we could perhaps arrange a swap. At the very least, if Milosevic refused a swap, we would have a significant public-relations advantage over him. But though I persuaded Washington to let us take the Serb prisoner into custody, and eventually another, the Administration was wary of a prisoner exchange.

In the meantime the Reverend Jesse Jackson was seeking to travel to Belgrade to gain the release of our three soldiers. When I learned the news, it was my turn to be wary. Normally, such efforts require offsetting agreements, and I had heard that Jackson was pushing for a bombing pause, which would play right into Serb hands.

On Sunday morning, May 2, we got the call from Joe Ralston in Washington indicating that Jackson had secured the soldiers' release and was traveling with them to Croatia. This was great news, especially since Jackson had said nothing about a bombing pause in return. We brought them to Ramstein Air Base and then to the nearby hospital.

My concern was the welfare of the soldiers and their families. I wanted to look after their health, to prevent their exploitation by the press, debrief them, and reintegrate them with their units, as quickly as possible.

We learned from the men that they had been struck with fists, hit, butt-stroked, and hit with the barrels of weapons when they were captured. One of the men was kicked severely in the face and had suffered a broken nose. Later they were struck on the back with fists and rubber truncheons during daily interrogations. These were beatings that could break men down emotionally, even if the physical scars didn't show. But it was obvious from the soldiers' reports that the Serb prison guards had been restrained from applying to our men the kinds of extreme physical abuse that could be overheard in nearby cells.

I was still angry about the incident, but at least we had our soldiers back. And Jackson had done it without costing us anything, so far as I knew.

Jesse Jackson was not the only person engaged in diplomatic efforts. During the NATO summit, Boris Yeltsin had called President Clinton to discuss opening a diplomatic track, and Viktor Chernomyrdin, the former prime minister of Russia, had been designated as the Russian president's special envoy. Chernomyrdin and Vice President Al Gore had talked on April 26, with the Russian demanding an end to the bombing as a condition to negotiations. Strobe Talbott, and later U.N. Secretary General Kofi Annan, had gone to Moscow for talks, and diplomatic discussions continued among the Europeans as well. Chernomyrdin flew to Washington on May 3 and met with President Clinton, and upon his return from Belgrade Jackson had apparently carried a letter to the President from Milosevic. At SHAPE we followed the movements but weren't informed on the details, so it was unclear how much progress was being made.

Then, on May 4, we received the first indication that there was consideration of serious progress. Brigadier General George Casey, from the Joint Staff J-5 office, was requesting our views on how we would make the transition from a bombing into a cease-fire, with Serb withdrawals, and an implementation force. What, we were asked, were our "red lines," the limits beyond which concessions to facilitate an agreement would compromise NATO's success?

The Joint Staff thinking was not to intermix NATO and Serb forces, so we would direct the removal of air defense weapons first, then verify by air a Serb ground force withdrawal over a period of about seven days. Then the NATO force would enter to stabilize the situation and assist the civil implementation organization in its early operations. After about six months, the NATO force could be drawn down substantially.

This coordination between the Joint Staff and the Commands was essential, and I was pleased to have been consulted at an early stage of the thinking. At the same time, I implored that we not cut corners in a rush to end the air campaign.

I penned my thoughts on an E-mail message: There had to be a genuine Serb withdrawal, total and fast, with no holding on to northern Kosovo. No compromise on NATO command and control of the force (the Russians could send in forces with the United States, as they had done in Bosnia). No border controls by Serbs over refugee return. No reconstruction for Serbia without an OSCE presence, open media, restrictions on police, turning in war crimes suspects, and so on. My message was to remember that we were winning and not to settle for half a loaf, because there would be no second chance with Milosevic, who had defeated every other international institution.

I was also encouraged to learn that, in conjunction with a trip to the G-8 summit, President Clinton was coming to Brussels on May 5 and then flying on to visit some of the airmen engaged in the campaign. It would be a welcome opportunity to place everything in perspective and to describe face-to-face the strategy and what needed to be done. The President's visit would also provide an opportunity to reinforce personally the message I had sent back to the Joint Staff.

The President began his visit by meeting with Secretary General Solana, while I and several others gathered in the briefing room on the ground floor. Then he came in, greeted us, and took his place in the center position between Solana and me. As he pulled out his chair to sit down, he turned to me in an aside, and asked, "I guess the Apaches are too risky to use?"

"No, sir," I replied, pausing for an instant to see whether we would discuss this now or move into the briefing. He turned quickly away.

Why did he feel this way? I wondered. Was it the two accidents?

Casualty estimates are notoriously bad, and no reliable mathematical models existed to predict the actual loss rates for the Apaches. The Apaches had never been used in war like this, so there was no experience to draw on. In the first briefing to the Chiefs on the Apaches back in April, I had resisted being drawn into loss estimates. At one point, Hugh Shelton had told me, the Chiefs had said that after the first Apache was lost, then the political pressures would force us to repeat the attacks with others until they were all lost. It wasn't logical—I certainly wouldn't have followed such a course. And we hadn't done that with the Stealth aircraft when the first one was lost. (After the war I heard that the White House was told that eventually half of the Apaches would be destroyed. I wondered if the White House wondered where these figures came from. There was also a plain lack of knowledge. At least one of the top Army leaders hadn't realized that the Apaches were equipped with a system to defeat some of the Serb antiaircraft missiles.)

But the President was already turning his attention back to Solana. It was time to begin the briefing. I hoped it wasn't the end of an opportunity to use the Apaches.

Following the briefing, we began a wide-ranging discussion, with Secretary Albright, Secretary Cohen, and General Shelton looking on. How much should be done to raise money for more refugee camps? What about the planning for ground troops? Are we ready for victory? What about the Apaches—when would they be ready to employ? Will we have huge losses with the Apaches? And so on.

To be ready with the peace support force when Milosevic surrendered, I pressed for a NATO activation order for ground troops, at least the limited plan for the Kosovo force, ready to enter in the event of an agreement. This would be a strong signal of resolve and a catalyst to expedite the readiness of NATO troops. I stressed that we had to continue our attacks on both the tactical and strategic axes. I urged that we prepare a plan to turn the KLA into a civilianized police force or some legitimate political institution. And I discussed the Apaches at length. I pushed hard to keep the door open for their use, but I didn't want to raise expectations until we had completed our rehearsals and I was satisfied with the targeting process. It was clear to me that I was responsible for the success of the Apaches, and I was determined that when used, they would be successful.

As I had always found him, the President was on top of the issues and asked the right questions, as did the Secretary of State and the Secretary of Defense.

As the meeting was concluding, Klaus Naumann brought up the need to have planned for a forced entry on the ground. This was his last full day as Chairman of the Military Committee, and as always, he spoke straightforwardly and with great conviction.

Then we were off to the air base visits, including time for the President to visit the three released soldiers and their families. For me, it was a chance to visit the airmen and commanders again, and for more informal dialogue with members of the President's team. These were men I had worked with as the J-5 and knew well. It was also the opportunity to discuss plans and intentions with Hugh Shelton.

Our first stop was at Spangdahlem Air Base, one of the U.S. air bases in Germany supporting the war. Secretary Cohen held a press conference, with Hugh Shelton and me participating. The Secretary continued to call on me to respond, so I guessed I had been "rehabilitated" for public exposure, despite my press conference the week before.

That day we were scrambling for the next big event to ratchet up the pressure on Belgrade, and we had planned more strikes on the night of May 7. Our intent was to create a series of Belgrade "packages" as we received approval for new targets. We would focus the strikes tightly on the elements of Milosevic's formal and informal command and control system for running military and police efforts throughout the country. This would help reduce his capabilities to continue the ethnic cleansing in Kosovo. We knew that this would be one of the most effective means of telling the Serbs that this was a struggle against Milosevic and ethnic cleansing, and not a war against the Serb people themselves.

One target was to be the Hotel Yugoslavia, which we believed to be the headquarters of the notorious indicted war criminal Arkan, a man who had earned a fierce reputation for brutal ethnic crimes in Croatia and Bosnia. His organization, Arkan's Tigers, represented the worst kind of profiteering from murder. We'd known about this building for some time, but before we could strike, we needed assurance that the hotel wasn't being occupied by legitimate civilian guests. Now we had that assurance.

Another target was to be the presidential hunting lodge and retreat outside Belgrade, where Holbrooke and the rest of our team had met with Milosevic, Karadzic, and Mladic in September 1995 and arranged a cease-fire and a withdrawal of Serb heavy weapons from Sarajevo. I remembered that Milosevic had said that the Bosnian Serbs were waiting 200 meters away, presumably in a bunker, so we searched the area for indications of the bunker and communications complexes.

We were also working other targets, including various military and police headquarters. On the 5th we received the completed target sheets for several more targets, including the headquarters for the Federal Directorate of Supply and Procurement in Belgrade. According to the target sheet, this agency was responsible for the coordination of arms trafficking. I looked at it and saw what looked like a three-story building with long rows of warehouse-like structures behind it. It was the same once-over I gave all the targets in my review—I was principally checking the risks of civilian casualties if we went ahead, and the proximity of any other significant structures. Along with the targets, we also maintained a comprehensive "no-strike" list, which we used to avoid strikes that might damage churches, hospitals, schools, embassies, and so forth. As I looked at this target, number 493, it seemed significant in isolating Serbia from arms imports.

As we toured facilities and talked in the rear of the presidential party, I reminded Hugh Shelton of our plans for Belgrade area targeting and handed him a stack of recently prepared target worksheets for Washington approval. He passed the worksheets to National Security Adviser Sandy Berger, who glanced at each, looked at the relevant data, and approved them for strikes. Of course, we would have to secure approval for the strikes from NATO countries and Solana, too.

I also weighed in again for the Apaches. I had been asking through staff channels, without success. "Sir, we are ready to do the last sets of rehearsals for the Apaches," I told Shelton. "Maybe one, two, or three rehearsals. And this is the time we need approval for the use of the long-range rockets that will provide suppressive fire for the Apaches."

"Okay, Wes. I don't think there'll be any trouble with this. I'll talk to Berger."

I left for Belgium late that afternoon satisfied that we were on track for success. The U.S. leadership was determined that Milosevic was going to lose. There was no softness that I could detect. President Clinton, in particular, was firm that we were going to win, not just avoid losing. And Clinton and Berger wanted Milosevic gone. No more dealing with him. In public the President had said, "We will continue this campaign in which we are engaged. We will intensify it in an unrelenting way until these objectives are met." It was a reassuring and welcome message.

TWELVE

RESISTANCE AND PERSISTENCE

I N THE FIRST WEEKS of May, Milosevic embarked on a political-diplomatic campaign designed to blunt NATO's will and eventually halt its actions. First, there was the release of the three U.S. soldiers, a gesture of good will, accompanied by a letter to the President. Then he released the Kosovar Albanian leader, Ibrahim Rugova, and his family, whom his troops had taken prisoner early in the campaign. On May 6 he proclaimed victory over the KLA and ordered a halt to his military operations in Kosovo.

Diplomatic efforts by all sides were ratcheting up. On May 6, the G-8 nations (Canada, France, Germany, Great Britain, Italy, Japan, the United States, and Russia) agreed to a seven-point draft peace plan to be taken to the United Nations for authorization. The plan called for the withdrawal of Serb military police and paramilitary forces from Kosovo and the entry of an effective international civil and security presence. There was no reference to NATO leadership in the plan, but privately we were assured that the international military force would be led by NATO, as had been the case in Bosnia.

At the same time Russia announced its intent to inspect the NATO forces in Macedonia, under the terms of the 1994 Vienna Document, which provided that nations could request to inspect maneuvers and troop buildups of greater than 13,000 soldiers. The Russian request was a problem, for it could result in the breach of operational security for our forces. It was entirely possible, in my view, that Russian observers could report sensitive locations back to the Serbs, who could then use their long-range rocket systems to strike us inside Macedonia. I had been objecting to this visit but was overruled by the political authorities. Fortunately, there was also a provision in the Vienna agreement that could justify protecting militarily sensitive sites and information. The Macedonians directed the Russians to land at a remote site and were unable to provide helicopter transport, thus further eating into the Russians' forty-eight-hour inspection period.

The Russian team finally completed its inspections on May 8 and departed. They had met with NATO officers but were unhappy that they were not provided detailed information about weapons, units, and locations. At NATO headquarters there was concern that the Russians had left disappointed and frustrated, and some thinking that NATO had left itself open to criticism. However, we succeeded in protecting our operational security.

At higher levels there was continuing discussion of what the international force deployed in Kosovo would look like, but I recommended retaining the original plan for Kosovo that we had devised before the start of the air campaign: a three star-level headquarters with five brigade sectors, and a NATO nation in charge of each sector. If the Russians had a sector of their own, they probably would not be answerable to the NATO command structure. I had worked with and carefully watched the Russians in Bosnia. We would not be able to share much intelligence with them, nor in a pinch, could we be certain that their loyalty to the Serbs wouldn't dominate their actions.

A week later the Russians demanded an inspection of the NATO forces in Albania, and simultaneously requested to inspect NATO facilities in Italy under the provisions of the Conventional Forces in Europe Treaty. Many NATO nations wanted to accede to these requests to help Russia return to more active cooperation with NATO in ending the conflict and in repairing relations in general. I was supportive, but with responsibilities for the operational security of our forces, I had to resist Russian demands for full disclosure of information and open inspections. I had political backing for my position from the United States and others.

In addition to working to shape any eventual agreement in both U.S. and NATO channels, our ongoing challenge was to explain our successes in the media and thereby sustain the air campaign in the face of the Serb "peace offensive." The more the European and American public thought we were winning, the less pressure they would exert to cave in to a weak compromise. Conversely, if the Russians or Serbs sensed the NATO effort collapsing, we could end up with no diplomatic solution at all. I did my best to remain upbeat and positive in public. A cheerful outlook was thus a source of "combat power."

Another complication was the fact that within most NATO countries the war had provided an opportunity for partisan political division. National survival may not have been at stake, but political futures were. In the United States, there was a certain degree of resistance by some in the Republican party who opposed President Clinton's policy for many reasons, including disliking the U.S. commitment—they might have called it "overcommitment"—to Europe. Even so, I never felt any lack of support for our airmen, sailors, Marines, and troops. In Britain, where Prime Minister Blair had committed himself to the success of the strategy, his opposition called for the use of ground troops and made light of the possibility of achieving success with "diplomacy backed by force." In most nations there were public demonstrations and various calls to end the bombing.

It was clear that neither the bulk of the military nor many members of the media understood what was happening in the war. Probably the rank and file military in most countries, and certainly in the United States, were frustrated that we hadn't gone full-bore after Milosevic and the Serb military machine from the outset. The media were in some doubt as to whether the air campaign was working or not, and continued to press for decisions on ground options.

In fact, the best evidence of the success of the air campaign came from Milosevic himself, as he struggled to find a formula to halt the bombing without depriving himself of his gains. On May 10, for example, Milosevic continued his "peace offensive" by announcing a partial withdrawal of forces from Kosovo. In the following days, however, we found no evidence of any withdrawal.

In fighting Milosevic on the public-relations front, we knew that NATO's greatest vulnerability was unintentional injuries to innocent civilians. We knew the political impact on our governments could be devastating if it were thought that innocent civilians were inadvertently bearing the brunt of NATO's air attacks.

On the morning of May 8 we were faced with two nearly simultaneous incidents of collateral damage. In the first case, a cluster bomb unit intended to destroy helicopters on a Serb airfield malfunctioned over the city of Nis, in southern Serbia. Destruction of these helicopters would have severely limited the ability of the Serbs to move their elite light infantry and would also have impeded command and control of Serb forces. According to what we were able to determine later, the weapon "functioned" at excessive altitude, scattering the bomblets short of their target and resulting in civilian deaths and injuries. It was a tragic accident. At that point some 1,500 cluster bombs had been dropped, and to our knowledge this was only the second malfunction.

Worse was what had happened overnight when we hit the Federal Procurement and Supply Directorate, Target 493, in Belgrade. I was awakened shortly after I'd gone to sleep by my operations officer in the chateau, who warned of news reports charging that we had bombed the Chinese embassy.

I pulled on a pair of jeans and stumbled down the hall to my study and the secure communications. We looked again at the target sheets, pulled out our map of Belgrade, and watched the television closely. According to our information, we couldn't have struck the embassy. It was located in the northern part of Belgrade, and we were striking in the southern area. Perhaps an errant Serb antiaircraft missile, but not us, not this time.

But one thing I had noticed about the Serbs' propaganda was that they seldom broadcast anything to the West about our strikes that didn't contain an element of truth. They had control of the ground. There were undoubtedly things they didn't let journalists see, but what they did allow reporters to see couldn't be easily refuted. As we watched the television coverage, we could see a burning building. Then we could see Chinese faces.

Two hours later we discovered the unfortunate truth. Target 493, the Federal Procurement and Supply Directorate headquarters, was erroneously located. The site we had bombed was in fact the new Chinese embassy. The bombs had struck the target. It was a tragic mistake. There was no "secret plan" or conspiracy to strike the Chinese. And it was irremediable.

There were frantic phone calls all night and into the next morning as we sifted the records to find out how such a mistake could have happened. The French liaison officer was in early to find out what had happened, and why, since France also knew about the target, though perhaps not its exact location. My intelligence officer, Brigadier General Neal Robinson, took full responsibility and offered to resign. I refused his offer; he wasn't actually responsible.

The truth was, we were engaged in a very complex targeting process in which the national agencies, over which we had no control, were charged with recommending targets that would meet our priorities. While it was true that at any stage, anyone could have contacted someone with very recent experience in Belgrade who might have recognized that the building pictured for Target 493 was the new Chinese embassy, the fact was that the recommendation came from a CIA official who had served in Belgrade and was screened by the appropriate people in the Department of Defense in Washington. The next day Secretary Cohen and CIA Director George Tenet took responsibility for the mistake.

Meanwhile we reviewed all of our approved targets, and those in process, to be sure that the photographs actually were the targets we were after. And we began to add even more information to our no-strike list. We were determined that this wasn't going to happen again, because Operation Allied Force had to continue and to be intensified. We had struck almost 1,000 targets, and there had been only eight incidents of serious civilian losses. I had to stand up for the airmen, who were flying the most precise and error-free campaign ever conducted, so far as we could see.

Over the next week, however, we seemed to be snakebit. On the night of May 13, two of our aircraft struck at a reported Serb police station outside the Kosovar village of Korica. We had noticed Serb equipment there previously, and we had reports that this set of buildings had been taken over by the police. That made it a legitimate target. Unmanned aerial vehicles tried to validate activity at the site that day, but a combination of weather and enemy action frustrated our efforts. The nighttime strike went ahead anyway. The pilots saw revetments, possible artillery pieces, and police vehicles, including an armored personnel carrier. But what we didn't know was that apparently more than a hundred Albanians had been locked overnight in the compound and told they would be shot if they tried to leave. Our bombs reportedly killed eighty Kosovar Albanians—the very people we were trying to help.

The next day we also heard that there were two near misses of International Red Cross convoys. Jim Ellis wanted to rule out attacking trucks, period. Mike Short was reminding me of the lack of strikes on Belgrade since the Chinese embassy incident. We had to settle it down, I said. No backing off. Generate more targets. And put any rule changes in writing. I acknowledged that we might have to make adjustments in what we were doing. I could sense the loss of momentum.

I knew that additional incidents were inevitable in an air campaign. As time went on, mistakes added up, and civilians suffered the most. In addition, there were reports of Serbs using the Kosovars as human shields under bridges and at other locations that might be likely targets.

But public pressure after the strike at Korica was intense. The NATO ambassadors were concerned; their governments were being subjected to widespread public criticism. Admiral Guido Venturoni, Klaus Naumann's successor as Chairman of the Military Committee, called to reinforce the expectations of the ambassadors. "Wes, you must be more careful," he said. "Please don't allow such incidents to occur."

"Guido, I understand what you're telling me about the reaction in the Council," I replied. "And we are revising procedures. But if we try to prevent all civilian casualties, we'll never strike another building. We've already ceased bombing trucks. There are human hostages under bridges, so we're not bombing bridges in Kosovo. There's an intense desire that we'll never have civilian casualties again. But we will—this kind of incident will happen again. It's inevitable." I wanted to defend our airmen and to give Venturoni the arguments he needed to reduce the unrealistic expectations of the ambassadors. "Guido," I implored, "you've got to continue to stand up for us in the Council— we're all in a tough predicament."

Despite the Chinese embassy incident, Washington remained

determined that the air campaign continue at a high level of activity. Hugh Shelton told me on May 12 that if we just hit Milosevic very hard for the next two or three weeks, we would get an agreement. The next evening we struck Serbia's electric power system for a third time, along with numerous other targets. I felt we were delivering our requirements thus far, though I was having difficulty securing French approval to strike at the heart of the Serbs' communications systems, which tended to be located near the center of most cities, substantially raising the risk to civilians nearby. Still we kept up the tempo, striking air defense, airfields, bridges, military facilities, radio relay sites, and petroleum facilities throughout Serbia. We just needed a fallback, a guarantee. That was the ground plan.

The British had come up with a slightly different twist to the problem of ground-force planning. While they fully supported my going ahead with assessing the options from the previous summer, they developed the idea of a halfway measure between the existing NATO planning for KFOR (under which NATO would be invited to Kosovo to enforce a diplomatic settlement) and Option B(-) (the direct invasion of Kosovo by NATO troops). They termed it the "semi-permissive" environment, a condition in which there was still no invitation to enter but well-organized resistance at the operational level had collapsed. NATO would enter on its own and "mop up."

The virtue of this proposal was that it would seem to require a smaller invasion force than Option B(-). And it was certainly tempting to believe that after weeks of attacks, the Serb forces ought to be virtually demolished.

The difficulty was that we could not guarantee any specific level of damage from the air, much less predict it. In the Gulf War, the planners had sought to destroy 50 percent of the Iraqi force from the air before the entry of the ground forces. But after a forty-four-day air campaign there, according to subsequent battlefield examination, only about 10 percent of the Iraqi force had been taken out from the air. And this had been in a desert with far easier flying conditions. Hugh Shelton and I were wary of the notion of "semi-permissive" combat, since it is more likely to be a condition determined after the fact, when resistance actually collapses, than it is to be predicted. If we built our plan on this, entered, and found ourselves bogged down with organized resistance, we would lose time and take unnecessary casualties. I believed it was important to stand firm on the full military requirements.

The arrangement we reached was a compromise, however, pending the review of Option B(-). We would update the basic KFOR plan and encourage nations to accelerate the deployment of their forces. This would give us a jump-start if we had to go ahead with an invasion.

Meantime I was still revising the Option B(-) plan. In meetings with the key Chiefs of Defense, the reception was generally favorable. Charles Guthrie, the British Chief of Defense, spoke of tens of thousands of British troops if necessary. Jean-Pierre Kelche of France explained his country's deployment, citing sizable French commitments overseas. The German Chief, Hans-Peter von Kirchbach, who was new in the position, was virtually silent, though he did state that a ground operation would be a big political problem in Germany. The Italians had only about 18,000 troops who could serve overseas, since they were still a conscript Army, and they already had several thousand troops committed in Bosnia, Albania, and Macedonia. Their Chief, Mario Arpino, said that he believed his nation would do what it could. But of course, these weren't commitments, just informal dialogue among military chiefs to help us in scoping the size of the U.S. force that might be required. When I factored in the hedging and qualifications, I could see somewhere between 75,000 and 100,000 NATO troops available, not counting the Americans.

However, my key commanders, looking at the possible revisions to Option B(-), were far from consensus on anything except the need to continue planning. Most mentioned the need for more aggressive economic and political sanctions, always a favorite of top-level military leaders. They were still sore over NATO's failure to put in place an effective embargo against petroleum resupply to Yugoslavia. Two commanders wanted to invade from the north, attacking Serbia (including Belgrade) through Hungary and Croatia. They felt this was the best solution because, they thought, it provided a long-term, regional solution. Two others preferred this plan because it was the doctrinally correct solution, decisive force aimed at an adversary's presumed center of gravity. An equal number felt that Option B(-), the effort against Kosovo, was preferable because it would be less likely to fracture NATO solidarity, would have less impact on Russia, and could be executed in time to return the refugees before winter. Two others felt that NATO solidarity would still be at risk under Option B(-), and the option should therefore be executed under only the most extraordinary circumstances.

I had promised Hugh Shelton that I would provide him with a workable ground plan, and so I continued to work on Option B(-) in the days following, ably supported by Dieter Stockmann, Ed Burba, Rupert Smith, and a multinational planning team provided by the Chiefs of Defense. Shelton had told me that if the air campaign didn't work, we would either have to tell Milosevic he won or produce a ground option. Faced with that choice, we in the military had to lead. Many of the other Chiefs of Defense felt the same way.

After working over the courses of action again, we began to see a way to proceed that would enable us to win on the ground, deploy in time to finish the fight before winter, and limit the U.S. contribution to roughly half the total force. On Monday, May 17, I arranged a special teleconference to brief my commanders on the concept and to take a sensing of how their thinking had progressed since the last session. I quickly sketched out the enemy situation, the likelihood that, after another three months of our air attacks and his continuing reinforcements within Kosovo, we would probably have reduced the Serb force by a third in tanks, by two-thirds in armored fighting vehicles, but perhaps by none in artillery and mortars. With reinforcing infantry and police we were probably going to face a Serb force of perhaps 50,000 to 60,000 troops within Kosovo. We had to assume it would be a prepared defense, with mines and bunkers, tying together villages in fortified zones and fighting within urban areas, at least initially.

My plan was to attack with decisive force. To be certain that we could make the penetration and exploit to finish the operation within a few weeks, I wanted six divisions, some light, some heavy, some mixed. U.S. Marine as well as Army forces would be needed. We would use avenues of approach through Albania as well as Macedonia, moving and fighting through the mountains as necessary. Some would attack by infiltration, others would have to make a river crossing. In every area, we'd be struggling with the difficult terrain as well as with the enemy. We would also exploit our helicopters and heavy armor at the appropriate time.

We would make the deployment in about seventy-five days. We had looked at the logistics problems, including road repair, movement of fuels, and forward movement of the heavy equipment. We hadn't nailed the final details but in scoping the problems, we felt it was all doable. Even the poor bridges in Albania could be bypassed by tracked bridges.

It was a modification and enhancement of the concepts on which I had briefed the Chiefs of Defense and the commanders. In recent days, as Rupert Smith and I had talked to military leaders in the Alliance, we could see support gathering for the necessary European troops. Informally, we were envisioning at least 35,000 to 50,000 British troops, 10,000 to 20,000 French, and at least 3,500 Italians. If everyone else contributed we would get other NATO troops of more than ten thousand, I figured. The Germans hadn't responded, even informally, but I was hopeful that in the end, Germany would not stand aside while its Allies shouldered the burden. With the American contribution, we could assemble the 175,000 troops we would need for the campaign.

Though I could sense a convergence around the concept we had developed, I made it clear that I wasn't yet ready to organize for the ground operation. In fact, I explained, I was not pressing to go in on the ground. The mission would be tough, and it would take the whole-hearted commitment of the nations to make it work. They would have to commit themselves to war. My job at that point, as I saw it, was to present a workable option. If the air campaign were to prove insufficient, we had to have an alternative. I hoped that we wouldn't need to use it.

I called Hugh Shelton shortly after my conference with the command. "Sir, just finished working through the assessment with my four-stars. Please tell the Secretary that I have a feasible ground option that can be executed this campaign season. We will get the refugees home. It's about 175,000 troops, with around 100,000 actually going into Kosovo to fight."

But before we'd implement any ground option, I was determined to bring the Apaches into play. With the air campaign reaching the limits of its usefulness, we needed to take risks up front, soon, and not defer them until later, when we would have to pay with the lives of our soldiers on the ground and ultimately, far more civilian casualties.

Despite Hugh Shelton's assurance during the President's visit that there would be no difficulty obtaining permission to do live-fire rehearsals using the artillery and rockets assigned to Task Force Hawk, I heard nothing from him on this for several days afterward. Meanwhile, Jay Hendrix had declared Task Force Hawk ready to fight, except for the rehearsals, and I was looking forward to another video teleconference with Secretary Cohen and the Service Chiefs to make my case for the Apaches.

But the feedback I was getting from Washington was disturbing. Several of the Chiefs still questioned the value of risking the Apaches to attack the tactical forces in Kosovo. Apparently, they didn't believe that the Serb forces there were in any way a center of gravity for Milosevic and saw no connection between the destruction of these forces and the successful conclusion of the campaign. Their view nicely suited the political climate in Washington, where it was feared that casualties might discredit the campaign. In fact, from the beginning of the campaign, some members of the Joint Chiefs had apparently questioned the value of our commitment in the Balkans, period. Ironically, the more successful the air campaign was in going after targets on the ground in Kosovo, the less likely would it be for the Chiefs to support using the Apaches.

All of the success we were reporting, and the determination of the political leaders to succeed, couldn't bridge this divide between those in Washington who thought they understood war, and those in Europe who understood Milosevic, the mainsprings of his power, and the way to fight on this continent. The Europeans also looked at the Apaches as a litmus test of the American commitment to the operation. Although the Americans were providing the largest proportion of the airpower, the Europeans seemed to feel that they were taking the largest political risks in the operation. Indeed, it was a European war, with refugees, troop commitments, and a clear economic impact on southern Europe.

On the American side, though, Hugh Shelton had told me that Washington wanted to pull back on anything that looked like we might be heading incrementally into a ground war. As he explained it, after talking to some of my subordinates on his last visit, he felt that we didn't need the Apaches. The Air Force and Navy jets were doing just fine against the Serb forces. In his view we wouldn't find the massed formations on the battlefield that we always practiced against, and that would justify the risks to the Apaches. I took issue with his interpretation. He didn't order us not to proceed to make the Apaches ready, however. It was an opportunity left open, one that promised more effective action against Serb ground forces.

So I had no illusions when I went into the VTC with the Secretary and the Service Chiefs on May 13, prepared once more to make the case for Hawk. Our first problem was with using suppressive fires against the air defense. According to standard Army procedure, we simply estimated where enemy air defense might be, based on the terrain and the force's operating patterns. But the Defense Department's lawyers insisted that before we could shoot at these locations now they had to be "observed," that is, they couldn't be "templated." The lawyers were going to define what "observed" meant. This was a requirement derived from the NATO Rules of Engagement that had been approved for the operation, without regard to the kind of needs we might have for the Apaches. By the lawyers' definition, someone would have to view the Serb air defenses through photography or TV within a few hours of the time the artillery was to be fired.

This would be fine in theory, but in a busy theater the vagaries of weather and the limitations of available assets would make it a standard that we would have trouble meeting. The intelligence team could look at, say, eight possible places for enemy air defenses—probably some piece of high ground along the border, but maybe a known site deeper in Kosovo. Before we could shoot our suppression, we would have to have visibility over what was there, updated within the last few hours. If we had seen only five of the locations, then only those five could be engaged. The commander would then have to either accept the added risk from the other three untargeted locations or call off the planned mission. Surely there had to be a better way. Never had we imposed such a standard on ourselves. There had to be a misunderstanding, I thought.

As I worked through the discussion on why we needed suppressive fires, it was clear that we weren't going to get the go-ahead with the live fire rehearsals until the issue of unobserved suppressive fires was worked out. So I couldn't report that the Apaches were ready, because we didn't have permission to do our live-fire rehearsals. Nor was I totally confident that we had the targets to justify taking risks with the Apaches. I didn't want to proceed on the basis of preconceptions. But I didn't want to give up on the Apaches, either.

On May 14 Hugh Shelton told me that a group of retired Army generals, whom he had seen at an Army aviation convention, had begged him not to use the Apaches in Kosovo. I warned him that if we listened to this kind of advice from people who weren't present at the scene, conclusions would be drawn that the Army can't do much. The next day I again visited Task Force Hawk in Albania, and I was impressed at its level of readiness. We were conducting twenty-four-hour tracking of possible targets, and we had figured out a way to live with restrictive guidance on "observed fires." I invited another Army four-star, this one on active duty, to come and validate the Task Force's work, with an eye toward offsetting the "graybeards" and Washington.

The resistance to the Apaches highlighted the problems facing Operation Allied Force, because by mid May we had gone about as far as possible with the air strikes. The next strategic targets would entail more risk of civilian casualties, and the French, among others, were resistant. Even though we were now producing more and more targets, the easy and obvious targets had mostly been hit. We had about completed attacking most high-level targets, too. And in Kosovo, concerns for civilian casualties were driving us to be more cautious in air strikes against Serb forces, just as the Serbs were becoming smarter. Further intensification of the conflict was going to be difficult, unless we committed the Apaches or announced a ground option.

The Apaches were strictly an American problem. The Europeans had already pronounced the Apaches more or less an embarrassment, and, in any case, I had retained them under U.S. control. The ground option, on the other hand, truly was a problem for NATO. In this effort I knew that Secretary General Solana saw the need for a follow-on option if the air campaign didn't succeed. There could be no future for NATO as we knew it without success in this mission. I knew that we would have support from Great Britain, Italy, and, eventually, France. Germany was officially silent, but I was not worried about its likely support. If the United States and these countries went in, we could count on most of the smaller allies, too.

However, in dealing with the United States, there were profound political difficulties. Most observers felt that a ground operation would certainly require a vote of endorsement by Congress, and the outcome of such a vote was unclear. Moreover, according to some, to call for a ground option meant acknowledging some degree of failure with the air campaign.

Just as important, going in on the ground was going to require a major additional commitment of resources from the Congress. It would weigh heavily on the Department of Defense, and opinion within the Pentagon was anything but united in backing the engagement in the Balkans.

As I considered the problem in Washington, I recognized the extraordinarily difficult position in which Secretary Cohen found himself. As a former senator he had great experience with Congress. Many of the senators were his friends, including several who had never supported U.S. engagement in the Balkans. But he was responsible for the U.S. military operations, and for all of our preparations. The Balkans was one of the Administration's most important foreign policy initiatives. Peace in Bosnia had come, thanks to the United States and the U.S. Armed Forces.

Secretary Cohen was also responsible for the future of the U.S. Armed Forces. He recognized, as did I, that the more deeply we went into the ground operations planning, the greater the threat to the overall Defense program that had been designed by the Pentagon, forcefully advocated by the Secretary, and approved by the Congress. I knew from our discussions that Cohen had never wanted U.S. troops sent into Kosovo, and I had continually tried to support actions and plans that avoided committing U.S. troops.

What we had not discussed was whether he would support a U.S.-led ground operation, if the alternative was to concede failure. No doubt he would not want to commit in advance to the idea of a ground intervention, I reasoned, for fear that it would make such an intervention more likely. Further, he may have been concerned about the rumored fractious attitudes within the Joint Chiefs. But we were approaching the moment of truth, at least in terms of making the decisions to begin preparations.

I wanted to be certain that I had strong NATO support for moving ahead with planning, so I arranged for Secretary General Solana and

Admiral Venturoni to come to SHAPE headquarters on May 19 to receive our ground options assessment work. I skimmed quickly through the technical details in order to focus on the conclusions— that we had a feasible option; that it could be accomplished before the winter; that preparations had to begin by June 1; that the preparation for ground operations gave us greater diplomatic leverage.

Solana was pleased that we had completed the assessment. He went back through the key points: how deploying forces now for the enhanced KFOR would feed into Option B(-); the need to commence preparations soon; the difficult position that Washington was in; where the troops would come from. When I raised the option of going in from the north, he just shook his head and waved it off. "You know it will not be acceptable to the nations," he said.

Solana was searching for a way to postpone a decision to commence the preparations. "How much can you do under the authority of KFOR?" he asked again. I had to draw some hard lines here. This was where the political dynamic had to yield to the military dynamic, I explained. We needed a full push for deployment, and some nations would need to call up reserves. This couldn't be fuzzed much longer. I was particularly concerned about Washington.

I had always been candid with Javier Solana. I was a double-hatted officer. I followed guidance and orders from the U.S. chain of command, but I was also responsible for the NATO operations. Usually, there was no conflict, but in this case there might be. The Secretary of Defense had made it plain enough for many months that he didn't want another commitment in the Balkans and that any necessary commitment should be minimized. But we had hit a wall here; there was no finessing this issue. I had done the assessment. I had to present it and follow through. For me, if it came to a choice between recommending ground troops or accepting failure, it was going to be ground troops. And we needed to make a decision to move in that direction soon.

OK, Solana said, and he promised to make it clear to the British and to the Germans that we had to have a fundamental decision at the end of the month.

Then I gave the Secretary General another letter on the ground option. I had written it to be the "clincher" after the brief, though I knew that it wasn't necessary today. The letter demonstrated at length how moving into ground-force preparations would exponentially increase our leverage against Milosevic, making it all the more necessary for a decision to be made by June 1.

I knew the real challenge was in Washington, however. On May 18 I had a private VTC with Hugh Shelton. It was a constructive discussion on the ground option, and we talked through many of the military details, including Allied contributions and the possible effect on the Russians, an aspect that worried him. On balance, though, he seemed supportive, arguing that we had to get on with our preparations or admit that we didn't have the stomach to do it. We arranged that I would come to Washington to brief Secretary Cohen and the Service Chiefs on the results of our assessment.

On the long flight across the Atlantic, I scanned my briefing again. I knew I still hadn't resolved the military's innate hankering to go deep into Serbia from the north, with a larger force, seeking a decisive military solution even at the expense of greater strategic and diplomatic difficulties. Many in the Army disliked the idea of going through Albania en route to Kosovo. As one of the senior officers told me, only half joking, "We don't do mountains."

I didn't want to make the political argument against this option, which Solana had given me—many American officers would have shot back, "we have to stand up for what's right militarily." But the more I looked at the northern option, the less I liked it on military grounds. For one thing, it was directed at Belgrade, a strategy that would be useful only if attacking Belgrade would force the Serb military to deploy and contest our advance. In that case, we would mass our capabilities and destroy the Serb military. But this was almost certainly a decisive reason for the Serbs not to respond in such a way.

If the Serbs resisted by falling back and moving deeper into Serbia, then our options were different. On a continental scale, Serbia might look small. But relative to the size of the force we would deploy, Serbia was big. It could swallow up several divisions, each consisting of 10 to 20,000 troops. To get to Belgrade might require more than one major river crossing. If we didn't "do mountains," then how good were we at major river crossings? I remembered how NATO troops struggled to cross the flooded Sava River from Croatia into Bosnia in January 1996, and the press coverage that followed.

What were we going to do with Belgrade when we got there? If the Serbs decided to resist, were we going to fight through the city block by block, using artillery and mortars?

In Kosovo, the bulk of the population would be on our side. Tens of thousands of Albanians would be begging to help us. Kosovo was small, too; once through the mountains, it was a matter of about sixty miles' advance to secure almost the whole province. But fighting our way through Serbia would likely be different. The Serbs were deeply patriotic, and given their tradition of partisan resistance during the two world wars, it was difficult to believe we could be welcomed there as liberators. The seemingly open terrain leading to Belgrade was marked by scores of towns and small cities, as well as some large urban areas. We wouldn't be able to bypass every one of these. It would mean early action in built-up areas, more casualties, destruction, and delay.

Upon my arrival, I met with Hugh Shelton in his office. I flipped through the briefing charts, highlighting the changes we had made since I met with him and the other NATO Chiefs of Defense, and discussed where we stood. I sensed support from him up to a point. This was rough, he said. As he saw it, it was necessary to draw a line and force a decision. If we were going to intervene on the ground this year, then preparations had to begin immediately. He said that he was sticking with my June 1 date and that his job was to make sure there would be no slippage in that decision. If the gang across the river couldn't make a decision by then, then the answer was, no ground option, he said.

I recognized a degree of ambivalence, but also agreed that we needed to force a decision.

As I prepared to leave, he added, "By the way, Berger asked me if it was all right to talk to you. I said yes, so he may call you. Hopefully, you'll support me on the 1 June date."

"Of course," I said.

That night Sandy Berger called to talk about the ground option. I described the plan in outline. Then came the question I knew to expect: "How long can we defer a decision, Wes?"

"We need to start preparations on 1 June," I said. "That's when we need the decision." Then I clarified, "Now, we don't need a decision to do a ground operation. That can come much later. We just need to decide to prepare for it, alert any reserves, begin the logistics move-ments, and start everything in motion. The plan won't be finished in all its details. But if we decide to begin preparations, we can make what-ever adjustments are required to make it work."

"Wes, let me just ask, can you push that date back a couple of weeks, to, let's say, 15 June?" he asked. So, this is what it was about—an effort to end-run the Chairman. But then, didn't he have the right to talk directly to the commander?

"Sandy, we can't. It's a seventy-five-day deployment, best case. That's no allowance for bad weather or screwups. Some slippage is inevitable. Don't push it back on us; don't risk that we'll have to com-mit our soldiers to fighting in the mountains in bad weather, or with-out the kind of preparations we need."

"Wes, I've got to have two more weeks."

"I don't see how we can do it. Anyway, what will we get out of two more weeks?"

"Maybe nothing, but we need more time. We're not ready here."

When Sandy Berger wants to work an issue, I thought, he really knows how to explore it from all the angles. At last, though, we con-cluded. "All right," he said, "I hear what you're saying about needing to decide to begin preparations as soon as possible. I'll keep that in mind. And let me ask you to reconsider and find some way that we can extend that deadline by a couple of weeks."

"OK, I'll reconsider, but I can't promise anything. I still think we need to decide by 1 June." I didn't give. Still, it was good to hear the seriousness with which Sandy was considering the ground option. He wasn't rejecting it, not by any means.

On the morning of the 20th, I walked down the Pentagon E-ring hallway to see the Army Chief of Staff, General Dennis Reimer. There is a tradition and a reserve about this office that inspires every Army officer who enters it. It is the tradition of George Marshall and Maxwell Taylor, William Westmoreland and Creighton Abrams, all legendary Chiefs of Staff. This was the office where Army Chief of Staff Carl Vuono had pinned on my first star in 1989.

Now I was entering this office almost ten years later, hat in hand, asking for the Army's support to help us win a war.

Reimer couldn't have been more hospitable. He welcomed me

warmly, offered coffee, inquired about the operation overall, and how he could help.

"Chief, I'd like to give you a quick look at the plan and ask your support in the tank briefing today," I said.

I flipped through the briefing slides I would present that afternoon, highlighting the key points and summarizing the conclusions. We talked about logistics, deployability, and several other aspects.

"Wes, I certainly support your planning," Reimer said, adopting a kind, even solicitous tone. "I think we should continue the planning. And we need to take a look at it back here, examine some of the work in detail, especially the logistics. And what about the option in the north?"

Of course, he hadn't studied the plan, and I didn't expect a full endorsement. The Army wanted its chance to help, to provide the expertise and assurance that the plan was as sound as possible. The Apache deployment, with the two crashes in training, was no doubt embarrassing in the internecine struggles within the Pentagon and in Washington. Good planning took time. In Operation Desert Storm, there was six months of planning after the forces began deploying, and they had at least begun with the rudiments of a theater war plan. Even for the quick take-down of Panamanian dictator Manuel Noriega in 1989, the planning had consumed months. It was certainly reasonable, preferable from the Army's perspective, and even prudent for the Army to want all these details worked.

But by the way Reimer said it, I knew instantly what was implied. It sounded like a stall—bring the plan back, find a dozen reasons to keep studying it until the window for operations closed, maybe defer it for eight months, maybe never have to execute at all. At least, wait to be ordered by the National Command Authority. No volunteering for these kinds of risks.

I remembered Reimer's maneuvers to try to prevent transferring the U.S. Army South headquarters from Panama to Puerto Rico in 1997. Besides, the planning for Kosovo was my responsibility, not the Army staff's. The logistics work had been done by well-qualified Army planners in Europe consulting with experts in the Pentagon and elsewhere. We had looked at roads, calculated repair requirements, fuel and ammunition requirements, arrival airfields, and ports. We had made the on-the-ground reconnaissance and double-checked it. We were working closely with Allies in theater, about whom the Army planners in the States knew little directly. I had deliberately waited to endorse the option until I was personally convinced it could be made to work. The Army was supposed to support and assist my efforts, not block them. Yet I had felt no rush of support from the Army staff to help me deal with the urgency of the situation. I was concerned.

In my own experience at the National Training Center, I had worked with scores of units as they went through their operations. "There are only two kinds of plans," I used to tell the commanders there: "Plans that might work and plans that won't work. There's no such thing as the perfect plan. You have to take a plan that might work and *make* it work." I wanted Reimer's support that what I was presenting was basically a course of action that could be made to work. With effort. With risks. To get more than a million and a half refugees home before the freezing Balkan winter, before the air campaign foundered, and before NATO consensus dissolved. But I didn't get it.

I walked back toward the river entrance to see Joe Ralston, the Vice Chairman, and talk through the plan with him. We sat around the small table in his office and flipped through the slides. As I concluded, I asked for his support.

"Wes, let me ask you this question," he replied. "Let's just say we implemented your plan, and then something went wrong in Korea, and we had to go to war there. What would we do? We do have 80,000 Americans there, and a treaty. So we'd have to do something."

"You'd fight it with other forces," I said. "You'd use the forces that have that as their assigned mission in case of war." I could see where this conversation was headed. It was the old "two major regional conflicts" argument.

"OK," he said. "But I care about oil, too, so what if fighting were to occur at about the same time in the Persian Gulf?"

"Well, you have other forces that could be used, or you could call up reserves. But if you needed the forces we're using, those forces would be unavailable for, let's say, about four weeks while we pulled out and repacked for the Gulf. But, Joe, there is no fighting in either place, and no likelihood of it in the near term," I protested.

I paused. We looked at each other across the table, where we had spent many hours over our three years of work together.

"Joe, surely you're not saying that we're going to give up and lose in the only fight we have going, in order to be ready for two other wars that are not threatening in any way now?"

"Well, it's the kind of question we have to ask," he said.

Sure, it was a logical question, I thought. But it wasn't a supportive question. The Chiefs were seriously considering withholding forces to be ready for the two nearly simultaneous hypothetical major theaters of war elsewhere, however unlikely, even if it caused the United States and NATO to lose the actual war in Europe.

I walked into the tank for the briefing just a few minutes before the scheduled start. One by one the Chiefs came in, the Vice Chairman, and the Chairman. Secretary Cohen didn't attend, which surprised me.

I went through the briefing. I laid out the plan as clearly and objectively as possible. But as I talked it through and fielded the questions, I sensed the skepticism in the room. Of course, the chiefs hadn't had their staffs work through the plan in detail. But they had heard the general outline through various channels, and through their staffs' pre-briefs. I couldn't push it to a decision; I didn't have the support. And I didn't want to give them a way to say no or to block my continuing work on this.

"So, this is just an In-Process Review," I concluded. "I intend to go back, do some more work on the option in the north, and then come back with more details."

There was nothing to disagree with. I had taken my soundings, and I had more work to do, I knew. It wasn't won, but it wasn't lost, either.

On the way out of the building, around 6:45 P.M., I stopped by to see Hugh Shelton. "I'd like to go see the SecDef, and give him a letter explaining where we are," I said.

"Sure, go ahead," he said, glancing at the letter but not reading it.

I went upstairs and knocked on the door. It was quiet on the third floor, and the Secretary was finishing off his last papers before leaving.

"Mr. Secretary, may I have just a few minutes with you?" I asked.

"Of course. Come in." He was cordial, as always. He gestured to a chair and looked up at me.

I reviewed quickly the session with the Chiefs, sketching out the plan. I was pretty sure that Shelton had read him in on the details. Then I said, "Sir, I'd like to give you a letter which lays out the political-military arguments in some detail."

It was very similar to the "clincher" letter I had given to Solana a few days before. I wanted him to understand that I wasn't asking to use ground troops to fight a ground war—not yet. I wanted to commence the preparations soon to gain the increased diplomatic leverage we needed to offset the mounting constraints on the air campaign. I wanted him to see the urgency of facing this decision.

"Wes, who else has seen this letter?" he asked, glancing around.

"No one," I said. "Hugh Shelton knows I'm bringing it up."

"OK, I'll read it."

I was satisfied. I had carried the issue as far as I could at this point. I had given my superiors my military advice. I sensed resistance from the Services, so this would be a continuing struggle. But then, it wasn't June 1 yet, either—we still had another eleven days. And we still had a chance to win.

I returned from Washington straight to Brussels to brief the North Atlantic Council on our progress in the air campaign, and to address in more detail the issue of collateral damages. We continued to be plagued by incidents causing civilian casualties. On May 19 there were charges that an errant bomb had hit a hospital in Belgrade, and on May 20 we made news by some limited damage to the residence of the Swedish Ambassador during a dinner party and to the residence of the Swiss Ambassador. The Ukrainians had even sent a letter calling my attention to the new address of their embassy in Belgrade.

It was a difficult session initially, and the atmosphere was tense as I began my briefing. But the ambassadors listened carefully as I reviewed the "measures of merit," the complexity of the campaign, and the progress we had achieved against the ground force targets. I then explained in the greatest possible detail the strike that had resulted in the collateral damages at the hospital. I had to have their continuing support, and I could see how much they appreciated the details.

Still, the session was tough. The ambassadors were angry at the collateral damages, and they questioned how long they could maintain their support for the air campaign. "How long do you expect us to put up with this?" one ambassador asked. As long as necessary, I replied, and we need to do more in each of our governments to support this effort. These kinds of incidents are inevitable with what you've asked me to do, I said.

Meanwhile, during the VTCs I continued to work at the target development process in the Combined Air Operations Center. We hadn't struck a Serb command post since May 11—too long. I was concerned that the new rules imposed since the Chinese embassy incident and other collateral damage incidents had become a reason to simply avoid the detailed target development work. If so, we had to strengthen our procedures.

Bit by bit, we did. On May 23 we added fifty new targets to the master target file, and on the 24th another one hundred targets came in. Some of our longer-term targeting efforts were paying off, too. We were now becoming more adept at assimilating various snatches of information, correlating them with imagery, and seeing patterns.

Inside Kosovo I sensed progress, too. Despite the restrictive rules of engagement, our intelligence efforts were seeing more deeply into the structures, activities, and locations of the enemy. We were receiving more reports about Serb desertions and mutinies, public demonstrations in the cities in southern Serbia, and difficulties keeping Serb units forward and engaged. It was promising but by no means decisive.

On the strategic axis, I determined after returning from Washington to package targets to make a sustained two-week effort to break Milosevic's will. We would hit more Belgrade headquarters and leadership targets, increasingly degrade the electric power system, go after the remaining line of communications, including the bridges in Novi Sad and the big bridges in Belgrade. We would also gut the core of Milosevic's communications structure by destroying the switching centers, reported to be under Serb military control. We now had the targets to do this, and ever more aircraft—over 850 aircraft now, including deployment of U.S. Marine Corps strike aircraft in Hungary. Bases were being readied in Turkey, and we were completing final arrangements to use Bulgarian and Romanian airspace.

I needed only the approvals of the targets, and that meant a willingness to accept the risks of greater numbers of civilian casualties. I briefed Washington on the plan in a video teleconference on May 24 and noted the numbers of targets that still required approval there. Washington reaction was generally favorable to this approach. This was the American way of war: strategic, heavy firepower.

Later that evening, I met with the British, Italian, German, and

French Chiefs of Defense to underscore our needs. We were succeeding in our attacks and keeping the Alliance united, I told them, but we needed to strengthen our efforts against Milosevic to get a prompt settlement. We needed more coercive pressure, so we would try to intensify our attacks on high-visibility, high-leverage targets over the next two weeks. The objective was to pressure Milosevic to capitulate. The group listened closely as I described the targets we needed to attack. I didn't sense the same approving attitude that I had seen from the American side.

The European chiefs cautioned that what I was asking was too difficult. A major collateral damage incident, one suggested, could drive Russia out of the negotiations. The impact of striking these targets is likely to be less than we were predicting—we must concentrate on attacking the forces in Kosovo. Collateral damage was a major consideration, said another. Even the most supportive chief reminded me that it was important to go after the Serb military and police.

I asked for their support in carrying to their political leaders that we had reached the stage of needing to make hard choices in the air campaign: the easy targets had been struck. And as far as collateral damage, I said, look what the Serbs had done to the Kosovars.

Yes, one replied, but there is a declining interest in the Serbs' crimes.

I could see that we were reaching the end of the strategic campaign, at least with a unified Alliance. If we weren't careful, we were going to be at a decisive point, but it would be a point of failure.

The next evening, I spoke to Javier Solana and explained the idea of our big push for strikes over the next two weeks, and the likely risks in terms of civilian casualties. Be careful, he warned, not to stir up a lot of concern in the foreign ministries about the possibilities of civilian casualties. I also spoke with several of the NATO ambassadors that evening. Of course there could be no civilian casualties, the French envoy told me. Paris would find any collateral damage unacceptable.

The next day I returned to Brussels to meet again with the ambassadors. I briefed them on the proposed campaign and discussed the strategic opportunity before us. Then I showed them what they had not yet seen—the complete system for predicting and reducing collateral damages, as applied to a prospective Belgrade target. I spoke for over an hour. Each of the ambassadors asked his questions, and most of the questions were technical, not hostile. By the end of the session, the atmosphere was entirely different. There were no objections to what we were doing.

As I was gathering my papers to leave, one of the ambassadors came up to ask, "That target you briefed, our embassy is within a block. Should I tell my people to evacuate at night and board up the windows?"

"Yes," I said.

Then another ambassador jumped in. "What about my embassy? We are four blocks away. Will it be all right if we just tape our windows?"

"No," I said, "board yours up, too."

"I will tell them to do so immediately," he said.

I knew that I had their personal support, more strongly now than ever before. But I also knew that that wouldn't necessarily win the foreign ministries' support in their nations.

Even Washington was having trouble, as a significant backlog of targets was waiting to be approved. Hugh Shelton phoned to say that we couldn't go after the railroad yards with the kind of heavy strike we needed because of collateral damage concerns; another target was disapproved by the lawyers on grounds that it lacked the necessary connection to the Serb military. I'm frustrated, he said; have your intelligence people look for the linkage.

Negotiations with the Russians were continuing, but without progress. Hugh Shelton sounded dispirited as he described the prospects. I knew that the ground option was increasingly important to our diplomatic efforts and so were the Apaches, though neither one seemed likely to get the U.S. approval we needed.

But I wasn't prepared to give up. I followed through on the promise I had made to the service chiefs to take a more detailed look at invading Yugoslavia from the north. We formed an additional planning team, relying heavily on officers from the headquarters of the U.S. Army in Europe, and worked out courses of action, force requirements, and timelines.

It wasn't possible, on purely military grounds, to dismiss totally the northern option. More troops would be required, but the access to Serbia from the north was much easier than movement through the Mediterranean, across the Adriatic, and through the mountains of

Albania. Though a northern operation would require a month or two of preparation time beyond the start date I sought in the south, the weather was different, and there would be no problem of mountains packed with snow. The countryside was more open, and it could be argued that this was more favorable to American doctrine and close air support, despite the problem of potentially several major river crossings and the towns and cities that would have to be secured.

However, there was no military answer to the problem of urban warfare in Belgrade, or the determined resistance of the Serb population along the way. The northern approach included the classic invasion routes, which the Yugoslav military would be well prepared to defend. Also, I knew that the political problems for NATO would be insuperable.

But there was enough military rationale to make for a good debate in American military circles, where the virtues of "pure" war-fighting were highly prized. The delay in timing would also appeal to those who wanted more time to plan, or simply hoped that with additional time, we could somehow avoid moving to the next step.

I was concerned. This was going to be the next struggle.

I also knew that I needed to line up European military support for the ground option as soon as possible. I especially needed to rebut the Pentagon's fears that the Europeans wouldn't be providing any significant numbers of ground troops. I was never sure where the continuing accusations against the Europeans originated—sometimes from the Hill, perhaps from conversations with the defense attachés in Washington, or perhaps it was just the natural skepticism that we often reflected in our military staff briefing papers. But I knew that this negativism corroded to our possibilities for success.

At my May 24 meeting with several Chiefs of Defense, I presented our assessment of the ground options and received a much different reaction than I had from the American service chiefs. All agreed that the larger option from the north was really not an option. They thought we had overestimated the threat in Kosovo. They believed that Option B(-) was feasible with even smaller numbers. And they wanted to work to reduce the deployment time to sixty days.

Was this the European way of war, then, to begin without assurance of decisive force, hoping to break the enemy's will, and then pick your way toward success at a cost of increased time and casualties? Armies had fought in the manner before, and won. But I would have to resist. The ground campaign would have to be swift and decisive—for reasons of timing, maximizing our chances for operational success, and minimizing the political risks attendant to a drawn-out campaign. No more Vietnams. And I would have to press to get the resources to do it right. Still, I welcomed Europeans' support and their determination.

The opposing transatlantic perspectives were clearly on display. The Americans favored a strategic air campaign, the European militaries were more ready to move in on the ground. I was in the center, trying to make both options work.

I also continued to work over in my mind the problem of the command and control arrangements. My commanders were pressing to learn the future organization. I was pretty sure that I couldn't do all the detailed work at my level, and there were sure to be enormous complications within the NATO chain if I were to follow General Eisenhower's precedent and not appoint an overall ground commander.

On the other hand, I couldn't wholly delegate the plan and the responsibilities to subordinates, either. The ground campaign would require the tightest orchestration of political and military insights and efforts. There would be many politically sensitive decisions—the decision to begin, the risks posed by limited training and deployment times, the acceptable levels of risks in combat, the involvement of the KLA, the development of the air support, the risks of civilian casualties. I would have to retain key authorities at SHAPE, for these decisions would govern the nature of the campaign.

I talked again to General Montgomery Meigs about the plan and the Allied reactions to it. Like many of us who had studied and reflected on military history and the art of war, he was inclined toward what he saw as the more decisive, northern option. But as I reminded him, and, as he acknowledged, as soldiers, we don't always get to fight where we want. We have to win where we fight.

It also seemed that we would have to win without the Apaches. On May 18 President Clinton had commented publicly that the Apaches probably wouldn't be used, suggesting that the risk to the pilots was simply too great. My problem was that the Administration had never reached an official decision on the Apaches, so far as I knew. If it had, I wasn't informed. I was still working on the target problem and the rules of engagement, and trying to handle the continuing issues that were raised. I had not given up, nor had I been told to do so. And from frequent visits to Jay Hendrix's headquarters I was increasingly persuaded that the Apaches could be useful, perhaps vital in strengthening the fight against the Serb forces in Kosovo.

But as we continued our preparations, the mood in Washington had turned increasingly hostile to Task Force Hawk. Particularly damaging was a May 20 story in *Inside the Pentagon*, personally attacking Jay Hendrix and claiming, among other accusations, that he would not allow the Apache sorties to appear on Short's Air Tasking Order. The article was apparently based largely on an E-mail sent by a disgruntled Air Force officer several weeks previously, as Task Force Hawk was organizing itself. The story's publication was symptomatic of the difficulties of operations that maintain open communications from all levels of the chain of command. A staff officer's misunderstandings, communicated without perspective to friends in other units, suddenly surfaced to make news weeks after it had been written, after the problems it addressed, if real then, had been corrected.

The perceived vulnerability problem—that the Serbs' SA-7 antiaircraft missiles could shoot down the Apaches—was not borne out by analysis. Flying low at night up narrow valley and through the mountains, moving in small formations, the Apaches would present a fleeting target to any Serb gunner. Nor was it clear that the Serbs even had night capabilities with these launchers. Anyway, the Apaches had defensive systems.

Of course we could never guarantee that the Serbs didn't have more advanced systems or that the Apaches would take no losses. Anything could happen. But the risks were certainly bounded, and they had to be weighed against the targets available and their significance. As I knew from my close observation of what we were hitting with airpower, there were many more targets available than our aircraft were striking.

An Army assessment team visited Task Force Hawk at my invitation, but for some reason they overlooked all of the joint support available, ignored the superb targeting process that Jay Hendrix had put into place, and discounted the value of striking Serb forces. While complimentary of the crews, the Army seemed to have no confidence in its own Apache weapons system in the most likely conditions in which it would be used. I simply didn't agree.

On May 25, I resolved to try once more to gain approval to employ the Apaches to attack those targets that could not be hit by the Air Force. I told Hugh Shelton that I would like to send in a written request outlining my plan. He said OK, and I put my request for authorization in writing. The plan was simple: fly up near the border, but not across, and, using the seven-kilometer range of the Hellfire missiles, strike Serb forces inside Kosovo. Adequately prepared, such a mission would be virtually risk-free. The Serbs would have great difficulty forward positioning air defense inside Albania, and the Apaches could move north, fire, and pull back in a matter of a very few minutes. It was a plan that offered the advantages of escalating the military pressure against the Serbs, assisting the Albanians in retaining control of their northeast, and preparing our forces for possible future operations. It also met the Europeans' need to see a further demonstration of American commitment and leadership.

I wasn't especially optimistic about getting a positive response. But I believed that in a campaign like this a commander has an obligation to push, and keep pushing, to get the resources he thinks he needs, until he is simply told, No. Success in war is at least in part a matter of determination and resolution, or as Rabin put it, persistence. Still, I would have preferred the target of my persistence to have been only the enemy, rather than the Pentagon as well.

PART IV

ENDGAME

THIRTEEN

HOLDING STEADY

O N TUESDAY, MAY 25, we began to hear rumors that Milosevic
was to be indicted by the International Criminal Tribunal. I had
been one of several individuals that Chief Prosecutor Louise
Arbour had spoken with as she began to take legal action against Milosevic. In our conversation she acknowledged that this would be a highly
sensitive decision, but she did not tip her hand as far as what evidence
she had. I told her that I would be happy to testify eventually, recounting how Milosevic had admitted advance knowledge of some of General Mladic's plans for Srebrenica in 1995.

On Wednesday evening I got a call from the State Department. It's
true, I was told, Milosevic will be indicted tomorrow. I was also
informed that some in the Pentagon and the White House were
unhappy about this.

I understood the concerns that some in Washington had. An indictment on war crimes charges would rule out the possibility of conducting direct negotiations with Milosevic. It might even harden his will to
resist, though this was unpredictable. But I was more concerned about
the attitudes of NATO governments, and from this perspective, I reckoned, an indictment was a huge win. Nothing was more likely to stiffen

the Allies' resolve and push us forward into a winning situation than this indictment. And there was just a chance it might be the kind of legal blow which could break Milosevic's will. In any event, it was done. As it turned out, it did harden European resolve and did not significantly affect the ongoing effort to bring the Russians into the peace effort.

That night I also received a phone call from Lieutenant General Robert H. "Doc" Fogelsong, the Assistant to the Chairman of the Joint Chiefs of Staff, who was traveling with Strobe Talbott and assisting in working out the details of the prospective negotiations with the Russians. Fogelsong reported that there had still been no progress on that front. It was, he said, kind of a game, with each side restating its conditions.

Fogelsong was part of a team thinking through the details of a transition from the bombing campaign to the entry of ground forces. I sketched out what I thought were some of the key principles: first, there had to be a verifiable and substantial withdrawal before we stopped the bombing; second, anything that was not withdrawing was still a target; third, we needed to put in writing a military technical agreement that would govern the post-bombing period. And we couldn't be too impatient. All this might take some time, certainly more than twenty-four hours.

On Friday Washington's mood on the talks became more optimistic. Chernomyrdin was in Belgrade, finding ways to make Milosevic accept an agreement. Milosevic announced that he could accept the G-8 Principles—cease-fire, Serb military and police forces out, an international security presence in, full return of refugees, and participation in a later political agreement to determine the final status of Kosovo—as the basis of an agreement. The next day, Secretary General Solana expressed cautious optimism that Yugoslavia's offer could signal the beginning of the end of the conflict. Meanwhile, in London, President Marti Ahtisaari of Finland, a member of a negotiating team that would travel to Belgrade, sounded a firm note in favor of continuing the air strikes even as the talks were moving forward. "If you do not first achieve a verifiable withdrawal of Yugoslav security forces from Kosovo," he told the press on Sunday, there might be a situation where "any bombing pause could be used by Serbian authorities to prolong negotiations forever." He saw it quite clearly, I thought.

In general, the Alliance seemed to be doing a good job publicly restraining its optimism and continuing to focus attention on the need to intensify the air campaign. I did the same.

I told the command that morning, "We don't want to let our hopes gallop away from reality. Milosevic doesn't want NATO troops, just a bombing pause. We are in the stalling and the protracting phase. It is important to continue with the intensification of the campaign."

I knew that I had to take a continuing strong role in shaping the agreement for NATO. The Germans reported that Milosevic was balking at the SACEUR being in the chain of command. Of course, one could argue that he should have no right to dictate the composition of the force, but I knew that it was entirely possible that his demands could be taken into account in any agreement. I was determined, though, that the operation would be under NATO command and control, and appear as much like the Bosnia command arrangements as possible.

Fogelsong called that evening to update me. He recognized that Chernomyrdin was trying to convince the German chancellor, Gerhard Schroeder, to endorse Milosevic's terms concerning the chain of command and other matters and he noted that "this town is quite upset with Cherno's attempt to split the Alliance." I reassured him that the government of Germany was not going to pull away from us no matter what the blandishments, but I also counseled him again that the operation had to be under firm NATO control. By that, I explained, there must be a NATO nation in command of each sector of Kosovo, so that we can share intelligence. We cannot have a Russian sector; the Russians could participate with us in our sector, but they couldn't have their own, or we would lose NATO control.

I also warned Fogelsong that the discussions might get personal, with references to the SACEUR's role in the bombing. He said he would do his best to keep us in the chain of command at the next meeting with the Russians, in Bonn on Wednesday, June 2. Please hang tough on the details, I urged.

Even as the diplomatic efforts were moving forward, my commanders and I had been watching for weeks as the Kosovo Liberation Army slowly rebuilt its strength. Throughout the month of May we had information about the KLA's recruiting efforts, and we had learned of its training camps in Albania. We had also received information concerning the KLA's continuing struggle in northern Kosovo, around the town of Poduevo, which dominated the key Serb line of communication north towards Belgrade. And we had observed as the KLA had held onto a small corridor leading from far northeast Albania into Kosovo through the village of Kosare. The continued struggle there often drew Serb forces out into the open, where we had a chance to strike at them.

By the morning of May 26 we had considerable information about the KLA's plans to attack into Kosovo. It appeared as though four or five battalions, perhaps 1,800 to 2,000 men, would be attacking over the top of Mount Pastrik, which formed the high ground northeast of Kukes and would be key terrain for us if we invaded Kosovo under Option B(-).

I was uneasy from the first moment I learned of the plan, not that my reaction would make any difference. What I evisaged were the green troops, lightly equipped, trying to make an infantry assault against the least degraded of the Serb forces. The Serbs would have the KLA vastly outgunned in mortars and artillery, and perhaps even outnumbered in infantry as well.

But I also recognized the full significance of the KLA offensive for us. If it were at all successful, it would draw several Serb battalions out of the villages and into the fight, where we could attack them from the air. We were starting to pick up lots of hits against the Serbs' mortars on radar. We just had to bring the aircraft in against them. Or, as Jay Hendrix noted, his artillery and rockets.

I called Ric Shinseki, the Army Vice Chief and soon-to-be Chief, and asked for his help in breaking the Apaches loose to help us at this time. I explained that we did not need to fire suppressive fires, because we did not need to go over the border at all. He seemed not to know about the message I had sent to Shelton requesting this employment of the Apaches.

By Friday, May 28, the KLA offensive on Mount Pastrik was going strong, though according to the reports I was receiving, it was light infantry against heavy forces. The Serbs were reinforced by lots of artillery and mortars, and the Kosovars were not able to secure their objective. They were encountering heavy fire from the Serbs.

I was encouraging the close exchange of information between Task Force Hawk and the Combined Air Operations Center (CAOC) in Vicenza. Hawk was in direct contact with the Albanian Army who, in turn, were monitoring the KLA, and many targets were being passed to the CAOC. In addition, Hawk was acquiring targets itself by using its artillery- and mortar-locating radar. I was especially anxious to take action on these radar detections, which we knew to be real-time accurate to within a few meters. Because the U.S. ground forces weren't permitted to engage the enemy themselves, they were trying to pass the locations to the Air Force pilots overhead who would have to visually search for the targets before they could attack them. Naturally, there were delays, and some targets were never found or struck.

As Mike Short saw it, we had a good system, and he could account for all forty of the targets that Task Force Hawk had passed to him. What he couldn't do was attack those targets in real time. Some were deferred until the next day. This delay was what we needed to continue to tighten.

"This is our best chance to avoid a ground operation, this next two or three days," I said during the daily VTC. "We've put this system together. We ought to just chew them up here."

I told Jay Hendrix to make sure we were giving feedback to the Albanian Army on how we were operating. Jim Ellis, who had operational control of both the CAOC and Task Force Hawk, spoke up; he saw policy questions about some of these issues, such as how close we would strike to possible KLA locations, and he wanted to help strengthen the relationship between Hendrix and Short and their two headquarters. Ellis was right. It was exactly what he needed to do. I told him to take the leadership on this and pull it together.

I also had to turn my attention to why we still had not received any word from Washington on our request for the engineers and port opening augmentation that we would need to commence preparations for the ground option. One of my staff officers explained what was going on. "Sir, they're really dragging their feet on it. And I don't know where the holdup is on it. I talked to the operations people yesterday trying to put a push on these things, but somewhere there's some real resistance to putting these horizontal construction battalions in." The days were passing, and each passing day raised the risks for our troops.

I knew that all the NATO governments were attempting to come to grips with the political issue of moving to the ground forces. The previous week I had received word from the German government that Secretary Cohen was coming to Bonn on May 27 for a meeting with the British, French, German, and Italian defense ministers, the purpose of which was to consider the ground option. The German defense minister sent word that he would like me to attend the meeting. It was logical to assume that there would be discussions about the plan and the requirements each nation would face.

Of course, I said, but I will need an invitation, and since Secretary Cohen called the meeting, he will need to invite me. Through two different channels my staff inquired about such an invitation, but we were told, no, there would be no invitation forthcoming.

According to the American version of the meeting, the five defense ministers agreed that the time for reaching decisions was near. There was interest in trying to strengthen the air campaign, and there was concern that diplomacy had yet to achieve results. All agreed it was a good thing to have approved an increase in the size of the authorized permissive entry force, KFOR. But the key problem was the ground option. The British argued strongly for it, while others were opposed. So, from the American perspective, it seemed that there would be no clear Allied support for ground operations. This was jarring, since it was not what I had been hearing.

But after the meeting in Bonn, I began to receive other feedback from the participating nations. In addition to the British, another nation said it was prepared to go ahead on the ground option, if that was the decision, and would participate. A second nation, sensing reluctance and caution from the Americans, chose to hold back. A third nation's feedback was similar in tone; it could not agree to participate at this time. But taken overall, the thrust was, if there's to be a ground option, the United States has to be a willing leader, then we can and will follow.

Later that evening I received a note from an unknown source, along with alleged memoranda of the secret conversations between Prime Minister Blair and President Clinton. The memoranda showed that Blair was continuing to argue for a ground offensive if necessary, and for decisions soon. And Clinton was in general agreement that he would do whatever was necessary to win and was moving toward a positive decision on the ground option. They agreed that others could be brought along. It wasn't a decision, to be sure, but if genuine, it was the best news I had received in weeks. And it was an important counterweight to the grim U.S. assessment from Bonn.

On Friday, May 28, I received the report of the U.S. Army Europe's deployment planning team, which I had charged with working the timelines for deployment of U.S. forces to Albania. The results were less than I had hoped. They had proceeded logically and systematically, but what they found was a requirement for more time. According to their estimate, we would be only partially deployed at the seventy-five-day point, leaving us with a reduced period to complete the fighting before the bad weather was likely to begin. However, this was only the U.S. heavy force piece of the puzzle. We still had the use of Macedonia and the European deployments there, and if we couldn't get enough heavy forces into Albania, we might have to make the main attack with the European forces through Macedonia. Or we might operate with a combination of heavy and light forces, with the Albanians playing a larger role. And we might slip the start date by a couple of weeks, or even stagger the start.

In any event, I wasn't going to be deterred by this analysis. I directed the team to use its work as a baseline, figure out how to tailor forces and loads, take risks with the deployment packaging, and determine if there were other means I could use to accelerate the flow of forces. I believed we still had at least two more weeks to nail down all the details. Unfortunately, I knew that the work we were doing was bound to flow back into the Pentagon, where it would feed the continuing Army resistance to moving forward with the ground operation.

In the ongoing struggle over the use of the Apaches and of the artillery and rockets to hit the Serb forces fighting the KLA on Mount Pastrik, I was mystified by the Pentagon's response. In their public statements, Defense officials seemed to suggest that I was the one who didn't want to use these assets. In a Department of Defense News Roundtable on Friday, May 28, Secretary Cohen was asked about the use of long-range Army missiles, or ATACMS, the kind I had been asking to use for weeks. His reply: "Well, the ATACMS would be conceivable in conjunction with the Apaches. And when a decision is made by

General Clark, if he believes it is appropriate to use the Apaches, he may very well use the ATACMS in conjunction with it…. To the extent that General Clark feels he'll be more effective and efficient with the Apaches, then he will make that recommendation."

Of course, this was precisely what I was recommending, and to underscore this, I sent another message to Hugh Shelton asking that the Apaches be employed, along with the ATACMS. Cohen's answer confirmed what I realized was happening all along, and it was precisely why I had put my request for the Apaches in writing. As my operations officer noted the next morning in his briefing to me, "Task Force Hawk is with the Chairman. I think that's code…." Clearly, there were problems.

By Saturday, the KLA offensive had stalled, and the Serbs were playing a cautious game to avoid being vulnerable to our airpower. The Apaches would have been an ideal tool for targeting the Serb heavy equipment positioned in the treelines at night, when, as Mike Short admitted, our aerial attack was least effective.

At that same Friday news roundtable, Secretary Cohen was shaping the public understanding in the United States. "There is no consensus for a ground force," he explained, referring to his meeting with the European defense ministers the day before. "And until there is a consensus, we should not undertake any action for which we could not measure up in the way of performance …. And so, there is a very serious question in terms of trying to push for a consensus that you really diffuse or in anyway diminish the commitment to the air campaign. The one thing we have to continue is to make sure that we have the Allies consolidated in strong support of the air campaign. They are. And they are in favor of its intensification, so that's where we intend to put the emphasis."

He apparently believed that if we showed any inclination to go in on the ground, we would lose support for the air operation. From where I sat in Europe, I couldn't see it the same way. Here, the air operation was in significant difficulty over the issue of accidental injuries to innocent civilians, which would inevitably increase as we intensified our efforts. Unless we showed the Europeans that we were prepared to go as far as necessary to succeed, including ground troops, several nations might soon favor taking the best offer from Milosevic and conclude the operation before more damage was done politically to their governments. They were looking for American commitment.

On Saturday I traveled with Javier Solana to Aviano Air Base in Italy to visit the aircrews and continue the public pressure on Milosevic. I was trying desperately to make the air campaign work. But I was under no illusions that we would make easy progress. Nor was it clear that we had a follow-on option if the current diplomatic efforts failed. I warned Solana that we were not yet on the required timeline to a forced-entry option, because the Pentagon had yet to approve the early deployment of the engineers who were critical to the plan.

During this period Joe Ralston called to discuss the issue of my returning to the States for a meeting between the President and the Joint Chiefs on Thursday, June 3. Hugh Shelton's executive officer had called earlier in the week to inquire whether I was coming, and in subsequent phone calls with the Chairman, I discussed the importance of the meeting and expressed a desire to attend. "Wes, the Chairman has spoken to me about your desire to be here when the Chiefs see the President," Ralston said. "But if you came back, your presence would put too much pressure on the Secretary to make a decision on the ground forces. It would raise press speculation and expectations."

"But, Joe," I responded, "aren't we ready to make some decisions? And how can you make them without me there?" It was true that my presence would raise expectations—normally the CINC would come in privately, but that would be difficult in this case—but still, who was going to present my ideas, and who would know them well enough to answer objections? No one on the Joint Staff understood my planning in that level of detail. This was going to be a controversial decision.

"Well, this session really isn't for a decision anyway," Ralston replied. "Chances are the war won't even come up. This is just routine picture-taking at the White House. They do this every six months or so. If we need you, we can always call you."

I was concerned. I was having difficulty moving the Apache decision forward, and it was far less significant than the ground-forces decision.

By Sunday morning, Washington was hedging its bets on the ground option. Someone had realized that if the deployment of the engineers was not authorized, then we would have made a decision by default to forgo a ground option. If the engineers were approved for deployment, we would keep the option alive without having to make a decision. We got the approval to move our own European-based engineers to Albania, and we received the coordinating draft of the order deploying the horizontal construction battalions from the States to Europe. The ground option was still alive.

The night before, we had continued our pattern of striking a full array of targets throughout Serbia and striking close enough to Belgrade to force the Serbs to sound the air raid sirens, but during the day on Sunday, our jets struck a bridge at Varvarin while civilians were crossing it. Unfortunately, as people rushed out from the village market to assist, the aircraft came back and struck the bridge again. The toll was put at nine dead and twenty-eight injured. If the bridge was a legitimate military target, why didn't we strike it at night, when no people were around? asked a local schoolteacher who was quoted in the press.

It was a good question, especially since the bridge had indeed been a legitimate target. We subsequently moved bridge attacks to nighttime. But the next day there were two fresh reports of civilian injuries, a strike on a military facility in Surdulica that had hit a sanitarium and an attack to close off a tunnel that had killed an Italian journalist. Pressure from NATO Headquarters in response to the incidents was intense. I explained what had happened, and once again made the case that if we were going to continue with the air campaign we would have to understand that incidents like these would recur. I could sense the increasing difficulty that Solana was facing in dealing with the issue of civilian casualties. It made the ground option even more important.

Even by the most optimistic estimates, the ground forces would take two and a half months before they were ready, and I still had the Apaches sitting on the ground in Albania, waiting for authorization to strike Serb targets in Kosovo. By Sunday, May 30, Jay Hendrix's Task Force Hawk was doing still better at picking up Serb locations on Mount Pastrik with the TPQ 37 Target Acquisition radar. Hendrix was passing the information to the Combined Air Operations Center. But as Jim Ellis explained, the Airborne Forward Air Controllers were continuously busy. They would be dropping a bird in the hand to go after these new targets when they came in. It was further reinforcement for the argument for the Apaches and the long-range rockets.

I was concerned that the Serb forces not be allowed to push the

KLA back across the crest of Mount Pastrik. I didn't want them looking down at our refugees in Kukes, calling artillery fire on the reser-
voir, or observing the airfield. Holding the top of that hill was
extremely important. I asked Ellis to put the priority on stopping the
Serb counteroffensive in that area, telling him, "We lose that high
ground, that's all ground that's going to have to be retaken. That means
we're going to pay in blood, with our soldiers' lives, for any ground
they lose over that crest."

I was also fighting another battle, one that was threatening to break
out into the open, as the press became increasingly aware of the tension between the Pentagon and me. I was doing my best to contain the
damage, but it was clear to reporters on both sides of the Atlantic that
the distance I was kept from the President and even from the Secretary
of Defense was complicating efforts to move the campaign forward.
On my recent trip to Washington I had fended off two *Wall Street Jour-
nal* reporters pursuing a potentially damaging story concerning the
Secretary of Defense's restrictions on me. On May 30, Steven Lee
Myers and Eric Schmitt published an inflammatory article in *The New
York Times*, asserting that my staff derisively called the Secretary "Senator" Cohen. So far as I knew, there was no truth to the story, and we
had tried to head it off. Once published, we tried to deny it, without
drawing even more attention to it. But a recurring theme was obvious—for whatever reason, the Pentagon and the National Command
Authority had kept their distance from this operation, rather than
embracing it from the outset. The distance was also apparent in many
teleconferences.

On Monday morning, we started receiving reports that the KLA was
barely hanging onto the top of Mount Pastrik. At the VTC I could not
have been clearer with Mike Short and Jay Hendrix. "By one o'clock," I
directed, "you're going to tell me what you're going to do to help the
KLA hold the top of that mountain. That mountain is not going to be
lost. We're not going to have Serbs on the top of that mountain. We'll
have to pay for the top of that hill with American blood if we don't help
the KLA hold it now. That's my number-one priority."

Hendrix was getting good radar detections of the Serb artillery firing at Mount Pastrik, and he wanted them shot immediately. He had
passed these to Short, but the airmen in the CAOC wanted the right

weapons to go after them. Unfortunately, that was the Cluster Bomb Unit, which had been pulled from us since the second set of civilian casualties. But in the increased close battle we were fighting around Mount Pastrik, we needed cluster bombs to go after the Serb artillery and antiaircraft positions. I had sent in a request several days earlier for permission to use CBU, but we had heard nothing. I asked John Jumper to push this through Air Force channels, too. "Call back now," I told him at 11:30 A.M. "Wake some people up and get us the permission to use CBU. And help Mike Short get the B-52's and B-1's in play on Mount Pastrik."

At 1:00 P.M. I reached Joe Ralston, just before his morning meeting at the Pentagon. I warned him of the collateral damage sensitivities— Solana and Venturoni had called to remind me of their concerns—and I reinforced my requests to use the ATACMS and artillery in the fight on Mount Pastrik. I also asked again for his help getting permission to use the CBUs.

Ralston said he would raise the issues and reported that the request to use the CBUs was at the White House for approval.

A few minutes later, the hourly update came in: eighteen aircraft engaging three tanks and a military vehicle—a suspected tank battalion in a treeline. We had aircraft over Mount Pastrik searching for targets, but they could detect no artillery fire.

I called Jay Hendrix. "Sir, it's a confused situation on Pastrik," he said. "The KLA holds some positions to the east, and I've passed ten good targets to the Air Force." Ground combat is almost always confused, of course, especially as it is occurring.

"Jay, please stay with the Air Force and follow up on this," I replied. "I want those targets hit." Hendrix was moving steadily into the role of ground component commander in Albania. I knew he would push and take a continued personal interest in the Air Force strikes.

Then Joe Ralston called back, to say that the White House was concerned by reports that foreign advisers were with the Serbs fighting on Mount Pastrik, so any approval of rockets and artillery "is not going to happen quickly."

We'd had reports like these before. Perhaps they were mercenaries. The Albanians alleged that at least one Russian captain had been captured fighting with the Serbs. But we had to go on with our mission. I doubted that foreign governments would be surprised by casualties, if they were putting in advisers to assist the Serbs.

By 5:00 P.M. Mike Short had diverted the B-52's onto the slopes of Mount Pastrik. "Sir, it's going well," he said. Of course, there was no way at that point to assess the damage done to the Serbs, but the reporting indicated that the KLA was still clinging to the top of the mountain.

It was early evening when the Army Chief of Staff, Dennis Reimer, called. He said he was surprised that we did not yet have authority to use the long-range missiles to hit the Serb forces around Mount Pastrik. I emphasized that if he wanted to help, then we would need U.S. leadership at this point to move ahead on committing additional assets and working for the follow-on ground option.

That evening I also received a response from Hugh Shelton to my two requests to employ the Apaches. The pivotal element revolves around the increased risks versus the potential gains, Shelton said. Could I provide data justifying the gains, in terms of targets not hit by other means? I said I'd get to work on it right away.

Late that night I received word that Secretary Cohen had authorized us to resume use of the CBUs against the Serb forces in Kosovo.

The battle to protect the KLA toehold over the crest of Mount Pastrik continued for the next two days. Our airmen were flying repeated strikes against Serb forces and areas throughout western Kosovo. Many of the strikes were against what the airmen reported as revetments, or mortar pits. I continued to hope they contained some real artillery, not just decoys, but they also reported striking tanks, armored fighting vehicles, and artillery. They reported occasional secondary explosions, too. And we were sending B-52 strikes in against border posts and staging areas.

Task Force Hawk continued to pass more targets than the airmen could strike, including some that reportedly could be seen by the Apaches from across the border. As I later told Shelton, of the fifty-one new targets, along with nine counterbattery radar detections that Hawk had submitted, only twenty had been struck by the Air Force. I asked again for his support in approving the Apaches.

In the midst of the battle for Mount Pastrik, I also received on Monday the revised movement timelines from the deployment planning team. This was everything I had hoped for. In a little over forty-eight hours, they had devised a plan that might work, and that we could make work. It demonstrated the feasibility of deploying and position-ing adequate combat power forward to Kukes to begin our operation on September 1. It looked imaginatively at the use of water transport and the improvement of the airfield in northeast Albania near Kukes. It astutely used Task Force Hawk as the initial force to move forward and secure the line of departure, with the Marines following as soon as pos-sible. Of course there were caveats. This plan took risks. But I believed the plan was workable with forceful leadership.

It was just-in-time analysis. I had arranged to see Javier Solana that evening and present him the results. In my own logic, I couldn't argue for a generic ground option; I had to have a specific plan, one that I knew could be made to work. I was now persuaded that I had such a plan.

This was the culmination of my thirty-three years of military ser-vice, combat in Vietnam, service in Army units, training at the National Training Center and in the Battle Command Training Pro-gram, personal observation, study, and research on military operations. It was not only military judgment; it was also personal judgment. Com-manders do that all the time, but here, I thought, there is a big differ-ence. I was actually advocating a new operation based on this specific plan. I often had worried about the civilian risks as we carried out the air strikes; this recommendation was far more difficult personally, for I knew that there would be casualties and suffering as we went through with this operation. Still, I had to push ahead.

Leadership manuals don't have much to offer in the way of advice in such circumstances, but I recalled a story related to me by General Alexander Haig when I worked for him in 1978. As a lieutenant during the early days of the Korean War, Haig had stood in the back of the room as General of the Army Douglas MacArthur had briefed the Joint Chiefs of Staff on his plans for the Inchon landing. The Chiefs had objected, according to General Haig, on the grounds that it was too risky. As I remembered the story, MacArthur had picked up his pipe and hat as if to leave, stood and said, "Gentlemen, you'll approve that plan or you'll have yourselves a new commander in the Far East."

I didn't foresee anything so dramatic, but I was under no doubt that I would have to fight to defend my judgment on this plan. There would be those in the Pentagon who would say it couldn't work. I would be "laying my stars on the table," as we said. If the plan were rejected, it would likely constitute a crippling lack of confidence in my command.

Secretary General Solana listened carefully as I ran through the specifics and described what we would have to do to make it work. I said that we had a feasible military option to secure Kosovo with ground forces, and that we would need between 175,000 and 200,000 troops to succeed. There was no need to make a decision to invade right now, I said, but the nations did need to decide now to initiate preparations, including detailed planning and the deployment of forces.

I warned there would be other difficult decisions: the capabilities of the KLA would have to be fully exploited (we had scrupulously avoided direct contact with them in Albania); political constraints on targeting must be relaxed; access to Serbia through Montenegro and up the Danube must be blocked; and other forces might need to be deployed around the periphery of Yugoslavia.

We had a detailed discussion, with Solana asking the searching questions. Would we be better off with this option than if we just halted the bombing? Was this the best option? What about Russia and China? Were our soldiers up to this? How should NATO proceed? We talked through the issues, and I left with the understanding that he would press to move ahead with this option.

But what was most troubling to Solana was the constant barrage of criticism from the governments about Serb civilian casualties. The pressures from France, Belgium, Luxembourg, Italy, and even Germany were becoming increasingly pointed. There were insinuations that NATO was trying to sabotage the negotiations by causing civilian casualties. He told me I had to correct the air campaign: no more strike mistakes.

I left for home certain that we were at the crux of the strategic issue. The air campaign was in serious trouble if it persisted on its present course. To strengthen the campaign it would have to be placed in context: "Better to risk a few civilian casualties now, than much greater casualties later, when we invade." As I saw it, pushing the Europeans toward the ground option would strengthen their determination to intensify the air campaign in the interim, and the combination of air campaign and ground threat might just be enough to break Milosevic.

The next morning, in response to Solana's directions, I ordered the airmen to rework the guidance on collateral damage. I knew we weren't going to eliminate it all, but we had to find a way to keep the strikes going. And I had to keep pushing the ground option, especially with Washington.

I was concerned about how to proceed. There was no doubt that returning to Washington for the Joint Chiefs' meeting with the President would increase public pressure there. But some in the Pentagon were reportedly working hard to discredit our planning efforts. I had to consider Secretary Cohen's position, too. It was clear he did not want to endorse a ground option, at least not yet.

Talking to Undersecretary Walt Slocombe, who was consulting with his French counterparts at the Ministry of Defense in Paris, I described the progress we had made in planning the ground operation. I then laid out the problem of conveying the recommendation to Washington. Slocombe was loyal to Secretary Cohen, but he had a judicial temperament, and I respected his integrity and his judgment. "Walt, I can't believe they're not inviting me back to brief the President at the meeting with the Chiefs on Thursday," I said. "I was ready to leave today. I just don't understand how the President could make a decision, one way or the other, without hearing from his commander."

Let me work it, he said.

On the routine VTC update that day I briefed Secretary Cohen, General Shelton, and the Service Chiefs on the ground force planning. Option B(-) was feasible, I said, and talked them through the detailed assessments we had made since my visit to Washington two weeks earlier. The Chiefs had questions but offered no indications of support. The VTCs still seemed like a scene from a courtroom, with a peering jury empowered to question the witness directly.

Shelton called back afterward to explain. Everyone wants details, he said, and we can't provide them because the political controls have prevented planning. Some of the civilians think we've been doing covert planning, he continued. Of course, we weren't.

I underscored the importance of moving ahead with the real planning.

He acknowledged as much, and then admitted that it was getting very frustrating.

Sure enough, a few hours later, the Navy Chief, Admiral Jay Johnson, called to tell me that he didn't like the fact that the numbers in the Option B(-) plan had changed between July 1998 and May 1999. To him, this raised a red flag about the quality of the planning. "Jay," I said, "the numbers changed because we didn't have a real plan—and we still don't. Anyway, the more we plan, and refine the plans, the more the numbers will change." It was just a fact, but Admiral Johnson's reaction was symptomatic of the problem of planning in the midst of a war.

That evening, Solana called to say that he had passed on my assessment of the Option B(-) to Sandy Berger. It sounded as if we were moving to line up White House support.

I then called Shelton to describe my conversation with Solana. "I'm also sending you a copy of the letter I gave him last night," I said, "and it has a summary of our discussion points. Can you please get it to the Secretary?" I asked. I didn't want the Secretary to be caught off-guard by anything coming indirectly through the Solana-Berger channel.

"So, your recommendation is Option B(-)?" Shelton asked again. I thought I had been clear enough.

Shelton said he was going to tell the President not to go ahead with B(-) unless we were really going to do it; no bluffing. But as I listened to him, I realized that I had little idea, and never had during the entire crisis, how the Commander in Chief or the Secretary of Defense were making their decisions. Wouldn't they have been able to make better decisions, and have them better implemented, I thought, if they brought the commander into the high-level discussions occasionally?

I always flashed back to the television footage of General Schwarzkopf going with General Powell to Camp David to brief President George Bush on his plans in the Persian Gulf. Somehow, that seemed to epitomize the relationship that a regional commander in chief was supposed to have with Washington.

There were probably reasons for keeping a distance, I reflected. Maybe the Washington people were simply too busy. Perhaps it was the need to maintain perspective, staying away from distracting details, or to try to minimize the appearance of U.S. leadership in the operation. But then, the targets were being approved at the highest levels. Or perhaps it was the need to preserve the rigid channel of communications running from the National Command Authority through the Chairman of the Joint Chiefs to me, and avoiding any hint that Shelton and the Joint Chiefs were being bypassed. I wasn't angling to sit in on meeting in the White House Situation Room. I had done enough of that as the J-5.

But under the Goldwater-Nichols Act, passed in 1986, the regional commanders in chief were supposed to be working directly for the National Command Authority, as the combination of the Secretary of Defense and the President was termed. The Chairman was their military adviser, but he wasn't in the chain of command.

As it had emerged in this case, it seemed to me that the distance made it difficult to convey intent, requirements, and opportunities. We couldn't look each other in the eye. In the Army we always made it a practice to work details and intent "two levels down and up." If you were a battalion commander, you had to understand the division commander's intent. If you were a brigade commander giving an order, you had to know what the companies in your battalions were doing.

Somehow, I had become just a NATO officer who also reported to the United States. I provided information and took orders, but without engaging in give-and-take political-military discussions, we didn't seem to be making full use of the unique potential of the SACEUR position. Of course, I was on the phone constantly with Hugh Shelton and Joe Ralston. But one thing I had always practiced in my own commands was to communicate directly on a fairly frequent basis, especially at the decisive points in the operations.

I had had many direct discussions with Javier Solana. Within NATO, I was authorized to speak directly with heads of state or any level of political official, and I had not been shy about doing it. But with my own national superiors, the communications weren't as close as they could have been.

Shelton then floated the idea of just arming the KLA, and letting its soldiers fight. "We could do a train and equip, and provide air support. What do you think?"

I was glad that Washington was considering doing something with the Kosovars. If we were going to send our soldiers in, they had to be there, too. But this halfway measure wouldn't help much. "Well, I agree that they're not getting anywhere with their conventional attacks on the Serbs," I said. "I always felt that if they were going to operate it had to be as guerillas, but that's no long-term solution. This is just a means of prolonging and enlarging the crisis."

Later that night Walt Slocombe called back with the answer to my concerns about briefing the President. He assured me that the word coming from the White House was that the President was not going to make a decision on the ground option without talking to me. I had been screened off; I had to hope that I would have my say before it was too late. I had heard that the Army was campaigning furiously against Option B(-), and I feared that the decision would be prepared against the ground option, before I could get in to argue against the Army's and the Service Chiefs' concerns.

Coincidentally, Senator John Warner, the chairman of the Armed Services Committee, had arrived for a brief stay and a troop visit on Wednesday, June 2. Senator Warner, of Virginia, had been an interested visitor on previous occasions, and we had had detailed discussions of NATO and its future, as well as the future of the Armed Forces in general. He wanted an update of the situation, and my assessment. Over several hours, as we had lunch and he participated in various activities and discussions in the headquarters, I gave him a full, candid review of the planning and decision process as I knew it. Late that evening, Walt Slocombe arrived from Paris and joined in the discussions.

That day I had a final opportunity to visit Albania, and see again the routes and forbidding terrain over which I had recommended we proceed. I just had to confirm it, again. And I had to see again Jay Hendrix's preparations to assume his role commanding the effort from Albania going against Kosovo.

As we circled the helicopter above the steep mountain slopes and the dark green lakes, I measured with my eye the widths of the road, and imagined the wide-eyed concerns of the young soldiers who would be driving their trucks, self-propelled guns, and infantry fighting vehicles up this road. They could do it, I thought. "Walt, Senator, what do you think?" I asked.

"Doable, doable," Senator Warner said. He had fought as a Marine in the Korean War. He knew rough countryside.

When we returned that night, Slocombe had a message that there was to be a foreign policy group meeting—the President, Vice President, Secretary of Defense, Secretary of State, and National Security Adviser—the next morning at the White House. It was believed that they were meeting to decide on the ground option. I had no idea what was being presented to the principals at the meeting; I hoped it was my latest assessment of the deployment timelines and my bottom-line assessment that Option B(-)was feasible. But I just had to have faith.

FOURTEEN

DIPLOMACY BACKED BY FORCE

BEFORE LEAVING FOR Albania on the morning of June 2, I received a memorandum from Doc Fogelsong on the results of Strobe Talbott's meeting in Bonn that day with the Russians, detailing the principles on which an agreement to end the fighting was to be based. It seemed to have maintained the "red lines" I had established, but just barely: it called for the withdrawal of "all" Serb military, police and paramilitary; it required a subsequent Military Technical Agreement to work out the details for the withdrawal of the Serbs and suspension of military activity; and it required "an international security presence with substantial NATO participation [to be] deployed under unified command and control and authorized to establish a safe environment," and under U.N. authority. A footnote explained that "substantial NATO participation" meant having NATO at the core, and that in turn meant a unified NATO chain of command under the political direction of the North Atlantic Council. Russia's participation was recognized to require additional agreements.

I had no doubt that Washington was determined to insure that NATO was in charge of the mission. Still, my political adviser, Mike Durkee, and I were uncomfortable. The reference to NATO authority was reduced to a footnote, and Russia's participation hadn't been defined. While we did have the existing NATO plan with its five brigade sectors, I knew that this could well be sacrificed, if necessary, to secure an agreement. We had already conceded to a far less robust legal regime than we had established for the enforcement of the Dayton Accords in Bosnia. I believed we were at the knife's edge of giving away the essential elements of success.

That evening Strobe Talbott called the chateau to speak to Walt Slocombe, who remained overnight after the trip to Albania. Talbott explained the details and context of the emerging agreement and confirmed that former Russian Prime Minister Viktor Chernomyrdin and President Marti Ahtisaari of Finland would indeed go to Belgrade the next day to present the agreement to Milosevic.

After the call, I asked Slocombe, who was with me in the study, "What do you think, will we get an agreement?"

"Unlikely, but worth a try," he said.

Thursday, June 3, was another day of battle rhythm; it was Day 72 of the war. We continued to balance the campaign on the four "measures of merit": avoiding aircraft losses, impacting Serb military and police in Kosovo, minimizing collateral damage, and maintaining Alliance cohesion. We continued to attack on two air axes—a strategic axis, targeting the integrated air defense system, command and control, lines of communication, fuels, ammunition, military industry, the electrical system, and special targets closely associated with Milosevic's control and command, and a tactical axis, targeting the Serb military and police forces in Kosovo, and their support.

The battle at Mount Pastrik was continuing, with the KLA holding on near the top of the mountain, and the Serbs pushing and preparing counterattacks, but trying to avoid the continuing NATO air effort in the area. Further north, KLA elements had pushed their supply corridor deeper inside Kosovo, according to reports. Our pilots were reporting substantial results from their air strikes. But we also had indications of Serb forces converging to mount a strong coordinated attack against the KLA penetration in the north.

The big event of the day, however, was that Ahtisaari and Chernomyrdin were flying into Belgrade to deliver to Milosevic the proposed framework for ending the strikes. If Milosevic refused outright, it would likely force the political leaders in NATO to move to the next steps in developing the ground force options and deciding to mount an invasion. If he accepted the proposal, he would have accepted all NATO's conditions in principle, including the pullout of all Serb military, paramilitary, and police from Kosovo. It would be taken as NATO success.

It would have to be followed, of course, by the development of the detailed proposal to pull out the forces and put the NATO force in place. And we would need authorities for that force. I foresaw a lot of hard work ahead for us, even if Milosevic accepted. We would prepare the NATO force and its orders, a process already under way. We would write and negotiate the detailed Military Technical Agreement governing the actual implementation of the NATO principles, so called to indicate that it had no "political" content and could therefore be left to the military to develop. We had already prepared a draft Military Technical Agreement, based on the Dayton provisions and the proposed Rambouillet Accords. Then we would work with the diplomats to design the sequence of events that would let us end the air campaign and enter with ground forces.

In fact there were several large political issues caught up in this. First, there was the matter of detailing the specific mandate and authorities of the NATO force that was to operate inside Kosovo. Without those details resolved, which we had labored over intensively at Dayton for the Bosnia mission, the force would be virtually powerless once it entered. These issues were inherently political. We wanted it made clear and unchallengeable that NATO was in charge of the mission, and that the commander on the ground could do virtually anything to assure mission success, just as in Bosnia.

A second issue was the possible Russian participation in the NATO mission. It made sense to keep the Russians involved, as we had done in Bosnia, because they had a certain influence with the Serbs, and because, in the larger scheme of European affairs, we wanted to bring the Russians aboard as a constructive participating power. I favored using the same model that had worked in Bosnia, where the Russians operated within a NATO sector and took orders from the SACEUR through a Russian deputy. But we had not yet succeeded in persuading them to adopt this same approach for Kosovo.

The danger was that the Russians would gain a separate sector that they would turn into a separate mission favoring the Serbs, meaning in effect a de facto partition of the province. Even in Bosnia, within the American sector, the Russians tilted toward the Serbs. A separate Russian sector in Kosovo would be seen by many in Europe as a NATO failure. It was clear that in their own sector the Russians wouldn't take NATO orders unless it suited them. I worried that some in Washington might see such a price as necessary to buy continued Russian engagement.

Third, there was the whole matter of how to proceed with the detailed negotiations while continuing the air campaign. It is the fear of every commander, I suppose, that what was won on the battlefield would be lost at the peace table. In 1991, Saddam Hussein kept his Republican Guards and remained in power. In 1973, when we ended the direct American participation in the Vietnam conflict, we agreed to accept the presence inside South Vietnam of a substantial North Vietnamese force, which became the fulcrum for the eventual North Vietnamese conquest of the South. Those talks went on for almost five years. And in the Korean War, the peace talks went on for almost two years, while the fighting continued.

In Yugoslavia, we had many experiences negotiating with Milosevic. His subordinates were perfectly capable of backtracking on his concessions, and until all details were agreed and ratified with signatures, nothing was solid. He was wily and stubborn. In fact, he might well accept the NATO conditions in principle and then work to stall and manipulate, hoping that NATO would lose its sense of direction. Things like this could happen in negotiations. I knew that we had to maintain our leverage over the Serbs until every detail was finalized, and this would mean that Operation Allied Force should continue and even intensify if we entered detailed discussions with the Serb generals. It would mean continuing to battle over the preparations for escalating Allied Force into ground operations should the detailed negotiations break down.

June 3 was also the day that the Joint Chiefs were having their "routine" meeting with the President. Inevitably the ground invasion option would come up for discussions. I had been assured that no decisions would be made, but I was anxious nevertheless. I would have preferred to be present, but had been ordered not to attend.

There was one piece of good news that morning. Through a contracted air service, the United States had at last dropped some food into northern Kosovo. We had arranged for there to be no NATO aircraft in the area during the contract flight, but the plane still took fire from the ground. Still it was a start, and if we were to sustain a resistance movement inside Kosovo until we invaded, this channel for food deliveries would be important.

In the morning VTC, I directed the airmen to keep the pressure on the Serb forces in western Kosovo, and especially those that might be moving against the KLA supply corridor. We would take advantage of every KLA effort to draw the Serbs into positions where we could strike effectively. We were making sure to avoid any strikes around Belgrade in order not to compromise or interfere with the Ahtisaari-Chernomyrdin visit.

With regard to the invasion option, I pressed to gain Joint Staff approval of additional engineer units to be deployed from the United States to help us with road construction in Albania. I learned that the Army was reluctant to move ahead without additional funding, and I couldn't help feeling that this was another "go-slow" effort.

If Milosevic gave in, we had to have KFOR ready. Here the nub of the problem was that those peacekeeping forces would have to start deploying immediately if the Serbs actually agreed to NATO's terms. But some nations felt that the NATO plan couldn't be finalized until the presence of the force was legally authorized by the consent of the Serbs and endorsed by the United Nations. Thus, the forces would have to be deployed and received under national control, not NATO control. This caused problems for the Macedonians as well as for Mike Jackson and his staff.

General Rupert Smith was working on the problem. KFOR, as he saw it, was "the biggest marvel of a command and control arrangement I've ever seen. It's the masses of different arrangements, units there on national authorities with unofficial relationships.... Jackson can't forward a request for something he doesn't know exists, and NATO can't send him something it doesn't know he wants.... Both ends have to work toward the middle."

By late morning Javier Solana was on the phone to see if I had heard anything from Washington. "From what I hear, and I have nothing clearly authoritative, Washington is leaning toward extending the air campaign and against a ground option," I told him, relying in part on what Senator Warner had told me the day before. "The U.S. Army is arguing against the ground campaign, according to what I'm told." In fact, the Army was allegedly seeking any alternative to Option B(-), arguing against taking the fight into the mountains; it was too much like Korea, Army officials reportedly contended. I knew I had little support from the Joint Chiefs for my plan. If the Army said the plan wouldn't work, then anyone else who disagreed could cite the Army as an authority. We were in danger of a war run by a committee on this issue, for sure.

I went back through the logic of the ground option that we had discussed Monday night. Solana acknowledged the importance of moving forward with planning and preparations. I felt that I had his strong support. But he was concerned about collateral damages; some countries were continuing to call and complain that we had injured Serb civilians. He didn't want to stop the air campaign, he said, but just reduce the collateral damage.

In the early afternoon, we got our first news from the Ahtisaari-Chernomyrdin visit. Doc Fogelsong called from Bonn, where he and Deputy Secretary Talbott had remained while Ahtisaari and Chernomyrdin had gone on to Belgrade. "They're making progress," he said, "and they may call you to work out the details of a withdrawal."

I broke off the call to move to the VTC with Secretary Cohen, General Shelton, and the Service Chiefs. I updated them on the feasibility of the Albanian operation, including the brilliant work by a British engineer who had planned the full use of the river and lake system to transport heavy equipment into northeast Albania. Each successive report confirmed my confidence that we could deploy rapidly and fully within northeast Albania. I briefed them on the ongoing air campaign and air reinforcement efforts as well as the European complaints about collateral damage.

Secretary Cohen seemed surprised to hear about European pressures to reduce collateral damage. It wasn't brought up to him the previous week in his meeting with the defense ministers, he said. Just push on with the bombing.

Then we discussed the plans for the next phase, the Serb withdrawal. Hugh Shelton asked a key question: "What about the Russian sector?"

Stay with the original plan, I said. Five sectors, Americans in the southeast. The Russians can come in with us, just as in Bosnia. I made clear that this wouldn't work if the Russians were really intent on putting in 10,000 troops, as some had suggested. But we could certainly handle a battalion, perhaps "a battalion coming right out of Bosnia, right over to Kosovo. That's the quickest and easiest way to do it."

The Secretary said "my recommendation" would be considered in Washington. I sensed that the issue of how the Russians would participate was unresolved within the U.S. government, or at least within the Pentagon. While perhaps no one wanted to "volunteer" a sector to the Russians, someone might compromise with the Russians on the issue of NATO control of all sectors as a last resort, I guessed. But if so, they didn't appreciate what was at risk. It would be up to me to push as hard as possible to secure a workable agreement that kept NATO in charge of all sectors on the ground.

In the midst of the VTC we got another call from Bonn, this time from Brigadier General George Casey, who was with Strobe Talbott and Doc Fogelsong there. The Serbs were now discussing sending their military chief, General Ojdanic, down to the border crossing with Macedonia. Be ready for a phone call.

I don't like the idea of meeting Ojdanic, I said. I'll have to consider whether to go myself or not. If I went, I would be meeting and negotiating with an indicted war criminal. There would be the issue of why we weren't immediately arresting him, and he, citing this, would be wary to come anywhere near our forces. I could sense this wasn't going to work. Secretary Cohen said that his reaction was that I shouldn't go personally; there's no need to move it up to such a high level at this point.

I had no sooner walked out of the VTC than Solana called again. He had heard that Milosevic had accepted the NATO conditions. In consequence, someone from Germany was asking that we not bomb any targets near cities this evening. Would that be possible? I was afraid of such a response from the Europeans; it amounted to undercutting the negotiating leverage we were gaining from the air campaign.

It was all phone calls the remainder of the afternoon. I determined to send Mike Jackson up to the border to do the face-to-face talks with the Serbs, and told Fogelsong in Bonn to convey this to the Serbs. I also asked Fogelsong to send us the text of what had been agreed in Belgrade.

But before long Fogelsong had disturbing news. It appeared that in the discussions thus far, Milosevic had accepted the agreed principles, including the footnote explaining that a substantial NATO presence would mean NATO command and control. "But," he reportedly said, "the Yugoslav parliament could never accept such a formulation. So, in order for the Yugoslav parliament to ratify the agreement, the footnote must be removed." This seemed to be the last legally sufficient reference to NATO control of the operation.

I had worked in the Balkans long enough to understand the game that Milosevic was playing. Everything in a peace operation depended on legal authorities. Everyone read the fine print in all the agreements, and every legal dispute was an excuse to delay and not to comply. One reason the Dayton Agreement was effective was the strong, unambiguous authority given to the military commander on the ground in Bosnia. I didn't want us to adopt a weaker agreement in Kosovo.

When Hugh Shelton called a few minutes later, I informed him of Solana's request not to bomb in or near cities. I had to keep Washington apprised of European views.

"Just keep bombing," he said. "Forget about the targets in Kosovo and go after targets in northern Serbia."

"I don't have enough of those targets," I said. "We'll have to hit them wherever we can, but I can't just strike in the north." The Pentagon, I could sense, was concerned that if we continued to strike Serb forces in Kosovo, the Serbs might use it as an excuse to avoid pulling out. It was precisely the opposite view of many Europeans, who felt that if we struck targets in Serbia, the Serbs might use civilian casualties as an excuse to continue repression in Kosovo. I was nearing the fork in the road, I sensed, where European and American views were totally divergent.

Shelton was still wrestling with the problem of Russian participation. "How many sectors are there, again?" he asked.

"Five," I said.

"Well, NATO could have three or four sectors," he suggested.

I continued to reinforce my original plan. "We need to bring them in with the U.S. No separate Russian sector. It compromises NATO command and control. We can't share intelligence with them, and we can't depend on them to do whatever may be necessary to make an agreement work." I had already seen Russian ambivalence in Bosnia, where they worked for us but reportedly shared intelligence with the Serbs and sometimes favored the Serbs in their daily actions.

Shelton was worried about whether such an arrangement could be made effective. Perhaps he felt that someone would be pressing for the greatest possible accommodation for the Russians. But, he noted, "If we're in there first, and we own the ground, that's the key."

Admiral Venturoni called to coordinate the timing and process of reaching an approved NATO Operations Plan. "Guido, please, right away, get the plan moving toward ACTORD," I requested, referring to the formal NATO authorization to begin. "I would like to have it approved and authorized tomorrow. It will take us between thirty and forty-five days to deploy. And you agree that we have to continue the air strikes?"

"I agree," said Venturoni.

By the end of the day, we had determined the basic concept of the Serb withdrawal that we would seek. We would have Milosevic begin the withdrawal from northern Kosovo; he would designate his routes and assembly areas, and those forces and areas wouldn't be hit. Forces in the south would be targeted until we had determined that he had complied with the agreement. The advantage to this plan was that it let us continue to apply airpower where the fighting was most intense, and at the same time, prevented Milosevic from falling back into northern Kosovo and retaining it as a kind of de facto partition. And when his forces moved to withdraw, we would expect to see their cannons turned to the rear or other visible indicators that they were no longer engaging in combat operations.

I spoke to Solana again at the end of the day, to tell him that it wasn't possible to honor the German request not to strike near cities. I reviewed with him all the changes I had made, assured him that we weren't going to bomb Nis again, where there had been civilian casualties and where popular discontent with Milosevic was rising, but I could not cut any more strikes.

Solana was not pleased, but he recognized that we were both in a corner. "I will not tell you what to do," he said. "But you are a very intelligent man. You know what the nations want. That is all I can say."

Joe Ralston called a few minutes later. I described my concept of the withdrawal and my approach to continuing the strikes. "We don't want to be accused of moving the goalposts," he said, seeming to imply that if we kept the pressure on the Serbs, we might jeopardize the agreement in principle that Chernomyrdin and Ahtisaari had just achieved.

"We aren't moving the goalposts," I countered. "The agreement calls for a total withdrawal of the Serbs, and that's what we'll get."

"There's a sense that striking the Serb forces in Kosovo is going to be a problem," he said. I explained again how the phased withdrawal would work, and asked for his support.

Then the French called to convey that President Chirac would like there to be no bombing in the northern part of Serbia. Here was the perfect opposition of the two countries' views of the correct strategy. This conflict had to be resolved above my level.

A few minutes after 7:00 P.M., the Serbs called from Belgrade. It was General Ojdanic. "I am authorized to meet with you," he said. "Let us meet at 10:00 A.M. Sunday."

I was surprised at the delay and wondered what Milosevic had up his sleeve "We can meet Sunday," I said, "but we could also meet earlier, and you must understand that until there is a Military Technical Agreement and we verify your withdrawal, we will continue to bomb."

After some moments of discussion, he agreed to meet on Saturday, and we determined that the location would be somewhere along the Macedonian border. "General Jackson will represent me," I said. "We will provide the Military Technical Agreement. And we expect you to agree to it quickly."

Then George Casey called again from Bonn, with a last wrinkle. The Russians may send their own general into the negotiations to back up the Serbs, he reported. I figured we would address that issue later, if necessary. For now, I had to go to Brussels for a meeting of the North Atlantic Council and a briefing from Strobe Talbott and Doc Fogelsong.

Talbott was cautious in describing the situation thus far. Milosevic's acceptance of the principles hadn't really been confirmed. It wasn't clear that all parties understood the NATO role. Russia's role had yet to be defined. And Milosevic's intent was uncertain. Was this more of a game, just to find a way to stop the bombing? Would Milosevic believe that he could take over the peace process and use it to his advantage? In any event, Talbott said, we need to be careful of proclaiming peace and victory—we don't have it yet.

During the discussion at NATO, I raised my concerns: to approve and implement the Operations Plan, put NATO in charge with no Russian sectors, and get the nations to start moving forces immediately. I was especially concerned that there be no withdrawal and no halt to the air campaign until the full Military Technical Agreement was signed. The bombing was our leverage to secure this agreement, I explained.

The diplomats had begun to wrestle with the complete sequence of activities required to end the campaign successfully. In order to secure the ACTORD for the NATO order, some nations required an authorizing U.N. Security Council Resolution. But to do that, Russia and China would insist that NATO stop the bombing. In order to stop the bombing, we were insisting on a demonstrable withdrawal of Serb forces. How much of a withdrawal was an issue that was continuing to be discussed. But before the Serbs could withdraw we were insisting that they complete the Military Technical Agreement. And so the NATO ambassadors were anxious to see and approve the Military Technical Agreement with the Serbs.

We had started drafting the agreement some days previously and had forwarded it to the Joint Staff, so that George Casey and his team could make sure that it fit within the continuing diplomatic discussions. That afternoon we had received the Joint Staff's rewrite of our document, which was more direct and explicit in removing all Serb forces—military, police, and paramilitary—from Kosovo. I liked it, and this was the version I submitted for NATO approval.

Meanwhile, the political pressure for reducing collateral damages had finally hit Washington hard. The Joint Staff asked that we submit our ideas on which targets would not be struck at this point, including electric power and cities. They added to the restrictions, limiting us to clearly military facilities outside urban areas and only those with low predictions of collateral damages. We canceled a few strikes immediately.

It was becoming clear, though, that NATO or not, the endgame was Washington's to win or lose. What had begun as a NATO operation was ending with a Washington-brokered agreement.

When I returned home that night I continued to work on the ground option, which we would need if the negotiations collapsed. At Senator Warner's advice, I prepared a message for Hugh Shelton arguing against indefinitely prolonging the air campaign. If Washington was really considering such an option, as Senator Warner had suggested to me in Albania the previous day, then I wanted to weigh in right away. I believed that, just as with the air strikes, we needed to keep the ground option moving forward, if possible, until the Military Technical Agreement was truly completed. I couldn't seem to get a firm reading from the Joint Chiefs' meeting with President on the ground option's status in Washington.

Overnight, the airmen reported good results in their strikes against Serb forces in Kosovo. The Serbs' counteroffensive efforts in the Mount Pastrik area had apparently ceased in mid-afternoon, and it appeared that elsewhere in Kosovo the Serb military and police were also pulling out of ongoing operations.

By the next morning, Friday, June 4, I had a new problem. Despite the fact that the draft Military Technical Agreement had been reviewed and revised by the Joint Staff, now it was loose in the interagency process with the Department of State and the National Security Council staff. I was told it was not yet approved. This was surprising, because it would have been normal to have the draft cleared by the White House and State Department before I was authorized to submit it to NATO. By early afternoon I was on the phone with Washington, trying to break it loose.

"I need to provide it to the Serbs as soon as possible," I explained, "or they won't be able to agree to it tomorrow."

A senior officer in the Pentagon explained the hold-up. "Sir, they just want to stop the bombing back here. That's the big push." In other words, he implied someone in Washington was concerned that we might be asking too much of the Serbs. Fair enough.

"Well," I said, "Doc Fogelsong has been with this process from the beginning, he's seen what's in the agreement, and he feels they'll accept it all."

For NATO, the best I could do was submit a letter containing the principles of the proposed Military Technical Agreement, citing problems in completing it in detail. Shortly after 2:00 P.M., Admiral Venturoni called to explain that my letter had been reviewed, and for the most part the principles I cited were acceptable. But it could be rejected by the NATO nations anytime up until 7:00 P.M. He added that the North Atlantic Council had also insisted on approving the Military Technical Agreement itself.

By 4:30 Joe Ralston was reporting Pentagon concerns with the Military Technical Agreement. "This is the only chance we've got to stop this air campaign," he said. "The Military Technical Agreement could torpedo the deal, and then we'll be blamed." I understood his logic perfectly, but the impact was that now we were thinking about watering down the agreement to make it easier for the Serbs to swallow. I wanted us to hold steady.

Hugh Shelton called a few minutes later to reemphasize Ralston's message. Just get in there on the ground, he said. Don't worry about the piece of paper. Say as little as possible to get NATO in there. Once we're in, it's a fait accompli.

I understood the guidance. Their concern was real, but I also knew the Balkans. The language of agreements did matter, and omissions would come back to haunt us. Our actions would be hamstrung without legal authority. Every step we took would involve securing consensus from national capitals, maybe even from the Serbs. We would be as powerless as UNPROFOR. But his phone call was all about intent; there were as yet no specific issues. Washington was just preparing me to accept the mark-up when it came in.

A little after 7:00 P.M., I hosted a VTC with Mike Jackson and Jim Ellis. They wanted to see the agreement that they would be discussing in twelve hours with the Serbs. I tried to allay their concerns. Echoing guidance from the North Atlantic Council, I stressed that this would not be a negotiation. It would simply be your laying down the conditions and their accepting them. Because it is politically approved, you won't have the authority to change anything in the document, anyway, I said, but if there's something now that you'd like worked, let me see what I can do. And we'll get you the document as soon as it's finished. You'll have to focus on the details of the withdrawal planning, what's there, what routes are they taking, where their assembly areas are, and so on.

One of my last actions that day was to send a letter to General Anatoliy Kvashnin, the Chief of the Russian General Staff, welcoming the participation of Russian peacekeepers in the Kosovo mission and inviting him or a senior representative to come to our headquarters and work out the details.

Later that evening, the Joint Staff passed back the Washington revisions on our draft. We passed it on to Solana, as well as to Jackson and the Serbs in the early morning hours of Saturday, June 5. The changes simplified some of the language, accelerated the Serb withdrawal to be accomplished in seven days, took out some of the details, and softened the emphasis on NATO command and control. It was designed to be "just enough" to let us halt the bombing and move into Kosovo, without being unnecessarily provocative to the Serbs or the Russians.

Saturday morning, all attention was focused on the scheduled meeting with the Serbs. Mike Jackson had worked all day Friday arranging the site, some 500 meters south of the border at the Café Europa, along the main highway linking Skopje and Pristina, the capitals of Macedonia and Kosovo. Jackson was ready for the negotiations, though with the last-minute changes to the agreement, it had been a busy night. We knew that directing the Serbs to complete the pullout within seven days was probably too tight, but that was what the political leaders had directed.

By 9:00 A.M. we had our first problem: the Serb delegation wouldn't come south of the border to the agreed meeting place. Instead, we were to go north of the border to their meeting place. It was the wrong way to begin. They would have to come to us, I reasoned. I had my political adviser, Mike Durkee, deployed to Macedonia to work with Jackson and to help keep me up to date on the atmospherics. He concurred with the decision not to go north just yet.

Solana called for an update. He was concerned to hear that the meeting hadn't started. Then Joe Ralston called from Washington. "Joe, we were late in getting them the information on the meeting site, and we sent them the agreement late, too, and then we sent in another version," I told him. "Why don't we give them some time to sort it out? We can work on them a little. They should be coming to our meeting place, that's why I didn't want us to go to Belgrade." The art was not to appear overly eager.

"Wait," he said. "I'll get guidance back to you."

Within a few minutes, the Pentagon directed that we ask the Serbs for security guarantees and move north to their site. I passed the instructions on to Mike Jackson, and informed Solana.

An hour later I reached General Ojdanic, to try to establish a better atmosphere for the meeting. I stressed that this was the day to sign the agreement. He was concerned, however, that their initial look at the document suggested it contained political elements wider than simply the instructions on how to withdraw.

The meeting did begin, several hours late, with the Serbs eventually agreeing to come south. Mike Jackson quickly heard the same sort of objections from the Serb team that General Ojdanic had given me. In addition, the Serbs were complaining that the seven-day timeline for withdrawal was too tight. They wanted fifteen days. Just stay with it, I said to Jackson, and be sure that you arrange it so that when they withdraw, step by step, you fall in with your forces right behind them. We were worried about a possible "security vacuum" resulting from a Serb withdrawal and no NATO entry.

Throughout the afternoon, the reports flowed in from the discussion on the border. As I reported to Solana, the atmospherics are fine in the meeting; Mike Jackson reports that they are seeking a means to withdraw in order to get the bombing stopped. They are quarreling with the content of the agreement, which they claim is political, and say that they have no authority to sign a political document. But they need to be empowered to sign the agreement. Apparently, they are not.

Solana was insistent: this is not a negotiation; it is not a discussion. They must accept the agreement, he said.

I understand, I said, but it may be necessary to apply more pressure on General Ojdanic and on Belgrade. I need to call him and threaten.

Then Ralston called. He was also wired into the negotiations through direct reporting from Fogelsong, who was at the scene. He wanted to help us meet Serb concerns. "Wes, the seven days' withdrawal was just an example," he said. "You can go to eight, nine, or even ten days."

I spoke with Hugh Shelton a few minutes later. He saw the need for applying pressure, and said he would support intensifying the bombing if the discussions weren't producing results. I appreciated his support on this issue, but it was clear that we had now established two parallel reporting channels, one to me from the site and another direct to Washington. So long as all instructions flowed through me, I reasoned, it could still work, but it would inevitably generate internal issues to be worked. I also sensed, from time to time, some differences between the guidance that came from the Vice Chairman and that from the Chairman.

In an effort to facilitate the discussions, I called General Ojdanic about 4:30 that afternoon. We disagreed about the nature of the Military Technical Agreement. He insisted that the discussions were only about the withdrawal; I insisted that the agreement authorizing the International Security Presence was essential and had to be completed now, before the bombing could be stopped. "Your government has already accepted it," I said. After a lengthy discussion, Ojdanic agreed to study the problem and come back to me in two hours. "Let's just get it done today," I pressed.

The Serbs weren't talking about giving up on the agreement, according to the reports I was receiving. These were serious discussions. I called Solana to update him on my phone call and to ensure his support for including the political authorities for NATO in the discussion. He agreed with me.

A few minutes later, Joe Ralston called. He was looking for some way to reduce the demands of the agreement. Just get a partial agreement, focus on the key articles, he suggested. But the Serbs were still on break from the talks, so there was nothing to be done at the time.

Shortly after 7:00 P.M., the Serbs called back, as promised. Your agreement is improper, they said. President Milosevic has called Finnish President Ahtisaari, and he agrees with us, the agreement should not discuss the structure and mandate of the International Force.

I couldn't accept this. If we allowed the Serbs to withdraw and stopped the bombing, we would surrender our leverage before we had compelled them to surrender their authorities in Kosovo. It was a prescription for trouble.

I called the Pentagon to express my concern. At Pentagon suggestion, I called Strobe Talbott, to argue against the interpretation the

Serbs had taken. "Strobe, we have to have the references to the force in that document. That's what gives the specific authority to the commander of the force. We can't let them get away with just demonstrating a withdrawal—if we do, we'll never get the authority we need to do the real work once we get into Kosovo." Talbott was supportive.

At the end of the day, I reported to Solana that the negotiations were confused, but by no means lost. It seemed that the Serbs wanted to do what was necessary to have the bombing halted. We just had to push them into the full agreement.

I directed Jim Ellis to be prepared for a more intensive air campaign for the next day.

When I awoke on Sunday morning, I was surprised to see that Washington had further revised the Military Technical Agreement, placing the mandate and authorities that the Serbs found objectionable into an Appendix. There was no mention of NATO in the document now, only KFOR. Conspicuously missing was the item requiring the Serbs to account for and release all Albanian missing persons. At least we were sticking with the seven-day withdrawal, though.

In an early morning phone call, Fogelsong explained that Washington's intent was to use the new document as a fallback. He had apparently worked on the document overnight with the Pentagon and the Washington interagency without our involvement. This was an effort to make the agreement easier for the Serbs to accept, without falling off our key requirements.

Solana was concerned when he learned of the changes. How can they do this? he asked in frustration. The previous approach had been cleared by the North Atlantic Council. He said he would talk to Washington in the afternoon and try to straighten it out. Sandy Vershbow, the U.S. ambassador to NATO, also expressed his concern that the deletion of the references to NATO was too weak to sustain the kind of authority needed by the North Atlantic Council.

Information that morning was that the fighting had been light in Kosovo, though Albanian sources reported that the Serbs were still there, biding their time. The airmen were working carefully within the constraints to maintain some air presence over Serbia, as well as continuing to strike the Serb forces in Kosovo. I asked Admiral Jim Ellis to prepare a large air package to go against targets in Serbia, and place the package on hold. I directed the intelligence staff to look at finding Serb assembly areas that we could strike in late afternoon with the B-52 and B-1 heavy bombers. I would need Solana's approval to order such a strike, but it could be important in achieving leverage to advance the negotiations.

Then Jay Hendrix broke in to our discussions. He had a different impression. Fighting was not slacking off on the ground in Kosovo. There had been over fifty radar detections of Serb mortars and artillery in the past twenty-four hours, he said. The Albanians were reporting heavy Serb attacks in the northern area of the Kosovo-Albania border. The Albanians said the situation for the units on the ground was critical. Hendrix's report deepened my concern that we had to maintain the air strikes, especially against the Serb forces in Kosovo.

The talks between Mike Jackson and the Serbs resumed at 9:00 A.M. The Serbs' position was hard. They were willing to withdraw, but only to the level of forces they normally maintained in Kosovo, in other words, down to some 25,000 troops. Then they would wait for a U.N. Security Resolution, specifying the composition of KFOR, before they withdrew any further. And they were insisting that even after we halted the bombing, they would retain the right of self-defense for their forces in Kosovo. (This meant that they could then charge that the KLA initiated all contacts.) In their view, any international force would operate under the United Nations, not NATO.

If we were to have accepted this version of the agreement, the air campaign would have achieved virtually nothing.

This was another example of Milosevic's style: we were going to have to struggle to regain the points he had already conceded in principle. I was going to do everything I could to prevent this struggle from reducing a NATO victory into a defeat at the end.

I reviewed the problem with Solana, who was still concerned about the deletion of the references to NATO in Washington's latest revision. Don't give them the newest draft, he said. But at noon we were directed by Washington to put the new draft in play. I asked for a little more time, while I consulted with Solana. Then Solana called back, saying that the document stood, go ahead with it.

At 2:00 P.M. Jackson reported that he had in fact given the Serbs the new draft document. He also reported that a Russian general had arrived to oversee the negotiations. The Serbs, over the next several hours, then began to alter the new document, taking out all references to "KFOR" and inserting the term "U.N." at every opportunity.

Fogelsong was also informally exchanging views with one of the Serb representatives. "Milosevic really prefers a NATO occupation to the Russians coming in, but of course he can't say so publicly," he reported the Serb saying in an aside. "I've told Washington, and they're intrigued." This was an old play in Serb practices: play off the West against Russia. I didn't believe it for a minute, and warned Fogelsong.

But Mike Jackson and his team kept the talks in session nevertheless, finally adjourning in the early morning hours. The Serbs had stuck to their basic line, no mandate or agreement on the troop presence before the bombing halt and the U.N. Security Council Resolution. Of course, once the bombing was halted, anything could happen in the United Nations to further delay and complicate our plans. I was still worried about the two key issues—NATO command and control over the operation, and the role of the Russians in the force. I wanted to get as much worked out as possible while we still had the leverage of the bombing working for us. At 2:00 A.M. on Monday we authorized Mike Jackson to release a statement calling for intensification of the air campaign.

When the talks resumed later that Monday morning, June 7, the Serbs made their position clear: they would begin to withdraw, there would be a bombing pause, followed by a U.N. Security Council Resolution, and then they would halt their withdrawal when they returned to their normal peacetime level of forces. This, of course, would mean no cease-fire, and no acceptance of the NATO conditions. Worse, after a bombing pause and a Security Council Resolution, it would have been difficult for NATO to raise the pressure again.

I called back to the Pentagon to report the latest developments. I saw it as another phase in Milosevic's resistance to NATO. It was typical of the "talk-fight, fight-talk" approach that the Serbs had used in their activities during the Bosnia conflict. They sincerely wanted to stop the bombing, and they were prepared to withdraw some of their forces to peacetime levels. They just wanted to play everything to their best advantage. And we knew that once we stopped the bombing, we would lose our leverage. We were at an impasse.

At the morning teleconference with EUCOM, I directed that all the engineer units we had tagged for Option B(-) continue to flow. We were still within my timelines for being able to execute this option, if necessary, so long as we got the engineers in to work on the roads in Albania. We had to use this period to intensify the pressure on Belgrade. The air campaign against Serbia itself was slipping away, however. As Mike Short explained it, under the existing restrictive guidance, there were almost no targets left for us to strike.

We had to reenergize the campaign, but how? Jim Ellis suggested striking the Novi Sad petroleum refinery. There was a low chance of collateral damage, but Washington had told us, in preparation for Ahtisaari's visit, not to make any strikes against fuel. And there was the possibility of striking Batanjica airfield, near Belgrade, which the airmen had presumed was also proscribed by the U.S. guidance. I checked; it wasn't, and I cleared them to strike it. Steve Abbott suggested re-strikes against certain electric power targets. "Get me the revised plan by 1300," I told Ellis. "Plan it, I'll argue it with Washington, and then we'll go get it. These are Washington's restrictions, not our Allies'."

I also pushed for more focus on the Serb forces remaining in Kosovo. The simple truth, I observed, was that Milosevic has put his army in jeopardy, and the more of it we could take care of now, the greater pressure on the Serbs to withdraw. Mike Jackson said that the Yugoslav Army was pretty chastened by all this, and I wanted to see them go back as losers.

Hugh Shelton called in after his morning meeting in the Pentagon. He was worried about the ground option, especially the logistics. People are worried about early snow in the mountains, he said. They want to look at going after Belgrade, or just keeping the air campaign going indefinitely. They're just "upset with all the deadlines," he continued.

"Sir, you need to get me back there to work on the naysayers," I pleaded.

"Wes, the Chiefs are down on the Albania option," he continued.

"Sir, you know we're encouraging Milosevic to stall by not following through with the ground option," I said. "We've got to get our engineers over here to improve the road."

It was one more phone call in a series of repeated requests to put the pressure on Milosevic.

Be very careful with the bombing, Solana warned me again that afternoon. The G-8 meeting is working the U.N. Security Council resolution, and this is the most important thing, he said. The idea was to fit all the pieces together smoothly—first the Military Technical Agreement, then the Bombing Suspension, then the U.N. Security Council Resolution, then the approval of the NATO Operations Plan, and then the entry of the international force. I was pleased to learn that the work on creating the draft U.N. resolution was proceeding in the absence of any progress in our negotiations on the Military Technical Agreement.

I knew that the NATO diplomats felt that we were walking along a dangerous edge in continuing to apply pressure during this critical phase. But it was the pressure of the air campaign and the continued work toward the ground option that were responsible for the progress we were making.

Throughout the day and overnight the air campaign continued. We did strike the Batanjica airfield and the oil refinery at Novi Sad, and the airmen reported impressive results from their continuing strikes against Serb forces in Albania, including secondary explosions indicating the presence of fuel or ammunition stores. The media gave prominent coverage to what they saw as the resumption of the air strikes.

On Tuesday, June 8, we received the results of the G-8 meeting, and they were not particularly encouraging. The Russians were still working to minimize the NATO role—the draft resolution recognized "substantial NATO participation," but dropped the footnote reference to "NATO at the core." We had thus weakened our legal position from "NATO-led," to "NATO core," to "substantial NATO participation" over the past two weeks. In addition, Russia was pressing to halt the bombing early and to restrict cooperation with the International Criminal Tribunal.

Some of the Western diplomats reportedly viewed the Russian attitude as "very constructive," since the Russians had not challenged the substantial NATO participation in the force. They felt that the footnote shown to Milosevic in the original Ahtisaari-Chernomyrdin document, which referred to NATO command and control of the international force, was legally adequate. I understood their perspective—the Russians had moved a long way from their position in late

March—but we had to be as certain as possible that we had the full NATO authority unarguably present and visible in the agreements. I wanted to be certain we had a workable agreement after we had given up our leverage.

Worse still, in response to the breakdown in the discussions with the Serb generals at the border, the Pentagon was further reworking the Military Technical Agreement. Joe Ralston called to discuss its elements with me. He wanted to secure a workable agreement, of course, but I was concerned that the changes left ambiguous the NATO role, and thus opened the door to a Russian sector. I reinforced these concerns when Hugh Shelton called in the early afternoon.

Ralston called back with a modification: Jackson would give the Serbs a letter, to be drafted by NATO, saying that he was in charge. The Pentagon was confident that the presence of our forces on the ground would by themselves ultimately assure us the outcome we wanted.

"But, Joe," I said, "please understand that Mike Jackson doesn't have enough strength on the ground to make an opposed entry against the Serbs if there is a problem with this agreement. NATO authority has to be present in the document." I was also worried that once again, NATO and Javier Solana hadn't received a full opportunity to participate in approving the new version of the agreement.

The back-and-forth dialogue with the Pentagon continued all afternoon. Solana finally received the revised Military Technical Agreement about 3:30 P.M. Washington had relaxed the timeline for Serb withdrawal from seven to nine days and had removed all references to NATO. The force was known as an International Security Presence, "KFOR." All that we had held onto was Mike Jackson's designation as the commander.

By late Tuesday afternoon, the exact sequence of events had been lined up. NATO would approve the Military Technical Annex, then Mike Jackson would present it to the Serbs. After the Serbs signed the agreement, it would enter into force. We would not bomb their withdrawing forces, or anywhere in Serbia, though we would continue to fly and strike forces in contact along the Albanian border. Once we verified the withdrawal, then we would pause the bombing and the U.N. Security Council Resolution could be passed. Then the NATO entry force would flow in behind the Serbs' withdrawing elements. We would consider the bombing suspended until the Serb withdrawal was completed.

Our military problem was going to be verification. We decided to rely on the unmanned aerial vehicles and such manned reconnaissance aircraft as were available. We would not be asking to put people in on the ground at this stage.

I went through our plans with Hugh Shelton, stressing that we needed time to make an adequate verification of the Serb withdrawal. He said that he had requested a meeting at the White House to work out some of these final details. The issues were moving very quickly at this point, I reflected. I expressed concern about the minefields along the border, which might delay our entry. He was concerned about Secretary of State Albright's forthcoming trip to Albania, he said. And we agreed that, in keeping with previous U.S. policy, we would not deploy U.S. forces into Macedonia until the Military Technical Agreement was signed.

Ed Anderson, the J-5, called a few minutes before 9:00 P.M. to ask how quickly the United States could enter Kosovo and whether we would be able to participate in the initial entry.

I described our plans and talked about an idea that Jean-Pierre Kelche had suggested, for French troops to attempt a heliborne occupation of the airport at Pristina, though I also reported that Mike Jackson seemed uninterested in this approach.

Coincidentally, that evening I also received an answer to my message of May 26 requesting to employ the Apaches in combat. The answer was no, not enough targets and too much risk. The Joint Chiefs had recommended that the Secretary of Defense disapprove my request last week.

At least I had an answer. Task Force Hawk had done a great job preparing for a difficult mission. By firing their long-range missiles without crossing the border, the Apaches could have had a significant impact on the Serb forces, with virtually no risks. To me the decision reflected either a continuing misunderstanding of the conflict or a profound lack of confidence in our troops and leaders in Albania. But now I was definitely clear to use them as part of the initial entry force into Kosovo.

That evening, Mike Jackson received the NATO-approved Military Technical Agreement and delivered it to the Serbs. But rather than a

prompt signature session, the meeting became a discussion and negotiation session that lasted all night and into the next morning.

That day and overnight we kept up the attacks on Serb forces in
Kosovo, including strikes by B-52 heavy bombers flying out of the
United Kingdom. There was a rumor from Albanian sources that one
of the B-52 strikes had killed 400 to 800 Serbs, but we had no way to
confirm this. By early Wednesday morning there were unmistakable
indications of Serb preparations to withdraw. Fighting had slackened
off, no targets were visible to our airmen overhead, and no artillery or
mortar fire was detected by the radars from Task Force Hawk.

It was also clear that we were moving toward a signature on the Military Technical Agreement. I had to get Javier Solana's permission for
Mike Jackson to sign, and the Serbs were waiting for approval from
Milosevic. Small changes were still being worked out. Would we control the borders to prevent the Albanian terrorists from having free
access? We would.

There were multiple lines of communications throughout the
negotiations. I was communicating with the Pentagon and NATO
headquarters on a minute-by-minute basis, responding to suggested
changes but also trying to retain the minimum essentials for NATO.
There was also an unofficial channel: Fogelsong was on the ground
with Mike Jackson, communicating directly back to Joe Ralston in the
Pentagon, and, I learned later, giving Jackson powerful "hints" about
what he would soon be directed to do by SACEUR. I also had an unofficial channel, with Mike Durkee in touch with Fogelsong and Jackson
and reporting to me, though this was strictly for information. And
Washington was working through White House channels with our
NATO allies, the United Nations, and the Russians on details of the
various agreements.

I did all I could to keep everyone informed as the issues flowed—
about the withdrawal of local police, the number of days allowed for
Serb withdrawal, and the language expressing how closely NATO
would follow the Serb withdrawal.

By early afternoon, Milosevic played one of his last cards: he
wanted to delay the Serb withdrawal until KFOR was present on the
ground. But KFOR couldn't be present on the ground until there was a
Security Council Resolution, and there could be no resolution until we

halted the bombing, and we ought not halt the bombing until the Serbs withdrew. I warned Solana it was a possible deal breaker.

By this point, Washington was calibrating each word. And we were trying to keep the talks going to prevent rumors in the press that they had broken down again. I told Jackson to do anything necessary to keep them going, but of course, this was after they had worked all the previous night without a break. "Keep them in there and just take a nap," I suggested.

By late afternoon, President Ahtisaari was again called on to explain the logic and details to Milosevic. This broke the last logjam in the discussions. And this further constrained any possible changes by us.

At 5:47 Jackson called to tell me that the Serbs had departed.

It was about that time that the French military representative came to see me. He couldn't get in, so he left a note. Remember the offer that General Kelche made to put the French heliborne troops into the airport at Pristina? he wrote. He called General Jackson to make the same offer yesterday and Jackson seemed to ignore him. I made a mental note to raise it with Jackson again.

Washington was still working on the issue of the Russian participation, and what should be done if the Serbs stalled in their withdrawal after we had halted the air campaign. The Pentagon seemed ready to support renewed bombing should the Serbs renege on the agreement, as well as supporting my recommendation that the Russians would not get their own sector.

But as we ended matters on Wednesday afternoon, there were still Russian objections to the command and control arrangements. The Russians wanted their own sector, in northern Kosovo, under their own commanders. They had floated the idea of a U.N. officer bridging the gap between NATO and Russian command lines.

Late that evening Mike Jackson called to inform me that he had achieved the signature of the Serbs on the Military Technical Agreement and had delivered to them the letter stating that KFOR would be operating under NATO command and control. I passed the completed agreement to Secretary General Solana for approval. The Serbs had refused to accept or acknowledge the letter on NATO command and control, and I also informed Solana of this. Still, we were upbeat: the withdrawal of Serb forces was to commence the next day. But they won't start until midday, Jackson warned, and they won't move at night.

It had been a difficult week of negotiations, but we had been largely successful in applying military pressure to move the agreement forward. We had preserved the sequence of activities, so that we would not give up the bombing until we had the agreement that we needed, and in its general construction the agreement seemed all right.

As I looked it over again, we had managed to retain Appendix B, which provided the specific authorities of the KFOR commander. The agreement did specify a complete withdrawal, though we had slipped back to eleven days for the timeline. Unfortunately, the Pentagon had dropped the return of Albanian prisoners. But the real weak point was that NATO command and control was not explicitly recognized. That meant that we would still have to work with the Russians to define their participation. Mike Jackson had pushed hard, and he had been pushed hard. He was getting a lot of instructions, trying to prepare the entry operation as he was negotiating, and I assumed he was keeping London informed, too. He'd had little rest for the past week, on top of the stress of the three months' deployment in Macedonia. We were lucky to have him, I thought.

Overnight we continued to fly aircraft into Kosovo, seeking targets. We used the B-52's one last time, and flew an A-10 aircraft against Serb artillery.

Thursday morning, June 10, was the day to begin cleaning up the loose ends of our operation. Once we got the verification of the withdrawal, then we would have what we needed to call off the remaining strikes and even pause in working the ground option. I had decided that the way to do this was simply to stop dropping bombs, without formally requesting any measures from the political machinery at NATO. That way, if we needed to resume the strikes, there was no formal diplomatic permission required, though the nations would have to agree informally, of course.

And we'd have to focus on the Russian participation. I had already dispatched my special assistant for Russian matters, Steve Covington, to Moscow to join Brigadier General Casey and Deputy Secretary Talbott for these critical discussions.

That morning with my commanders we reviewed again the KFOR entry plan, the sectors, and the timelines. We were now entering a new operation. Assuming the Serbs actually withdrew, and we were expecting to see a substantial withdrawal, then we would enter the next day, Friday, June 11. Even the U.S. forces would be on hand for this, despite all the delays caused by the sticky political situation in Washington and the notification requirements to Congress.

In a VTC, I went over the four new "measures of merit" I had established for KFOR: deploy smoothly and quickly; avoid anarchy—get all Serb forces out, stop any crimes of revenge or Serb ethnic cleansing, and give full support to the International Criminal Tribunal; provide humanitarian assistance to the greatest extent possible; and protect your force, especially from minefields.

Mike Jackson did not want to take advantage of the French offer to secure the Pristina airfield. He had concerns, he said. For one, there was a lot of unexploded ordnance there that could hurt our troops. And the early occupation of the airfield wasn't that important. He had other uses in mind for the helicopters, in order to move quickly through the Kacanik defile north of Skopje. He planned to be in Pristina the following night in any case, and he would coordinate the details of his plans with the Serbs in their meeting scheduled for 2:00 that afternoon. I didn't push for the French option; Jackson was the commander on the ground, and he didn't want to do it. How to enter Kosovo was his responsibility at this point.

Meanwhile I was fending off the anxious calls from Brussels inquiring whether we would terminate the air strikes early. We have to wait for the actual, substantial movement, I said, which was not expected until around 1:00 P.M. I was handed a note around noon that day, passing a message from Sandy Berger: "The United States is quite content for the SACEUR to be judicious and cautious in assessing whether the withdrawals have begun." I was surprised. I hadn't been receiving communications from Berger during the operation.

As we were awaiting first word on the withdrawals, Steve Covington called from Moscow. We have real problems, he said. Talks had been going on all morning, and the results were discouraging. Talbott had instructed Casey to tell the Russians that "the KFOR train has left the station and the Russians need to cooperate or they'll miss the train." But by mid-morning, the Russian military, led by Colonel-General Leonid Ivashov, was proposing a combined Russia-NATO force under the leadership of the Permanent Joint Council, a NATO-Russia consultative body, with Russia having its own sector. They also inquired about the status of the airfield at Pristina. On the other hand, Covington reported, the meeting was congenial in tone. Perhaps Ivashov was just a hard-liner and did not speak for President Yeltsin or others in the Russian government. I broke off the phone call to meet with Secretary Cohen and the Joint Chiefs on the teleconference. After reassuring the Secretary that we had done all of our planning and were well positioned for the entry, I told him about the situation with Russia. This is the political-military point of main effort, I said, and this is where we'll either succeed or fail.

I sketched out the way we had handled the Russian troops in Bosnia, which we were pushing for here in Kosovo, and then contrasted that with what the Russians had proposed in Moscow. It is "co-leadership" they're asking for, I said, with SHAPE bypassed and no unity of command. It won't be operationally effective. The Russian troops need to be inside a NATO sector, preferably the U.S. sector.

If they produced a 5,000-to-7,000-man Russian force, would your solution still work, I was asked.

Of course it can, I said.

The Secretary and the Joint Chiefs took in my comments but didn't indicate any support. That's the way it usually was on these VTCs. I talked and made requests. They listened and asked questions. I answered. The VTCs were mostly for passing information and requests upward.

Javier Solana had hoped to be able to conclude everything by 3:00, the time of his regularly scheduled press conference, and so at 2:30 he called to check on the status of the withdrawal.

"Javier, we just don't have enough movement yet for me to say, one way or the other," I said. "And I am worried about the Russians." I relayed the Russian demands for their own sector and the kind of independent control that would signify a partition of Kosovo.

A few minutes later, though, we began to receive indications of highway movements and other "tippers" that a withdrawal was under way. After consulting with Jim Ellis, I called Solana back, about 3:15. "Javier, we assess that a withdrawal is under way," I said.

"Thank you, Wes," he replied, and dashed off to his press conference.

I called Joe Ralston to tell him that we had verified the beginning of the withdrawal, though, as I noted, no tanks or artillery were moving, just the "rear area" personnel, trucks, and logistics.

At 3:36 I directed Jim Ellis to suspend the air campaign. Operation Allied Force was done. Finished.

We had determined that once we verified the commencement of the withdrawal, it wasn't feasible to continue to bomb in some places and not others. More important, this cleared the way for the U.N. Security Council Resolution.

A few minutes later the President called to congratulate us on the campaign. I thanked him for his support and the call, but I told him that one problem remained: we had to prevent the Russians from having a separate sector.

I explained my reasoning, as I had done with the Secretary of Defense. I felt by his reaction that the issue was still open in his mind.

A few minutes later Mike Jackson called to report that following his meeting with the Serbs he had decided to delay entry by a day, until Saturday, June 12. They needed more time to move their equipment up the few roads in southern Serbia and had asked for an additional day. I approved the delay, subject to confirmation by Solana.

Around 6:00 P.M., George Casey called from Moscow, explaining that the Russians really wanted their own sector. He proposed that we consider a small Russian sector, and then put most of their forces in a NATO sector.

I was acutely uncomfortable with this, and told him so.

Two hours later, Javier Solana called. The U.N. Security Council Resolution had just passed in New York. It was over. Done. He was ecstatic.

"Wes, Wes, you have won, you have done it," he said. He explained the outcome in New York, and the reaction of the press in Brussels. His voice was warmer than I had heard for many weeks. He was not only happy, he was also enormously relieved. "You will be my friend for life!" he said.

It was indeed a happy moment. I felt immeasurably lighter. I relaxed, for the first time in weeks.

I slumped into the backseat of the Mercedes as we made the short drive back to the chateau. I was at least as tired as Mike Jackson, I thought. But it was over, almost. And, like Solana, I was happy and relieved. The stress of the relationship with the Pentagon had been the worst part, I thought, and maybe that's over now. The President's call was a good sign.

That evening we forwarded the execute order to AFSOUTH: "You are directed to deploy KFOR into Kosovo." The operation was under way.

FIFTEEN

PRISTINA AIRFIELD

ON THURSDAY, JUNE 10, most of us in NATO were focused on verifying the Serb withdrawal and suspending the bombing. None of us fully appreciated how fast events were moving in Moscow.

During my VTC with Secretary Cohen that afternoon, I expressed concern that the Russians might hold hostage the U.N. Security Council Resolution to use as leverage to obtain their separate sector. Washington wisely advised Strobe Talbott to draw the Russians into discussions and keep them there until the resolution passed in New York. At that point, we reckoned, Moscow would have less leverage. For whatever reason, the Russians didn't block the resolution as it moved to passage.

But the discussions met Russian intransigence nonetheless. Shortly after 5:00 P.M., Colonel General Ivashov rejoined the military discussions and, using the American delegation's own analogy, stated that Russia had decided to "take her own train." After discussions inside the U.S. delegation, where someone had reportedly raised the idea of giving the Russians the French sector in the north, George Casey called me. I again warned strongly against giving the Russians a sector. Apparently the U.S. delegation dismissed the idea.

But a few minutes later the Russians indicated via a document sent to the Americans that they placed a great emphasis on the Pristina airfield, referring to it by its actual name, Slatina Airfield (which initially confused the Americans), and that they intended to ensure Russian access to the airport. Steve Covington apparently warned that there was some possibility that the Russian detachment in Bosnia could be sent into Kosovo to secure the airfield preemptively, but after some discussion the Russian document was apparently discounted.

George Casey forwarded to me the points made by the Russian deputy foreign minister, Alexander Avdeyev, in which he laid claim to a Russian sector and stated Russia's intent to use Slatina Airfield for deployment. I saw the paper the next day.

On Thursday evening, however, the Russian brigade in Bosnia received instructions to begin preparations for movement, and by the early hours of Friday morning, Major Ken Chance, our liaison officer with the Russians in Bosnia, had concluded that they could in fact be moving into Kosovo. Chance had just taken up this position, having previously worked for Steve Covington in my headquarters in Belgium. He called Covington around midnight to report his concerns. The American delegation reportedly decided to raise the issue with the Russians in their meetings that morning.

When I arrived at the office on Friday, I went through the normal morning update discussions with Pete Chiarelli, spoke with Mike Jackson, and raised my general concerns on the Russian issue with Javier Solana. Then, just as I was walking out of my office to move toward the NATO VTC, Chiarelli came in with a message from Major Chance, who was concerned enough to call directly to SHAPE, in addition to reporting through normal channels.

Chiarelli repeated Chance's report. "Sir, the Russians are moving forces from the assembly area at the Bijelina airfield toward the bridge crossing the Drina River into Serbia. It is about 200 personnel. The remainder of the brigade will remain in Bosnia for now." Their mission reportedly was to occupy Pristina airfield and receive reinforcements.

At the NATO teleconference there was conflicting information. SFOR only knew that the Russians had received a warning order to be prepared to move. I directed SFOR to find out what was really happening and slow down the Russian deployment. This violates the agreement with SFOR, I said, where we had arrangements that they would provide four months' notice before removing any troops.

And I was clear in my intent to KFOR: "I want to ensure that KFOR gets there first. I don't want to be welcomed by a Russian battalion that claims to dominate the airport and then have to negotiate with the Russians for the use of the airport."

The danger was that if the Russians got in first, they would claim their sector, and then we would have lost NATO control over the mission. I had closely observed the double standard the Russians had applied while working for us in the Bosnia mission. They took care of the Serbs, passing them information, tipping them off to any of our operations, and generally doing their best to look after their "fellow Slavs" while keeping up the pretense of full cooperation with us. And in Bosnia we hadn't given them their own sector. If they had their own sector in Kosovo, they would run it as a separate mission, and Kosovo would be effectively partitioned.

I was interrupted by a phone call from George Casey in Moscow. He read over Deputy Foreign Minister Avdeyev's talking points from the previous evening and reported that Colonel General Ivashov had told him that "within six hours of your deployment, we are going into the north and take the sector we want." I'm not certain they could really do this, Casey added.

I am certain, I said. They can move those units, believe me. How fast, I don't know, but if they start moving today, who knew?

In Casey's view, the signals coming from Moscow were mixed, with the foreign ministry taking a decidedly softer line than the military. He was awaiting the results of a meeting that Talbott was having with Ivanov, and he was hopeful that this would clarify the Russian position.

After returning to and concluding the VTC, I held Mike Jackson and Jim Ellis behind, to continue the discussion on the Russians. They were going to meet Secretary Albright, who was visiting Skopje that morning, but they would stay in close touch with the situation. Jackson confirmed that he did have the option of going by air to Pristina if necessary, using the French offer to lead.

Shortly after I returned to my office, I got a call from SFOR, following up on the Russian situation. It was Major General John Sylvester, the ranking American in the absence of General Meigs, who was temporarily in Germany.

"Sir, the Russians are not moving," he said. "But I would like to know where you heard this."

This was a relief to hear, but it didn't explain the earlier report. And it wasn't conclusive. "John, just go back and be certain, please," I said.

Not long after, Sylvester called back to correct his earlier report on the Russians. "They did move out of their cantonments this morning," he said, "sixteen trucks and sixteen armored vehicles. They coordinated for a police escort to cross the bridge at Bijelina ... and they are beginning to move across the Drina River now."

This was conclusive. We had a problem. The Russian threat to establish a separate sector was now real.

I knew, though, that in this case I had to get political guidance and support for any action. I tried to contact Javier Solana—I had been trying since George Casey had reported Colonel General Ivashov's threat—but he was unavailable.

I then called Joe Ralston in Washington, waking him, and told him that the Russians were moving from Bosnia into Kosovo. I had developed a routine of calling Ralston early and Shelton late. It seemed to work for everyone. This was the very situation I had feared, where we lacked the legal authority to deny the Russians their call for a sector. This was the case in which Shelton and I, in several previous conversations, had talked about "getting in there first." Ralston had told me the same thing.

"Joe, don't you think we have to at least consider a military response to this?" I asked.

Yes, I do. Why don't you go ahead and work that, he suggested, adding that he would handle the Washington end of the problem and get back to me with further guidance.

I huddled with my key leaders at SHAPE, and by 10:30 had raised Mike Jackson. "This is a warning order," I said, "but I want you to get ready to move by air to occupy Pristina airfield." Jackson acknowledged the warning order.

Still unable to reach Solana, I called U.S. Ambassador Sandy Vershbow. He would need to be informed, in any case. Vershbow's response was immediate. "Don't we need to get to Pristina before they do?" he asked.

Solana finally called at 11:20, just after I'd gotten off the phone with Vershbow. He was already aware of the problem, having heard from Washington that Talbott was being returned to Moscow to continue the discussions there.

I told him I was considering whether there were any military options.

He had guidance for me. "I am recommending you move to Pristina airport as soon as possible," he said.

"Javier, I just want to be certain that you are comfortable that I have the authority to order this," I asked, to be clear.

"Yes, of course you do. You have ACTORD," he said emphatically.

So I had NATO support, but I knew there was much more to be done before an operation like this could be executed.

Joe Ralston called shortly before noon. I explained that I had given Mike Jackson a warning order for the air movement to the airfield and that I had Solana's support. He had different guidance now from Washington: Send in a small element; this shouldn't be a military confrontation, just explain that this is for coordination and information flow. Of course, you'll have to tell the Serbs. Think about it, he said, and come back to me with a recommendation.

Then I reestablished communications with Jim Ellis, who had gone to the airfield in Macedonia to meet the Secretary of State and had been drawn into an extended conference call on her aircraft, as she consulted with Talbott, Secretary Cohen, and the other "principals" in Washington.

Ellis reported that the Washington consensus was that we needed to get a NATO presence on the ground before the Russians arrived at the airfield. The question was, how? We discussed some of the difficult aspects of the operation that Jackson was looking at, including the air defense and what to do in the event of a confrontation. Neither of us had seen Jackson's plan at this point. It seemed that we would need someone at the airfield of sufficient rank to deal with the Russians on a peer basis—which meant a major general—and that if he went in with too small a force, he might be pushed aside by either the Serbs or the Russians. I was still thinking in terms of the guidance I had worked with Hugh Shelton over the previous week, and was interested in determining whether we could put in a substantial force.

Ellis was also concerned that KFOR was to have a coordination meeting with the Serbs in less than an hour. What should we say?

"Jim, don't tell the Serbs anything until we know what we're doing." I said. "We can't be asking permission for something at this point; for now, just keep the dialogue open."

Then I lost communications with him.

I called directly to Mike Jackson to get an update on the planning. He had two British companies (about 250 troops), he said, and the French were offering most of a battalion (about 350 soldiers). He proposed to tell the Serbs at 1:00 P.M., about one hour before the first elements of the force would arrive at the airfield, under the most optimistic of his planning assumptions. No confrontation, I stressed.

There were many details as we talked, and I was highly uncomfortable with the idea of just launching two companies to the airfield by helicopter. I wanted to sit down, at least over the VTC, lay out the plan, and discuss it before we executed it.

As we were continuing to review our options, Jim Ellis arrived at Jackson's headquarters and joined the conversation. As we compared the guidance we had received, it was even clearer that we were some way from having a plan put together. Ellis reported that he himself had been directed by Washington to get to the airfield. I explained to Ellis that I had already told Washington that this was not a good idea at this point. And how many forces did we really need? To do exactly what? What were the standards for sustainability and survivability? What were the plans for the close air support to accompany the helicopters? How would we call in the air support if we needed it, since the tactical air capabilities were still on the ground on standby in Aviano, Italy?

Rupert Smith came in to my office to join the conversations. He was concerned that we were heading into a confrontation, whether we wanted one or not. I agreed with him.

Hugh Shelton called in a little after 12:30. I updated him on the status of the planning, centered on the idea of getting a "substantial" force to the airfield. He gave his assent.

I checked directly with the Combined Air Operations Center, to confirm whether we were moving any of our aircraft forward to support an operation. We were not. The CAOC was trying to observe the Russian movement and the frontier between Kosovo and the rest of

Serbia with the Predator unmanned aerial vehicle. "Please check with AFSOUTH and get the support package for the close air support aircraft under way," I said.

Walt Slocombe called from the Pentagon. I described our planning, and the current intent to send in a substantial force, if we could get it all coordinated and it made sense.

"That sounds exactly right," he said. "And we need to get some U.S. personnel in that force, too. Let's get the Marines. But you'll have to get approval from the Secretary of Defense, of course."

Immediately Jim Ellis was on the phone to update on the planning. We can put in two battalions, he reported.

Taking the cue from Slocombe, I asked Ellis to check on whether we had any of the U.S. contingent available to participate, and if so, to put them on alert.

Ellis was also getting information directly from the Secretary of State's party at the airfield. "Secretary Albright says Russian Foreign Minister Ivanov claims that the Russian troops are not going into Kosovo. But we are getting reports of six transport aircraft with 600 troops on the move out of Russia."

This felt like high command in crisis. Not war, but a serious position nonetheless. The phone lines were jammed with incoming calls, information and guidance were cutting back and forth across command lines and skipping echelons. The top people were spending too much time talking, and not enough planning and thinking. This, I reflected, was like what happened in warfare when you "got inside the other fellow's decision cycle." This was why it was so important to seize and retain the initiative in operations, thereby forcing your adversary to respond. Strategic commands weren't like battalions—they didn't have a football drill to issue orders or a playbook of responses. That was even more true in an Allied command, where more than one set of political leaders was involved.

Of course, we weren't at war, nor did we want to be. This was a further constraint on our options. We had to work our way through this, I thought. So far, we were on course for doing that.

I called Secretary Albright, just to get her direct read on the situation, since she was in my area, and her staff was feeding us information. I brought her up to date on the planning, and warned her that the Russians certainly were in collusion with the Serbs on this move. I wanted her to have this information when she next spoke with Ivanov.

At 1:20 Jim Ellis was back on the phone. He said he understood the warning order I had given to Mike Jackson, but he was concerned about how much force might be required. We can't get everyone and everything we need in there, he said, and that makes the risk extremely high. What's the risk of waiting a while?

I was sensitive to what Ellis was saying. I hadn't seen any details of the plan either, and shared his and Jackson's concerns. "I'm not sure myself what the other options are at this point," I told him. "But we don't want to lose the airfield."

I had to drop off with Ellis to take a call from Joe Ralston, who wanted specifics on where we stood in moving toward the operation. "Have the Serbs been told?" he asked.

"Not yet," I replied, going on my own guidance to Ellis and the absence of any report to the contrary.

"What's the status of the helicopters? How soon could we lift off?"

"We're at about thirty minutes or less, if we were to give the order," I said. I had directed them to get ready, but they still owed me back-brief on the plan. That was still to come.

Ralston emphasized that we had to get a senior American officer in on the first lift of birds. He then speculated on what was behind all of this. It's the military on its own. They won't stop. This is like a coup, he said. If so, it was even more dangerous. But I had no information to support such speculation, one way or the other. I had to assume the worst.

Rupert Smith and Dieter Stockmann were in and out of my office all morning and into the afternoon, listening, and commenting whenever there was a break in the steady stream of phone calls. Smith had just gotten off the phone with Mike Jackson. He sat down in the small chair close to my desk, looking worried.

"SACEUR," he began, "Mike is concerned about the operation. He has identified five specific risks." He began to enumerate them: the risk to the just-negotiated Military Technical Agreement, which called for a smooth and synchronous occupation by KFOR as the Serbs withdrew, rather than an insertion into the airfield; the risk that helicopters might get shot down by the Serbs; the risk of a confrontation with the

Serbs at the airfield; the risk that the Serbs would blow the bridges and tunnels north of the Macedonia border, cutting off the force and leaving them unable to be reinforced from the ground; and the risk of some confrontation with the Russians.

I was glad to see the risks laid out systematically. It was the kind of analysis we would need before we went forward. We would now need to deal with the risks, mitigating each to the extent possible. Then we would have to decide on whether the gains were worth taking those risks. That decision, ultimately, was up to the nations. I just had to set up the military option.

But this was the first time I had seen my deputy so troubled. "So, what are you recommending at this point, Rupert?" I asked. "Do you think we shouldn't be doing this?"

"Well," he said, "I think you should certainly be planning this option, but don't fly them yet."

Smith went on to say that Jackson was labeling the operation a high risk; however, he continued, "we can do it."

Before we could advance the conversation, Hugh Shelton was back on the phone. He had talked to the British Chief of Defense, General Sir Charles Guthrie. I understand the British want to hold, he said.

"They are getting soft, I think," I replied, "and if we're to go ahead, you'll have to deal with Charles Guthrie."

I recounted the risks that Jackson had enumerated, and added my own thoughts. The most troubling to me was the fact that the road from Macedonia up to the airfield was easily interrupted. We knew that the bridges and tunnels on the route had been rigged with demolitions. We had to expect that these would be destroyed, forcing us to develop alternate routes and significantly delaying any ground reinforcements. I didn't want a group of paratroopers stranded at the airfield for several days if, in the worst case, we ended up in a confrontation. Despite our airpower, there was still a lot of Serb armor and artillery in the area, and they still retained sufficient low-altitude air defense weapons to make helicopter reinforcement costly once the shooting started. I had no doubt we would prevail, but the risk was there. We would have to work the airpower.

Still, I said to Shelton, the Russians have already requested transit for their reinforcing aircraft through Hungarian airspace. If they get a substantial force into the airfield, they will be able to do exactly what Colonel General Ivashov has threatened—take the area in the north, declare it their sector, and, in effect, partition the province. This is the worst scenario, I continued. It will mean that we achieved almost nothing from the campaign. There had been continuing press speculation that what Milosevic wanted in the end was a partition that allowed the Serbs to retain the northern part of the province. In this area they were in the majority. This was also where the major mineral wealth was located.

"What do your commanders think?" Secretary Cohen asked, as he came in on the conversation.

"They consider it high risk at this point," I said, "and so do I. That doesn't mean we shouldn't continue to work this, though. We have to see what we can do."

I didn't want the operation prematurely canned. We just hadn't worked it thoroughly enough to give up. The conversation ended with my reviewing the positions of the nations on the operation and Washington promising to work on it.

I was back almost immediately with Jim Ellis. It was now shortly after 2:00. Ellis had just been informed that the French would not participate. That took away two of the four companies Mike was counting on. What's the status of the planning overall? I asked.

I've just had a look at the order, and it's not ready, he said.

Ellis was concerned about the possibility of combat once the force got on the ground. He didn't want to write off several hundred troops.

"Of course we're not going to do that," I said.

But, in order to beat the timelines, we've got to get the force in the air, he continued, exasperated.

"Wait," I said. "We're still working it at this level. You continue the planning. I'll get back to you."

We were operating at the margin of what an Alliance can do in a not-quite-war situation. I had to rely on the commanders to plan the operation. They had to fix the details, and they had to believe in their own plan. But ultimately, the decision to go ahead shouldn't be the military's. This was going to be an operation with substantial political risks and costs, as well as benefits. It required political support and approval. As Supreme Allied Commander it was my responsibility to approve the military work in the plan and recommend to the Chiefs of Defense and the political level that we go ahead with it. At the same time I was trying to keep the nations in support, so that the commanders would have the assets to plan with.

This was a situation that constituted a strategic challenge to the Alliance. The threat of a Russian sector in the north had placed the whole premise of KFOR at risk. We were in this situation, I believed, because the West hadn't been firm enough in dealing with what we knew to be a contrary Russian agenda. The Russians very bluntly had given us adequate warning that they disagreed with NATO control of the mission, but we had cut the language very fine. We had left too much room for their interpretation, which could lead to a partition.

Now it seemed to be up to the military to correct the Russian view by changing the facts on the ground, if we could. The nations would have to back us up.

Russian aircraft were reported to be taking off from Moscow, and trying to enter Hungarian airspace.

Rupert Smith rejoined the dialogue, having just consulted with the British authorities. "London's interest is waning," he said. "Without the two French companies, Jackson says he doesn't have enough force."

Just before 2:30 Charles Guthrie called from London, concerned that we lacked combat power. I offered another problem that had been nagging at me: if the Russians really wanted to enter and establish a sector in the north of Kosovo, they could simply drive across the border, even if we blocked the airfield, and plant their flag. Reinforcements could be flown in to airfields in Serbia and driven in. So there was a chance that we could be outmaneuvered even if we seized the airfield.

Guthrie said that he had never trusted the Russians, but he warned that we would need very strong political backing to undertake an operation like this.

At 2:38 Hugh Shelton was back for another update. I explained that we needed to plan for the use of U.S. forces to replace the French. We had two airborne infantry companies that we had moved in from Task Force Hawk that morning, plus the Apache helicopters. And the Marines were arriving from their landing in Greece.

Plan for it, Shelton said. He recommended checking with the Serbs at this point, so their reaction could be factored in.

At 2:52 Jim Ellis reported that the Serbs had already been told. They reacted immediately and said that a NATO move to the airport was impossible. I told him to meet me with Jackson on the VTC in twenty minutes. I knew I had to pull this together.

At 2:54 Joe Ralston called back for another update. How soon could you move? he asked. "In fifteen minutes," I said, "at least for the Brits. I don't know yet about the status of the Americans."

After Ralston and I hung up, I turned to Rupert Smith, who was still in the chair by the desk. "We just can't do it with only two companies," I said.

"I agree," he said.

But I hadn't given up on the option. Maybe we would get the two U.S. companies. We'd have to check on their sustainability. We had the Apache helicopters, as well as the Italians' Mangusta helicopter gunships. I was concerned about how we would manage the close air support. If the Serbs did oppose us, then I wanted the fight to be over quickly. We had about six hours of daylight remaining. We weren't expecting the Russians before early evening, so we still had time, if, on balance, we chose to do it.

At 3:05 Hugh Shelton called. British support was weak, he said, and Ivanov had repeatedly assured Secretary Albright that these forces weren't going in to Kosovo, that the Russian movement was a "mistake." There were still concerns with the details. In view of all that, Secretary Cohen thinks that we shouldn't go forward. What about just standing down for now?

There was no political support, now, from the U.S. side. "OK," I said, "I'll keep them on fifteen minutes' notice while we continue to work the details that we can here."

But I was unable to mitigate the risks adequately as I thought about where we were. There were too many unresolved issues. There had been no detailed back-brief, and no rehearsal. The air and ground elements hadn't worked together before. The logistics were uncertain. My commanders were full of doubts and reservations. I couldn't direct or recommend an operation like this until my commanders and I could review the plan and believe in it.

I assembled the team on the VTC and told them to stand down, as we went further into the details of the planning. I asked Smith to pull together where we were and recommend next steps.

There were a number of things wrong during the planning effort, I thought—too many phone calls, not enough collaboration in working the details between headquarters, and ultimately, we hadn't achieved closure before we lost political support. This was an alliance trying to transition from peace operations into a potential war-fighting requirement. I had pushed hard, but even with the best leaders and systems, which we had, there are tasks that can't be done in time unless they have been prepared and rehearsed. Especially difficult was the "calculus of risk." We had been in a mindset to minimize risks, so every risk in the prospective airfield occupation jarred people, up and down the chain of command. It would have been far easier to have worked the planning from the other direction, going from readiness for war into something less demanding. There were many other "what ifs."

It was odd, too, that the French pulled back their offer of participation, since they were the ones who had been most keen on the airfield option in the first place. But we had been right to look at the military option, I sensed.

I hoped that Foreign Minister Ivanov was correct when he told Secretary Albright that the Russians were going to stop before they entered Kosovo. But just to be certain the Russian plan was disrupted, we asked Romania, Hungary, and Bulgaria to deny the Russians overflight permission.

The remainder of the afternoon and early evening was quiet. The reported movements of the Russian airborne forces had tapered off. Around 9:00 P.M., Hugh Shelton called. We compared information on the reported Russian air movements and ground movements and agreed that the Russian convoy had stopped in Serbia, somewhere near the Kosovo border. We also discussed the Russian sector issue. It sounded as though someone in Washington was still floating the idea of compromising with the Russians by giving them a sector. Each time I talked with Washington, I sensed the hesitancy. People listened, but they never quite agreed. They just didn't say, "Got it." Instead, they were always looking for me to give an opening to them.

"Sir," I said, trying to reinforce my position, "NATO command and control is required. That means a NATO brigade in charge of each sector. If we give the Russians any possibility of an independent sector, no matter how small we say it is initially, we've lost the principle of NATO command and control."

A few minutes later, Joe Ralston called to ask my support for a congressional delegation to visit Macedonia and Albania in the middle of this. I asked him please deflect them. Then I went back through the issue on the Russian sector again: "Joe, this is the last issue where we will have to draw a hard line. But if we don't draw the line here we'll end up with partition. I am not in a position to know if we can trust what the Russians are saying about this move, but my instinct is that something bad is going to happen.... The Russians are in a domestic position where it makes sense for them to push a confrontation. The U.S. is in the domestic position to avoid a confrontation. But, Joe, if we let the Russians have their own sector, this kind of problem will be replayed a hundred times on every issue."

I had done all the talking; he had listened, but I could tell that I still hadn't hit home. I couldn't see the Washington perspective, but what I had to do was stake out my own position as clearly and as forcefully as possible. As far as I could tell, Washington hadn't stopped listening to me.

Probably, the Joint Staff was preparing to help achieve an interagency consensus. That was the way the policy process worked. In this case, it meant that you had to lean on the CINC. I wanted to be helpful but had to present my best judgment. This was no time to back down on this fundamental issue. It was the workability of the mission—indeed, even the future of NATO—that was at stake.

Madeleine Albright called sometime before 11:00 P.M., as she was preparing for another conversation with Ivanov. She reassured me that Ivanov had promised her that the Russian forces would not cross into Kosovo prematurely. She had been pleased with the way the Russians had helped us so far, she said, and hoped that we could coordinate the movement of forces with a similar teamwork.

A few minutes later, Hugh Shelton called to tell me the White House had decided to delay the NATO entry that was scheduled for the next morning. There was a hope that if we delayed NATO's entry into Kosovo, the Russians would delay entering as well. The White

House wanted to avoid any chance of a confrontation. I protested the idea of the delay, but there was nothing to be done. The decision had been made.

We talked again about how to solve the issue of the Russian sector. Now people in Washington seemed to be working on the idea that maybe there could be a neutral sector, not under a NATO member nation, and the Russians could work with us in that sector. But if they could work in a neutral country's sector, then they could work in the U.S. sector, I reasoned. We shouldn't be compromising on NATO command and control of the mission.

I called Jim Ellis to pass on Washington's guidance to delay the NATO entry. I knew Jackson would be upset.

It was almost 1:00 A.M. on Saturday, June 12, when my special assistant, Colonel Dave Edgington, pushed me out. "Sir, you've got to get some rest," he said.

Less than an hour later, Edgington called me in the bedroom. "Sir, the Russians are in Pristina. They're being welcomed as heroes."

I pulled on my jeans and sweatshirt and went in to work the phones. Sure enough, the 200-man Russian element that had departed early that morning from Bosnia was being hailed in the streets of Pristina, in a scene shown over and over again on television. We began a blizzard of phone calls that extended over the next three hours. I had three phones in the study, and I continuously had one in each hand, with Edgington working the third.

My first call was to Javier Solana.

"Javier, have you seen the TV? The Russians are in Pristina," I reported.

Solana already knew, and he had talked to Washington. "But they said they were not going to Kosovo at all. Now the Russians are saying this was a mistake and they will be pulled back. What do you think?"

It was what I had hoped would not happen but had feared all along. They'll go to the airfield at Pristina, I said.

I spoke to Rupert Smith, and to Guido Venturoni. Charles Guthrie called to commiserate on the doublecross by the Russians and to find out why we weren't planning to enter Kosovo in the morning. He had felt, as I did, that delaying our entry was a mistaken decision before, and it would be a bigger mistake now.

Shortly thereafter, Ivanov issued a statement acknowledging the deployment to Pristina as "unfortunate" and declaring that the Russians would be withdrawn. A few minutes later, the news organizations reported that the Russians had arrived at Pristina airfield.

Solana and I conferred. I assured him that Jackson's forces would move in as rapidly as possible early that morning, and that we would reach the airfield to dispute Russia's control.

Somehow over the last few hours Washington had now taken an ever increasing roll in the operations. Decisions were being made quickly. I called Hugh Shelton again. "You have to get this order changed," I said. "After what the Russians have done, we have to enter as soon as possible. They are completely overestimating the risks here."

About a half hour later, Shelton called back. Sandy [Berger] has reviewed the situation and changed his mind. Go ahead with your plans to enter.

On Saturday morning there were indications of a second group of Russians leaving Bosnia to move to the airfield at Pristina, and I was still receiving indications of a Russian intent to reinforce the group at the airfield by air, landing paratroopers straight from Moscow. As we received reports from Moscow on Russian intentions, the situation seemed headed for a partition. Colonel General Ivashov had reportedly told the Americans that Russia intended to protect the Serbs in northern Kosovo. According to Ivashov, the Russians would not cooperate with NATO.

At the morning update teleconference at 9:00, Mike Jackson was confident in the operation. It was under way at last, and he predicted he would soon be at the airfield—perhaps in as little as three hours. Jackson was confident that he could handle the Russians. He spoke Russian, and, he said, he was going to be very nice to them. His approach was to win their cooperation by providing them logistic support, then gradually exert influence through control of the logistics. This was in keeping with our desire to have no confrontation.

But we also had to prevent a partition, and for that we had to prevent any reinforcement of the initial Russian element. We had apparently held them off during the evening hours as Hungary, Romania, and Bulgaria denied Russia overflight. I directed that we recontact the

American embassies in each country and reinforce the importance of their continued firm stand. Given the geography and their historical precedents, I knew that this was very difficult for these nations. I wasn't optimistic.

Some were speculating that the whole action was a military coup. I didn't have enough information to judge. Then at 10:20, Mike Jackson called to report that the Russian military attaché in Macedonia had just delivered to him a letter specifying that Pristina airfield was in the hands of the Russian ministry of defense.

"Mike, reject the letter. Find the guy who delivered it and turn it back," I directed. He said he would try.

The lead NATO forces were making steady progress, often with assistance from the Serb forces they were bypassing, it seemed. But there was a considerable number of mines and wire obstacles. The three hours stretched to four, then five, then six.

Most of the day was marked by agitated phone calls from Brussels, as hour after hour went by, and the KFOR elements had not reached the airfield at Pristina. Jackson reported that he understood his instructions and was pushing the pace to the best extent possible. He had initially had the option of employing a heliborne force forward, but had now decided to commit them on the ground.

Meanwhile, I continued to call Chiefs of Defense and ambassadors from Hungary, Romania, and Bulgaria to reassure them and ask their continued support in keeping the airspace closed.

One of the commanders then called me to ask what we were going to do if the Russians violated Hungarian or Romanian airspace? Would we shoot down the transport aircraft? It was a serious question. It would be decided at the highest levels, of course, not by us. But it was the right question to be asking.

By late afternoon, the lead elements of the NATO force were approaching the airfield. The weather had turned sour, with heavy clouds and a thunderstorm in the vicinity. Jackson reported that he intended to do a press conference from the airfield at 7:00 P.M., though the Russians were being " a bit awkward."

Washington had also arranged for a meeting in Macedonia with the Russian representatives. This meeting proved disappointing, also. I had sent Steve Covington, along with my Operations Chief, Major General

John Dallagher. They reported that the Russians wanted their own sector and were intent on bringing in 10,000 troops. They would not participate with their initial unit in the American sector, as we wanted, until the decision had been taken to give them their own sector.

In the early evening Joe Ralston called, after a meeting of the Deputies Committee in Washington. They were also worried about the possibility of the Russians flying in additional troops. You might want to block the runways, he suggested.

"Yes, good idea. I've been thinking about it, too, but don't see how we can do it. Apparently the British troops never actually reached the airfield."

Why don't you use the Apache helicopters, he said. They belong to us, and the Deputies support it.

"I have Washington support for this?" I asked.

He confirmed that I had support and that Washington would like me to do this.

Subsequently, I called Jim Ellis and passed along my instructions. Jim, I want you to use the Apaches to block the Pristina runways during the hours of darkness so the IL-76 transports can't land. This isn't "business as usual." NATO has been deceived or misled by about everyone in the Russian government at this point—we can't believe their promises. We don't want to be forced to decide whether or not to shoot down Russian aircraft if they violate Hungarian or Romanian airspace. So, you work this with Mike Jackson. If you need more resources, let me know. We've got to get ahead of the flow of events on this; we have to anticipate what we need.

The details would have to be filled in by Ellis and Jackson, of course, and I expected to hear back from them.

In the meantime I called the NATO force in Bosnia. I had to keep them connected to the overall effort. "The Russians knew four days ago that they were going to move out of Bosnia and into Kosovo," I told them. "Now, let's think how we can cut that force off from the flow of reinforcements in Bosnia."

Lieutenant General Mike Wilcox, the British Deputy Commander for Operations in Bosnia, was concerned. Trying to isolate the Russians didn't seem smart, and if we blocked the bridges over the Drina River, we would have political problems with the Serbs, he felt.

I left the problem with them, but told them we wouldn't block the bridges.

This was typical of the problems of crisis action in a peace operation, I thought. They were trying to work their own mission in Bosnia, and I didn't want to drag them into the Kosovo problem. But the Russians had already connected the two operations. It would have to be watched and possibly worked later.

At this point we appeared to be heading toward some sort of political-military confrontation. The real danger, it seemed to me, was that we could no longer rely on what the Russians said. We had to be prepared to head off their actions and not wait for their promises to be proved empty.

Jim Ellis called back around 10:00 P.M. Jackson has given the order to organize the Apache force, he reported, but he is really troubled. He says his mission is strictly humanitarian and peacekeeping; he doesn't have the legal authority in his order to do anything like this, and the Russians might react. And he doesn't have any extra forces; everything now is committed except the Americans, and nothing else will arrive for the next four days. He wants to stay with his approach, just to gain the Russians' confidence, despite the difficulties he had with them today, Ellis continued. Anyway, there's such terrible weather right now that the Apaches couldn't fly in over the mountains tonight. What do you want me to do?

It was an extended conversation. I rebutted the points on the nature of the mission, the lack of authority, and the risk. It seemed that Ellis was just reporting Jackson's view, but I wanted to be certain that he understood the authorities correctly. It also seemed to me that we had identified the least-risk option for interdicting the possible flow of reinforcements. If the Russians came in quickly, before our force was fully deployed, they would seize the sector they wanted in the north, forcing us into a more risky confrontation at that point. Of course, I could do nothing about the weather. And I was scheduled to leave before dawn the next morning to fly to Macedonia and see Jackson face-to-face. Just leave it for now, I said. I'll work on it when I see him.

On the early morning flight down to Macedonia on Sunday, I called Solana, shared my continued misgivings about the Russians, and explained the operation I had ordered to block the runways. I've got U.S. authority to use the Apaches, I said. Solana said that he agreed with the proposed action.

I arrived at Jackson's headquarters in the abandoned shoe factory just as his morning staff update was concluding. His commanders were gathered in the conference room, seated on folding chairs, and concluding the run through the briefing charts. There was a real team spirit about the command, and they had been through difficult times over the last three months.

"SACEUR, can I have a word with you in my office now?" Jackson said as we were leaving the briefing.

Once inside, it was a frank discussion. Amidst the serious issues Jackson seemed angry and upset. There was a lot of emotion. I had expected to discuss the issues. I hadn't expected the emotional tenor, but I probably should have.

We exchanged views on the role of Washington versus the role of Brussels, the authority of the Strategic Commander versus the responsibilities of the commander on the ground, the nature of the crisis itself, and the implications. It was a rapid-fire exchange and became too personal, which I regretted but couldn't seem to prevent.

"Sir, I'm not taking any more orders from Washington," Jackson said.

"Mike, these aren't Washington's orders, they're coming from me."

"By whose authority?"

"By my authority, as SACEUR."

"You don't have that authority."

"I do have that authority. I have the Secretary General behind me on this."

"Sir, I'm not starting World War III for you...."

This was getting out of hand, and I tried to turn down the temperature. "Mike, I'm not asking you to start World War III," I said. "I'm asking you to block the runways so that we don't have to face an issue that could produce a crisis.... It doesn't have to be a confrontation.... You will have the position.... They will have to challenge you." I tried to walk through some details as I had thought about the possibilities.

"Sir, I'm a three-star general; you can't give me orders like this.... I have my judgment."

"Mike, I'm a four-star general, and I can tell you these things."

It was a clash of perspectives and command styles, experience and intent, and, I sensed, a clash born of fatigue and frustration.

Jackson was an operational commander. He was focused on the task at hand, and, as he explained it, the peacekeeping mission was on track. He had established a fragile liaison with the Russian forces. The Russian force was isolated at the airfield. In his view the airfield had no value. There was no point in confronting the Russians there. They could always be dealt with later. Reinforcements could be isolated. Besides, in his view, my orders fell outside the NATO mission mandate. KFOR's only purpose, he said, was to facilitate the return of the refugees.

I saw the problem in strategic terms. This could be a defining moment for the future of NATO. Would we or would we not be able to conduct our own peacekeeping missions? Would Russia be co-equal with NATO in this operation? Would Russia get its way by deception and bluff or by negotiation and compromise? Would we have an effective operation or another weak U.N.-type force?

Moreover, the airfield was precisely what the Russians wanted. I didn't want to face the issue of shooting down Russian transport aircraft if they forced their way through NATO airspace. If they were able to land a large force, then we would be in the position of having to contain them, which could force a confrontation where the odds were less favorable to us. I wanted the runways blocked to head off any Russian temptation to reinforce and challenge us.

Blocking the runways at this point didn't necessarily mean a confrontation, I reasoned. The airfield was quite large and there weren't enough Russians to fully occupy it, let alone defend it. Once we were physically on it, it was as much ours as theirs. I expected that when NATO met the Russians with determination and a show of strength, the Russians would back down. They didn't have the strength to back a confrontation with us and they knew it. The mere act of moving toward them would strengthen our diplomatic leverage in the continuing negotiations to define Russian participation.

I couldn't deny that there was risk involved in this. And I didn't have all the answers. Helping to supply some of those answers was Jackson's job. In the event we couldn't arrive at the answers, I was prepared to modify or retract the orders.

However, I already had NATO authorization to act, as least from

Solana. And in the North Atlantic Council meeting on Saturday, some of the nations, especially some of the larger Allies, had been outraged by the Russians' actions.

In the British system, a field commander is supported. Period. That is the rule. A field commander is given mission-type orders, not detailed and continuing guidance. It is a wonderful, traditional approach, one that embodies trust in the commander and confidence in his judgment as the man on the scene. The American military has always aspired to this model, but has seldom seemed to attain it.

My experience couldn't have been more different than Jackson's. In my service, I had seen frequent oversight by higher headquarters, repeated questioning of seemingly insignificant details, and surprisingly little autonomy for field commanders. Sometimes it was just nervous superiors, unwilling to accept the possibility of below-standard performances by subordinates. But sometimes there was a logic to it, when a commander needed guidance, when an organizational transformation was under way, or when the issues had an impact beyond that commander's particular endeavors or needed careful weighing of the political component. Dealing with the Russians was such an issue; it was essentially a policy matter. Military advice would be considered, but it might not be the final word. In democratic societies, whose militaries were under effective civil control, it was natural to expect such policy matters to be decided by civilian policymakers. And modern communications had made it possible.

Indeed, "focus on the decisive point" was the whole lesson that had begun for the U.S. Armed Forces in the 1960s. If higher headquarters *could* observe, supervise, or control, then higher headquarters usually *would* observe, supervise, and control. There were the stories of President Kennedy talking to the captain of the destroyer that was intercepting the first Russian ship to challenge the U.S. naval quarantine of Cuba in 1962, of the White House directing the bombing targets during the early stages of the Vietnam operation, of Army commanders hovering over Vietnam battlefields in helicopters, giving orders but not sharing risks, and of course, all the experience of the fine tuning of the U.S. operations in Haiti in 1994 and the NATO air missions in Bosnia in 1995.

The American military sometimes fought hard against these tendencies, of course, which were believed to infringe on commanders' authorities, causing them to look over their shoulders and hesitate. In the free-wheeling seminars at the Army Command and General Staff College or at the Army War College there was often a lot of posturing. "We" would never allow that to happen, "we" trust our subordinates, and "we" will guard against this kind of pressure from above. People would brag about not answering their radios, or making themselves unavailable for telephone conversations. Maybe it happened occasionally. Once.

But we also saw what happened when the right questions weren't asked by people at the top, and when a lack of attention to detail and specific guidance had led to tragedy. Wasn't that one of the lessons of the bombing of the Beirut barracks in 1983? Wasn't that what lay behind the 1993 tragedy in Mogadishu, Somalia?

I had found that success wasn't as much a matter of rebuffing higher headquarters as of dealing with them constructively. Higher headquarters and higher commanders often had good ideas. You had to engage; there had to be give and take. Perspectives had to be exchanged. So when higher headquarters asked, "How many?" or "Review for me how you intend to ...," then, at least in our American system, we usually practiced a doctrine of "unlimited transparency." And when higher headquarters gave directions, we did our very best to comply.

It was more than mere loyalty or discipline. We also practiced a doctrine of synchronizing around the intent of the higher commander. We might give our own views, but we usually did everything we could to accommodate the intent of our superiors, even when they were demanding and far from ideal. This tendency toward centralization and the tolerance for it was part of the maturity that generally permeated the upper ranks of the American military structure.

Jackson and I had been through the ambiguities and complexities of this operation for months. The negotiations were especially grueling, I knew, because of the centralized control and stream of changes over which neither of us had much control. We both knew very well that this was a multinational organization, where the views of all nations, and especially the most powerful, will always have to be taken into account.

Jackson's concerns needed to be seriously addressed. I decided to start at the top: his Chief of Defense, Charles Guthrie. Jackson remained under his national command authority, even though he was serving under me. If there were questions about whether NATO had the legal authority to issue such an order, or his duty to comply, this was the right place to begin. Besides, the ultimate authority in this case would lie with the U.S. and British governments, not the NATO leadership in Brussels. The two Allies from World War II, together again, shaping the future. Guthrie had been generally supportive of me throughout our work together, and I felt that he could help me redirect the discussion.

"Charles, I'm here with Mike Jackson, and we're discussing the order I've given him to block the runways at the airfield. He has some reservations about policy and authority." I then briefly sketched some of Jackson's concerns and my answers.

"Wes, let me speak to Mike," he said.

I handed the phone to Jackson, who moved off to the side of the room to explain the situation and his views to Guthrie.

After a few minutes, Jackson handed me the phone, "Sir, CDS will speak to you, please."

"Hello, Wes. Well, I must say that I agree with Mike, and so does Hugh Shelton."

I was stunned. Hadn't the go-ahead I received come from Joe Ralston? Speaking for Washington?

"I see," I replied. "Well, Charles, I got this guidance from Washington, so I'd better call Hugh. I'll get back to you after I've spoken to him."

It was about 3:00 A.M. in Washington when I reached Hugh Shelton. I explained what was happening, described the call to Charles Guthrie, and concluded, "And he says you agree with him. I don't understand. Joe Ralston called me and gave me these, well, instructions. I guess I could have said no, but I wouldn't have gone ahead without your support. Do you not support what I've ordered?"

Well, I knew that Joe was passing this to you, he said. And I supported that. But I did agree with Charles last night that we didn't want a confrontation—but I support what you're doing."

Jackson and I resumed our discussion while Shelton tried to reach Charles Guthrie in London. I reiterated my directions to Jackson, explaining carefully that if he didn't follow my directions, he would have to resign his position. He acknowledged this and accepted instructions to order NATO troops to block the runways. At his suggestion, I let him order British ground troops for this mission instead of the Apaches. The armored vehicles would have been far more effective than the Apaches—but, no doubt at least in part because he strongly objected to my instructions within the British national chain of command, London refused to allow its troops to comply with Jackson's NATO order.

It was not disobedience of orders, however, nor, technically, was it insubordination. It was just a striking example of what was to become an increasingly open "secret" of NATO operations: NATO commands were like puppets, with two or six or sometimes dozens of strings being pulled from behind the scenes by the nations themselves, regardless of the formalistic commitment of forces.

NATO commanders' orders were subject to hour-by-hour scrutiny and possible veto from nations. It was a practice that had apparently originated in U.N. operations, called "red-carding," where nations just temporarily drew back their forces from certain actions or operations ordered by higher commanders. In the operations in Bosnia, we had seen a few cases where nations' forces simply refused to go along with orders, allegedly based on instructions from home, but usually fed by the subordinates on the scene expressing their concerns. And we had seen it during the air campaign, when nations abruptly ordered their pilots not to fly certain missions or strike particular targets. It was a situation that the U.S. officers hadn't faced personally, because they seldom worked for international authorities. But if orders from an international authority conflicted with Washington's orders, they would certainly have obeyed Washington.

It wasn't against the rules of the Alliance, either. It was well understood that nations always retained ultimate authority over their forces and had the right to override orders at any time, if they chose to do so. In practice almost every nation had special teams monitoring its forces, ready to cry foul at the least deviation from expectations.

It was a miracle we had made it as far as this, I thought, without a major blowup.

So what we had in this case was not an "authority problem," as it may have appeared at first blush, but rather a "policy problem." Wash-

ington and London apparently disagreed, at some level, on how to
address the threat of an independent Russian sector and a de facto partition.

During the morning Shelton was unable to work this out with
Guthrie. Then I was told that Secretary Cohen would speak with the
British defense minister, George Robertson.

This was a case where the five-hour time difference worked against
Washington. The British government was alert and active. In the United
States only the military was available. The British had serious concern
about the possibility of a confrontation at the airport. They won't like
this in London," I was warned by one of my political advisers. The
British preferred to follow the original course laid out by Jackson, believing that any additional Russian troops arriving at the airfield could be
sealed off with minimal risk.

Washington didn't want a confrontation either, but there was something different in the American perspective, a greater self-confidence
when facing the Russians, more mutual understanding, and much
deeper consultative arrangements. The pattern of the Cold War had
been European reluctance to face the Soviet Union without the active
participation and leadership of the United States. Action now would
again take strong leadership from Washington.

Instead of blocking the airfield runways, the British troops moved to
block the roads leading from the airfield. Jackson prepared a letter disputing the Russian claim to control the airfield. There was nothing more
to be said, pending the outcome of the political level discussions between the United States and the United Kingdom. Jackson and I parted.

A few minutes later I told the press that we were proceeding exactly
as planned, despite the "bizarre" Russian dash to the airport. I
explained that the airport wasn't crucial for KFOR and that the Russian actions were a political problem, which needed to be resolved in
political channels.

Elsewhere in Macedonia, George Casey and some of my NATO
team were meeting with the Russians. The atmosphere was cordial but
unproductive. The Russians were still demanding their own sector. As
talks got under way in Moscow later in the day (Strobe Talbott had
flown back the night before), the Russian position actually hardened, as
Russia attempted to reap the political benefits of its military ploy.

On my flight back to Belgium that afternoon, Hugh Shelton called to explain that the British were still refusing to block the runways. Later that night I heard that nothing had changed after the phone conversation between Secretary Cohen and Minister Robertson.

I wasn't surprised. Operations need a lead nation, and normally the nation with the largest force has the loudest voice. On D-Day Eisenhower, not Montgomery, was the Supreme Commander, because we had by far the larger force. In this case, the troops at the front were British. The largest of the national contributions was going to be British. They were in the crucial sector of Pristina. As for the United States, we had pledged not to deploy our troops before there was an agreement. So we were late in arriving for the entry on June 11 and 12. We had consciously sought to avoid leading the Kosovo force, so the British had provided the commander on the ground. And the British would provide much of the voice for the mission, whatever the lines of authority on NATO organization charts. I hoped the British approach would work.

I thought back to the words of a U.S. senator, as he explained the mood of at least some in Congress in addressing a top-level political-military strategic conference in Germany, before the start of the air campaign. "America," he had said forcefully, "is a reluctant leader." He had been urging the Europeans to do more and take more responsibility. Now they were. I remembered thinking as the senator had spoken that we might not always like what others would do when they led.

As I settled into the evening's work at the chateau, the phone rang from my staff in Germany. "Sir, we've heard Russian air transports are moving again. They could be heading this way."

If so, it would be the third night's test of the courage and steadfastness of Hungary, Romania, and Bulgaria. Limiting the scale of the Russian presence at the airfield, and thereby forcing them into negotiations, again would depend on these three small countries.

The information on the movements was unclear. Hugh Shelton led a two-hour conference call with the Principals Committee—Berger, Albright, Cohen, and others—scattered around Washington as we sorted through the intelligence and Russian intent. There was another call to Ivanov, who said that the Russians weren't going to try to bring in more troops. The President had spoken to Yeltsin that day.

Now we just had to work the problem of Russian participation so they didn't get their own sector. The Serbs had to withdraw completely, and we had to deploy the NATO force and fulfill our obligations to demilitarize the KLA.

Over the next few days, we made progress in each area. Despite the President's conversation with Yeltsin, the Russians continued to try to fly in reinforcements, this time by landing them in Bosnia, but were blocked diplomatically and procedurally. Mike Jackson and our team worked out limits on the Russian control of the airport in Pristina, while we continued to use diplomatic means to block the entry of additional Russian forces. Secretary Cohen and Secretary Albright traveled to Helsinki, Finland, to meet with their Russian counterparts, and, in what were perhaps Cohen's finest hours as Secretary of Defense, he and the Secretary of State held the NATO line to prevent the Russians' receiving their own sector. Not until the agreement was fully completed in Helsinki did the first Russian reinforcements arrive. We had talked them down from their original figure of 10,000 to about 3,600. Some people were surprised at how good the Russian troops and equipment looked, but I wasn't. I had always respected them.

The Serbs conducted a withdrawal under pressure from the KLA, who continued to snipe and harass them as they pulled back. General Ojdanic phoned me often, urging NATO to fill in behind his units, provide security, and take care of the Serbs remaining behind. We continued to receive reports that some of the "stay behinds" were military and police and that the Serbs had hidden arsenals, too. But, almost on schedule, a little more than eleven days after they began, the Serbs' military, police, and paramilitary were gone. There were mines left behind, a few decoys, and a few destroyed armored vehicles.

As KFOR and the news media entered in force, they were amazed at the relatively little damage done by the bombing. Whole sections of towns and cities had been razed, but by the Serbs rather than by the Allied aircraft. NATO forces, as they came in, began to work immediately assisting with humanitarian relief and working through presence, patrols, and person-to-person dialogue to dampen the explosive rage of the Kosovar Albanians. It took more than two months before the force was at full strength, but we had succeeded in establishing control and reducing the levels of violence.

The Albanian refugees poured back. Their return was unstoppable, at least by the United Nations, which had hoped for a more orderly and measured return. This was reported to be the largest spontaneous return of refugees in Europe since World War II.

We had our cease-fire. NATO was there, and in charge, supporting the United Nations. This was success.

SIXTEEN

THE GOOD FIGHT

ALONG WITH THE SWELL of refugees returning to Kosovo during late June and early July came an increasing number of what we called "distinguished visitors." One of the first was Secretary of Defense William Cohen, who met with some of our troops and with Albanians in the American sector. He also visited with our airmen at Aviano, Italy. It was a warm summer day in Kosovo, and thousands of Albanians were on the streets of Urosevac, eager to show their gratitude to the Americans. I was impressed by the deep emotion of the Albanian crowds. In his speeches to the troops and to the airmen, Cohen was generous in his praise for our command. I appreciated the kind personal letter he sent to me, too.

President Clinton arrived in Macedonia on June 22 to visit our troops, though he didn't at that time go into Kosovo. It was a pleasure to see him and his family, and he seemed to take a real satisfaction from what had been achieved. Sandy Berger and Jim Steinberg were ebullient. It was done. NATO had succeeded. They felt sure that Milosevic would be gone, perhaps soon.

After the visit in Macedonia, I flew back to Germany with the presidential party on the C-17 cargo plane that was temporarily serving as

Air Force One. People were moving around the airplane, conducting business, and chatting. In the midst of several conversations, a very high member of the President's party sat down beside me and asked, speaking personally, if I was getting along all right with Secretary Cohen.

I mumbled that things seemed to have worked out OK, and put the comment aside. Of course, there had been a succession of frictions with Secretary Cohen, and with Hugh Shelton, too. But in war, when major issues are at stake, frictions and frustrations are bound to occur. I believed that with the end of the war, and after Cohen's recent visit, those frictions would subside.

On June 24, Javier Solana and I went together to Pristina. Contrary to some of the early Serb propaganda, the capital of Kosovo had been little impacted by the air campaign—just a few precision strikes against Serb police and military facilities. There was joy in the streets that day, as Solana and our party were mobbed by enthusiastic supporters. Until that time, I had not allowed myself to feel the impact of what NATO had accomplished. But now, it was undeniable. Operation Allied Force was a victory for these Albanians who had been harassed, attacked, and eventually evicted by the hundreds of thousands from their homes and from their country. It was more than just a victory for NATO. It was a personal victory for all of us who worked to bring attention to Milosevic's plans in Kosovo, and fought to halt and eventually to reverse the ethnic cleansing.

Milosevic hadn't gone all out in the conflict with NATO; his most basic objective was to preserve his own power and authority. Apparently, he never valued Serbia's control of Kosovo above his own survival, despite boasting to Klaus Naumann and me that "Kosovo is more important than my head." When it became clear that Serb actions couldn't destabilize neighboring countries or split the Alliance, he shifted his tactics. When it became clear that continued resistance in Kosovo threatened his survival, he gave in to NATO's demands.

As I reflected on why Milosevic surrendered, I came to see a combination of factors at work: the impact of the air campaign, which, though measured, was steadily expanding and which Serbia was incapable of resisting; the threat of a ground invasion, which the Serbs could see building rapidly around Yugoslavia, with the strength of Task Force Hawk and the forces coming into KFOR. A ground attack would have destroyed large portions of the Yugoslav military and police, weakening the final bastions of Milosevic's power, and made his efforts to disguise defeat impossible. For Milosevic, a final factor must have been the lack of any significant outside assistance, as Serbia was surrounded by increasingly hostile neighbors and received no material support from Russia.

The Russians, of course, did their best to claim credit for Milosevic's change of heart. But the settlement was in their interest, too, for they needed a more constructive relationship with the West. They had been unable to help Serbia resist, and the prospect of seeing NATO forces destroy the Serb army and smash its way into Yugoslavia would have been an even deeper blow to Russian geostrategic interests and wounded pride than the agreement they helped encourage.

Of course, even after accepting NATO's five conditions in his meeting with Ahtisaari and Chernomyrdin, Milosevic and his government continued efforts to create a more favorable implementation of the agreement. Had we stopped the bombing on June 3, as many wished, the Serbs might have succeeded in vitiating the essence of NATO's conditions, achieving (with possible Russian collusion) a de facto partition of Kosovo.

With the fighting over, there was important work to be done on the ground in Kosovo. Troops were continuing to arrive for KFOR, though we didn't anticipate being up to full strength until autumn. The situation on the ground was progressing well, with KFOR moving steadily to assert control over the troubled areas and reduce the levels of violence. However, the situation in Montenegro was troublesome and portended some violence. There remained the likelihood that Milosevic had left behind in Kosovo some of his police units in civilian clothes with communications and weapons hidden, ready to foment trouble on a moment's notice. The Kosovo Liberation Army had moved into the vacuum the local institutions and police left when the Serbs departed, and KFOR was trying to prevent the KLA from seizing political legitimacy without adhering to its promise to demilitarize itself.

At the end of the campaign, the Serb forces were organized enough to move out in relatively good order. We observed their departure from the air in about the numbers we had expected. When they occupied their assembly areas and the bomb-blasted facilities outside Kosovo, we also noticed a number of missing systems from their artillery, tank, and infantry units. Over the course of a few months, these units were refilled. Perhaps this equipment was destroyed or damaged and later replaced, or perhaps it was just removed for periodic preventive maintenance activities.

When the press reported that the Serbs were pulling out a lot of equipment in good condition, there arose an immediate controversy about how much of the Serb force we had actually destroyed in Kosovo. That wasn't surprising. Our strikes against Serb ground forces drove most of the men and equipment into hiding, many in Albanian villages and facilities. General Ojdanic and his commander in Kosovo, General Pavkovic, were adding to the controversy about how much Serb materiel we had destroyed, especially after they were promoted and decorated by Milosevic following their withdrawal.

I ordered a complete survey to account for each hit that NATO had claimed. We knew, for example, that we had struck a number of decoy systems. Teams were to examine every location where we had claimed a hit. If no sign of a hit was there, then I asked for an explanation of what had led us to claim that we had hit something. I knew we hadn't been fabricating figures, but I also knew that we would never be totally satisfied with the answers we got. That was why I had opposed "battle-damage bean-counting" throughout the campaign.

In late July I met with my commanders in the American chain of command in London. It was a routine we tried to manage every four to six weeks—have a social event with the wives in the evening, followed by a half day's discussions of the key issues. And London, the location of the U.S. Navy's headquarters in Europe, was a favorite meeting place. At this time we were unwinding emotionally from the intensity of the battle, putting the war and its lessons in context and trying to anticipate future challenges from Milosevic and others in the region. But we especially enjoyed the social event the evening before, as we went to the musical *Buddy*, the Buddy Holly story, one of London's longest running plays.

Holly was one of the heroes of our generation, one of the first real rock and roll artists. This was a genuine person, a man who had made a tremendous impact on our music, and who lived a beautiful life before a tragic and untimely death. He also recalled for us the innocence of the late 1950s. The lyrics we all knew so well came back, and as I left the next day for a long-deferred visit to Lithuania, the rhythm and words of the last song kept echoing in my mind: "Rave on! It's a crazy feeling ... Rave on! You've got me reeling ... Rave on! It's a crazy feeling."

I thought about my team in the meeting, and about how far we had come in the past year. There had been no new problems with the Pentagon since the end of the negotiations; in fact, tension with Washington was largely gone. Operation Allied Force was over, and we had won. It was a "crazy feeling."

That night, as we were dining with Lithuanian President Valdas Adamkus, a soldier from my communications team came to the table and interrupted the conversation. "Sir, General Shelton is on the phone and says he needs to speak to you on an urgent matter."

I had forgotten. Shelton's aide had called earlier in the afternoon and said that his boss wanted to talk to me at 10:00 P.M. I had intended to call after the dinner was over. It was now 10:10 P.M.

"Excuse me, Mr. President, I'll have to take this call," I said, as I got up and walked outside to look for the secure communications setup.

We had only the cell phone with us. I took it from my communications sergeant, "Yes, sir," I said to Shelton, "sorry not to be with you on time. I had heard you needed me at 10:00 P.M., but we weren't finished here. And I don't have the 'secure' with me."

Shelton said it was all right, no secure phone was needed. He wanted to inform me that Secretary Cohen had made the decision that I would come out of my command in April 2000.

I stood there, stunned. Was I being relieved of duty? And why now? SACEURs were expected to serve at least three full years. They are usually asked to extend for a fourth. But now, having just completed my second year at NATO, I was being told that my term would end in nine months.

The timing of the phone call was a surprise as well. I had just been in the States for a conference with the other regional commanders in chief and had spent a full day with Hugh Shelton. He had said nothing.

Back in the autumn of 1998, at a dinner in Rome, Secretary Cohen had told me that I would have two more years in the position. The evening had been a rare respite from the frictions with the Pentagon, as Cohen's wife, Janet, exclaimed to her husband, "Bill—with a Jewish father, Wes has the same background as you!" The sparkle of the evening was like a small nugget that my wife, Gert, and I could look back on with warmth, as we discussed whether we should ask for an extension to a fourth year. But we weren't quite able to resolve our own mixed feelings. I was engrossed in the work in Europe, but by July 2000 we would have been abroad for four years, and we were thinking about going home.

Yet somewhere in the back of my mind I had been half expecting something. I had pushed very hard to make the strategy work in the Balkans. Almost from the start there had been frictions, and, after Shalikashvili's retirement in September 1997, it had been a cool relationship with the Secretary and his team. The warning signs continued during Operation Allied Force as well.

I asked Shelton why Secretary Cohen had made this decision, and why now. To depart early, after public speculation during the war about my difficult relations with the Pentagon, would look bad for everyone. Were they just clumsy? Or was this the result of the buildup of bad feelings? Were they trying to get back at me? I was at a loss to understand.

Shelton explained that Joe Ralston, the Vice Chairman, was the only possible replacement for me as SACEUR, that his four years as Vice Chairman were to end in February, and so, by law, he would need to be in a new position within sixty days or he would be forced to revert temporarily to two-star rank. Therefore, I would have to come out early. Anyway, he went on, I had served longer than the average SACEUR.

It didn't wash. I was sure that legal arrangements could have been made to enable me to complete three full years. And I knew that the excuses about the average SACEUR tenure weren't factual. So, was this just a way of easing me out early, without admitting it?

Still, I hoped that there might yet be a graceful way out for everyone, if I could just explore it a minute with Shelton, but he needed to get off the phone. "Look, Wes," he said, "I have to tell the Secretary that I've notified you. He's in Japan and he told me that I had to have notified you before 4:30 Washington time, so I have to break this off and call him."

Shelton and I agreed to continue the conversation later. I returned to the restaurant for dessert with President Adamkus. I had my game face on, but it was a dark moment.

About forty-five minutes later, as soon as I returned to the privacy of my hotel room, I picked up the secure phone to my communications team and asked them to reconnect me with Shelton. There were always frictions in operations, I thought. I remembered the stories from the Gulf War, about senior officers shouting and screaming at each other. But the leadership kept it tucked away. Pulling me out early was going to confirm and publicly surface the tensions with the Pentagon, detracting from what had been a superb team effort.

But before I could reach Shelton, another call came in. "Sir, there's a, er, I think, Bill Graham, holding on the line for you. Would you like to talk to him first?" The communications officer sounded uncertain about the first name.

Graham? Senator Bob Graham? Don Graham, the publisher of *The Washington Post*? "OK," I said, "put him through."

"Hello, General. This is Bradley Graham of *The Washington Post*. I just heard that you were to be replaced next year by General Joe Ralston, and wondered if you could confirm it."

I knew Bradley Graham (no relation to his ultimate boss, Don Graham) from occasional contacts at congressional hearings and around Washington. His call put me on the spot, because Shelton and I had not finished our conversation, and obviously we needed to coordinate. And I still hoped to ride out the lack of support from the Pentagon. I knew that if this story hit the papers, it would be locked in concrete, regardless of whether Shelton would reconsider after another discussion. I tried to hold Graham off.

"Well, Bradley, I have heard something like this, but maybe this is just a rumor," I said.

"Hey, General, we've known each other a long time. Now, tell me straight, OK? I've got an official leak that says you are to be replaced by Joe Ralston. Now what I want to know is, when were you consulted and what do you think about it?"

I was trapped. Someone had tipped off Graham, and he was going to run with the story, with or without a quote from me. I asked how long I had to answer. He told me his deadline was in three hours.

I tried Shelton; not available, in a meeting. Secretary Cohen?

Preparing for morning meetings in Japan and not willing to accept my call. I called my staff at SHAPE, the Secretary's public affairs officer, Ken Bacon, and anyone else I could think of who could help me at this moment. Solana, I discovered, was in the hospital and also unavailable.

Finally I got Shelton on the phone. "You know this is going to play as a negative, Hugh?" I said.

"It is?"

"Yes, but all you have to do is correct the leak and say it's just rumor."

"OK. Let me talk to my public affairs officer. Wait—I'll get back to you." A pause. "No, it just won't work; the SecDef's office has already sent information to the Congress notifying them of the change."

Finally Secretary Cohen accepted my call in Japan. "Sir, this is going to play negative with the press," I began. "What should I say?" But as I tried to get into the tough questions, he closed me off.

"Well, the decision has been made that Joe will replace you. And you should know it's been cleared by the White House." The Secretary then broke off to go to his meetings, and his only advice to me was this: "Just say that you'll continue to do your job."

Pentagon spokesmen claimed that giving Ralston my job was the only way he could be persuaded to stay on active duty. Ralston called me the next morning to say he had nothing to do with this. Whatever the motives, it was done.

The standard NATO procedures would have called for circulating the proposal for my replacement through the Secretary of State for her concurrence and then into NATO for the other nations to concur. That had not been done, but it didn't matter. The decision had been made and punctuated by the press.

As for me, I was an American officer. I served at the pleasure of the President and the Secretary of Defense. While many were surprised that the decision was being announced so prematurely I certainly wasn't the first officer who was going to leave early, and I intended to give everything I had until the very end.

The publicity lasted for a few weeks, echoing through Europe. The White House denied responsibility, and there was reportedly a lot of internal heat about how the decision had been executed. The President was asked about my removal in a press conference in Europe and expressed complete satisfaction with my performance. "I had nothing to do with it," he told me privately. Secretary Cohen was generous in his praise of me in later European trips. The Allies and my command were enormously supportive. They recognized important work ahead.

For my part, I tried to make the most of every remaining day in command.

Over the next few months, KFOR continued its work in Kosovo amid periodic rumors and threats that the Serb military and police were preparing to force their way back. The troops did a fine job of reducing the level of violence in the province, while also succeeding in building strong teamwork with the U.N. mission there.

A number of the Serbs fled the province before KFOR arrived, and later many relocated to the relative safety of all-Serb communities. The troops worked hard to guard the remaining Serbs, even as they prepared to protect Kosovo from a Serb military encroachment. The KLA was formally disbanded, but the hard feelings from the war lingered on. Some of the Albanians retained their weapons and a thirst for revenge. KFOR was challenged to constrain the efforts of a few extremists to reignite war across the border in southern Serbia.

We also avoided confrontation with the Russians. They moved into most of the areas to which they were assigned, where they operated within the NATO sectors headed by the French, the Germans and the Americans. They turned over responsibilities for air traffic control and logistics at Pristina airfield to the British but retained a key role controlling access and security there. They denied NATO access to the former Serb command facilities at the airfield, even when entry was requested by the highest authorities.

Everyone was pleased that we had avoided a confrontation and hoped to strengthen relations with Russia by constructive work together on the ground. The British, who had objected to blocking the runways, and many others, believed this success proved their case that any risks at the airfield had been unnecessary. Some, however, took different interpretations. Eastern European officers who were veterans of service with the Soviet Army said, "The Russians took NATO's measure and found you wouldn't react—it was a key element in their decision to renew the war in Chechnya." Within the command we worked hard to put the memory of those days behind us.

There were continuing rumors about special arrangements between the Serbs and the Russians. In one area, around Orahovac, Albanian citizens simply refused to allow the Russian forces to operate, citing the participation of Russian mercenaries in the Serb ranks. At one time, the Russians threatened to pull out from the mission for political reasons, but on the ground the troops got along well. I awarded medals to several Russian soldiers who gave first aid and assistance to some injured Americans.

I made many visits to Kosovo during my remaining time in command. We always flew into the airport at Skopje, Macedonia, and took a helicopter north, over the mountains and up the Kacanik defile to Pristina.

The autumn of 1999 was warm, and the snows were late in arriving. So I had many flights on which to study the rugged terrain that our ground operation would have fought through. I looked at the trail network and estimated the steepness of the slopes. I could see in my mind's eye how our soldiers would have worked their way behind the Serb positions, striking them from above and the rear, penetrating at night using advanced optics.

On this particular route, it would have been a British division making the attack. Rupert Smith and I had spent many hours discussing how it would be done. He was confident it would have succeeded, and so was I.

I also thought a lot about Task Force Hawk, and the plans to bring the American force through Albania. We would never prove who was right in combat, but we had, at least in the case of the U.S. Army, exposed some issues that would need serious consideration in the years to come. I loved my Army service, especially the men and women I served with and their families. My family and I had given more than thirty years to this institution, and to our country. It meant many moves and a lot of hardship for us, but I believed, and they supported me. I regretted that I wouldn't be around, in uniform, to continue the work.

But each time I flew, I thought about the attacks we would have launched, and the toll they would have taken on our militaries and on the civilians. I was happy that they had never come to pass. There were no NATO soldiers' graves on those rugged mountains, no villages destroyed by NATO forces, and no wasted countryside.

We had succeeded not with main battle but with coercive diplomacy. It was a modern war. But because they wouldn't call it a war, we couldn't call it a victory.

But our Allies knew. And so did our adversaries.

On May 3, 2000, I changed command at SHAPE with Joe Ralston. It was a dark, chilly day. The new NATO Secretary General, George Robertson, the former British Minister of Defense, passed the flag between us. During the outdoor ceremony there was light blowing sleet, but I was buoyed by the warmth of so many friends and colleagues who stayed behind in the cold to say farewell in the Army custom. Spontaneously, most of my personal staff drove to the airfield at Chievres for a private farewell as we boarded the jet for the flight home.

A few weeks later I stood on the sunny parade field at Fort Myer for my retirement parade. General Ric Shinseki, now the Army Chief, stood beside me as my host. Secretary and Mrs. Cohen sat in the stands. The Canadian Chief of Defense, General Maurice Baril, had flown in that morning and presented me with Canada's Military Service Cross. It was the last in a series of very high decorations I had received from our Allies. Shinseki presented me with the Army Distinguished Service Medal and the first U.S. Kosovo campaign medal, which all the U.S. personnel who participated in the campaign were supposed to receive. Steve Abbott and Pete Chiarelli had worked miracles to win service approval of the campaign medal, and I was pleased to see it before I retired.

But my thoughts were on my family and especially on my West Point classmates, many of whom were there among the large crowd in the reviewing stand. I was one of the last members of our class left on active duty. Thirty-one had died in Vietnam. I thought about our years at West Point, about Duty, Honor and Country, about the discipline, and the close friendships, and the folk music we listened to—Peter, Paul, and Mary, Trini Lopez, Bob Dylan. Especially about Dylan. Maybe he put it the best, when he sang:

> *How many roads must a man walk down*
> *Before you call him a man? ...*
> *How many years can some people exist,*
> *Before they're allowed to be free?*
> *How many times can a man turn his head*
> *Pretending he just doesn't see? ...*
> *How many deaths will it take till he knows*
> *That too many people have died?*

Dylan said the answer was "blowin' in the wind."

I think many of us felt that wind. I know I did. I had been the J-5, responsible for advising General Shalikashvili on our U.N. policies in 1994, when we stood by as nearly a million Africans were hacked to death with machetes in Rwanda. I had seen the aftermath of the vicious ethnic cleansing in Bosnia, before the U.S. pledge of ground forces helped to end the fighting.

In the post–Cold War world, it had taken too long, and too many people had already died. But I was proud that our country and our Alliance had learned, that we didn't "turn our heads," and that we hadn't stood aside to permit another tragedy in 1999 in Kosovo. And I was proud to have been part of that effort, even if it brought the end of my military service.

It made me recall one of my friends from Oxford, U.S. Army Captain Alex Hottell, a West Pointer from the Class of 1964. After we stayed up late one night discussing life and death and Vietnam, we finally came back to the adage, "If there's nothing worth fighting and dying for, then there's nothing worth living for."

Alex was killed in Vietnam in 1970. But he believed in serving his country. He stood for something.

As of this writing, Slobodan Milosevic is in jail in Yugoslavia. There is real hope for democratic transformation and peace. His Army commander, General Dragojub Ojdanic, was dismissed from his post as minister of defense. I hope they will soon be in The Hague, along with the others, standing trial for their crimes. Unfortunately, there is low-level fighting in southern Serbia and in northern Macedonia, as old grievances are being addressed by force, despite NATO's presence nearby.

As for me, the adage that Alex and I spoke of that night at Oxford rings truer than ever. One of life's greatest gifts, I've found, is the opportunity to fight for what's right. There is so much more to be done.

CONCLUSION

A T THE NATO defense ministers' meeting in Toronto, Canada, a
few months after the war, a special discussion was held on lessons learned during Operation Allied Force. One defense minister began his remarks by suggesting that perhaps the most
fundamental lesson was that "we never want to do this again." If the
remark was meant to be humorous, no one laughed. It had been a difficult and painful experience, and perhaps many in the audience sympa-
thized with the sentiment expressed.

The conflict was complex, controversial, and, to the public, often
confusing. Some people said it should never have been fought. Others
said it could never be won. Even in the end, many were questioning
what had been accomplished.

Though NATO had succeeded in its first armed conflict, it didn't
feel like a victory. There were no parades except by the joyful Albanians
returning to Kosovo. The military and the diplomats within NATO
were simply relieved that the operation was concluded, and they were
absorbed in the next mission, working on the ground inside Kosovo.

Yet coercive diplomacy had worked. NATO's five conditions were
met: a cease-fire, Serb military and police out, international security

presence in, refugees returned, an opportunity for a political settlement. Moreover, a ground invasion was avoided, no airmen died, the precious Danube bridges in Belgrade were not struck, the war did not spread into the surrounding states, and the financial costs were surprisingly little.

Any endeavor that is both successful and painful is all too apt to be forgotten, and its lessons are likely to be painful, too. Searching for lessons reminds us of poor judgments, lost opportunities, overstressed emotions, quarrels, and tribulations. Also, deeper issues will inevitably be exposed, issues that will require rethinking cherished programs and popular agendas. But none of this should mean that lessons shouldn't be sought. We have to understand both how and why we won and how we can do better in the next modern war.

Every war is unique. Just as in chess, where games begin similarly only to diverge in unpredictable ways, no particular military engagement is likely to be repeated exactly. Nevertheless, lessons must be drawn from past experiences. While no error in military history is more chronicled than armies preparing to refight the last war, only to discover they had failed to prepare for the next, the art is to identify the significant features and then to discover their causes. With this information, it may be possible to forecast how patterns may evolve over time and what must be done to deter, prevent, or if necessary, win the next war.

What we fought in the Kosovo campaign was a limited war: limited means–limited objectives. It was coercive diplomacy, the use of armed forces to impose the political will of the NATO nations on the Federal Republic of Yugoslavia, or more specifically, on Serbia. The NATO nations voluntarily undertook this war. It was not forced on them, nor was it strictly defensive, in the ordinary sense. In that regard, the strategic and political context was wholly unlike those of conventional conflicts like World War II. Instead it was much more like the interventions of an earlier era, but this time for the far different reasons of regional stability and humanitarian assistance.

In such actions the "big battle" philosophy that dominated much of Western military thought during the twentieth century must be modified. While nations have always aimed in war to gain their objectives with the least cost, in modern war, achieving decisive political aims may not require achieving decisive military results. Wars can be won through battles never fought, as much as through the "battles of annihilation" taught in the military textbooks. Operation Allied Force showed us how this can be done, under the right conditions.

Modern war can be expected when adversaries are not major and the issues at stake do not threaten the immediate survival of the great powers. This is a circumstance that is likely to be repeated.

However, the features of Allied Force may compromise a broader pattern, since they reflect both modern military technology and current political forces and relationships. NATO actions in the campaign, and the operations in Bosnia that preceded it, offer a powerful glimpse of the modern way of war, well beyond the limits of coercive diplomacy.

The features of this war that captured so much public commentary—the surprise and lack of preparedness at the outset, the planning and adaptation of the operation during the conflict, the dependence on Allies, the exclusive reliance on airpower, the reluctance to accept friendly casualties, the horror of civilian casualties on any side, the struggle to move to a ground campaign, and the impact of the media—are each driven by deeper factors. Some of these factors are fundamentally fixed; others may evolve over time. Some factors are practically beyond our control; others may be transformed by our own efforts.

Fully understanding what happened there will take years. But I believe there is an urgency to drawing the early lessons that can't await the full historical record. We succeeded in this operation, but we have to understand precisely why and how, if we are to adapt successfully to face the challenges ahead.

One of the most obvious features of the conflict was the West's lack of preparedness when conflict actually began. This is likely to be a pattern which we will see again, despite all efforts.

In the Kosovo campaign we witnessed all the historic reluctance of democratic nations and their political leaders to resort to the use of force, or the threat of its use, and to put lives at risk. As NATO tried to muster leverage against Milosevic in the months before the ethnic cleansing reached a point that conflict became inevitable, our own deep-seated ambivalence vitiated our policies. Throughout the summer of 1998, when the conflict was preventable, some questioned the facts on the ground, or the Serbs' intent: "How many villages have really been destroyed? Perhaps they are only directing their efforts against the terrorists." Others distributed blame: "The Serbs are just responding to the attacks from the KLA." Some nations insisted on prior authorization from the United Nations. The result was that we could not present an unambiguous and clear warning to Milosevic that he had to halt his actions.

When the extent of the humanitarian crisis forced NATO nations to agree in the fall of 1998 to a clear threat against Milosevic, he did in fact call off his campaign temporarily. But when the Serbs began to break their promises to NATO—sometimes in response to the KLA— by deploying new forces against the KLA in late December, and even after the massacre of Kosovar civilians at Racak in mid January 1999, NATO nations were again reluctant to act militarily, even to prepare fully for what was becoming inevitable. To be clear, Racak did mobilize popular opinion, but instead of taking the military steps that had been prepared, nations tried again to negotiate a solution. All along, Western nations had been dealing with the emerging problem of Kosovo on the basis of a political dynamic, following the traditional pattern of diplomacy, identifying through discussion and dialogue the compatible interests between the parties to the dispute. And then, having identified these interests, Western diplomats sought negotiated agreements through compromises. They attempted to create good will and understanding through open, transparent discussion, and to use artful language and ambiguities to bridge the remaining issues. This is essentially a process of bargaining, a pattern seen again and again in the western world, whether in back-room political maneuvering, labor disputes, or trade negotiations.

But to create an opening for dialogue, negotiation, compromise, and consensus, the West had to rely on the threat of force from NATO to convince Milosevic that continued repression in Kosovo would lead to unacceptable damage to other interests. Milosevic would not willingly compromise his definition of sovereignty to permit Western diplomatic intervention. It was a little like breaking up a fight between two quarreling schoolboys, one of whom was an overpowering bully, by threatening to take him to the school principal for punishment. A lot depends on how the bully views the threat posed by the principal.

This threat, in turn, raised troubling political, legal, and even military issues for NATO. What made this situation worth considering the use of military force? What would be the reaction of other powers, especially Russia? How much would it cost? These political questions led to legal issues. Would the U.N. Security Council authorize such actions, as it had done in the case of Bosnia? If not, what would be the legal authority for such threats?

The political and legal issues resulted in obstacles to properly planning and preparing military forces and, coming full circle, reduced the credibility of the threat. In the United States, the Roberts Amendment, enacted to inhibit U.S. military activities in the Balkans, prevented timely reconnaissance, participation, and deployment of the U.S. forces. In Europe and the United States, repeated political concerns inhibited the kind of detailed NATO planning in the summer and fall of 1998 that might have promoted a more credible and more effective threat. At the defense ministers' meeting in Villa Mora in September 1998, the lack of legal authority caused almost every NATO government initially to reject Secretary Cohen's appeal to authorize a NATO threat. The refusal of the Pentagon to countenance U.S. ground forces in Kosovo in October 1998 reflected a reluctance in Washington to undertake another mission in the Balkans and a National Military Strategy obsessively oriented on fighting hypothetical conflicts in two other theaters. Even in March 1999, with the prospective failure of the Rambouillet talks, the Pentagon sent the aircraft carrier USS *Theodore Roosevelt* away from the Adriatic and into the Persian Gulf, despite impending conflict in Europe. Milosevic could hardly have missed this signal of ambivalence.

The United States has also suffered from an almost decade-long partisan debate about its role in the post–Cold War world. Much of this debate actually centered on the Balkans, which the Democratic Party introduced as an issue in the 1992 presidential campaign. The result was a partisan divide that did much to complicate the Clinton Administration's ability to make and sustain commitments in Bosnia and to prevent the slide into war in Kosovo. Similar partisan bickering could well arise to bedevil U.S. actions elsewhere in the world where there is a similar lack of strategic clarity.

Military thinkers like to plan for perfect operations, in which there are clear objectives, unambiguous political guidance, "mission-type" orders, a defined exit strategy, and popular consensus at home. And while U.S. military planning is well advanced for operations in Korea and the Persian Gulf, this is not so much the case for potential conflicts elsewhere in the world. Strategic planning takes months to complete and requires detailed information from hundreds of units and organizations. It will not be possible to foresee and plan for every contingency, despite the military's best efforts. Military leaders traditionally find it difficult to act in such circumstances.

As for NATO, political approval from each member nation has been necessary before any military plans can be developed, and the general political reluctance in the West to signal readiness to use force means that the Alliance's military planning will almost inevitably be too slow. When called to act, the plans are unlikely to go far enough to deal with the range of contingencies that might arise.

The Serbs, meanwhile were taking measures to absorb the NATO air strikes, if necessary, and even to block a ground intervention from Macedonia. Forces in Kosovo were reinforced, air defenses were readied, key assets were dispersed and hidden. Meanwhile, the campaign of ethnic cleansing was quietly begun by striking key persons such as doctors among the Kosovar Albanian population.

Ultimately, NATO succeeded in Kosovo in part because many of the member governments could not afford to fail. These governments had limited the objectives and methods of warfare, but they had not limited their own commitment, and so their own political survival was at stake. Ironically the very controversy that the operation aroused helped to propel it to success.

Another factor was at work, too. This conflict about Kosovo became a test of NATO's role in post-Cold War Europe. NATO itself was at risk of irrelevance or simply falling apart following a defeat. Even those governments that could have survived operational failure could not afford to lose NATO.

Political leaders will always be circumspect in risking their governments and NATO on a military operation. But in other ways, the success of Operation Allied Force does open the door for its repetition elsewhere. In the first instance, there is now historical precedent for the use of force to intervene for purposes of humanitarian relief.

Further, Western publics have seen that such operations can succeed if properly executed.

Surely, the key lesson must be that nations and alliances should move early to deal with crises while they are still ambiguous and can be dealt with more easily, for delay raises both the costs and the risks. Early action is the objective to which statesmen and military leaders should aspire.

However, democratic societies don't easily resort to the use of force, or the threat of its use. The political and legal problems that undercut military preparation for Kosovo constitute a fundamental pattern that will likely reappear in future crises. And this means that military forces are likely once more to have to adapt and modify plans while pressing the fight forward.

What, then, caused the severe internal struggle about the strategy to be followed during the war? Here is a second element that is a likely pattern in modern war, however unpleasant.

Using military force effectively requires departing from the political dynamic and following the so-called "Principles of War" identified by post-Napoleonic military writers a century and a half ago. Every military officer learns them in early training. Most of us spend a lifetime understanding how to apply them.

As formulated in modern American studies, the Principles of War are defined to include having a clear *objective* and relying on *unity of command* to focus all efforts toward this aim. Plans and operations should be *simple* in conception, *mass*ing forces at the most critical points, relying on *economy of force* in the peripheral areas, and achieving *surprise* over the enemy. Forces must attend to their *security*. Decisive results are obtained from *offensive* action and *maneuver*.

The operation in Kosovo violated almost every one of these principles as it began. Any first-year military student could point to the more obvious inconsistencies between our efforts and the requirements posed by the Principles of War. The air campaign began with one objective—drive the Serbs back to the negotiations at Rambouillet—and quickly moved toward other aims, such as halting the ethnic cleansing, and then, after the NATO summit, the five conditions endorsed by the G-8 foreign ministers—a cease-fire, the withdrawal of all Serb forces, the return of all refugees and displaced persons, the presence of a NATO-led international force, and subsequent participation in a political settlement.

Unity of command was nominally through my headquarters, but in practice national command chains continued to shape and drive the campaign through connections directly to NATO-assigned forces and sometimes bypassing NATO, including in the negotiations to end the fighting. Even within my U.S. chain of command, my subordinate component commanders were reporting to, and no doubt influenced by, members of a committee in Washington composed of the four Service Chiefs, the Chairman and the Vice Chairman of the Joint Chiefs of Staff. And because there was no pre-agreed strategy, unity of effort suffered.

While the air campaign was simple enough in concept, its execution was repeatedly constrained and distorted by political forces such as hope that just a few strikes would compel Milosevic's surrender, thirst for a bombing pause, fear of civilian casualties, exaggerated fear of the Serbs' military capabilities, and the American military's reluctance to risk the Apache helicopters. The air campaign began with enough forces to punish the Serbs, but it lacked the mass and capabilities needed to halt the ethnic cleansing. Even when more aircraft arrived, differing concepts of strategic airpower constrained the application of the airpower against the most sensitive targets. Throughout the campaign, and especially as it contemplated ground intervention, the Pentagon was distracted by its preference for focusing on Northeast Asia and the Persian Gulf, despite the fact that the only real conflict was in Europe. Other nations, such as France, also kept a wary eye on balancing their operations in various areas.

Surprise was compromised early and often, from the delivery to the Serbs of portions of the campaign plan in October 1998 through the warnings of imminent attack in the final hours after the withdrawal of the OSCE "unarmed verifiers." Possible strikes against many sensitive targets were disclosed by repeated public discussion during their approval, particularly the strikes against targets in Belgrade.

Security was also at risk early in the effort, when nations were unable to achieve unity of command of their forces in Macedonia under Lieutenant General Mike Jackson and the ACE Rapid Reaction Corps. And we continued to worry about the safety of our aircrews as some of their targets seemed to be anticipated by the Serbs, or perhaps compromised inadvertently or by espionage.

Publicly ruling out a ground effort at the outset took away the threat of decisive maneuver and offensive action, however wise or necessary such statements may have been for political reasons. It must be said that the Serb military had already made defensive preparations to counter a threat, and whether Milosevic would have been compelled by more rhetoric is unclear. Nevertheless, the statement compounded the Alliance's difficulties in transitioning to war.

In order to succeed, we were in a process of continuous adaptation, moving from an initial military effort driven by political dynamics toward a more effective military campaign oriented on the Principles of War. We expanded the air campaign from the initial strikes directed at 51 targets, executed by a force of 366 aircraft, to a target base of almost 1,000 targets and a force of about 900 aircraft, with more en route. We resisted efforts to pause the bombing. Despite U.S. military resistance, the Apache attack helicopters were deployed to Albania, backed by a corps-level headquarters and a full Army brigade of ground combat power. Though the Army and the Joint Chiefs succeeded in blocking their use in battle, the force conveyed a powerful image of a ground threat, and would have been its lead component. Planning and preparations for ground intervention were well under way by the end of the campaign, and I am convinced that this, in particular, pushed Milosevic to concede.

This transition from the political dynamic to a military dynamic was a continuing struggle on many fronts. We worked with and worked through the sensitivities of some Allies, the concerns and instincts of diplomats, the self-interests of nations in the region, and the egos, judgments, and experience of some colleagues in uniform, especially in Washington. I had to take positions, privately and publicly, that pushed the Alliance into adaptation. Driving this transition during war may have been the principal contribution of the strategic headquarters.

Surely, a key lesson—and an old one, that we tried many times to impress during the emergence of the crisis—is that once the threshold to use force is crossed, nations cannot easily escape from the need to succeed. It is always preferable, though not always possible, to have agreed on the strategy for full success before the first aircraft is moved or the first shot fired. The corollary, however, is that even in the absence of an agreed strategy, it is sometimes possible to succeed through adapting during war.

This was not the first time that a military campaign departed from its original ways and means, but it may have been the most far-reaching adaption in decades. Certainly recent operations, in Grenada, the Falklands, Panama, and the Persian Gulf, never attempted such a metamorphosis, because none of them occurred in such a complex political and legal landscape, with so many constraints at the outset. They were more conventional in purpose, and more military in design. They achieved their objectives directly through the application of military force—driving out opposing leaders or regaining territories. They took place not in Europe, with all the historic and legal sensitivities imposed by the aftermath of a disastrous century of war, but on simpler battlefields. And they lacked the intricate political machinery of NATO, a mature Alliance of nineteen sovereign nations.

But in the end, the strategic adaptation was all the more powerful because it represented a unified Alliance, not a single nation. In that sense, the political power of NATO's member nations enabled us to reinforce the military actions and achieve a military success at remarkably little cost in Allied lives and resources. We paid a price in operational effectiveness by having to constrain the nature of the operation to fit within the political and legal concerns of NATO member nations, but the price brought significant strategic benefits that future political and military leaders must recognize.

A third feature of the operation, and one that will be sought again, is the integrated, allied nature of the campaign. Despite the appearance of American domination of the command chain, this was very much a NATO operation. European allies vigorously participated in targeting and strategy and, near the end, made key decisions regarding Pristina airfield. The United States could not have operated unilaterally in the area. Allied contributions during the campaign were substantial. France provided almost one hundred aircraft, the second largest number behind the United States. Air bases were provided by Germany, France, Greece, the United Kingdom, Italy, Belgium, the Netherlands, and later Hungary, the Czech Republic, and Turkey, and every nation's bases played some role. While the United States provided all of the stealth aircraft and most of the refueling and electronic warfare assets, the Allies flew some 40 percent of the strikes.

On the ground, America's European Allies bore a disproportionate share early in the campaign. At the start of Operation Allied Force, there were more than 2,000 NATO soldiers in Macedonia, waiting to be assigned as part of KFOR, none of whom were Americans. In addition, the NATO force was made responsible for coordinating the force protection for the 350 Americans, formerly serving under U.N. operational control, who remained in Macedonia. When American ground troops entered the theater in strength as Task Force Hawk, they received support from both the Albanian government and the NATO force deployed to Albania to assist with refugee support.

Where the American role was dominant was in planning the air operation. The reason was basic. NATO itself had no intelligence. NATO only received national intelligence and then disseminated it. It had no collection and little analytic capabilities. Nor did NATO possess the means to conduct battle damage assessments. Other NATO member countries also lacked intelligence collection and battle damage assessment capabilities. In fact, 99 percent of the target nominations came from U.S. intelligence sources. In this area, and in this area alone, due basically to lack of European capabilities, the operation assumed an excessively national character.

It was also clear that most NATO nations were prone to misunderstand the interests their Allies saw engaged. The German government, for example, had spent great sums to support Yugoslav refugees living in Germany, and it wanted no more. Italy was not just a transit point for refugees but also a substantial investor in Yugoslavia. Greece was a large investor in Serbia and also had strong religious and cultural ties. Turkey had historic and religious ties with the ethnic Muslims in Bosnia. France had historic ties with Serbia and Montenegro and, like other NATO nations, sought commercial interests there. Other Allies had more remote interests in the specifics on the ground but still very real concerns for stability in the region and an end to the conflict there. Such interests have in fact been a driving force behind the European Union's pursuit of a European Security and Defense Program.

For each nation in the Alliance, NATO's engagement in the Balkans, and especially the operation in Kosovo, was a domestic political issue. In most countries the political opposition to the government used Operation Allied Force as leverage against the government, though not always from the same angle. In the United States, for example, the Republican Party developed several mutually inconsistent critiques: first, that there should be no U.S. involvement; then, if there was, that the air campaign wouldn't work and that a ground operation would be required. Had the Administration opted for the ground campaign, then almost certainly there would have been criticism of the plan, its cost, and risks. An authorizing vote in Congress would have been demanded, a hurdle whose risks were probably not fully appreciated in Europe.

In Europe, there were other problems. In Great Britain, the Blair government was attacked during the first days of the air campaign for its ineffectiveness in stopping ethnic cleansing. There the opposition seemed to be insisting on a ground campaign, perhaps largely to embarrass the government. In France, with its strongly pro-Serb orientation, the pressure was to minimize the destruction caused by the air campaign, and especially the civilian deaths. In Germany, the Green Party, holding the foreign ministry, had always been pacifist in orientation; now it was called to defend the use of force within its own ranks. It generally resisted the idea of a ground campaign. In Italy, the new coalition that took power in October 1998 was led by a former Communist, whose party was far less persuaded of the rationale for the operation than he was himself, but for Italy, the war provided a significantly increased voice in NATO and European politics. And in Greece, the government was contending with a strong Communist Party, which objected to NATO itself and to all aspects of the war. Greece was concerned about the problem of Albanian migration, however, and this, along with the strategic importance of NATO, provided the rationale for Greek support of the operation.

North Americans sometimes failed to appreciate the immediacy of the problem for Southern Europeans, too. Italy, for example, opened new airbases during the conflict, using nearby hotels to house the Allied airmen. But because the airmen were thrifty visitors, the tourist industry along the Italian east and south coast lost money. The fishing industry, also, was impacted by the ordnance dumped in the Adriatic. In Hungary there was growing anxiety for the fate of the 370,000

Hungarians living in northern Serbia. Not only did each strike on cities like Novi Sad threaten their safety, but in retaliation the Serbs began to intensify the repression of their Hungarian minority.

Giving nations an appropriate voice in the campaign was essential to maintaining Allied unity, making the target clearance process all important. However, it was also true that the less opportunity given for discretion by the nations, the better for military effectiveness, since almost every country could question or suggest alternatives. So, we had to get the balance right between sharing information and requesting approvals. At first we were able to restrict detailed target approvals to the U.S. channel, but others then sought detailed access, and the process continued to open. There were many horses pulling the wagon of Allied cohesion on the air campaign—close, continuous communications were maintained by heads of government, foreign ministers, and defense ministers—and despite differences in national perspectives, we had enough horsepower to achieve the approvals we needed. Also, the Alliance itself acted as a kind of shock absorber, enabling ministers to express publicly their reservations about a particular target or activity, but then privately accept the Allied consensus to move ahead with the campaign. While NATO operated on a basis of consensus, in which any one dissenting nation could block an action, the NATO ambassadors themselves spoke with remarkable courage to their own ministries in generating support for the campaign. They were acutely conscious of the interests of NATO as a whole, not just their own nations. The three new members, Poland, the Czech Republic, and Hungary, must have found it especially challenging to enter NATO just as it went to war for the first time, but they did their part in supporting the Alliance.

Almost every step beyond the first strikes required from SHAPE a kind of political reconnaissance of our Allies and partners. In some cases, we would work through the U.S. ambassador in the country that would be affected. In other cases, I sent Rupert Smith to talk with the government or visited them myself. Sometimes Mike Durkee, my political adviser, would work with the ambassadors and their staffs in Brussels. And I always checked my moves with Javier Solana. In each instance it was necessary to make the military case for the requirements and then determine how the attendant political complications could be resolved.

In the American channel there were constant temptations to ignore Allied reservations and attack the targets we wanted to strike. It was always the Americans who pushed for the escalation to new, more sensitive targets (those in Belgrade, or those associated personally with Milosevic and his cronies), and always some of the Allies who expressed doubts and reservations. For a U.S. Administration anxious to finish the operation and avoid the problems of a ground intervention, these Allied reservations were, no doubt, exasperating.

But though there was discussion in U.S. channels about striking unilaterally, we never did. We always maintained that no single target or set of targets was more important than NATO cohesion. This was the most crucial decision of the campaign, and one of its most important lessons, for it preserved Allied unity and gave to each member of NATO an unavoidable responsibility for the outcome. This made it a true Allied operation—a pattern for the future.

One of the most controversial features of the campaign was the decision at the outset to rely exclusively on airpower. The allure of airpower puts a greater responsibility on the Air Force to adapt its capabilities and strategies far beyond what exists or was worked in Operation Desert Storm, the persistent reference point.

NATO's reliance on airpower reflected the needs and goals of coercive diplomacy, despite the widespread skepticism about attacking an enemy with airpower alone. "We used airpower in Afghanistan," several Russian military leaders once told me, "and it failed for us. It will fail for you, too." But reliance on the air threat was natural for NATO. First, it had worked in 1995, against the Bosnian Serbs, albeit in conjunction with a powerful Croat ground campaign. Second, it promised a low-cost, low-risk statement of political intent. And third, it left open other, more difficult, and costly options. It seemed to be the military means best suited to carry the nations' political dynamic forward.

Writing in *The Daily Telegraph* shortly after the conclusion of Operation Allied Force, the British military historian John Keegan credited air power with the victory. And it's true that air power in Operation Allied Force demonstrated great evolution from the days of the end of the early air power enthusiasts seeking an alternative to the horror of trench warfare.

The process began its development after World War I, the results were first seen in World War II, when the B-17, B-24, and B-29 aircraft conducted daylight, high-altitude precision bombing against enemy transportation and industrial facilities. These were massed raids, however, requiring fleets of aircraft to carpet bomb and swarms of fighter aircraft for protection. Moreover, they caused large numbers of civilian casualties. During the Vietnam War, the relatively inefficient air strikes of Operation Rolling Thunder were eventually upgraded using laser-guided weaponry to attain radically new levels of effectiveness. One illustration was the attack on the Thanh Hoa bridge over the Red River just outside Hanoi in 1972. The bridge had been subjected to 700 strikes during the years of the war and had never been destroyed using the old bombing techniques. And the heavy air defenses around it had shot down eight American fighter bombers. But in the first attack with the laser-guided bombs, the bridge was destroyed. It was the beginning of a new era of warfare.

Modern fighters such as the F-15 and F-16 greatly strengthened air attack operations. In the early 1980s, the Israeli Air Force used these planes to destroy the Iraqi nuclear reactor Osirak I and to launch a long-range strike at Yassir Arafat's headquarters in Tunisia, hundreds of miles away. American capabilities were also growing, as we demonstrated in the 1986 punitive strike against Libyan leader Muammar Qaddafi, which was accurate enough to hit his tent.

But public attention wasn't focused on the radical improvements in air capabilities until the next big U.S. air operation, Operation Desert Storm. Here the capability for precision strike was joined by the capability to minimize or elude detection by enemy air defense radars, the Stealth technology. With the new F-117 Stealth fighter-bomber, it was possible to attack ground targets even inside heavily defended zones. These two technologies were highlighted day after day in the forty-four-day air campaign that led the ground action in the desert. The TV scenes of the bombs striking exactly on the cross hairs of aircraft shelters and bunker ventilator shafts fired the public imagination, and within the military, the term "precision strike" became the mantra for a new way of warfare.

After Operation Desert Storm, the United States continued to expand its reliance on precision strike. In 1993, Tomahawk Land Attack Missiles were used against Iraq in a quick strike intended as punishment for an Iraqi assassination attempt against former President George Bush. In 1995, precision strike capped off the limited air strikes that helped us secure the Dayton Agreement in Bosnia. In 1998, precision strike was used against the terrorist training camps of Osama Bin Laden in Afghanistan. And all through the summer and autumn of 1998, a complex series of strikes was planned, then postponed, then replanned, and finally executed against Iraq as Operation Desert Fox.

It had taken eighty years of development, hundreds of billions of dollars, numerous wars—but we had moved decisively beyond trench warfare, it seemed. Airpower and the cruise missiles that were part of precision strike could hit targets accurately, so accurately that the results seemed guaranteed. This was real "action at a distance"; it kept the attacker far away from the effects of the weapons, and when combined with Stealth and other protective measures, dramatically limited the likelihood of friendly losses.

Precision strike had a further virtue: it was controllable. Targets could be picked with great certainty that they would be struck and little else affected. "Messages" could be sent to opposing leaders. The strikes could start small, as small as a single missile. At any time, the strikes could be called off, the force dispersed. Even the logistics were part of the attraction—fewer systems, less mess in setting up the operation or ending it.

Because precision strike was controllable and relatively small, it could be executed by professional militaries, not requiring mass mobilizations of reserves or other political disruptions. Financially, a campaign of precision strike also seemed less disruptive. Although the weapons were individually quite expensive, with some of the cruise missiles costing a $1 million or more, the overall cost for the campaign would still be much less than deploying and sustaining thousands of troops.

We should be careful, though, about extolling the air operation in Kosovo as a pattern for future success, for it also a manifestated the limits of airpower, even high technology airpower, as an independent military instrument. In this manner the air campaign provided clear warnings about the direction of some U.S. military thinking.

We have relied too much on the clear air, clean ground characteristics of our training areas in the American desert. This has given us the precision strike and high-altitude unmanned aerial vehicles, and it has given some the clever idea that it is within our grasp to know everything about any given 200 kilometers square, and that by so doing, we can dominate the outcome of a battle with minimal risk and central control, with a couple of smart people making the key calls.

Not yet.

Future battlefields are more likely to resemble Kosovo than the Iraqi desert. There will be clouds, vegetation, villages and cities, and civilians whom we don't want to harm. There will be environmental hazards like toxic chemical or nuclear storage to limit our strikes. And there will be laws, journalists, and widespread public visibility of actions.

Even with the best-intentioned efforts, "precision strike" will need augmentation by "precision acquisition and identification" of targets. We will need specific information, in real time. We will need to see underneath clouds and inside buildings. We will want to know whether the men on the tractors and inside the buses are soldiers or civilians. We will want to know whether trucks are carrying food or weapons. We will want to know who is in the underground facility, civilians or military, families or opposing leaders.

Then, we will want to take specific actions against the targets whether they are inside buildings, underground, or under camouflage nets. The actions might not be lethal force. Instead we may want to detain, restrict, or disperse.

Neither the specific information nor the range of actions can yet be done from a distance. Instead, we will need to place people on the ground to observe and listen. They may have to come close, even face-to-face, with those we oppose. No doubt they will have fabulously powerful communications and other technologies. But they will also require physical courage and a willingness to take physical risks.

Technology may enable us to reduce the size of this "forward" force, which may be supported by unmanned aerial vehicles and other means of information collection and firepower. But for every means and measure there will likely be a defensive countermeasure. In the near term, at least, the margin of victory will be courageous individual soldiers, or perhaps soldier-police such as the Italian *carabineri*—a military organization fully trained, organized, and equipped for police work—who are able to make the critical decisions on which the prosecution of the campaign will rest.

We have already seen examples of this type of warfare. The U.S. operation in Panama in 1989, Operation Just Cause, was such an action. In the space of a few minutes, U.S. forces conducted twenty-seven separate airborne assaults, heliborne and amphibious landings. Heavy firepower was used when necessary. The actions took place among a civilian population. And after a few days, resistance was broken and the opposing leader detained. There were casualties, among both the civilian population and the American forces. But the results were decisive, and democracy was restored to Panama.

Another feature of the campaign that will recur is the compelling need to prevent civilian casualties. Both we and the Serbs realized at the outset how critical this issue would be. It was the most pressing drumbeat of the campaign: minimize, if not eliminate, civilian casualties.

While precision strike was a dramatic leap forward over the firebombings and carpet bombings of World War II, each incident of accidental harm to civilians sent shock waves up and down through NATO. In part, this was a direct result of that conflict's doctrine of "total war," and in the aftermath of World War II, international legal efforts to reduce the costs of war to noncombatants were intensified, most notably in the 1949 update of the Geneva Convention. The media, especially television, also played a role in publicizing the horrors of war, as graphic visual images offered maximum impact.

There was another factor at work during Operation Allied Force. Serbia had been seen historically as a European state. In the nineteenth century, Serbian Christianity opposed the Ottoman Empire's Islam in Europe's southeast corner. In World War I, Serbia had been an ally of Britain and France against Austria and Germany. The West had created Yugoslavia in the peace agreements at the end of that war. During World War II the Yugoslav Communist resistance, led by Marshal Josip Broz Tito, had been assisted by the West. This sympathy had carried over into the early postwar years, when Tito's resistance to Stalin won him sympathy and support from the West. Tito further strengthened his position through Yugoslavia's leadership of the Non-Aligned Movement, a kind of "third bloc" that emerged during the Cold War. Yugoslavs migrated throughout Europe seeking jobs. Western tourists visited Yugoslavia's spectacular Dalmatian coast. By the 1980s, Yugoslavia was considered the most progressive and enlightened of the states still under Communist control. The Serbs were Europeans, and this meant that the operation against Serbia was, in the 1990s atmosphere of European integration, akin to a European civil war.

In fact, there was a sense among some that NATO was fighting on the wrong side. During the operation, a French general told me, privately, "Sir, do not fight against the Serbs. They are the best fighters in the French Foreign Legion and the best fighters in Europe. They have all left the Legion now, saying that 'NATO is attacking my country.' And, sir, do not forget, only Serbia stands between Europe and an 'Algeria' in Europe." Of course, this wasn't the official policy of France. Most Frenchmen supported the war. But it was a sentiment I had heard expressed more than once unofficially.

Finally, with NATO's intervention premised on humanitarian needs, it was difficult to defend the intervention logically and politically if it was causing more harm and damage than it was preventing. This balance—the injuries and damage we inflicted accidentally versus those inflicted deliberately by the Serbs—continued to run through the private and public discourse during the campaign.

The balance was also a practical political consideration during each aspect of the campaign. It began with the charge by some critics that the NATO bombing was somehow responsible for the Serb ethnic cleansing campaign in Kosovo, as though NATO should have taken into account the potential Serb reaction to the air strikes, even if the Serb reaction was illegal and immoral. This was, first, an error in fact. The Serb ethnic cleansing began before the start of the air campaign. This was also a double standard: if it could be expected that the Serbs would behave improperly (as they always did), then the West was wrong in taking a legal course of action that could have given them the excuse to behave illegally. It was a little like blaming policemen carrying arms for the fact that criminals use guns.

But the underlying rationale was more compelling. Harming the Albanian civilians whose mistreatment had been the source of NATO's action in the first place was morally, legally, and logically abhorrent. Every Albanian death or injury was a tragedy, doubly so if the result of NATO actions. Our humanitarian concern extended equally to the

Serbs. This was not a war against the Serb people, as NATO leaders often stated. We worked intensely to avoid harming innocent civilians on all sides.

There was also the rising hope that the conflict would encourage the Serb people themselves to rebel against Milosevic. The growing signs of civil disobedience in southern Serbia had to be encouraged by protecting the people there, not harming them.

Along with the desire to avoid civilian casualties, there was continuous commentary on the fear of NATO to accept military casualties. This, unfortunately, is unlikely to be unique to this operation.

Of course, using friendly personnel on the ground risks friendly casualties. Neither political nor military leaders will want to take these risks. But our adversaries will exploit our reluctance by facing us with the dilemma of either inflicting accidental injuries to civilians or risking our own people on their territory. For the Europeans, memories of the slaughter and devastation of the two world wars remained strong even decades later. For the Americans, it was the drawn-out conflict in Vietnam that defined contemporary political-military culture. The weekly grind of the American losses, long after the government had given up its aim of winning, brought a disillusionment similar to that afflicting the British and French in the post-World War I period.

The U.S. military, and especially the Army, was deeply affected by the Vietnam War and its aftermath. Senior officers, feeling victimized by a political system that had ordered them to fight but denied them the authority and objectives of victory, and cost them the approbation of a large part of the American public, resolved never to fight another Vietnam again. The new, post-Vietnam Army was to be built around "heavy forces"—tanks, armored fighting vehicles, self-propelled artillery, and helicopters. It was designed to interweave the Reserve and National Guard forces so that no serious military operation could be contemplated without calling up Reserves and mobilizing National Guard forces, thus forcing the political leaders to secure public approval before committing troops to an operation.

The end of the draft left the Army with the problem of building a new self-image, and a new relationship between the ranks. In the Volunteer Force, the country at large no longer provided its young men for service; the Army now had to recruit men and women itself. In competing for soldiers, the Army had to become a far more caring institution in order to attract the young people who were seeking stable jobs and family benefits. The net result was an Army that was far more capable of sustaining its people, and more interested in doing so.

These changes were echoed in the other services. Air Force, Navy, and Marine pilots, for instance, sought to avoid a repetition of the Vietnam experience, where they had endured combat tours of several months' duration, facing enemy fire on many missions, risking death or imprisonment, and living with the long-term pain of seeing their colleagues imprisoned for years in North Vietnam. For the pilots, the post-Vietnam challenge was to avoid a repeat of the losses suffered in extended air operations.

In other words, it wasn't just the politicians who were pushing the military to avoid casualties. We were feeling the impact of deeply rooted organizational forces from within the military itself.

Before Operation Desert Storm in 1991, casualty estimates were running as high as 20,000, a figure that contributed to the political unease with which Congress greeted the operation. But by taking extraordinary care to avoid casualties—just 148 killed—popular support was maintained.

The failed raid on Mogadishu, Somalia, in 1993, in which eighteen elite U.S. Army soldiers were killed, was especially significant in shaping Americans' attitudes toward casualties. This was a combat action gone awry. Our best soldiers had made several critical tactical mistakes, including the loss of surprise, the lack of an effective reserve, and a breakdown in effective command and control. But these mistakes had come in an operation that had enlarged beyond its original scope and purpose without clear strategic guidance.

What had emerged, over a period of many years, was a distinction in the minds of political leaders, the media, and the public. If war were forced on us, then casualties would be expected. If we were engaged in wartime operations to turn back aggression against our allies, then casualties would be regrettable but more or less accepted. But if we put ourselves into operations voluntarily, in pursuit of forward presence or engagement, or in efforts to stop war or provide humanitarian assistance in far-off lands, then casualties would be far less acceptable.

"Voluntary" operations that incurred casualties might not be sustainable. Period. All senior military leaders sensed it.

(It is interesting to note that the same pressures were not operative on our European Allies. France, and to a lesser extent the United Kingdom, suffered loss after loss in peacekeeping operations in Bosnia and elsewhere. Those risks, while regrettable, were considered part of the duty.)

In that context, the results of NATO operations in the Balkans, and Operation Allied Force in particular, were truly remarkable. Not a single NATO soldier has died from direct hostile fire in over four years of engagement and combat in the Balkans. There have been accidents, to be sure, and several men have died as a result of land mines, but not in direct combat. Even when we lost aircraft, the pilots were recovered. Operation Allied Force has thus set a high standard for future operations. We have shown that it is possible to intervene without losses. It probably will be the standard by which other operations are measured.

But it is time for the military in the United States, in particular, to put the legacy of Vietnam and even Somalia behind us. It will be necessary to take risks in war. It will be up to the military to mitigate these risks—by sound preparations, bold action, integrated political-military strategy—but we will not be able to escape them. And we cannot pass all the responsibility to the politicians above us.

A final aspect of this war—the reluctance to enter a ground campaign—could likely be an emerging pattern as well. Like the preference for airpower, this was foreseeable, and not just because of the likelihood of casualties.

The twentieth century taught that land campaigns were almost the precise opposite of what air campaigns aim to be. Operations involving land forces were slow, expensive, costly in terms of lives, often indecisive, and usually entail unpredictable consequences. For every Plan Yellow, the German blitzkrieg that tore apart the French and British defenses on the Continent in 1940, there were a dozen far less successful efforts: the inconclusive amphibious landings at Gallipoli in 1915 and Anzio in 1943, the breakout at Caen in June 1944, or Operation Market Garden, the 1944 airborne action to seize simultaneously a number of bridges along a single road extending deep into enemy territory, chronicled in Cornelius Ryan's book, *A Bridge Too*

Far. Even successful operations often had unintended consequences, like the American push to the Yalu River in the autumn of 1950, which provoked Chinese intervention in the Korean War. Some operations that achieved military success ignited their own political opposition, like the U.S. strike into Cambodia in 1970, which generated powerful anti-war resistance at home.

In the case of Kosovo, significant financial costs were also a consideration in Washington. Under the restraints of the Balanced Budget Amendment, no operating funds were available for a major military undertaking. Securing those funds from a Congress controlled by the opposition party would have subjected the Administration to high stress, political trade-offs, and perhaps operational restraints, even if ultimately the funds were provided. Those funds would inevitably have subtracted from the ongoing efforts of the armed forces to sustain their readiness, fulfill their obligations elsewhere, and address the serious lag in procurement and modernization they were facing. Other nations faced similar concerns, and I was well aware that facing up to the financial needs would have carried a high political price.

Organizational factors worked strongly against the ground planning as well. Inside the Pentagon, U.S. planning has tended to follow a deliberate planning cycle that enables full consideration of movement planning, operational trade-offs, and costs. These are the strategic plans, basically departure, movement, and arrival plans. The actual warfighting plans emerge from formations and organizations within the prospective theaters of operation. Various sections, communications, transportation, and so forth, have opportunities to make certain their needs are included, and the services normally review these plans as well. A year or two to produce one of these fully coordinated plans is not unusual.

In a crisis, short-term, more limited plans can also be produced, and relatively quickly, building on the existing plans developed by the commanders in theater. But in the case of Kosovo, there simply was no detailed planning. There was no strategic consensus in Washington. Even if there had been, U.S.-only planning would have been unrealistic, since we never had any intention of fighting alone. Nor could we have done effective U.S. planning without visiting the theater, which was impossible under the restrictive provisions of the Roberts Amendment, which forbade spending money for intervention in the Balkans unless certain prerequisites and reporting requirements had been complied with. Detailed NATO planning would have required political authorizations that just weren't possible.

It was the interplay of these organizational factors and political matters that restricted the planning, especially as it became clear that an invasion of Kosovo would require far larger commitments than we had already given in Bosnia. What made our task more difficult was the fact that military planners typically operate under near "worst-case" assumptions. This is the conservative way to plan, and providing a buffer for the unexpected, the best way to handle political authorities. So it was reasonable for the Pentagon's planners to project a campaign that would take longer, require more forces, and cost more than might actually be the case in practice. Indeed, this has been one of the reasons that the Services don't resist calls for planning and reportedly urge that it be undertaken carefully before complex operations. The Washington-savvy leaders among them probably believed that the surest way to kill our engagement in Kosovo was to plan a ground operation in excruciating detail. But I believe there were also some who simply believed that the best way to prevent our ever employing ground forces there was to refuse to plan for the possibility.

As the air campaign got under way, the political factors became dominant in Washington. Planning for a ground force could be seen as an admission the air campaign might not work. This would have required a defense of the wisdom of the initial strategy, and also might have opened an opportunity for greater congressional restrictions.

These kinds of pressures, to avoid ground intervention planning on the one hand, or to worst-case it and expose it on the other, are probably permanent features of the political scene in Washington and perhaps elsewhere. Whether they will be significant in the next war will very much depend on the nature of the interests at stake and the degree of consensus behind the policies. It is difficult to imagine any administration, or NATO for that matter, encouraging planning for major ground campaigns and war with every use of coercive diplomacy or humanitarian intervention. Still, maintaining uncertainty in the minds of adversaries remains a key tenet of strategy, and that will often require being prepared to go beyond the limits of airpower. There are simply tasks that can't be done from the air. Flexible, agile ground forces are required, along with strategic transport to deploy them and sustain them. And, in the final analysis, "boots on the ground" are more likely to be decisive in the long term. This means having the requisite ground capabilities and the will to use them if necessary.

Finally, a feature of the Kosovo operation that will inevitably be repeated is public scrutiny through the media. Western military leaders must contend with a new media environment in waging modern war. The Western print and television media were a battlefield fixture, driven by entrepreneurial spirit, a thirst for the real stories, and a quest for personal respect and recognition. Most among the media in the Balkans had a deep understanding of the issues and the character of the people behind them. Many journalists had strong personal opinions, which they worked to keep away from their reporting. But they were experts, nevertheless. And they had to be dealt with; they were a big part of what we called "the strategic environment."

In the Gulf War, the military authorities were wary of the media. All of the senior commanders there had seen the press at work in the Vietnam conflict, and most of them wanted nothing of it. The press was fundamentally uncontrollable once you let them in. They asked difficult questions and came with their own opinions—likely different on social issues than the military mainstream. If they wrote something they thought was favorable about you or your troops, they might damn you with faint praise or the kind of attention to small details that showed the wrinkles and pimples in the skin of any organization. Public pity wasn't welcomed by the Army. Even if you escaped the unflattering magnifying glass of the press, if your name was in print, you were likely to arouse the envy of many colleagues in uniform.

But in the Balkans we weren't able to shut out the press, and even if we could have, we shouldn't. The Gulf War lasted only a few weeks, and its ground component only four days. For a prolonged campaign, of indeterminate length, you must retain public support. It was one of the key lessons from Vietnam.

By the late 1990s, twenty-four-hour news programs drove the intensity of the media coverage. Networks like Sky News and CNN pushed for as many details as possible. Camera teams were at NATO headquarters, many of our airbases, in national capitals, and in Belgrade. News and comment were replayed numerous times throughout the day. We knew at the outset that feeding the information machine was critical to sustained public support of the campaign. And we knew that the broadcasts had to be monitored and corrected, if necessary. I kept the television on continuously in my office and in the chateau. When the television coverage was incomplete, or the commentary inaccurate, we called to offer information or to request clarifications and corrections.

A representative incident occurred in the final days of the campaign, as a CNN announcer repeated at fifteen-minute intervals, "Despite the negotiations, NATO continues to bomb." To the commentator or producer, this may have seemed like an obvious inconsistency and a mistaken policy. So, I called the network to explain that the story reflected a misunderstanding: it was the bombing that was responsible for causing the negotiations; if we stopped it, we would likely lose the negotiations. The news header was altered.

Javier Solana himself devoted considerable personal time to the press and media. He gave daily interviews, and he participated in reviewing and approving the daily NATO public briefings. By all reports he was scrupulous in returning phone calls and providing the most detailed and accurate information.

At the outset we tried to limit the amount of information on the details of the airstrikes in order to retain as much surprise and operational security as possible. We wanted time to gauge what was known and how much had to be released. But it took only a few days before we could see that we had to open up considerably. We allowed greater media exposure of our air operations, including press and media presence at several air bases. We also kept seeking to present more information in the daily briefings at NATO. As Solana directed me a few weeks into the campaign, "Wes, you must find ways to make the briefings more *interesting*." That we hadn't anticipated. *Interesting*. He was right.

We both worked intensively to draw out the facts from within the NATO military echelons. Civilian injuries were handled at the command levels; these weren't routine public affairs staff actions. We built complete staff elements inside NATO and at SHAPE to follow up on urgent information requests. This was information "extraction," because we were literally pulling up raw information from within subordinate commands. This was unorthodox and painful, and we had to guard against incomplete or misleading information.

Ultimately, even these efforts were inadequate. The Serbs, reflecting the totalitarian methods at the heart of communist rule, were excellent in organizing press coverage and directing it toward NATO mistakes. From the outset we had seen that the Serbs would do all they could to portray the NATO strikes as targeting civilians, rather than the Serb military and police. For the first few weeks we avoided playing into their plan, but eventually, the accidents and misfortunes inevitable in any air campaign took over. The fact was, the Serbs were on the ground and we weren't. They had an immediate advantage in knowing what happened when the bombs struck and, when the result was embarrassing to NATO, they could assure world media coverage faster than we could investigate and explain it.

They had the advantage in time and space. They had access to the media representatives in Belgrade. And though they did their best to avoid coverage of NATO's successes, we found that there was usually an element of truth when they shone the spotlight on NATO's failures. Meanwhile we labored each day, refraining from public comment until mid-afternoon.

The consequence was an enormous burden on the alliance's top leadership. Day after day we found ourselves working to explain and clarify. After the first weeks, we were on the defensive. We couldn't keep the focus on the Serbs' continuing transgressions. Where, we wondered, were the pictures of the Serbs' continuing atrocities? Where were the compelling eyewitness stories and snapshots of the ethnic cleansing, the brutality and destruction. In this war, a camera inside Kosovo would have been worth a dozen strikes on Serb vehicles. But such stories were relatively few, and difficult for the media to gather.

In that respect, the Serb ethnic cleansing of Pristina in the early days of April must stand as one of Milosevic's greatest strategic blunders. It fully engaged Western opinion, and while it continued, made a strong impression. It was a key factor in sustaining the air campaign during the early weeks before the NATO summit. Milosevic must have sensed this, for after a few days he restricted the flow of refugees and tried to conceal the kinds of crimes that so turned public opinion against him. In the end, he achieved some success with his strategy, for after a few weeks, in the absence of new levels of outrage, media interest in the sprawling misery of the refugee camps waned.

The Chinese embassy strike was thus a huge gift to the Serb propaganda effort. So were the repeated incidents of strikes impacting off their targets and hitting Serb civilians. By the end of May, NATO was under sustained and intense pressure to avoid collateral damages. We simply eliminated targets from our list and pared down the impact of the campaign. The weight of public opinion was doing to us what the Serb air defense system had failed to do: limit our strikes.

The impact of this hasn't been lost on military or political leaders in the West. Attention to the media will be a must for any future campaign. For small, limited-duration special operations, secrecy is still possible if it is carefully planned. But for sustained operations, public support will be essential. This, in turn, can only be gained by accepting the restraints of public opinion and sensibilities on future operations, just as our nations and our Alliance did in Operation Allied Force.

Beyond all these patterns of modern war, as we experienced it in Kosovo, one of the biggest questions posed by Operation Allied Force concerns the future of the North Atlantic Treaty Organization itself, and the role it will play in the world of the twenty-first century. NATO is not a "full-service institution." It is only a political-military alliance. NATO doesn't control economic affairs, have a seat at the United Nations, or routinely post ambassadors abroad. It is not a state. It has no intelligence collection facilities. Its budget is achieved solely through national contributions by its member nations. Its operating procedures are governed by rules prescribed by member nations. Its forces are assigned by nations and can be even more easily re-assigned away. Its Secretary General is beholden to the member nations and looks to them for support and direction.

Finding the right place for NATO in the pantheon of international and European institutions has not been easy. Nations are rightly jealous of their prerogatives, and it was clear early in the Dayton discussions in 1995 that the major European powers sought to prevent what they feared would be an American-dominated NATO military force in Bosnia from establishing authority over non-military matters, even though they could probably see the exceptional value of military leverage in civil implementation. European fears were complemented by the American resistance to "mission-creep." Taken together, these concerns resulted in restrictions on NATO early in its endeavors—preventing it from undertaking certain police-type actions, restricting its ability to act in support of refugee returns, stifling its involvement in collecting information and combating corruption—which have served to delay the full implementation of the Dayton Agreement.

An important opportunity was also lost in the talks with the Serbs at Rambouillet, when NATO representation was resisted by the nations hosting the talks, and where, unlike at Dayton, the military annex to the negotiations was not promptly brought into play. One explanation was that NATO's presence and early discussion of the military annex might offend the Russians, whose assistance was sought in dealing with the Serbs. Another explanation was that NATO presence and the discussion of the military annex would introduce prematurely the military dimension of the diplomacy. But this was a case in which the military dimension would have added significantly to the leverage on the Serbs to accept a diplomatic resolution. A credible NATO presence might well have softened Milosevic's resolve to seek conflict.

In recent years France's role in the Alliance has been unique. Having stood for over thirty years outside the integrated military structure, France has often tended to view NATO's role more narrowly than do other member nations. In the mid-'90s, many within the Alliance tried to encourage French reintegration into the military structure. The return of the French Chief of Defense to meetings of the NATO Chiefs of Defense was warmly welcomed, as was France's appointment of a Military Representative to NATO's Military Committee. Today, there is extraordinarily good teamwork in the actual conduct of the operations. The French have often reminded us that when the Alliance has called, they have stood firmly with the others. And it is true. But in its strategic outlook, France has seemed to stand apart, as a distinct force within Europe, pursuing a variety of initiatives to give greater voice to French concerns and interests within Atlantic and European institutions. France was a leader in the insistence on a distinct European security and defense identity within NATO, and later, independent of NATO. French efforts were also behind various proposals that would have enlarged the role of other security consultative organizations in Europe.

Much of this effort has appeared to be directed quietly and steadily against American influence. I could sense a proud rivalry, which I respected and sometimes admired, among some in the French military and diplomatic service. As one of my French colleagues explained to me, "France will speak for Europe, even if no one else does."

In truth, there were strong reasons based on historical experience, for some of the French reservations in dealing with the United States. Ambivalent American support to French efforts in Indochina after World War II, disapproval of French actions that helped precipitate the Suez crisis of 1956, disagreements over the nature and pace of decolonization, and misunderstandings over nuclear strategy and the sharing of nuclear know-how all contributed to French concerns. The United States, no less than other countries, has tended to pursue its own interests and beliefs, as it sees them.

But Europe still has many voices and points of view, French concerns notwithstanding. We were continually approached by representatives of other European nations, expressing their views, usually differing with France. In fact, the United States has historically served inside NATO as a balancing agent, sought by several of the smaller European nations whose voices are often overridden by the larger European powers.

The challenge for NATO's member nations is to harmonize differing national interests and points of view, in order to use the expertise and influence of the Alliance early in a crisis, when NATO can be effective in deterring or preventing conflict, not later, when the only question is whether to fight. Like any complex institution composed of sovereign states, NATO has the means for reconciling these divergent views and generating the consensus required for action. Each nation is represented in numerous NATO bodies, ranging from the North Atlantic Council and the Military Committee to numerous more specialized, lower-level bodies. But there has always been within NATO a foundation built upon bilateral and multilateral consultations and informal relationships, always with the understanding that it is NATO itself, not these informal groupings, that must make the decisions. Sometimes the weight has been borne by the Anglo-American "special relationship."

Recently, periodic, informal discussions have been held within the so-called "Quad"—the United States, Great Britain, France, and Germany—or, as in the Kosovo campaign, the "Quint," the Quad plus Italy. Each grouping has roused concerns among those nations not participating, just as the prospect of a "European Union bloc" within NATO raises anxieties among the United States and other non-EU members. "Transparency" into these groups is now increasingly important.

As the NATO processes worked, at the military as well as the political levels, I was persuaded of the basic soundness of NATO decision-making. NATO decisions are made by consensus, which means that any nation can stop NATO's actions at any point that formal decisions are made. But during Operation Allied Force there was a continuous network of formal and informal consultation at all levels, even frequent visits to my headquarters by ambassadors and Chiefs of Defense. Opinions were sought and, by and large, heeded within the overall direction and purpose of the operation.

However, it was also true that nations generally influenced NATO actions in proportion to their commitment of forces. Those nations that contributed the most carried the greatest weight in the Council, in the military decision process, and in the informal consultations. Those that contributed less influenced less.

Realistically, the relative powers of member nations tend to be recognized in all multinational organizations, including NATO. The United States had always had the greatest power and the greatest influence. But during the Cold War the problem was that the United States was not vulnerable in the event of war in the same way as its European allies, and there were continuing concerns that the United States would somehow become "decoupled" from its European allies.

Ironically, a similar rift was a factor in the Kosovo crisis, because American commitments to potential crises in the Persian Gulf and Korea took priority in U.S. policy over problems in Europe. During the summer and fall of 1998 the United States seemed more concerned with Saddam Hussein's violation of the U.N. sanctions regime in Iraq than with the potential of another crisis in former Yugoslavia. This meant that NATO was depending for leadership on a nation whose priority security interests lay elsewhere. This is not an impossible situation, but the manner in which Washington expressed and acted on its priorities, however reasoned they may have seemed to the Americans, did not always inspire confidence among several European nations.

Differences between France and Washington on how to respond to Saddam Hussein's defiance of the United Nations particularly stressed relationships during this period, distracting attention from the continuing problems with Milosevic, and chilling the exchange of information, plans, and intent that could have strengthened NATO's response when it came time to use force in Europe. When the United States and Great Britain used air and missile strikes against Saddam Hussein in December 1998, France abstained. The strains lingered.

However, Washington's leadership was especially significant when it came to dealing with the Russians. Thirty years of diplomacy, from détente through the opening of the Kosovo campaign, indicated that Russian issues could be addressed more successfully in U.S.-Russian bilateral talks than in multilateral NATO-Russian discussions. During the war, several NATO nations met with the Russians. But it was the U.S.-Russian channel that ultimately carried the weight of the diplomacy. Russia, after all, still sought recognition as a second superpower, at least in its historic areas of influence. Dealing with the United States conferred that status. And there were longstanding personal relationships at several levels that reinforced this predisposition.

Using bilateral relationships to reinforce NATO's efforts required close consultation with the Allies. This was the rub within NATO as the campaign drew to a close. The pace of events seemed to overrun the ability to evaluate alternatives and to forge consensus through various channels of consultation. It left us with an information void and a "policy gap" among the Allies that gave us the confusion over how to respond to the Russian occupation of the Pristina airfield.

These stresses and strains within NATO take on added significance today with the emergence of the European Union's Common Foreign and Security Policy. If NATO is to retain its central role in transatlantic security, then both Europe and the United States must use it as their primary consultative and decisionmaking forum. NATO must have full transparency into all EU security discussions and an implicit "right of first refusal" on meeting any European security challenges. The United States must make clear that it will participate and will not "refuse" in future contingencies.

Transatlantic differences in perspectives at the military level within the Alliance emerged as well. As Rupert Smith and I worked our way through the air campaign and into the planning for the ground operation, the divergences between U.S. military doctrine and a European approach emerged with increasing clarity.

First, there were major differences on how rapidly to escalate the strikes. In U.S. military thinking, we seek to be as decisive as possible once we begin to use force. This meant that the sooner we could strike the most sensitive targets, the greater the coercive leverage against the Serbs.

France seemed to have a different view, however—to limit the strikes at the lowest possible level and to leave implicit the threat of more destructive strikes. As one French officer explained, "We believe we must save the best targets, so that Milosevic will know that he has more to lose in the future than he has lost thus far."

The underlying reasons for this difference are less clear. But as I came to understand it, the American view focuses on the outcome of the conflict; it recognizes that consensus for the use of force is difficult to sustain, and that public opinion coalesces behind success. The French view was more far-sighted; it sought minimal physical and psychological impact on Serbia and the Serbs with the aim of speeding postwar reconstruction and reconciliation. The American and French positions also reflected their distinctive historical experiences, cultures, and geography. But advocates of both positions eventually recognized the need for escalation.

The United States and many of its Allies were at odds on where to apply the main effort of the air campaign. Reflecting a fifty-year emphasis on the strategic use of force by an independent Air Force, most Americans believed that the best and most rapid way to change Milosevic's view was to strike at him and his regime as hard as possible. We had done this against Qaddafi in 1986 and attempted it against Saddam Hussein in 1991.

Most Europeans saw the need to strike at the Serb forces actually conducting the ethnic cleansing, especially the Serb forces within Kosovo. This was the more direct approach and avoided the culturally and legally more difficult problem of attacking targets in a nation's capital.

Even in terms of moving toward a ground campaign the United States and its allies brought different perspectives. The United States sought to succeed without the use of ground troops. Despite the military leaders' recommendations to plan for ground operations, the civilian leadership resisted. The President's statement that he "had no intent" provided the initial rationale, but strong political and organizational forces were at work throughout the campaign.

The Allies, on the other hand, had moved their forces into Macedonia even before the air campaign began. Some had been willing, as early as the autumn of 1998, to place their forces on the ground inside Kosovo. But the Europeans wanted no repeat of the events of the early 1990s in the Balkans, when the United States gave advice but refused to risk its own people on the ground. They may have also recognized that without the U.S. ground forces, they lacked sufficient power to assure success.

When it came to planning the ground action, the Americans and the Europeans were also moving in different directions. There is an American way of war, developed in the two world wars, last practiced in the Gulf War: muster an overwhelmingly large force; prepare and train it; then use it to achieve militarily decisive results. Lately, it had come to be known as the "Powell Doctrine." This accounted in part for the American military preference for a northern option, which they believed would be the end of the Serb military machine and of Milosevic's regime.

The Europeans, on the other hand, had experienced dozens of colonial and post-colonial battlefields where they fought outgunned and outnumbered. Often they won, as in the Falkland Islands in 1982, where British forces overcame severe disadvantages of geography and numbers to prevail. The European officers saw a leaner campaign, focused on Kosovo, characterized by more flexible and daring tactics. They were prepared to take greater risks with their troops and to ask for less from the supporting arms such as artillery and airpower. They were also far more realistic in recognizing the political and strategic infeasibility of the northern approach.

The differences in perspective in the land campaign were never fully recognized publicly, as there was no need to invade. But as a set, these differences between the Europeans and the Americans on how to use force should be addressed by NATO in the future.

There was much made in the press that this was "war by committee." And it is true that NATO agreement was required in many cases and sometimes was difficult to obtain. But there was also a purely American committee at work. This was the committee of the Joint Chiefs of Staff. By law, Hugh Shelton and Joe Ralston, the Chairman and Vice Chairman, were empowered to represent me, a U.S. regional commander in chief. The Chairman is the principal military adviser to the Secretary of Defense, the President, and the National Security Council. But the Chiefs collectively seemed to have great power. Perhaps this derived from the White House's reluctance to go against the Chiefs—though at least one member of the Chiefs vigorously opposed the operation—or perhaps it was the way that the Secretary of Defense or the Chairman preferred to use the Chiefs to buffer and analyze field advice, or just their style of communications, or the difficulties they themselves had in managing the Chiefs. For whatever reason, there appeared to be a far higher degree of "leadership by committee" than existing U.S. legislation requires. In practical terms, this seemed to constrain my ability to act every bit as much as any transatlantic difference ever did.

Under the terms of the Goldwater-Nichols Act of 1986, the Chairman of the Joint Chiefs of Staff was elevated above the other Service Chiefs and designated the "Principal Military Adviser" to the Secretary of Defense, the President, and Congress. At the same time, the role of the "Combatant Commanders," or regional commanders such as the Commander of the U.S. European Command, was strengthened in an effort to establish a clear and strong chain of command for the conduct of operations.

In Operation Allied Force, the provisions and intent of this legislation were severely challenged, as tension revolved around whether I had been given adequate authority and resources to accomplish my assignments. I continually argued for more resources and systems with which to escalate the campaign. Secretary Cohen (who as a senator had been one of the authors of the Goldwater-Nichols legislation) repeatedly assured that I would be given what I thought was necessary. But the reality was somewhat different.

On many key issues, I learned, some of the Service Chiefs frequently weighed against my requests, first on the deployment of the Apaches and later on their use, sometimes on the use of long-range rockets to strike Serb air defenses, and on the particulars of the ground plan. In the June 3 White House meeting that I was not allowed to attend, General Dennis Reimer, the Army Chief, was reportedly briefing the President that he didn't feel that it would be possible for the Army to deal with the rugged terrain of northeast Albania.

It is the responsibility of the Chairman to use his influence to deal with what is in some respects a natural tension between Service Chiefs, who are responsible for a longer-term view, and the regional commanders responsible for the immediate response to crises. It was apparently intended within the legislation that the Chairman would stand up for the CINC and compensate for the CINC's lack of access in Washington, in order to reduce the natural tendency of "war by committee."

The Chairman can ask the Service Chiefs to review any of a CINC's requests, to question them and offer alternatives. After all, Washington has to decide how to allocate resources among the various competing commands, and the Services are also the custodians of their personnel and resources. But in this case, the Chiefs couldn't see the full dimensions of the conflict or NATO's response. In retrospect, perhaps fuller, earlier consultation with the commander in the field would have helped Washington come to grips with its strategy—and, for example, to look beyond the heavy emphasis on targets—earlier in the campaign. The strategy Rupert Smith, Dieter Stockmann, and I articulated in my office at the outset of the campaign could have been most usefully presented to the national capitals, and particularly to Washington, though none recognized it at the time. When this viewpoint was presented at the summit, the need to "isolate the theater" was immediately recognized by the President and other heads of state.

There were no procedural or legal limitations that would have precluded such consultation. It simply wasn't done. Instead, the Chairman and Vice Chairman and I spent hours on the telephone exchanging information and pushing strategic ideas piecemeal as they apparently responded to the needs of their superiors, worked the fractious Chiefs, and tended the American strategy within the interagency. Perhaps the air campaign looked so simple that no greater consultation seemed required, but the appearance of simplicity was certainly deceptive. The operation was enormously complex in practice. Or perhaps the underlying isues that a comprehensive strategy would have exposed were too difficult.

There is a legal conundrum, however, in the way that U.S. military advice is given and received. By law, the Joint Chiefs are advisers to the President. But they can only be responsible for U.S. operations, or the U.S. component of an Allied operation. The legislation takes no account of the different responsibilities of officers in NATO positions, such as SACEUR. As Supreme Allied Commander, Europe, I was responsible personally to each of the NATO member nations for the overall accomplishment of the mission. There was no way for me to hand over this responsibility to the Joint Chiefs of Staff, to the Chairman of the Joint Chiefs of Staff, or even to the Secretary of Defense. As a U.S. commander, I would have to regard the hesitations of my superiors as implicit orders, but in NATO, I could not always accept them as such. Instead I was bound to continue pushing the strategy until instructed otherwise.

As for the quality of the Joint Chiefs' advice, I knew that the Service Chiefs were not present in the theater nor working the operation from the perspective of the commander. So far as I knew, none of them had seen and studied the terrain in northeast Albania, and it seemed that at least one was almost looking for reasons why the ground attack in Kosovo would not work rather than how to make it work. They and their staffs were, of course, talking to their component commanders, my subordinates in theater, to get their information. They were entitled by law to present their views as military advisers to the President. But the U.S. regional commanders in chief have no such right, though they work directly for the Secretary of Defense. Their access is controlled by the Secretary and influenced by the Chairman. Bringing the theater commander into closer contact with the full decisionmaking apparatus of the U.S. government, and the President, would probably have aided in the conduct of the campaign.

A key underlying factor, derived from the inherent conflict of the Pentagon's National Military Strategy and need for congressional support, was the lack of a unified U.S. national strategy for dealing with the Balkans. The greater the costs and risks of the operations there, the greater the tensions within the U.S. government. At the outset, when the first troops were deployed to enforce the Dayton Agreement, Pentagon restrictions on the mission of the Implementation Force were acceptable because implementation was more or less proceeding, especially on the tasks of the military annex. But as it became clear in the summer of 1997 that a more active military effort was needed to assure military success, the Pentagon's resistance seemed to increase. As the crisis in Kosovo deepened, and especially with the beginning of Operation Allied Force, the institutional split between the State Department and the Pentagon seemed to become much more open and debilitating. Tending this split seemed to have required daily efforts by the National Security Council staff. But it also left to the commander in the field the responsibility for pushing and working on strategic issues ahead of Washington consensus and in opposition to the Pentagon's innate reticence. This in turn probably contributed to the Pentagon's reluctance to allow the theater commander to engage Washington directly on strategic issues.

However, I always retained the authority as Supreme Allied Commander to speak directly to the head of any NATO government, including the President of the United States. I considered doing so several times. This was a trump card that I knew I could use to get the ground force briefing to the President at the appropriate moment. But I also understood that this would carry a very high price. It might not be playable more than once. I never had to use it.

I saw other factors at work in these difficulties within the chain of command. First, the Kosovo operation really did pose significant policy and doctrinal problems for the Joint Chiefs. The commitment to use force in the Balkans violated the National Military Strategy, as many in the Pentagon seemed to interpret it. This wasn't the war they wanted to fight. And the Air Force doctrine of strategic attack wasn't totally appropriate to NATO's requirements. Second, the Services naturally fought to restrict an operation that threatened their longer-term health by disrupting modernization and consuming "ready" units. This is a natural tension between the Services and the commander that constituted a "hidden agenda" during the Chiefs' consideration of my proposals. This hidden agenda may also have been encouraged by some of the partisan congressional resistance to the operation. Third, Secretary Cohen had a continuing strong opposition to planning and preparing a ground operation. It was a matter of his perspective and responsibilities, which I respected and tried to support, even though I viewed the Congress and Allies somewhat differently, and despite my own NATO responsibilities to prepare for follow-on options until ordered to stop. Finally, there may have been other factors at work. Some in the Pentagon had worked for two years to restrict my interactions within the broader U.S. government, for reasons that were never entirely clear.

But military organizations and their leaders must be agile enough to deal with the actual and changing requirements of battle as war unfolds. That was why the Goldwater-Nichols legislation sought to strengthen the hand of the CINC. I never saw any indication that war was threatened in any other theater. We could have afforded to do whatever might prove necessary to succeed. Nor should the Services place their long-term plans above success in the operation at hand. When nations commit their military forces to combat, the operations have to succeed. The Services knew this well (this was why they had always seemed to fear that the air campaign would lead to a ground effort), but some seemed to resist their obligation to win. And some in political positions, perhaps inevitably, viewed military advice primarily as a political problem to be managed rather than a resource to be developed and used. There was also within the Pentagon a reluctance to allow the regional commanders to engage fully along the broader political-military axes necessary to do their jobs.

Finally, personal factors always impact organizations. People make a difference; they are not interchangeable. Military history is replete with examples of the clashes of personality, skills, and ambition, but the test of military leadership is to make the best decisions and recommendations for mission accomplishment, taking into account the personal qualities of team members and colleagues.

Some may argue that because the campaign was ultimately successful, this Washington structure was not harmful and provided a required check on the commander. This view is incomplete. Steady, unrelenting pressure from the theater was a necessary tonic to the competing priorities and interests in Washington. It was integral to the success of the operation. Field commanders are expected to make precisely this contribution to campaign efforts. Commanders have to push to make operations succeed. The art is to get the balance right.

Problems of competing priorities, access to authority, and personality weren't unique to the United States. The other NATO members carefully monitored the plans and activities of the forces they had placed under NATO control and weighed relative priorities, too. A few nations were cautious in using their forces and sometimes refused to accept requirements from the NATO command chain. Even so, these exceptions were overshadowed by overwhelming support from within the Alliance, and especially from my colleagues among the Chiefs of Defense Staff.

Many in Europe clearly understood the extent to which NATO itself was subject to this committee of U.S. Service Chiefs and to higher authorities in the U.S. chain of command, whose priorities seemed so different from those of the European governments. For Europe, Operation Allied Force was a significant and pressing conflict. For some of my American colleagues and superiors in uniform, it was at times a distant and troublesome distraction. Allied military campaigns will always have to accommodate differing national perspectives and interests, but in this case these transatlantic differences fueled significant tensions between sovereign nations fighting this common campaign.

The nations themselves had to bear in mind differing national perspectives; they bore the ultimate responsibility for achieving Alliance harmony. But it was also up to NATO—the Secretary General, the Chairman of the Military Committee, the full range of NATO institutions, and the NATO military command structure—to help bridge these different perspectives, and NATO officials did so. From where I sat as SACEUR, I could see NATO's marvelous cohesion on a daily basis, surviving despite the stresses, and I was particularly grateful for the support of so many European, Canadian, and American colleagues.

Nations use diplomacy as a means to advance their interests. But when the interests are significant enough, when dialogue, negotiation, and compromise can't gain traction, and when nations believe their military advantage is sufficient, they will again employ "threat" to provide additional leverage.

Once the threat surfaces, however, nations or alliances are committed. Following through to preserve credibility becomes a matter of vital interest. Credibility is the ultimate measure of value for states and international institutions. Inevitably, sacrificing credibility carries long-term consequences far greater than the immediate issue, whatever it is. And both sides in the dispute are affected—those who have received the threat as well as those who have issued it.

This suggests that if coercive diplomacy is to succeed at the lowest possible cost, greater emphasis must be placed on the diplomacy at the outset. Ministers and heads of government should be personally engaged when the threat behind the diplomacy is still veiled and vague, before the first aircraft or ships have been positioned. But while non-military coercive measures should be used first, military advice is needed early, too. Once the commitments have been made, the military must focus on making the decisions succeed.

Inevitably, a certain momentum ensues. Events proceed from diplomacy backed by discussions of threat, to diplomacy backed by threat, to diplomacy backed by force, and finally to force backed by diplomacy. In the earliest discussions, civilian and military leaders must recognize, as many of us did, that once the struggle of competing wills ensues, it may not be possible to stop before reaching the end of the road.

Military operations may be thought of along a similar spectrum of intensity, running from mere military presence at the lowest end to all-out war at the upper end. U.N. peacekeeping operations in the Middle East, where blue-bereted soldiers are simply present as a symbol of both governments' acceptance of an agreement, represent the low end. The air strikes and tank battles of the Gulf War represent the high end.

Operations in the Balkans during the 1990s showed that Western capabilities were challenged by operating in the middle part of this spectrum. We had to take sides, and sometimes to use force in limited ways, to gain the political ends sought. On the ground, we found ourselves struggling to assess the appropriate degree of risk. It was difficult to integrate political and strategic issues into the tactical considerations. In the air, we found ourselves seeking the information and discrimination necessary to use force decisively in environmentally and politically constrained circumstances.

This is the difficult region of "not quite war—not quite peace." This includes limited war, pre-and post-conflict operations, and "nation-building." Make no mistake: if we are to avoid war this region needs further thought and perhaps different training, equipment, and forces.

At the political levels, clear, realistic aims are essential. Greater attention must be given to the integration of civilian and military activities. Military activities on the ground must reinforce civilian aims, within the limits imposed by military capabilities and resources. It must also be recognized that intervention to enforce peace will never be neutral; some parties will always be more heavily impacted than others, and all will attempt to use the force to advance their political aims. The civilian components of such missions will also be heavily dependent upon the military for security and enforcement of their decisions.

In undertaking operations in this part of the spectrum, militaries need to take into account higher level political considerations, some of which are too subtle or variable to be incorporated into the relatively fixed rules of engagement. Militaries also need clearer guidelines on when to accept risk. And militaries have to maintain their esprit and sense of purpose, as well as their capabilities for fighting at the top end of the spectrum of military operations. All of this can be done, with good military leadership.

However, civilian leaders must understand the limits of what can be done with military efforts alone. Operations must have sound, achievable political aims. Political leaders have to find the courage to make hard choices—like final-status determination in Kosovo—before the military efforts simply become untenable on the ground.

But there are also requirements for police activities, ranging from investigations of crime through reaction to civil disturbances and urban violence, and the fact is that most militaries are simply not capable of performing such functions effectively and should not be the primary element responsible for them. In these middle-range interventions, nations will have to create a full range of deployable, robust police-type capabilities as well as providing a legal and judicial structure to support their responsibilities.

For the U.S. Armed Forces, the requirements posed by Operation Allied Force and its aftermath revealed cracks and strains. Yet not enough has been done thus far to repair them. In Kosovo my commanders and I found that we lacked the detailed prompt information to campaign effectively against the Serb ground forces. Most of the technologies we had been promoting since the Gulf War were still immature, unable to deal adequately with the vagaries of weather, vegetation, and urban areas, or the limitations of bandwidth and airspace. The discrete service programs didn't always fit together technically. And the officers who operated the programs were not qualified to work across service lines and did not understand the full range of national capabilities. Far greater attention is required in this area. I worried about the nature of Joint skills even among senior officers.

Our planning and movements systems are still cumbersome. In the case of Kosovo, some of this was generated by overly cautious Pentagon attitudes restraining the commanders in the field, but for the most part, this is the American approach to war. We have been schooled on planning by using big matrices, with every cell to be filled before moving forward. We have learned a passion for detail, but not necessarily how to compromise for the sake of urgency. Surely with all modern capabilities, we can be much more timely in deployment planning, as well as operational analyses and preparations.

The efforts to produce a more deployable Army force, using lighter-wheeled vehicle technologies, are moves in the right direction. But for the Army much more will be required. Kosovo showed the obsolescence of some of the great organization we built after the Vietnam War. The equipment was either too heavy (like the Abrams tank) or wearing out and underdesigned (like the Apache, a phenomenal platform but one that won't fly in bad weather and has had fleet-wide maintenance problems). Moreover, some leaders were still relying on Cold War thinking, seeking massed groups of enemy targets for the Apaches, rejecting risks until "vital" national interests were at stake, and expecting the luxury of greater planning and decision time than may likely be available in the current environment.

Most important, the service cultures and career patterns need to adapt to retain and develop high talent for what will be increasingly complex demands. If we seek initiative, energy, and creativity, then younger leaders will need more authority. They want to feel the same kind of challenge as their peers in the civilian economy. They seek early opportunities to test their judgment, and recognition for their efforts. Most want to earn advanced civil degrees. In fact, these were the opportunities that soldiers of my generation received during the Vietnam conflict. They also expect more time with their families, and they aren't inclined to feel the same, continuing loyalty to large organizations.

Perhaps the Goldwater-Nichols legislation needs another look, too, if it has encouraged the military to create and sustain a Pentagon military strategy at odds with overall national requirements. Nothing can mandate the Secretary of Defense's close communication with the regional CINCs, and the Pentagon's procedures in this war were clearly within legal limits, even if they seemed out of line with the intent of the legislation. However, encouraging the regional CINCs to communicate and coordinate broadly within the U.S. government, while keeping the Pentagon informed, will surely yield benefits in both policy formulation and execution. It would also be useful to recognize within the Goldwater-Nichols framework the distinctive responsibilities of officers placed in Alliance positions.

On a global scale, the United States operates from a position of great strength. Our values and institutions are the envy of most other nations. Our economy has been the sparkplug of world economic growth. Our universities attract much of the finest academic talent. Our entertainment industry sets world standards. And especially among the former Warsaw Pact countries and many of the newly independent states of the former Soviet Union, the United States is a beacon of hope and an inspiration for reforms. Indeed, so great is the respect for the United States that our interests, especially economic interests, are sometimes advanced by the actions of others, without conscious efforts by the American people. And we are fortunate to have built and sustained during the Cold War strong alliances in the Pacific and in Europe.

But as events in the Balkans illustrated, American leadership will sometimes be required to advance our interests. When we lead, we will find that others sometimes expect not just advice and resources but our presence, too. They will expect us to share in their risks, and to help carry the burdens, even when our interests may not be affected as directly as theirs.

What I learned during my time in Europe was that the strongest force in the world is an idea whose time has come. In Europe, and in much of the rest of the world, freedom, human rights, international law, and the opportunity to "be all you can be" are those ideas today. For the most part, these are our own American values. And they are ideas whose formulation and dissemination owe much to American example and leadership in the past.

Because we live and extol these values, the United States enjoys a solid ethical basis for its power, a supportive community of like-minded nations and international institutions, and a moral force that extends our influence. Preserving these ideas and projecting our values should therefore be ranked among the most important of American interests.

To do so will require humility, generosity, and courage. We must still recognize and respect the strong convictions of others, especially when they disagree with us. No doubt our ideas will appear challenging or even dangerous to some. We have to balance our pride in our heritage with humility in our rhetoric. Living up to our values will cost resources that could always be used elsewhere. We can't do everything. But doing what we can will likely mean that we occasionally send our men and women abroad, into ambiguous, dangerous situations.

But these are the burdens we must carry, if we expect to maintain the benefits we currently enjoy. They provide hope for others, and a purpose beyond our own prosperity. "Shared risks, shared burdens, shared benefits"—it's not only a good motto for NATO, it's also a good prescription for America's role in the world.

ACKNOWLEDGMENTS

THIS BOOK is a personal memoir. It is not intended and could not be a complete record of the activities during this period or an objective accounting. I recognize that this record is likely to be as controversial as Operation Allied Force itself. The record will also be imperfect, despite incredible help and assistance. The responsibility for the omissions and errors of fact or understanding are mine alone. I am enormously grateful for the many family, friends, and colleagues who assisted me in getting the facts correct, presenting the issues, and remembering the contrasting perspectives and clash of emotions.

I would like to thank my executive officers and special assistants who helped me record the facts and my impressions during the operation, and later helped me confirm information and perspectives: Army Major General (then Brigadier) George Higgins; Army Brigadier Generals Pete Chiarelli and Bud Thrasher; Navy Rear Admiral (then Captain) Mark Milliken; Navy Captains Mark Ferguson, Jamie Kelley, and Gary Lehman; Air Force Colonels Dana Atkins, Dave Scott, and Dave Edgington; Marine Colonel Robert Blose; Army Colonels Dennis Dimengo, Charley Kuzell, Stephanie Hoehne, Mike Phillips, and Keith Walker; U.K. Army Lieutenant Colonel David Limb (now deceased); Italian Navy Commander Giuseppe Messina; and German Air Force Lieutenant Colonel Rolf Stichling.

I also wish to thank the historians and librarians at SHAPE and in Washington who helped me collect, organize, and store a vast amount of material: Greg Pedilow, Commander (U.S. Navy Reserve), Elizabeth Milliken, Susan Lemke, and Robert Montgomery; as well as my two faithful researchers: Jacky Hardy and Aaron Moberg-Jones.

Friends and members of governments and media inspired me to write this story, patiently read and commented on portions of drafts, provided facts, incidents and missing memory, corrected mistakes and misimpressions, or helped me deal with the many conflicting emotions and perspectives that the war brought out: Admiral (ret) Steve Abbot, former Secretary of State Madeleine Albright, Lieutenant General Edward Anderson, General Mario Arpino, Nancy Bekavac, Samuel Berger, Brigadier General John Brown, General (ret) Edwin Burba, Major General John Caldwell, Alistair Campbell, Major General George Casey, Carole Corcoran, Arnaud de Borchgrave, Steve Covington, Counsellor John Duncan, Minister Michael Durkee, Stewart Early, Colonel (ret) Jay Ferrar, German Air Force Colonel Konrad Frehtag, Colonel (ret) Alan Gropman, Secretary of State and General (ret) Alexander Haig, former Deputy Secretary of Defense John Hamres, Ambassador Chris Hill, Ambassador Richard Holbrooke, Lieutenant Colonel Tony Ierardi, General Jean-Pierre Kelche, Patricia Kelley, Admiral Luuk Kroon, Mark Laity, Jack LeCuyer, Jim Locher, Colonel (ret) Douglas MacGregor, General (ret) Sir Jeremy MacKenzie, Doug Martin, Commander Eric Massa, Colonel (ret) Jim McCallum, General (ret) Klaus Naumann, Dana Priest, Joe Reeder, Ambassador Larry Rossin, Major General (ret) Robert Scales, Greg Schulte, Lieutenant Colonel Jay Silveria, Walt Slocombe, General Rupert Smith, High Commissioner Javier Solana, James Steinberg, General Dieter Stockmann, Colonel Peter Stromberg, General (ret) Gordon Sullivan, Strobe Talbott, Ambassador Sandy Vershbow, Lieutenant Colonel Gil Villahermosa, most of my executive officers and special assistants, and others who must remain unnamed.

I would like to express my appreciation to my agent, Morton Janklow, and to my editor, Paul Golob, and publisher, Peter Osnos, who were brave enough to take a chance on an unpublished author. I am truly grateful for their skill and support as I worked to capture the incredible issues and stresses of operations in the Balkans.

Undertaking the review and the writing of this book would not have been possible without the encouragement and support of my colleagues at Stephens, Inc., the Little Rock investment bank which has welcomed me into the private sector, and I am especially grateful to Vernon Weaver, Doug Martin, Jon Jacoby, Curt Bradbury, and particularly Warren Stephens and his father, Jackson.

Most importantly, I am profoundly thankful for the love, support, and assistance of my family—my wife of thirty-three years, Gert, and our son, Wes. They endured the stress and turmoil of the campaign and its buildup, as well as the pain of the aftermath. Gert had the misfortune of hearing our team fight the war from my study every evening with my staff. It was probably the ultimate form of "bringing the work home from the office," an unfortunate practice I have been guilty of for years. She gave hospitality and hope to our many visitors, and listened to my frustrations and worries, and together we drew encouragement from our faith, our friends, the shared experience of over thirty years of experience in a difficult profession, and our belief that our country and the other nations of NATO would never allow Milosevic to succeed in his ethnic cleansing. My son, working in California at the time, was drawn in, too, by concerns for his security, love for his family, and his continuing interest in the Army and international affairs. Without them neither this book nor my military service would have been possible.

INDEX

PublicAffairs is a new nonfiction publishing house and a tribute to the standards, values, and flair of three persons who have served as mentors to countless reporters, writers, editors, and book people of all kinds, including me.

I.F. STONE, proprietor of *I. F. Stone's Weekly*, combined a commitment to the First Amendment with entrepreneurial zeal and reporting skill and became one of the great independent journalists in American history. At the age of eighty, Izzy published *The Trial of Socrates*, which was a national bestseller. He wrote the book after he taught himself ancient Greek.

BENJAMIN C. BRADLEE was for nearly thirty years the charismatic editorial leader of *The Washington Post*. It was Ben who gave the *Post* the range and courage to pursue such historic issues as Watergate. He supported his reporters with a tenacity that made them fearless and it is no accident that so many became authors of influential, best-selling books.

ROBERT L. BERNSTEIN, the chief executive of Random House for more than a quarter century, guided one of the nation's premier publishing houses. Bob was personally responsible for many books of political dissent and argument that challenged tyranny around the globe. He is also the founder and longtime chair of Human Rights Watch, one of the most respected human rights organizations in the world.

———

For fifty years, the banner of Public Affairs Press was carried by its owner Morris B. Schnapper, who published Gandhi, Nasser, Toynbee, Truman and about 1,500 other authors. In 1983, Schnapper was described by *The Washington Post* as "a redoubtable gadfly." His legacy will endure in the books to come.

Peter Osnos, *Publisher*

Win A Free Vac

1. What time of year did you visit the Myrtle Beach area?
   ❑ January–March ❑ April–May ❑ June–August
   ❑ September–December
2. What was your reason for visiting the Myrtle Beach area?
   (select only one) ❑ Business ❑ Convention ❑ Vacation
   ❑ Honeymoon ❑ Family Reunion ❑ Golf
3. Was this a family vacation? ❑ Yes ❑ No
4. Have you visited the Myrtle Beach area in the past 5 years?
   ❑ Yes ❑ No
5. Do you visit the Myrtle Beach area more than once per year?
   ❑ Yes ❑ No If yes, how often do you visit the area?
   ❑ 2-4 times ❑ 5 or more times
6. What area do you stay in while visiting Myrtle Beach?
   ❑ North Myrtle Beach (Little River to Briarcliffe)
   ❑ Myrtle Beach (Shore Drive area to Myrtle Beach State Park)
   ❑ South Myrtle Beach (Surfside Beach to Pawleys Island)
   ❑ Conway (Waccamaw Pottery west towards Conway)
7. What is your main reason for vacationing in Myrtle Beach? (select one)
   ❑ Beach ❑ Theaters ❑ Golf ❑ Shopping ❑ Nightlife ❑ Location
8. Which of the following services, if any, did you use while
   vacationing in Myrtle Beach? ❑ Hospital/Emergency Care
   ❑ Dry Cleaners ❑ Car Repair ❑ Movie Theater ❑ Pizza Delivery
   ❑ Spas/Nails/Hair Salon ❑ Jeweler ❑ Locksmith ❑ Video Store
9. Select one of the following as your favorite Family Activity
   while visiting Myrtle Beach: (select only one)
   ❑ Beach ❑ Putt Putt ❑ Dining ❑ Nightlife ❑ Water slides ❑ Golf
   ❑ Amusement Parks/Race Cars ❑ Live Theater ❑ Fishing
10. While vacationing in Myrtle Beach, did you visit other nearby
    areas such as: Charleston ❑ Yes ❑ No or Wilmington ❑ Yes ❑ No
    If yes, how long was your stay in this area?
    ❑ 1-3 days ❑ 4-6 days ❑ 7 or more days

lease print:

Name

Address

City   State   Zip

Phone [   ]   Date

❑ Male ❑ Female   Age: ❑ 18–25 ❑ 26–35 ❑ 36–45 ❑ 46–55 ❑ over 55
         Annual Household Income: ❑ Under $25,000 ❑ $25,000–$49,999
                                  ❑ $50,000–$99,999 ❑ Over $100,000

Mail to *Strand Magazine Survey*
1357 21st Avenue N., Suite 102
Myrtle Beach, SC 29577

Show Schedule

The Ice Castle Theatre

March 23 - August 31 .... "Footloose on Ice"

March 23 - April 21 .... "Footloose on Ice"
featuring Nancy Kerrigan, Scott Davis

September 18 - October 31 .... "Halloween On Ice"

October 2 - October 31... "Halloween On Ice" featuring Nancy Kerrigan

November 16 - December 30 .... "Merry Christmas on Ice"

December 31.......................... New Year's Eve Celebration

Legends in Concert

February 9 - November 3 .... Show of the Stars

November 5 - December 15 .... Holiday Show

December 26 - 30............................. Show of the Stars

December 31 .... New Year's Eve Show

Medieval Times Dinner & Tournament

February 7 - November 23.............. Dinner Show & Tournament

February 14.................................. Valentine's Day Show

April 15 .... Easter Show and Easter Egg Extravaganza

May 13...................................... Mother's Day Show

November 22 .... Thanksgiving Show

November 19 - December 30................ Christmas Dinner Show

December 31.......................... New Year's Eve Extravaganza

Spirit of the Dance

June 1 - October 31 .... Spirit of the Dance 2001 Show

November 1 - December 31 .... Holiday Spectacular

Times and dates of shows are subject to change. Call theater for specific times.

SWITZERLAND

AUSTRIA

SLOVENIA

Aviano
Air Base

Ljubljana

Sava R.

Trieste

Zagreb

ITALY

CROATIA

Rakovica

Bihac

BRIONI I.

K
R
A
J
I
N
A

Kms.

75

0

75

Miles

Zadar

Raska

Nis

Kursumilja

SERBIA

Banjska

Leskovac

Podujevo

Kosovska
Mitrovica

Srbica

Drenica

Pristina

Pec

Golgovac

Kosovo Polje
Pristina Airfield

KOSOVO

Stimle

Gnjilane

Djakovica

Malisevo

Racak

Prizren

Kukes

Skopje

Kms.

20

0

20

Miles

MACEDONIA

ITALY

TYRRHENIAN SEA

MONTENEGRO

ALBANIA